CALIFORNIA WOMEN AND POLITICS

California Women and Politics

From the Gold Rush to the Great Depression

Edited by | Robert W. Cherny | Mary Ann Irwin | Ann Marie Wilson

UNIVERSITY OF NEBRASKA PRESS • LINCOLN AND LONDON

In memory of Mildred Nichols Hamilton

© 2011 by the Board of Regents of the University of Nebraska
All rights reserved
Manufactured in the United States of America
∞
Library of Congress Cataloging-in-Publication Data
California women and politics : from the gold rush to the
Great Depression / edited by Robert W. Cherny, Mary Ann
Irwin, and Ann Marie Wilson.
p. cm.
Includes bibliographical references and index.
ISBN 978-0-8032-3503-8 (pbk.: alk. paper)
1. Women—Political activity—California.
2. California—Politics and government.
I. Cherny, Robert W. II. Irwin, Mary Ann, 1955–
III. Wilson, Ann Marie.
HQ1391.U5C347 2011
320.9794082′09034—dc22
2010046714

Set in Quadraat by Bob Reitz. Designed by R. W. Boeche.

CONTENTS

List of Illustrations   vii
Preface and Acknowledgments   ix
Introduction   xi

1. "I Do Not Like the White Man . . .
   He Is a Liar and a Thief"
   Testimonios and the Politics of Resistance   1
   LINDA HEIDENREICH

2. "Going About and Doing Good"
   The Lady Managers of San Francisco, 1850–1880   27
   MARY ANN IRWIN

3. "Woman Is Everywhere the Purifier"
   The Politics of Temperance, 1878–1900   59
   JOSHUA PADDISON

4. "Continually Doing Good"
   The Philanthropy of Phoebe Apperson Hearst, 1862–1919   77
   MILDRED NICHOLS HAMILTON

5. "Neutral Territory"
   The Politics of Settlement Work in San Francisco, 1894–1906   97
   ANN MARIE WILSON

6. "Citizen Bird"
   California Women and Bird Protection, 1890–1920   123
   MICHELLE KLEEHAMMER

7. Saving Redwoods
   Clubwomen and Conservation, 1900–1925   151
   CAMERON BINKLEY

8. The *Civitas* of Women's Political Culture
   The Twentieth Century Club of Berkeley, 1904–1929   175
   SANDRA L. HENDERSON

9. "We Want the Ballot for Very Different Reasons"
   *Clubwomen, Union Women, and the Internal Politics
   of the Suffrage Movement, 1896–1911*   209
   SUSAN ENGLANDER

10. "Awed by the Women's Clubs"
    Women Voters and Moral Reform, 1913–1914   237
    TERESA HURLEY AND JARROD HARRISON

11. "We Are Not Keen about the Minimum Wage"
    *Union Women, Clubwomen, and the
    Legislated Minimum Wage, 1913–1931*   263
    REBECCA J. MEAD

12. "No Undue Familiarity"
    *Gender, Vice, and the Campaign to
    Regulate Dance Halls, 1911–1921*   289
    MARK HOPKINS

13. "Hearts Brimming with Patriotism"
    *Katherine Edson, Alice Park, and the
    Politics of War and Peace, 1914–1921*   309
    EUNICE EICHELBERGER

14. Historians, Politics, and California Women   339
    MARY ANN IRWIN

    Contributors   369
    Index   373

ILLUSTRATIONS

Photographs

1. Rosalía Vallejo de Leese and family, ca. 1850 — 12
2. San Francisco Protestant Orphan Asylum — 33
3. San Francisco Ladies' Protection & Relief Society Home, 1865 — 35
4. Dorcas J. Spencer — 65
5. "Comparative Cost of Liquor" chart — 67
6. Benjamin Ide Wheeler conferring with Phoebe Apperson Hearst, 1912 — 89
7. Lucile Eaves in 1910 — 108
8. Harriet Williams Myers — 124
9. "Frank Chapman and His Legion of Women" cartoon — 129
10. Louise C. Jones and Carrie Stephens Walter, 1900 — 159
11. Clubhouse of the Twentieth Century Club of Berkeley — 183
12. Anna L. Saylor — 197
13. Lillian Harris Coffin, Mrs. Theodore Pinther Jr., and Mrs. Theodore Pinther Sr. — 212
14. The Barbary Coast, ca. 1910 — 254
15. "How to Dress on $12.50" cartoon — 278
16. Dance Hall Girls Storming Roche's Office — 301
17. Katherine Philips Edson — 311
18. Alice Park — 322

Tables

1. Annual Cost of Operation, San Francisco City Hospital, 1853–1857 — 44
2. Approximate Cost per Inmate at SFLP&RS Home, Alms House, and Industrial School, 1872–1879 — 47

PREFACE AND ACKNOWLEDGMENTS

In some ways, the origin of this anthology dates to a time in the late 1980s when Susan Englander came to me to discuss a topic for her master's thesis. She wanted to look at the role of San Francisco's working-class women in the campaign for woman suffrage in California. I told her that I had serious doubts that she'd be able to find enough sources to be able to do a thesis, but, after she insisted that she was confident that the sources were there, we agreed that she'd start research on that topic. I was happy to be proven wrong, as Sue developed an outstanding thesis. Her thesis was the first of a number of similarly impressive theses or seminar papers I received relating to California women and politics in the late nineteenth and early twentieth centuries. At some point it became clear to me that several of these theses and papers fit together in a coherent whole, tracing the complex and varied role of California women in politics from the Gold Rush through the 1920s. I began to think that I should put together an anthology. Unfortunately for the realization of that idea, I had, at that time, accepted time-consuming responsibilities with the academic senates of my campus and of the California State University system.

However, during the year when I was serving as academic senate chair at San Francisco State, Joel Kassiola, my dean, provided funds (for which I am very thankful) for a graduate assistant to help organize the anthology. Ann Marie Wilson agreed to undertake the project. I gave Ann a list of theses and copies of seminar papers and asked her to contact the authors and ask them if they would be interested in revising, updating, and condensing their work for the project. She and I were pleased that everyone agreed. Later, when Ann was deeply involved in her doctoral studies at Harvard, we recruited one of our essayists, Mary Ann Irwin, to assist with further editing and with expanding to a full chapter the historiographical part of the introduction that we had written. Finally, we recruited a former San Francisco State student, Linda Heidenreich, to contribute a chapter based on her doctoral research. The results have amply justified my initial sense that there was a coherent story in the various theses and seminar papers.

Ann and Mary Ann join me in thanking each of the authors for their willingness to update their work and to fit it into the constraints we gave them. And we also thank Ann Baker and Matthew Bokovoy of the University of Nebraska Press. Matt saw the value of the project early on and was there for us when we encountered obstacles. We thank him especially for recognizing the importance of having the anthology available in time for the hundredth anniversary of California women's suffrage in 2011.

Robert W. Cherny

INTRODUCTION

These essays convey the remarkable extent and intensity of women's political participation in California from the Gold Rush through the 1920s. Perhaps the greatest lesson we find in these pages is that suffrage was by no means the only—or even the most important—turning point for many women's engagement with public life. California women were deeply involved in politics long before they won the vote in 1911, and they remained deeply involved afterward, pursuing a range of agendas that included everything from temperance and moral reform to conservation, trade unionism, and settlement work.

Downplaying the significance of suffrage, however, immediately raises an important question: how do we define "politics"? Like others before us, we have followed the expansive definition offered by Paula Baker, finding politics in "any action, formal or informal, taken to affect the course or behavior of government or the community."[1] Thus, by politics we mean not simply the activities of voting, campaigning, or holding public office, but also the larger processes that guide governments in allocating resources and exercising authority. By this definition, politics includes lobbying officeholders, collecting signatures on petitions, engaging in discussions of policy questions, and sometimes just showing up. The women discussed in these pages—women who demonstrated, carried picket signs, heckled or listened respectfully, hosted tea parties to discuss dairy sanitation, moved from bird-watching to bird protection, or wielded a spear—were all behaving politically.

In composing this anthology, we began with a number of questions derived from previous studies of women in U.S. politics.[2] One set of questions considered regional distinctiveness. Despite the large number of works published on American women in recent decades, few have focused centrally on women and politics in California. By examining women's activism in one place, it becomes possible to see individual women both reacting to new situations and participating in a variety of activities, to observe how various groups and individuals pursued political goals and interacted with each other in the process, and to examine the ways that these things changed over time. This volume seeks to answer some basic questions: What were women's contributions to political life in California?

How were public agencies and policies shaped by women's demands? How are the experiences of women in California different from those of women in other parts of the nation?

Given previous work, we also began with questions regarding the intersections of ethnicity, class, and gender in California. How did working-class, middle-class, and upper-class women conceive of their roles in public life? Did each of these groups ascribe the same meanings to the category of "woman"? If not, how did differences in gender ideology influence their respective activities, tactics, and goals? Given that nearly all of the women who led the organizations and activities explored here identified themselves as white, what roles did race and ethnicity play in their understandings of themselves and their polity?

Other questions focused on the internal structures of women's political activism. How did women configure themselves in organizing for change in California? How did women's tactics and objectives correspond with those of men, who still essentially dominated the formal world of politics? To what extent did middle- and working-class women work together, or apart? What were the salient variables in shaping their particular alliances? And how did different groups of women—organized into women's clubs, settlement houses, labor unions, and the professions—work with different groups of men? Did women's tactics and objectives change over time and, if so, how?

Finally, we asked questions about progressivism and suffrage.[3] How did the rise of progressivism shape women's politics in California? Did progressive ideals change women's tactics and objectives, or was it the other way around—that is, did women's involvement in politics significantly shape California progressivism? And what difference did the winning of woman suffrage make for the women of California? California women won the right to vote in 1911, at the height of the progressive movement, when the national political arena was filled with rhetoric about woman suffrage, and when citizens were hotly debating what—if anything—would change if women were allowed to vote. Did the vote appreciably change women's understandings of their rights and obligations as citizens? How did suffrage alter organized women's tactics, goals, and justifications for action? Just how were politics in California different after 1911?

In seeking answers to these questions, our goal throughout has been to look broadly at the ways that California women participated in the formation of public policy. The authors in this collection found women engaged in a wide range of political action—both within and without the electoral process—sometimes acting as individuals but usually as members of woman-led organizations. Nearly all of the essays acknowledge the significance of the women's club movement. In chapter 8, for example, Sandra Henderson views the politics of clubwomen through the lens of one particularly effective Bay Area group. Charitable organizations were crucial as well. The essays by Mary Ann Irwin (chapter 2) and Mildred Nichols Hamilton (chapter 4) explore the powerful connections that emerged between women's philanthropy and politics. Women also found political influence through moral reform: Joshua Paddison (chapter 3) looks at the California branch of the national Woman's Christian Temperance Union, while Teresa Hurley and Jarrod Harrison (chapter 10) consider the role of clubwomen in closing California brothels, and Mark Hopkins (chapter 12) examines the broad coalition of groups that sought to regulate commercial dance halls. Michelle Kleehammer and Cameron Binkley (chapters 6 and 7) focus on women's work in what we today would call the environmental movement, while Ann Marie Wilson (chapter 5) considers the nexus that emerged among women social scientists, settlement workers, and organized labor in the course of a campaign to enforce new child-labor regulations.

Though each chapter has a different author, and though each chapter considers women's politics in different circumstances, individual women move easily across the pages, just as they did in real life. Alice Park, Louise LaRue, Katherine Philips Edson, and Phoebe Apperson Hearst were all keenly interested in a variety of social issues in California; thus, it is not surprising that these women were involved in several of the political undertakings discussed here. Several organizations also appear in multiple chapters, including the California Federation of Women's Clubs, the Woman's Christian Temperance Union, San Francisco's California Club, and the Friday Morning Club of Los Angeles.

Electoral politics is another theme that receives attention in nearly all the chapters, even though none focus expressly on the state suffrage movement, or on the 1896 or 1911 campaigns to amend the state constitution. Gayle Gullett covers these topics admirably in *Becoming Citizens: The*

INTRODUCTION

Emergence and Development of the California Women's Movement, 1880–1911. To be certain, Susan Englander (chapter 9) focuses centrally on the suffrage issue, but she uses that issue to explore those issues that divided middle- and upper-class women from women unionists, even as those same groups managed nonetheless to unite behind the banner of suffrage.

Despite our focus on politics rather than suffrage, suffrage inevitably appears in several chapters, where it was sometimes an objective and sometimes a tool. For some women, including the clubwomen described in chapters 6 through 8, gaining the franchise seemed to have little effect on their political lives. In other instances (e.g., those discussed in chapter 10), some women were quick to seize upon the vote as a new and powerful lever to accomplish long-standing policy objectives. For one of those objectives, a legislated minimum wage for women, the class divide appears again in Rebecca Mead's study (chapter 11). In this regard, California provides a particularly interesting site for exploring women and politics: it was an urban, economically diverse state where women achieved suffrage at a time when the national suffrage movement was still debating what difference women would make if they were to exercise their citizenship as voters. What California women did with the vote in 1911 and after may reflect, more than anything else, their understandings of the national rhetoric regarding the importance of woman suffrage.

All in all, these chapters form a cohesive narrative that traces women's political activism from the philanthropy of the Gold Rush era and Gilded Age, through the temperance activism of the late nineteenth century, to the kaleidoscopic array of activities comprising progressive reform. Yet, even though the chapters convey the impressive range of women's political activities, some of the answers to our initial questions are not as well developed as we would have liked. Foremost among these unanswered questions is that of race. As will become clear, the large majority of women in this book came from northern European backgrounds. Although the women discussed here represent a variety of classes, religious faiths, and ethnic backgrounds, no woman of African or Asian descent appears centrally in any of the following chapters. Latinas and Native American women represented the majority of the region's female population prior to the American conquest, but only Linda Heidenreich (chapter 1) is able to tease from the record the politics of indigenous women and *Californianas* (women of Spanish or Mexican descent born in California). This volume's emphasis on white women reflects, in part, the reality that whites comprised 95 percent of the state's population during most of the period under review. Nonetheless, these chapters raise important questions about the racial exclusiveness of the public sphere in California—and about the ability of historians to construct a more racially inclusive narrative of the past. While white middle- and upper-class women left behind volumes of personal and organizational papers, the traces left by California's politically active women of color can be much more difficult to find. Mary Ann Irwin (chapter 14) considers these difficulties in a broad survey of the relevant literature and offers suggestions for future research that we hope will produce even broader definitions of women's politics in California.

Before proceeding to the specifics of women's politics, it might be useful to consider, more generally, the context in which these activities occurred. As noted above, California is an especially rewarding location for examining women's political activism, for a number of reasons. The diversity of the economy, the presence of a major city, the ethnic and religious diversity of its people, and a complex class structure all make California an interesting laboratory for the study of women's politics. During the period covered by this volume, California was growing much more rapidly than the nation as a whole. In 1880 California's population ranked twenty-fourth among the thirty-eight states. By 1920 it had moved up to eighth among forty-eight. While a significant part of this growth was in southern California, most of the state's population nonetheless resided north of the Tehachapi Mountains, the traditional dividing line between California's northern and southern regions—more than 90 percent in 1880, and 60 percent as late as 1920. Not until the 1920s did southern California gain the majority of the state's population.

In the 1850s the new state was also more racially diverse than the rest of the nation. A quarter or more of all Californians were African American, American Indian, Asian, or Latino. Though the state had become 95 percent white by 1900, it still included significant communities of Chinese and Japanese, plus smaller numbers of immigrants from elsewhere in Asia. California was also home to a number of small but well-established African American communities and one of the largest populations of Native

Americans of any state. After about 1910 growing numbers of Mexicans joined existing Latino communities that dated as far back as the pre-conquest and gold rush eras. Even the numerically dominant white population was more ethnically and religiously diverse than the nation as a whole. Before 1920 half or more of all white Californians were immigrants or the children of immigrants, with Irish, German, and British the largest groups, followed by Scandinavians and Italians.

Other demographic features are important as well. The women of California engaged in politics as residents of a highly urbanized and economically diverse state. At the 1900 census, more than 40 percent of Californians lived in its ten largest cities, and the state had a higher proportion of its population living in metropolitan areas than all but a few other states. In 1900 nearly a quarter of all Californians lived in San Francisco; another quarter lived around San Francisco Bay or in the coastal counties between Monterey and Mendocino. San Francisco remained the state's dominant metropolis until at least World War I, ranking among the nation's ten largest cities between 1870 and 1900. The city fell to eleventh place only in the 1910 census, after the devastating earthquake and fire of 1906.[4] San Francisco's banks and corporations dominated the economic life of much of the Pacific coast and parts of the intermountain West. Its port handled a large share of imports to and exports from the entire Pacific coast.[5]

The effect of class distinctions can also be readily observed. Exploitation of California's natural resources, commercial agriculture, rail and water shipping, manufacturing, and other enterprises created extremes of wealth that were unusual in the West. San Francisco's extremes of wealth—and poverty—inspired Henry George's *Progress and Poverty* and prompted Jack London to some of his most searching analyses of class and character. From at least the 1880s onward, northern California—especially San Francisco—was also a stronghold for unionism.[6]

It is in this complex setting that the essays presented here find women challenging the boundaries of the public sphere. Acting alone and in groups, California's women asserted their rights to liberty and self-defense, to respect in city thoroughfares, to equal education and to equal economic opportunities for themselves and their children. Although some women discussed here worked primarily to benefit others, along the way many accrued influence, prestige, and other personal benefits. Class and race always mattered. Sometimes, as in the case of charity work, elite white women had the political blessing of like-minded men. At other times—as in the campaigns against brothels, dance halls, and saloons—middle- and upper-class women faced opposition, not only from same-class men but also from women whose livelihoods were threatened. Women's political causes often failed to synchronize across the clefts created by class and race. White women's reforming energies often failed to mesh with those of minority women, who cared more about the rights denied to them as second-class citizens or as aliens ineligible for citizenship. But as the following chapters reveal, despite their differences, California's women leaders had one important objective in common: a polity in which women had the power to shape public policy and to create their own destinies.

Notes

1. Paula Baker, "The Domestication of Politics: Women and American Political Society, 1780–1920," *American Historical Review* 89 (1984): 622.

2. There have been so many works in the past few decades that have shaped understandings of women and politics for this time period that it is difficult to select a few that have been more significant than others in formulating the central questions that we sought to have our contributors address. Nonetheless, these works stand out: Susan H. Armitage, "Revisiting 'The Gentle Tamers Revisited': The Problems and Possibilities of Western Women's History—An Introduction," *Pacific Historical Review* 61 (1992): 459–99; Baker, "Domestication of Politics," 620–647; Karen J. Blair, *The Clubwoman as Feminist: True Womanhood Redefined, 1868–1914* (New York: Holmes & Meier, 1980); Ruth Bordin, *Woman and Temperance: The Quest for Power and Liberty, 1873–1900* (Philadelphia: Temple University Press, 1981); Nancy F. Cott, *The Grounding of Modern Feminism* (New Haven CT: Yale University Press, 1987); Ellen Carol DuBois, *Harriot Stanton Blatch and the Winning of Woman Suffrage* (New Haven CT: Yale University Press, 1997); Estelle Freedman, "Separatism as Strategy: Female Institution Building and American Feminism, 1870–1930," *Feminist Studies* 5 (1979): 512–529; Lori D. Ginzberg, *Women and the Work of Benevolence: Morality, Politics, and Class in the Nineteenth-Century United States* (New Haven CT: Yale University Press, 1990); Joan M. Jensen and Darlis A. Miller, "The Gentle Tamers Revisited: New Approaches to the History of Women in the American West," *Pacific Historical Review* 49 (1980): 173–213; Suzanne Lebsock, "Women and American Politics, 1880–1920," in *Women, Politics, and Change*, ed. Louise Tilley and Patricia Gurin (New York: Russell Sage Foundation, 1990);

Robyn Muncy, *Creating a Female Dominion in American Reform, 1890–1935* (New York: Oxford University Press, 1991); Mary P. Ryan, *Women in Public: Between Banners and Ballots, 1825–1880* (Baltimore: Johns Hopkins University Press, 1990); Anne Firor Scott, *Natural Allies: Women's Associations in American History* (Urbana: University of Illinois Press, 1991); Kathryn Kish Sklar, *Florence Kelley and the Nation's Work: The Rise of Women's Political Culture, 1830–1900* (New Haven CT: Yale University Press, 1995).

3. "Progressive" is a slippery term that historians still struggle to define precisely. Here, we define "progressivism" as a broad and dynamic process of political change composed of many specific reform movements and shifting coalitions of self-interested groups uniting temporarily over specific issues and behind specific political leaders. For a similar approach, see Tom Sitton, "John Randolph Hayes and the Left Wing of California Progressivism," in *California Progressivism Revisited*, ed. William Deverell and Tom Sitton (Berkeley: University of California Press, 1994). See also William Deverell, "Introduction: The Varieties of Progressive Experience," 1–14, in the same volume. For participants in such movements, we have used "progressive," and have limited the use of "Progressive" to those who took part in the separate political party by that name.

4. Gayle Gullett, *Becoming Citizens: The Emergence and Development of the California Women's Movement, 1880–1911* (Urbana: University of Illinois Press, 2000).

5. Data on population comes from the various federal censuses. In calculating the population north of the Tehachapis, Santa Barbara and Ventura counties were included in southern California.

6. William Issel and Robert W. Cherny, *San Francisco, 1865–1932: Politics, Power, and Urban Development* (Berkeley: University of California Press, 1986); Philip J. Ethington, *The Public City: The Political Construction of Urban Life in San Francisco, 1850–1900* (New York: Cambridge University Press, 1994); Michael Kazin, *Barons of Labor: The San Francisco Building Trades and Union Power in the Progressive Era* (Urbana: University of Illinois Press, 1989); and Neil Larry Shumsky, *The Evolution of Political Protest and the Workingmen's Party of California* (Columbus: Ohio State University Press, 1991).

CALIFORNIA WOMEN AND POLITICS

1. "I DO NOT LIKE THE WHITE MAN ... HE IS A LIAR AND A THIEF"

Testimonios and the Politics of Resistance

LINDA HEIDENREICH

In 1874 in Monterey, California, Rosalía Vallejo de Leese spoke with Henry Cerruti, a research assistant for Hubert H. Bancroft, the author and bookseller who was producing a multivolume history of California. Her purpose was to recount her memory of the so-called Bear Flag Revolt in the spring and summer of 1846, when a group of European American men came to the Napa-Sonoma region, stole goods from *Californio* ranches (that is, the homes of men and women of Spanish-Mexican descent whose families lived in California before the arrival of the Americans), subjected the indigenous people of the region to unbridled violence, and on June 14 proclaimed a California republic, complete with a flag depicting a grizzly bear. Soon after, John C. Frémont, an officer in the U.S. Army, arrived with troops; in the area on a surveying mission, Frémont took command. In mid-July, Frémont and the Bear Flaggers learned that the United States had declared war on Mexico in mid-May. At the end of the war, in 1848, Mexico ceded California and other territories to the United States. By 1874 the account of those events prevalent among the then dominant European American population of the region painted the *Osos* (Spanish for "bears," a term used both by the filibusters of 1846 to describe themselves and by the Californios to describe the filibusters) as heroes—men who challenged Mexican rule in California and brought liberty and republican institutions to the region.[1]

Vallejo de Leese, however, described the Osos as thieves, rapists, and "rough looking desperados."[2] She narrated her account in Spanish, the language of her community before the Americans seized California. Her narrative presents a counternarrative of the events of 1846 and, in the process, it seeks to preserve and protect her culture. Her decision to present her version of those events, and to do so in Spanish was deliberate. From the time of the American conquest onward, she had refused to speak with the newcomers who had taken control of California, and she had forbidden her children from speaking English in her presence.[3] In her own words, as translated by Cerruti: "Those hated men inspired me with such a large dose of hate against their race, that though 28 years have elapsed since that time, I have not yet forgotten the insults they heaped upon me, and not being desirous of coming in contact with them I have abstained from learning their language."[4] Yet on June 27, 1874, she spoke with Cerruti and, "through clenched teeth," dictated a narrative that directly challenged the European American version of the Bear Flag Revolt.[5]

Her statement may not seem political on its face but, in fact, it represents an effort to challenge existing configurations of power, to preserve Californio values that were then under attack—including attacks using the more usual forms of politics—and to pose an alternative to the histories constructed by the "rough looking desperados" who came to power between 1846 and 1848.[6]

Vallejo de Leese's statement may be considered a *testimonio*, or testimony. The term *testimonio* can be traced to the time of the Spanish conquest of the Americas. Yet its modern definition—describing testimonies that are political critiques of specific historical events and that are voiced by the people under attack—was not established until 1959 during the Cuban revolution.[7] Perhaps the best-known testimonio is that of Rigoberta Menchú, whose graphic testimony of the Guatemalan civil war brought international attention to both Menchú and her people. Scholars now use the term to apply to a narrative by an eyewitness whose purpose in testifying is to draw attention to a desperate situation (e.g., oppression or poverty), or to correct a widespread perception that differs from the author's personal experience. Recent scholars have begun to treat as testimonios many of the late-nineteenth-century dictations by Californios, Californianas, and indigenous (California Indian) women. By treating these sources as testimonios, the political nature of those narratives becomes apparent.[8] Genaro Padilla's groundbreaking study, *My History, Not Yours*, examined many Californiana/o testimonios, drawing attention to women's testimonios as a form of resistance, and placing the testimonios in the larger political context of their time. Rosaura Sánchez, Beatrice Pita, and Bárbara Reyes have published several Californiana/o testimonios; most recently, Rose Marie Beebe and Robert M. Senkewicz published a volume of women's testimonios, many seeing publication for the first time. Of course, it was Rosaura Sánchez's *Telling Identities* that brought a critical and multidimensional analysis to the documents, forever changing the way that scholars approach these texts.[9] Similarly, Antonia Castañeda, Emma Pérez, Deena González, Vicki Ruiz, Miroslava Chávez-García, and Bárbara O. Reyes have established a body of scholarship in which Chicanas and Californianas are the center of analysis, one that examines women's efforts to maintain their own cultural values and identities in the face of strong pressure to conform to the views of the conquering European American majority.[10]

In order to do this work, Chicana historians have used a concept called the *decolonial imaginary*. In the 1990s the historian Emma Pérez developed the idea of the decolonial imaginary to explain how some of the most important historical events and facts are phenomena that most historians are not trained to see. According to this idea, war and other acts of conquest and domination make it difficult for conquered people to be political and to leave historical records in the same way as the dominant groups. In order to understand the politics of people who are not part of the dominant group, historians need to look for sources where there appear to be none. The historian needs to ask questions such as, "Where are the gaps in this historical record?" "Whose point of view is missing from this document?" "How did the people who did not hold political offices or own property understand the events of their time?" In other words, historians need to look at the gaps in the dominant way of understanding history, the nation, and politics, and to start research there.

This essay looks at the gap surrounding Californianas' and indigenous women's voices in California politics in late-nineteenth-century California. It asks "How did Californiana and indigenous women understand the historical events of the late nineteenth century?" and "How were these women historical actors?"[11] This essay presents testimonios by three women, Isidora Filomena Solano, Rosalía Vallejo de Leese, and María Higuera Juárez. Isidora Filomena Solano grew up in a Chiuructos (California Indian) community, a community that resisted Mexican colonization long after the establishment of California's mission system. Vallejo de Leese belonged to one of the wealthiest families in the region prior to the U.S. invasion—her brother was Mariano Guadalupe Vallejo, once both comandante general of northern California and the largest landowner in northern California. María Higuera Juárez grew up in a military family at the San Francisco Presidio.[12] Between 1846 and 1848, these women lived in what are now Napa, Sonoma, and Lake counties, areas north of San Francisco Bay. In the late nineteenth century, all three women spoke back to the European American society that had invaded their worlds and attacked their property holdings, language, and culture.

All three narratives come to us through someone else. María Higuera Juárez's stories come from her children and grandchildren. The testimonios of Rosalía Vallejo de Leese and Isidora Filomena Solano were filtered through the pen of Henry Cerruti. In the 1870s, when Bancroft began collecting documents to write his voluminous *History of California*, he sent assistants to interview Californianas/os so that he could include their information in his narrative and produce what he considered an objective history. Yet those narratives were not presented directly. The Californios dictated their stories in response to specific questions, which questions have not survived. Bancroft's agents wrote down the stories, filtering their subjects' words through the agents' own cultural understandings and, sometimes, translating from Spanish to English.[13] Thus, these narratives are all mediated—that is, the only version we have comes to us through someone other than the original narrator. More importantly, we must keep in mind the politics of those agents; the testimonios of Vallejo de Leese and Solano were mediated by individuals who benefited from the conquest of California.

Yet through these mediated narratives, Solano, Higuera Juárez, and Vallejo de Leese successfully challenge the dominant European American histories of their time. All three women engage what the scholar Lourdes Torres has termed "active memory," recounting the past in order "to confront the violence and silences of the past."[14] In doing so, the three women construct a different version of the past—a counternarrative that can be used by Californianas and Chicanas in the future.

By the time that Solano, Higuera Juárez, and Vallejo de Leese chose to speak back, it was the conqueror's story that had come to dominate histories of northern California. Throughout the latter half of the nineteenth century, as European Americans moved into the provinces taken from Mexico, they redefined the region as "American," solidifying a definition rooted in their own histories and understandings.[15] This redefinition was sometimes written in blood. Accounts from the 1870s through the early twentieth century tell of resistance by Californianas/os and indigenous peoples. When an Oso beat Sinao, a Suisun (California Indian) man with a cat-o'-nine-tails, Sinao lassoed the perpetrator, dragged him out of town, and then fled the area, never to be seen again.[16] Responding to the labor exploitation, beatings, thievery, and sexual violence of the European American men who had moved onto their land, Pomo (California Indian) peoples living by Clear Lake killed two of the perpetrators.[17] In Napa, when a European American man by the name of Preston shot and wounded Manuel Vera, Vera shot back.[18]

Most of this resistance was met with further violence. In response to the killing of the two men by Clear Lake, the United States Army slaughtered more than five hundred Pomo men, women, and children. In response to Vera's action, the men of Napa blackened their faces, stormed the county jail, and lynched him.[19] To avoid retaliation, some indigenous peoples, Californianas/os, and other communities in northern California found new and creative ways to maintain their language and cultures and to thereby resist white rule. Those in power responded by creating English-only policies in the public schools, demonizing ethnic neighborhoods, passing laws that indentured indigenous youth, and imposing white Protestant culture as normative.[20]

Violence was also used to physically remove indigenous peoples from land desired by European American settlers. In 1851 the U.S. Cavalry forcibly removed many indigenous peoples to reservations north of Napa.[21] Determined to take revenge on real and imagined cattle thefts, white settlers rode into Wappo-, Patwin-, and Pomo-speaking villages and rancherías and, in some cases, killed entire communities of men, women, and children. Napa newspapers printed accounts of white men "hunting" indigenous peoples.[22]

Those who had gained dominance through attempted genocide, war, theft, and law also constructed themselves as heroes.[23] By the 1860s a group known as the Pioneers of California began hosting annual celebrations of the Bear Flag "revolt" in Sonoma. It posted ads in Napa newspapers inviting all pioneers—but especially those who had "served on the side of the United States"—to come celebrate. Those who gathered toasted the men who stormed Sonoma, roasted an ox "in the old style," and then ran a Bear Flag up a flagpole.[24] Reminiscences by European American men who participated in the Bear Flag incident appeared in the local press, recollections that sometimes described the Californios as either "Mexicans [who did] not labor themselves" or as "greasers."[25] In the 1870s, as the Osos began to die, the *Napa Recorder* printed obituaries that constructed their deeds as heroic.[26]

The mythologies promulgated by the Pioneers in newspaper accounts and reunions were explicitly gendered. They not only constructed white men as heroes but also depicted Californianas as welcoming maidens. Even as women such as Vallejo de Leese and Higuera Juárez were resisting white rule, European American men were creating fantasies that constructed ethnic Mexican women as sexually available. By the 1870s images of the sexually available Californiana appeared both in eastern papers and in local periodicals.[27] In the *Napa Reporter*, for example, an author calling himself "Bear Flag" described Californianas as "señoritas" who desired European American men, especially men with "rosy cheeks and light hair."[28] Yet as Rosaura Sánchez noted in her analysis of the Californiana/o testimonios, the myths that European American men constructed around Californianas stood in dramatic contrast to the actual resistance rendered by the Californianas at the time of the invasion. According to Californiana/o accounts of the invasion, many Californianas, even those who were married to European Americans who sided with the United States, actively resisted the invaders.[29]

Recent scholars tell us that the construction of new local and national narratives and the subordination of indigenous or other previous histories and myths are an integral part of colonizing processes.[30] In the Napa-Sonoma region, the subjugation and attempted genocide of indigenous peoples was normalized by the argument that Wappo- and Patwin-speaking peoples (California Indian groups) were "fading away."[31] At the same time, European Americans glorified their dominance through a narrative that treated the newcomers as heroic "pioneers," and by describing incidents such as the Bear Flag "revolt" as heroic. Thus, it should be no surprise that Solano, in her testimonio, defended the lifeways of her people, or that Vallejo de Leese and Higuera Juárez specifically challenged the Bear Flag incident in their narratives, challenging what had become the dominant narrative in regional newspapers and the popular press.

When Cerruti transcribed the women's histories, the communities of Solano, Vallejo de Leese, and Higuera Juárez had been under attack for three decades. Responding to violence with violence had proven fruitless—and, at times, highly dangerous. By the 1870s counternarratives had become just one of several strategies by which Californio and indigenous communities fought back. The three narratives constructed by Solano, Vallejo de Leese, and Higuera Juárez all present the lawlessness and violence of European American men in such a way that, out of context, a reader might question why these women even spoke to Bancroft's agent, or why they would pass such stories on to their children. Yet, in the context of the dominant discourse of the time—with "lazy greasers," "fading" Indians, and "heroic pioneers"—we can see that these counternarratives were acts of resistance. In each, the speaker was attempting to create a space different from the one in which she was living.

In order to understand the significance of this space, we must turn to the concept of *sitio y lengua* (space and language), developed by Emma Pérez and other recent scholars.[32] According to these studies, a people must have their own language and space in order to survive and flourish. When colonizers come into an inhabited space, they not only claim the physical space but also seek to erase the language and the histories of the previous inhabitants—thus subjugating not only the people but also their histories and their ability to reconstruct those histories. Pérez argues that without language there is no memory.[33] In preserving or reconstructing histories, one can create a space—in the past—that sustains the community and allows it to imagine a different future. Thus, when Vallejo de Leese and Higuera Juárez found themselves in a space occupied by European Americans, where their language was banned from the public schools, and where the prevailing stories of conquest normalized white rule, they used their stories to create a different space. In all three of the narratives, the women reclaim their pasts—not only their personal pasts, but also their communities' pasts. In doing so, they create narrative locations that can be used by future generations—narratives that allow us, as Pérez puts it, to "decolonize a historical imaginary that veils our thoughts, our words, our languages," and to decide which history we want to survive, need to survive.[34] With these questions and theories in mind, let us turn to the narratives of Isidora Filomena Solano, Rosalía Vallejo de Leese, and María Higuera Juárez.

Isidora Filomena Solano

> Sutter forced the Jalquineros [California Indians] to exchange hides and dried fish for liquor; he had an Indian woman, not from California, she was a Canacha Indian who arrived in a boat with him—I do not like the white man much because he is a liar and a thief, my compadres Peralta and friend Bernales had many cows, Sutter lied to everyone, took everything, and gave nothing in return.[35] —Isidora Filomena Solano

In her testimonio, Isidora Filomena Solano refers to herself both as Chiructos and as Satiyomi. Wappo-speaking people did not refer to themselves as Satiyomi, but Spanish and later Mexican settler-colonizers did. Thus, we can deduce that she was most probably from a Wappo-speaking community, a group whose history in the region may have extended more than eight thousand years.[36] Like other indigenous people in northern California, the Wappo were a hunting and gathering people whose culture and political economy were shaped by gender roles and by trade networks that reached up the Pacific Coast.

The Wappos' geographic location between the Coast Miwok and Pomo meant that they were at the center of a regional trade network, harvesting clamshells from Pomo territory and working them into disks with which to purchase awls, carrying baskets, split-stick dice, and arrows.[37] Because of the role of trade throughout northern California, such communities were multilingual. People from other linguistic groups came to various villages to trade and then stayed to celebrate or worship together. Communities shared goods, stories, and languages, and most communities included people functional in at least three languages or dialects. About or shortly before the time that Isidora was born, this trade network was disrupted. In 1810 the Carquin people—the last of the communities standing between the Patwin people and Mission San Francisco de Asís—converted to Catholicism. The Patwin moved northeast, into the Napa area, to escape the Spanish missionaries and soldiers.[38] (Sem Yeto, Solano's future husband, came from one of these Patwin communities.)

As a young woman in a nineteenth-century Wappo-speaking community, Isidora lived among women who gathered acorns, fruits, herbs, and tubers. Many were expert weavers. Some women, like the men in the community, were trained in sanding, shaping, and drilling shells for trade; on occasion, women sometimes hunted small game. Isidora also lived in a world fraught with conflict. From time to time, Patwin-speaking peoples attempted incursions into their territories. Although these attempts escalated after Mission San Francisco Solano was established in the Sonoma area, trade and gathering continued.[39]

Then, in 1835, Isidora's world was turned upside down. Sem Yeto converted to Catholicism and became a trusted ally of Mariano Guadalupe Vallejo. Called "Chief Solano" by the Californios, Sem Yeto and his troops rode with Vallejo and his troops on campaigns against other indigenous peoples. This alliance allowed Sem Yeto to gain control over most of the indigenous peoples of the region. In 1835 Vallejo and Sem Yeto campaigned against Isidora's people. As he had in the past, Vallejo allowed Sem Yeto to keep any goods or women taken in the fighting.[40] Sem Yeto took Isidora, bringing her back to Mission San Francisco Solano, where the mission priest could train her as a Christian wife.[41]

By the time of the Bear Flag incident, Isidora had daughters working as servants in the household of Mariano Guadalupe Vallejo. Sem Yeto had gained special status, including the right to carry arms and to have a color guard; his people also had the right to refuse baptism, although such privileges did not extend to Sem Yeto's own family. When the European Americans invading Sonoma threatened violence against the men in the Vallejo family, Mariano feared Sem Yeto would retaliate, so he told Sem Yeto to leave. Sem Yeto went north, seeking a place where there were no white people—no European Americans and no Californios. He reached what was most probably Alaska and did not return for twelve years.[42] And so Isidora Solano was left to labor as a single mother; she raised eight children and watched all but one of them die.[43] European Americans and Californios stole or swindled from her the land that she and Sem Yeto had once held. Thus in her old age, Solano lived in a house on Mariano Guadalupe Vallejo's property, remembering her life before the "blancos" (whites) came, and supported by her only child, the one who had not died of disease or "sadness."[44]

Among other things, Solano's testimonio provides evidence of her very existence. Unlike Vallejo de Leese and Higuera Juárez, she does not appear on any census roll.[45] Unlike her husband, Sem Yeto, she rarely appears in any other testimonio or memoir of the time. When she does, it is a brief mention, as in the memoirs of Platon Mariano Guadalupe Vallejo, which note that Sem Yeto "left behind a wife, known by her Christian name Isadora [sic]. Also three daughters."[46] Solano's testimonio, then, restores her to the historical record, as it restores the lives of indigenous women generally. In modern terms it would qualify as a *recuerdo*, a document that tells a history and that contains information about the lifeways in a community's past, a recollection that weaves together history and other knowledge.[47] Her testimonio covers three categories: indigenous life before the *gente blanco* (white people), the dishonest acts of the European Americans, and how Solano came to be alone, living on the property of Mariano Guadalupe Vallejo and possessing "nothing." The testimonio is rich and many layered.

It is worthwhile to consider the structure of her narrative. Solano begins her life history in the present, stating that Californios such as Remijio Berryessa, Gonzálo Ramírez, and Salvador Vallejo still visited her, still called her "princess." She explains how she came to hold her title and how she survived two waves of gente blanco colonizers. She specifies that she did not choose Californio culture: "Before I was baptized, I belonged to the Chiructos tribe, and [Sem Yeto] . . . stole me. My father, along with many others from the Satiyomi[,] pursued him, but could not overcome him."[48] She follows the story of the kidnapping with an account of her acculturation, recalling, "Father Quijas, who baptized me, gave me the name Isidora Filomena, he taught me to be charitable to the poor, submissive to my husband, and compassionate with prisoners."[49] Solano does not speak of her acculturation negatively; instead, she stresses the values she was taught at the mission. Thereafter, she became the wife of Sem Yeto, known to Californios as "Chief Solano." Her account of Californio culture, before the European Americans came, is complex. At the same time that she recounts the violence of the Californios, she also notes their positive attributes. Thus, her account of her own survival is also a history of both her people and the Californios.

Although it is a mediated narrative, Solano's account of her life before the whites arrived is among the most detailed of the surviving narratives from an indigenous woman of her time. In it, Solano disputes prevailing stereotypes. In the 1870s, for example, white newcomers specified that the indigenous peoples were "fading away" and that they were dirty and lacking in industry.⁵⁰ The Californios, depicting themselves as the bearers of civilization, had spoken similarly about Patwin- and Wappo-speaking peoples.⁵¹ Solano's testimonio, however, stressed the abundance of food and material wealth before colonization, and noted how clean her people were: "We lived our lives with joy, we loved to bathe, because bathing makes you strong . . . my people always had white teeth that we cleaned with branches of ash trees."⁵² Food was in abundance, both plant food to be gathered and wild game to be hunted, and "*todos teníamos casas de tule*"—everyone had a home of tule reeds. Solano also spoke of her skills. Like other women in her community, she knew the herbs of the region and used them for making soap or curing illnesses.

Solano's narrative challenges white mythologies of Yankee industriousness in two places. On page two, she boldly asserts, "I drink a lot of liquor and I do this because I no longer possess my land, teeming with livestock, because the white men stole everything; nothing was left." Both Sem Yeto and Isidora Solano had once strongly opposed the sale of liquor to their people. Seeing the destruction that alcohol brought, Sem Yeto had fought the incursion of missions and presidios into the north, in an attempt to keep the substance out of his community.⁵³ Isidora continued to speak out against it, even after she turned to alcohol as an escape.⁵⁴ In her narrative, it is a drug she turns to only after being defeated by the whites—and it is a tool used by whites to subjugate indigenous peoples.

Solano specifically challenges the reputation of John Sutter. A Swiss immigrant, Sutter came to North America in the 1830s. After living both in the United States and in Mexico, he received a Mexican land grant in 1840, in the Sacramento Valley. There he built a fort and encouraged European Americans to settle in the region. Sutter exploited the labor of the indigenous peoples of the region. He sometimes traded liquor for hides, and he sometimes recruited California Indians to labor and then gave them nothing in return but mush from a trough. Sutter gave jobs and land to European Americans and sometimes forced the local peoples to work for them.⁵⁵ By the late nineteenth century, his name appeared in regional European American histories as a heroic founding father, but in Solano's account he is a thief who stole from both indigenous peoples and Californios, a man who "lied to everyone, took everything, and gave nothing in return."

1. *Rosalía Vallejo de Leese with spouse and children, ca. 1850.*
Courtesy San Mateo County Historical Association, San Mateo County History Museum.

Thus, Isidora Filomena Solano provides a counternarrative that challenges the dominant white narratives of her time. The richly textured and oppositional text rejects the invaders' stereotypes of indigenous peoples and, at the same time, informs readers of indigenous lifeways before the arrival of "gente blanco." Her testimonio forthrightly asserts that neither Mexicans nor European Americans uplifted her people. Instead, they replaced one culture with another one, and then yet another. Solano depicts violence against her community under both Mexican and European American rule, and asserts the corruption and dishonesty of an iconic pioneer. While Rosalía Vallejo de Leese and María Higuera Juárez also construct critiques of Euro-American invaders, neither acknowledge the violence against indigenous peoples perpetrated by their own society.

Rosalía Vallejo de Leese

During the whole time Frémont and his gang were in Sonoma, robberies were very common: ladies dared not go out for a walk unless escorted by their husbands and brothers—among my servants I had a young Indian girl about 17 years of age; and I assure you that many a time John C. Frémont sent me orders to deliver her to the officers at the barracks, but by resorting to artifices I managed to save the unhappy girl from the fate decreed to her by the lawless band.⁵⁶ —Rosalía Vallejo de Leese

Rosalía Vallejo de Leese grew up in Monterey, a member of the Vallejo family that dominated northern California in the middle of the nineteenth century and forced indigenous women, such as the daughters of Isidora Filomena Solano, into servitude. Vallejo de Leese's father, grandfather, and two brothers were all military officers, working to colonize northern California for Spain and then for Mexico. Her childhood was privileged yet harsh. The family was literate, with the boys studying with a public tutor and the girls studying at home. Though the family income was higher and more stable than that of regular soldiers, there were few luxuries. Men left the presidio for weeks at a time to fight indigenous peoples, leaving landed women at home to guard property, care for children, and manage the household. In 1818, when Hippolyte de Bouchard sacked the town and presidio of Monterey, Rosalía was among the children taken south and inland to Mission San Antonio.⁵⁷

Vallejo married outside the military. Her brother, Mariano, had wanted her to marry Timothy Murphy, an acculturated Irishman, but she chose instead to marry Jacob Leese. Originally from Ohio, Leese was a convert to Catholicism and a naturalized Mexican citizen.⁵⁸ A successful businessman in Yerba Buena (now San Francisco), Leese built a large home and attached a general store. In 1841 he received a land grant in the Sonoma region, and the family moved to Sonoma, the town and presidio established by Rosalía Vallejo's brother Mariano. Leese built a family home on the plaza and bred horses on their land grant.⁵⁹ Leese was not an officer, but he and other European Americans in the area served in the local militia. Thus, Vallejo de Leese continued to live in a militarized society. They had several children before Leese abandoned the family.⁶⁰

When Rosalía Vallejo de Leese sat down to speak with Henry Cerruti, she did not focus on the lifeways of her community prior to 1846—perhaps because, by the 1870s, she had returned to Monterey, where a significant Californio community still resided. Where Solano had only her memories and a wedding dress (which Cerruti took with him when finished his interview), Vallejo de Leese had her memories, her children, and a very small piece of property.[61] So it is possible that Rosalía felt she did not need to recount the lifeways of her community. It is also true that her brothers Mariano Guadalupe Vallejo and Salvador Vallejo—who provided two of the most substantial testimonios—also spoke with Cerruti and provided detailed accounts of life before the arrival of European Americans.

Whatever her reasons, Vallejo de Leese focused her account on the Bear Flag incident. In it, she portrayed Frémont and Sutter as anything but heroic. Like Solano, she wrote of these men as liars and thieves, and of Frémont as a rapist and a thief, thus providing a powerful counter-narrative. Like Solano, she also created a space where she, as a historical subject, resisted European American domination.

Unlike the usual narratives of the Osos, in Vallejo de Leese's account lawless violence saturates the Bear Flag episode. Frémont and his men attempted to murder her brother, to burn her and her unborn child, and to rape a young woman working in her household. Her recounting begins when, at half past five in the morning, she was awakened by a neighbor and informed that "a band of 72 rough looking desperadoes" had surrounded her brother's house. She rushed to the scene to find "Colonel Prudón hastening to the rescue of Captain Salvador Vallejo whom a ruffian called Benjamin Kelsey was trying to murder in cold blood." Prudón rescued Vallejo but was then detained along with Salvador and Mariano Guadalupe and brought to Sacramento, where they "were delivered to the tender mercy of the arch fiend John A. Sutter."[62]

Vallejo de Leese's narrative depicts the multiple ways that women resisted the invaders. According to her account, Frémont received news that Captain Padilla and his men were on their way to take Sonoma back from the Osos. Frémont sent for Vallejo de Leese and ordered her to write to Padilla, telling him to return to San José. Vallejo de Leese flatly refused, and she says, "but Frémont, who was bent on having his way, told me that he would burn our houses with us inside of them if I refused." She recalls, "I consented, not for the purpose of saving my life, but being in the family way I had no right to endanger the life of my unborn baby."[63]

Vallejo de Leese also addressed the sexual violence and threats of sexual violence perpetrated by the Osos. In this, her narrative intersects with those of male testimonios and histories of the U.S. conquest. Antonio María Osio, for example, wrote of the attempted rape of one of the daughters of Don Angel Castro, a landed Californio living in southern Alta California.[64] Salvador Vallejo likewise wrote of Frémont's men riding through the Napa Valley and sexually assaulting indigenous women.[65] In both men's and women's counternarratives, Frémont and his men are rapists. Yet in both Salvador Vallejo's and Antonio Osio's accounts, the women remain nameless.[66] Osio and Vallejo present women as historical objects, people to whom violence was done. Vallejo de Leese, on the other hand, is no object; she writes of herself as a historical actor, a woman responsible for protecting her home, family, unborn child, and the servant who worked for her. Under the circumstances, self-protection was no mean feat. In those moments when women are safe, according to Vallejo de Leese, it was because they were "escorted by their husbands and brothers" or, at other times, because they "resorted to artifices."

Vallejo de Leese's narrative, like that of Solano, challenges the dominant narrative. European Americans were not virtuous and industrious people who brought civilization to the region. Instead, they arrived in a culture-laden space, a *sitio*. In confronting myths of European American heroics, she, like Solano, marked off a space for herself in the past. Where Vallejo de Leese's narrative, like those of the men in her community, recounts the Bear Flag incident from a Californio perspective, noting the violence of the Osos, including the sexual violence of Frémont's men, her sitio is not just a Californio space but an engendered, Californi*ana* space.[67] It is a historical space where women are empowered—where they make choices and resist. By leaving a narrative of those actions, they make it possible for later generations of women to visualize a different past and, perhaps, to imagine a different future.

María Higuera Juárez

In August 1846 General Frémont passed by the Rancharia with one hundred and fifty men. Sixty of them came to the Juárez rancho and, while Don Cayetano was away, stole cattle and horses and saddles. They approached the house and attempted to take a very handsome saddle belonging to Señora María Juárez. She threatened to attack them with a heavy spear with which she was armed and which she could adeptly use and they rode off without her saddle.[68] —Vivien Juárez Rose

Like Rosalía Vallejo de Leese, María Higuera Juárez was born into a military family that lived at the far north of Mexico's territories. Her father was an officer at the San Francisco Presidio, as was his father before him.[69] As a young girl she received the training a young woman needed in a colonizing society—among other things, apparently she was taught to use a spear.[70] We do not know if this was part of her formal or informal education, but from the testimonio of Californianas in southern Alta California, we know that many presidio women were skilled with weapons. María and the other women in her family were also skilled at riding horses, at times participating in community rodeos.[71] At the age of twenty, María Higuera married Sergeant Cayetano Juárez in the chapel at Mission San Francisco de Asís (Mission Dolores). Two years later, she and Sergeant Juárez moved to Napa, which was then part of the district of Sonoma, where Mariano Guadalupe Vallejo helped Juárez obtain a grant of 8,856 acres.[72]

Once settled in Napa, Higuera Juárez's life was one of labor. She supervised servants, but she also labored alongside them, cleaning and cooking, and traveling to the river to do laundry. Like the Wappo and Patwin people who preceded her, she gathered local herbs, such as angelica and nettle; she also used rosemary, an herb introduced to the region by the Spanish colonizer-settlers.[73]

Higuera Juárez lived in a society where military violence was normal.[74] Her husband was wounded in an 1829 campaign against Native peoples, just forty miles from their home. His body always bore the scar from the arrow that lodged in his leg.[75] He stayed at the presidio for weeks at a time. While he was away, Higuera Juárez was responsible for protecting herself, her children, and the family property.[76] By the time of the Bear Flag incident, the family's land holdings were second in size only to the Vallejos in the Napa area.[77] She and Cayetano had eleven children, a family larger than that of the average Californio family of her time.[78]

The account of Higuera Juárez was published independently, without the mediation of Bancroft or his agents. Thus, her narrative provides information about the women Cerruti—for whatever reason—did not interview. It is worth noting that Bancroft's staff collected fewer than fifteen testimonios from women. The rest, nearly one hundred narratives, were those of men. In Bancroft's master narrative of the era, men were typically the actors, and the women were acted upon. As Genaro

Padilla indicates, Bancroft "was chiefly interested in supplementing the political history of California, which meant that men who held office, rancheros, military officials, soldiers, or traders" were called on to record their recuerdos.[79] Yet Padilla suggests a secondary cause for the disproportion in testimonios given by men and by women: for some women, refusal to speak to Bancroft's agents was, in itself, an act of resistance. Higuera Juárez's husband provided Cerruti with the shortest testimonio in Bancroft's collection, so one wonders if perhaps his wife simply refused to speak with his agents.[80] Whether we have no testimonio from Higuera Juárez because Bancroft devalued women's words, or because she herself refused to speak with Cerruti, or some combination of the two, we do have Higuera Juárez's recounting of an event in the Bear Flag incident. This recounting indicates that Californianas who left no written records were not necessarily silent: they spoke to their children. Thus, women's voices and accounts of resistance may appear in family stories and records. Higuera Juárez's story was eventually written down by a great-granddaughter, Vivien Juárez Rose, who committed family stories and histories to paper and then sifted through family records and newspaper clippings, old bills, and report cards to verify as many facts as she possibly could.[81] The collection assembled by Higuera Juárez's granddaughter points to the many locations we must plumb if we will recover women's counternarratives of resistance.

Not surprisingly, the history passed down by María Higuera Juárez has much in common with the testimonio given by Rosalía Vallejo de Leese. The story is much shorter and focuses on a single event, but it likewise addresses the Bear Flag episode and confronts the heroic myths surrounding Frémont and the Osos that dominated the popular press of her time. In her narrative, Higuera Juárez was at the family rancho while her husband was away in Sonoma. As in the past, she was in charge of managing the household, family, and property in her husband's absence. Thus, when Frémont's men rode through the Napa Valley and to the Juárez rancho, it was she who met them at the door—"with her spear in her hand."

Higuera Juárez's account, as passed down through her children and their children, challenges the narratives of the heroic Osos, views that depict Californianas as passive or as welcoming "señoritas." In Higuera Juárez's counternarrative, Frémont's men were would-be thieves, attempting to steal a woman's property—the saddle of Higuera Juárez—while her husband was away. The image of Higuera Juárez, spear in hand, standing off Frémont's men, stands as a powerful corrective to the hagiographies that filled northern California's local press in the late nineteenth century.

What does it mean to engage in a politics of resistance? In northern California in the late nineteenth century, indigenous women and Californianas found their space and language invaded. The violent resistance mounted by the men of their communities proved disastrous, as European American men met physical resistance with violence. By the time the women gave their testimonios, the California legislature had instituted English as the official language in public schools and Spanish was seldom taught at all.[82] Laws had normalized many aspects of white Protestant culture and the indenture of indigenous peoples. And so women found new means of resistance, mounting their opposition as racialized women with words and histories. A very small number of women spoke to Bancroft's staff, and others, such as María Higuera Juárez, passed their histories on to children and grandchildren.

The records left by all three women represent an oppositional politics that continues to challenge traditional accounts. In a time when the Osos were depicted as heroes, these women wrote of them as rapists and thieves. The women here challenged the stereotypes of indigenous women and Californianas that filled the white mind, and wrote themselves into the historical record as actors who resisted white rule. In doing so they constructed a sitio y lengua in the past, a historical place in which they resisted, a location to which future generations of indigenous women and Chicanas might reach to imagine and build different futures. Bancroft did not mention the existence of women's testimonios in his work, yet in the late 1980s historians such as Antonia Castañeda found the testimonios and letters of Californianas in his collection at the Bancroft library. Castañeda and others used the material, as had the women who left their stories, to once again challenge dominant narratives of early California history.[83] The founders of Mujeres Activas en Letras y Cambio Social (a Chicana feminist organization) drew on the newly emerging field of Chicana/o studies and on family histories, recuerdos, and testimonios to articulate a Chicana feminist politic for the twentieth century.[84]

The narratives of Solano, Vallejo de Leese, and Higuera Juárez remind us of the power and politics of history. Historical narratives are tools with which dominant groups establish power. They are also tools with which others resist power. Historical narratives—even those that seem to be lost in the "gaps" of time—can help later generations organize and rebuild community.

Notes

Portions of this chapter originally appeared in Linda Heidenreich, "The Colonial North: Histories of Women and Violence from before the U.S. Invasion," an essay in Aztlán: A Journal of Chicano Studies 30, no. 1 (2005): 23–54, published by the UCLA Chicano Studies Research Center Press. Excerpts also appeared in chapter 4 of Linda Heidenreich, This Land Was Mexican Once: Histories of Resistance from Northern California (Austin: University of Texas Press, 2007). Many thanks to Aztlán and to the University of Texas Press for their permission to use this material.

1. Dale L. Walker, Bear Flag Rising: The Conquest of California, 1846 (New York: Forge, 1999), 117.

2. Rosalía Vallejo de Leese, "History of the Bear Party," MSS C-E 65:10, p. 1, Bancroft Library, University of California, Berkeley, California (hereafter "Bancroft").

3. Genaro Padilla, My History, Not Yours: The Formation of Mexican American Autobiography (Madison: University of Wisconsin Press, 1993), 149.

4. Vallejo de Leese, "History," 6.

5. Padilla, My History, Not Yours, 25.

6. Américo Paredes, David Gutiérrez, and others mark the United States–Mexico border and the region claimed by the United States as its Southwest as "Greater Mexico," in recognition of its socioeconomic and cultural reality. See David Gutiérrez, "Migration, Emergent Ethnicity, and the 'Third Space': The Shifting Politics of Nationalism in Greater Mexico," Journal of American History 86, no. 2 (September 1999): 484.

7. Rosaura Sánchez, Telling Identities: The Californio Testimonios (Minneapolis: University of Minnesota Press, 1995), 7.

8. Chéla Sandoval, "U.S. Third World Feminism: The Theory and Method of Oppositional Consciousness in the Postmodern World," Genders 10 (Spring 1991): 1–24.

9. Rosaura Sánchez, Beatrice Pita, and Bárbara Reyes, Nineteenth Century Californio Testimonial, Crítica Monograph Series (San Diego: UCSD Ethnic Studies/Third World Studies, 1994); Sánchez, Telling Identities; Rose Marie Beebe and Robert M. Senkewicz, eds., Testimonios: Early California through the Eyes of Women, 1815–1848 (Berkeley: Heyday Books, 2007).

10. Antonia Castañeda, "Presidarias y Pobladoras: Spanish-Mexican Women in Frontier Monterey, Alta California, 1770–1821" (PhD dissertation, Stanford University, 1990); Antonia Castañeda, "Sexual Violence in the Politics of Conquest: Amerindian Women and the Spanish Conquest of Alta California," in *Building with Our Hands: New Directions in Chicana Studies*, ed. Adela de la Torre and Beatriz M. Pesquera, 15–33 (Berkeley: University of California Press, 1993); Antonia Castañeda, "Engendering the History of Alta California, 1769–1848," in *Contested Eden: California Before the Gold Rush*, ed. Ramón A. Gutiérrez and Richard J. Orsi, 230–59 (Berkeley: University of California Press, 1998); Deena J. González, *Refusing the Favor: The Spanish-Mexican Women of Santa Fe, 1820–1880* (New York: Oxford University Press, 1999), 3–11; Emma Pérez, *The Decolonial Imaginary: Writing Chicanas into History* (Bloomington: Indiana University Press, 1999); Vicki Ruiz, *From Out of the Shadows: Mexican Women in Twentieth-Century America* (New York: Oxford University Press, 1998); Miroslava Chávez-García, *Negotiating Conquest: Gender and Power in California, 1770s to 1880s* (Tucson: University of Arizona Press, 2004); Bárbara O. Reyes, *Private Women, Public Lives: Gender and the Missions of the California* (Austin: University of Texas, 2009).

11. Pérez, *Decolonial Imaginary*, 5.

12. Sánchez, *Telling Identities*, 216; Myrtle M. McKittrick, *Vallejo, Son of California* (Portland OR: Binfords & Mort, 1944), 9, 89; Vivien Juárez Rose, *The Past Is Father of the Present: Spanish California History and Family Legends, 1737–1973* (Vallejo CA: Wheeler Printing, 1974), 12; Isidora Filomena Solano, "Testimonio," MSS C-E 65:12, Bancroft.

13. Sánchez, *Telling Identities*, 6–29. For Hubert Howe Bancroft and Manifest Destiny, see also Lisbeth Haas, *Conquests and Historical Identities in California, 1769–1936* (Berkeley: University of California Press, 1995), 171–74; Castañeda, "Presidarias y Pobladoras"; David J. Weber, *The Mexican Frontier, 1821–1846: The American Southwest under Mexico* (Albuquerque: University of New Mexico Press, 1982), xvi–xvii.

14. Lourdes Torres, "Violence, Desire, and Transformative Remembering in Emma Pérez Gulf Dreams," in *Tortilleras: Hispanic and U.S. Latina Lesbian Expression*, ed. Lourdes Torres and Inmaculada Pertusa (Philadelphia: Temple University Press, 2003), 237.

15. Alexander Saxton, *Rise and Fall of the White Republic: Class Politics and Mass Culture in Nineteenth-Century America* (New York: Verso, 1990), 321–47; Ronald Takaki, *Iron Cages: Race and Culture in Nineteenth Century America* (New York: Oxford University Press, 1990), 80–193.

16. Salvador Vallejo, "Notas Históricas Sobre California," 1874, MSS C-E 22: 149–50, Bancroft.

17. William Ralganal Benson, "The Stone and Kelsey Massacres," in *The Way We Lived: California Indian Stories, Songs and Reminiscences*, ed. Malcolm Margolin,

166–73 (Berkeley: Heyday Books, 1981); Virginia Hanrahan, "Historical Napa Valley" (mimeograph, Napa County Library, Napa, California, 1948), 93–97.

18. "Lynch Law," *Napa Reporter*, May 9, 1863, p. 2.

19. Hanrahan, "Historical Napa Valley," 97; "Lynch Law," 2.

20. State of California, *Statutes of California, Sixteenth Session* (Sacramento: Government Printing Office, 1865–1866), 398. For the Treaty of Guadalupe Hidalgo and its protection of the Spanish language in conquered territories, see Richard Griswold del Castillo, *The Treaty of Guadalupe Hidalgo: A Legacy of Conflict* (Norman: University of Oklahoma Press, 1990); and Francisco Martínez, "California Blue Laws as Symbolic Expressions of Nativism in an Increasingly Diverse and Changing Society," California State University, Sacramento, March 2000, unpublished paper in the author's possession.

21. Victoria Calkins, *The Wappo People: A History of the California Wappo Indians as Revealed through a Series of Conversations with the Tribal Council* (Santa Rosa CA: Pileated Press, 1994), 23; Yolande S. Beard, *The Wappo: A Report* (St. Helena CA: Malki Museum Press, 1977), 34.

22. George C. Yount, "Narrative as Told to Orange Clark," n.d., MSS C-E 5189B: 85–86, Bancroft; Beard, *The Wappo*, 36–39.

23. See also Albert Camarillo's and Leonard Pitt's treatment of the Land Act of 1851 in Albert Camarillo, *Chicanos in a Changing Society: From Mexican Pueblos to American Barrios in Santa Barbara and Southern California, 1848–1930* (Cambridge MA: Harvard University Press, 1979), 114, and Leonard Pitt, *The Decline of the Californios: A Social History of the Spanish-Speaking Californios, 1846–1890* (Berkeley: University of California Press, 1966), 83–107.

24. "Meeting of Pioneers," *Napa Reporter*," June 8, 1861, p. 1; "Meeting of Pioneers," *Napa Reporter*, March 14, 1874.

25. See, e.g., "Reminiscences of 'Old Times,'" *Napa County Reporter*, June 15, 1861, p. 1.

26. See, e.g., "The Death of Captain Grenville P. Swift," *Napa Reporter*, May 1, 1875, p. 3; "Another Pioneer Gone," *Napa Reporter*, March 18, 1876, p. 3.

27. Rosaura Sánchez, *Telling Identities*, 197–200; Haas, *Conquests and Historical Identities*, 85, 102, 173. See also Padilla, *My History, Not Yours*, 109–52; Tomás Almaguer, *Racial Fault Lines: The Historical Origins of White Supremacy in California* (Berkeley: University of California Press, 1994), 60–62.

28. "Reminiscences of 'Old Times,'" *Napa County Reporter*, April 13, 1861, p. 1.

29. Sánchez, *Telling Identities*, 198.

30. See, e.g., Frantz Fanon, *Black Skin, White Masks*, trans. Charles Lam Markmann (New York: Grove, 1967); Frantz Fanon, *The Wretched of the Earth*, trans. Constance Farrington (1963; reprint, New York: Grove, 1963); Albert Memmi, *The Colonizer and the Colonized*, trans. Howard Greenfeld (1957; reprint, Boston: Beacon, 1991); Homi K. Bhabha, *The Location of Culture* (New York: Routledge,

1994); Ernest Renan, "What Is a Nation?" in Nation and Narration, ed. Homi K. Bhabha (New York: Routledge, 1990). See also Eric Hobsbawm, The Invention of Tradition (New York: Cambridge University Press, 1983).

31. For the attempted genocide of indigenous peoples, see Lindsay Glauner, "The Need for Accountability and Reparation: 1830–1976, The United States Government's Role in the Promotion, Implementation, and Execution of the Crime of Genocide against Native Americans," DePaul Law Review 51 (Spring 2002): 911–61.

32. Emma Pérez, "Sexuality and Discourse: Notes from a Chicana Survivor," in Chicana Lesbians: The Girls Our Mothers Warned Us About, ed. Carla Trujillo, 161–71 (Berkeley: Third Woman, 1991).

33. Pérez, "Sexuality and Discourse," 172–74.

34. Pérez, Decolonial Imaginary, 27.

35. Solano, "Testimonio," 2. "Sutter mandaba indio jalquineros que cambia licor por cueros, pieles, pescado seco; Sutter tenia mujer india, no California, era india Canacha que con el llega en buque—no quiero mucho el blanco porque muy embustero y ladron, mi compadre Peralta y amigo Bernales tenia mucha vaca el Sutter engaño todo torna nada paga." Solano's grammar is not always standard; Spanish was her third or perhaps even fourth language. Translations throughout are the author's.

36. Charlie Toledo, "Native Americans of the Napa Valley" (Valley of the Legends Historical Fact Sheet: Napa, California, 1997), 3. Earl Couey, interview by author, tape recording, Napa, California, August, 28, 1998; Jesse O. Sawyer and Alice Schlichter, Yuki Vocabulary, University of California Publications in Linguistics, vol. 101 (Berkeley: University of California Press, 1984), 1; Albert L. Kroeber, Handbook of the Indians of California (Washington DC: Government Printing Office, 1925), 378–79; Michael J. Moratto, California Archaeology (San Francisco: Academic Press, 1984), 537–38.

37. Harold E. Driver, Wappo Ethnography 36, no. 3, of University of California Publications in American Archeology and Ethnology (Berkeley: University of California Press, 1936), 194; Robert Heizer, The Archaeology of the Napa Region 12, no. 6 Anthropological Records, 227–28.

38. Heizer, Archaeology of Napa, 242–46; Randall Theodore Milliken, "An Ethnohistory of the Indian People of the San Francisco Bay Area from 1770–1810" (PhD dissertation, University of California, 1991), 20.

39. Jesse O. Sawyer, English-Wappo Vocabulary, vol. 45 of University of California Publications in Linguistics (Berkeley: University of California Press, 1965), 7; Beard, The Wappo, 47; Victoria Patterson, "Evolving Gender Roles in Pomo Society," in Women and Power in Native North America, ed. Laura F. Klein and Lillian A. Ackerman (Norman: University of Oklahoma Press, 1995), 133.

40. Marcus Edmond Peterson, "The Career of Solano, Chief of the Suisuns" (Master's thesis, University of California, Berkeley, 1975), 25n14.

41. Solano, "Testimonio," 12.

42. Platón Vallejo, Memoirs of the Vallejos: New Light on the History, before and after the Gringos Came, Based on Original Documents and Recollections of Dr. Platón Vallejo (1914; reprint, Fairfield CA: James D. Stephenson, 1994), 71–73; Peterson, "Career of Solano," 75.

43. Solano, "Testimonio," 2.

44. P. Vallejo, Memoirs, 71; Solano, "Testimonio," 2. Vallejo suggests the daughters died "from sadness and world-weariness."

45. Bureau of the Census, 1860 Census of Sonoma County; Bureau of the Census, 1870 Sonoma County; the author also searched for Solano in Familytree.com.

46. P. Vallejo, Memoirs, 17.

47. Tey Diana Rebolledo, Infinite Divisions, 17–18.

48. Solano, "Testimonio," 1. "Antes de ser bautizada . . . yo pertenesco a la tribu de los Chiructos, y [Sem Yeto] . . . me robó. Lo perisgio mi padre junto con muchos Satiyomi, pero no pudo vencerle."

49. Solano, "Testimonio," 1. "El cura Quijas que me bautisó y me dió el nombre de Isidora Filomena, me habia enseñado a ser muy caritativa con los pobres, muy mansa con mi marido, y muy compasida con los prisioneros."

50. Almaguer, Racial Fault Lines, 111–13.

51. See, e.g., S. Vallejo, "Notas Históricas," 39–46. For similar portrayals in the English-language press later in the nineteenth century, see Guadalupe Vallejo, "Ranch and Mission Days in Alta California," in Century Magazine 41 (December 1890) available at http://www.sfmuseum.org/hist2/rancho.html, accessed May 4, 2002.

52. Solano, "Testimonio," 2. "Viviamos a gusto—mucho gusta nosotros bañarse porque limpieza da fuerza . . . mi gente tenia siempre dientes blanco que limpia con palo llamado fresno."

53. Peterson, "Career of Solano," 22.

54. Solano, "Testimonio," 4.

55. Dale L. Walker, Bear Flag Rising: The Conquest of California, 1846 (New York: Forge, 1999), 46–50, 65–90. See also Hubert Howe Bancroft, History of California, vol. 5 (San Francisco: The History Co., 1886), 104; Solano, "Testimonio," 4.

56. Vallejo de Leese, "History," 5.

57. McKittrick, Vallejo, 8–9.

58. Sánchez, Telling Identities, 216.

59. Lin Weber, Old Napa Valley: The History to 1900 (St. Helena CA: Wine Ventures, 1998), 36–38; McKittrick, Vallejo, 193.

60. Sánchez, Telling Identities, 216.

61. The property was valued at $1,000, according to the U.S. Census of 1870. At that time her children and some of her grandchildren lived with her in Monterey. Also according to the census, several families in their neighborhood had Hispanic surnames and parents who were born in California.

62. Vallejo de Leese, "History," 2.
63. Vallejo de Leese, "History," 4.
64. Antonio María Osio, *The History of Alta California: A Memoir of Mexican California*, trans. Rose Marie Beebe and Robert M. Senkewicz (Madison: University of Wisconsin Press, 1996), 148–49.
65. S. Vallejo, "Notas Históricas," 133.
66. Osio, *History of Alta California*, 223; Marie E. Northrop, *Spanish-Mexican Families of Early California: 1769–1850* vol. 1 (Burbank: Southern California Genealogical Society, 1987), 95, 107.
67. Here I used "engendered" in the manner of Antonia Castañeda and Bárbara O. Reyes, to draw attention to the ways in which the space was a gendered space. See Castañeda, "Engendering the History of Alta California," and Reyes, "Nineteenth-Century California as Engendered Space."
68. Juárez Rose, *The Past Is Father*, 6.
69. "1790 Padrón de los vecinos del Presidio de San Francisco," MSS CA-50, 1:85–91, Bancroft; *Presidio de San Francisco Lista de la Compañía*, 1782 in the Z. S. Eldredge Collection, C-R9, carton 3, Bancroft.
70. Sánchez, *Telling Identities*, 155, 191. See also Apolinaria Lorenzana, "Memorias," in *Crítica: A Journal of Critical Essays*, University of California, San Diego Critical Monograph Series (Spring 1994): 12, and Juárez Rose, *The Past Is Father*, 12, 32.
71. Juárez Rose, *The Past Is Father*, 5, 12, 23.
72. Juárez Rose, *The Past Is Father*, 17.
73. Juárez Rose, *The Past Is Father*, 32; see David Weber, *Mexican Frontier*, 216, for a discussion of Californianas with similar routines.
74. Cynthia Enloe, *Maneuvers: The International Politics of Militarizing Women's Lives* (Berkeley: University of California Press, 2000), xii, 3.
75. Juárez Rose, *The Past Is Father*, 4.
76. S. Vallejo, "Notas Históricas," 104.
77. Lyman L. Palmer, *History of Napa and Lake Counties* (San Francisco: Slocum, Bowen, 1881), and Lyman L. Palmer, *A Napa County History* (Office of Napa County Superintendent of Schools, 1956), 10–13.
78. Juárez Rose, *The Past Is Father*, 1–2.
79. Padilla, *My History, Not Yours*, 110.
80. Cayetano Juárez, "A Few Notes Referring to Cayetano Júarez, Captain of California's Militia in 1841," MSS C-E 67, Bancroft; Juárez Rose, *The Past Is Father*, i. According to Juárez Rose, "[Bancroft] sent an assistant to the Tulocay Rancho. Júarez considered this a 'slight,' so—gave out only a rambling account to the 'underling' that had been sent!"
81. The end product was Vivien Juárez Rose's *The Past Is Father of the Present*. Juárez Rose then had the family documents archived at the Bancroft.
82. Mariano Guadalupe Vallejo, "Recuerdos Históricos y Personales Tocante

al la Alta California," in *Crítica: A Journal of Critical Essays*, University of California, San Diego Critical Monograph Series (September 1994), 142.

83. Antonia Castañeda, "The Political Economy of Nineteenth Century Stereotypes of Californianas," in *Between Borders: Essays on Mexicana/Chicana History*, ed. Adelaida R. Del Castillo (Encino CA: Floricanto, 1990), 213–36.

84. Antonia I. Castañeda, "Presidarias y Pobladoras: The Journey North and Life in Frontier California," in *Chicana Critical Issues*, ed. Norma Alarcón, Rafaela Castro, Emma Pérez, Beatriz Pesquera, Adaljiza Sosa Riddell, and Patricia Zavella, 73–94 (Berkeley: Third Woman, 1993); Beatriz M. Pesquera and Denise A. Segura, "There Is No Going Back: Chicanas and Feminism," in *Chicana Critical Issues*, 95–116; Lillian Castillo-Speed, "Chicana Studies: An Updated List of Materials, 1980–1991," in *Chicana Critical Issues*, 199–262.

2. "GOING ABOUT AND DOING GOOD"

The Lady Managers of San Francisco, 1850–1880

MARY ANN IRWIN

On February 5, 1856, the attorney Frederick Billings gave a speech honoring California's first charitable institution, the San Francisco Protestant Orphan Asylum. Using a metaphor that captured both the spirit and the reality of local benevolence, Billings described charity as a beautiful woman: "Beautiful as charity may be when she simply gives a cup of cold water to him who is thirsty—when she guides the steps of the blind—when she sits by the bed of sickness—when she cares for old age no longer able to care for itself—beautiful as she is in all her ways, she is never so beautiful as when in the form of a woman she takes the hand of the orphan child, wandering and lost in the confusion of the tumultuous city, and guides it to a home."[1]

In equating charity with women, Billings was more accurate than he probably knew. Women's charities were at the heart of social welfare provision in San Francisco in the period 1850 to 1880. Indeed, the central feature of poor relief in this era was the city's reliance on woman-led charities for social welfare services, especially services to women and children.

Women's benevolent associations served San Francisco in a surprising variety of ways. "Lady managers," as the leaders of women's charities often identified themselves, reaped personal rewards for their labors, including lavish praise for their altruism and piety (and occasionally their beauty).[2] In the process, local women moved the issues that concerned them most onto the agendas of state and local leaders. Poor families relied on women's charities for services the city did not provide, especially aid to women and children. Citizens supported woman-led societies because women's charitable work held down municipal spending and thus limited the corruption that seemed to follow expansion of the public sector. Elected officials relied on women's privately funded welfare programs to avoid raising taxes and thereby incurring voter wrath. In turn, by their charitable activities, local women expanded the scope of municipal administration and shaped the city's evolving structure of public services. Women's charities were thus a central feature of the local political economy. Moreover, the influence of local women's groups often extended beyond the city limits. Because San Francisco was the economic and political center of California in this era, women leaders influenced developing state social welfare policies and programs. In sum, charity work gave women leaders a substantial form of political power.

As they reshaped local welfare services according to their own lights, San Francisco's lady managers fashioned significant public roles for themselves. Excluded from the vote, women operated within a political structure that ran parallel to—though not independent of—the formal, male-dominated political structures. Working within their own same-sex organizations, local women exercised a form of political power that did not require the ballot. As a result of their labors, public welfare policies came more closely to reflect the priorities and concerns of influential women volunteers.[3] Like their eastern sisters, San Francisco women took part in a larger retooling of U.S. culture, a process that ultimately affected U.S. government and political thought, changing popular expectations regarding the government's responsibility to provide for the welfare of citizens.

Women's voluntarism was absolutely essential in Gold Rush San Francisco, where the population expanded far more rapidly than public resources. From about eight hundred in 1848, the city's population soared to more than 36,000 in 1852 to nearly 150,000 in 1870.[4] An "instant city," as one historian put it, San Francisco faced problems common to mature, eastern cities but without comparable administrative and bureaucratic development.[5] Before the Alms House opened in 1867, the only public relief available to the indigent was room and board at the jail or City Hospital.[6] San Francisco's only other public welfare institution was the Industrial School, which served only juveniles. Not surprisingly, these institutions were no match for the city's growing population and recurring economic and public health crises.[7]

Despite the obvious deficiencies of San Francisco's public welfare system, political considerations made its expansion impractical. As was true in other cities of this period, taxpayers demanded inexpensive, efficient municipal government.[8] Indeed, allegations of waste and corruption toppled San Francisco's city government in the 1850s. Local businessmen claimed that politicians were squeezing "outrageous taxes ... from the citizens" and spending them on "fine horses" and "luxurious living."[9] In the elections of 1856, vigilante-businessmen won key municipal offices and immediately cut local taxes by 40 percent. Municipal funding for social welfare fell steadily as a proportion of the city budget, from 14 percent in 1860, to 11 percent in 1880 and 8 percent by 1898. From the "Revolution of '56" through the end of the century, public welfare expenditures consistently failed to keep pace with the city's growth. The dominant political ethic of low taxes compelled politicians to curtail any expansion of public services, including welfare.[10] Instead, local officials relied on private charities to provide relief to the poor.

To meet the emergencies and everyday needs of citizens, San Franciscans established volunteer fire companies, volunteer militia, benevolent societies, and all the other service associations typical of nineteenth-century communities.[11] As the Gold Rush brought thousands of men to the city, various ethnic and fraternal groups organized to provide members and others with food, shelter, and medical attention.[12] During the cholera epidemic of 1850, for example, the Odd Fellows spent twenty-seven thousand dollars setting up a temporary hospital; members prepared meals, nursed the sick, and buried the dead.[13] One observer noted that the men "contributed money and exertions as freely as if their lives had been devoted to the exclusive function of human kindness."[14]

Women arriving in the 1850s built upon this tradition of voluntarism. To the seventeen or more existing male-led benevolent societies, the newcomers added a half dozen or so more of their own. These associations ranged in purpose from spreading the gospel to tending the sick and destitute. The number of female-led charities continued to grow over the next three decades, quickly becoming an essential component in the city's network of public and private social welfare services.

Bowing to the notion that men and women occupied distinctive spheres, San Franciscans formed separate, same-sex benevolent associations.[15] Most male-led charities served men, and women's charities provided services primarily to children and their own sex. Public welfare programs observed the same etiquette. Many of California's earliest county hospitals, for example, refused admission to women and children. Only specialized private children's hospitals admitted children, but prior to 1875 San

Francisco did not have one.[16] The only other unofficial public aid that might have been available to women and children—political patronage—was usually reserved for voting-age males.[17]

Women's charities thus filled a critical gap in public and private welfare services. Beginning with the founding of the city's first woman-led charity in 1850, San Francisco women practiced what we might call "lifeboat benevolence," a particularly feminine version of charity in which women and children always came first.

San Francisco's first social welfare institution—indeed, the first in California—was an orphanage founded by women. The total number of children in Gold Rush San Francisco was only one thousand or so, but the few left orphaned required immediate attention.[18] In 1850 Elizabeth Waller, the wife of superior court judge Royal Waller, learned of five children orphaned by cholera. Waller called a meeting of churchwomen to consider the best means of caring for these and other dependent children, and the San Francisco Protestant Orphan Asylum (SFPOA) was born.

The San Francisco Ladies' Protection and Relief Society (SFLP&RS), another of the city's oldest charities, was formed to meet the needs of dependent women. Tradition holds that the SFLP&RS began when a young woman came to San Francisco to join her gold-hunting brother. When the brother failed to meet her ship, a fellow passenger directed the girl to a house on Minna Street, but the house proved to be a brothel. Alone and friendless, she wandered the streets in mounting panic until she noticed a woman observing her from the window of her home. Trusting to the solidarity of her sex, the girl ran to the door begging for protection.[19] Her benefactor, the wife of A. B. Eaton, a Presidio officer, promptly called a meeting of local women, and the result was the San Francisco Ladies Protection & Relief Society.

SFLP&RS founders agreed that "almost every arrival from the Atlantic and other parts of the world" brought women who were left "destitute in our city by the decease of their natural protectors on their passage hither."[20] Founders vowed that they would personally "render protection and assistance" to the "sick and dependent women and children" who came to them for aid.[21]

San Francisco men approved wholeheartedly of women's charities. Contrary to the image of San Franciscans as reluctant citizens, business and political leaders responded enthusiastically when volunteering women came to call.[22] Local men heaped cash, goods, and even real estate upon the SFLP&RS. In 1860 Horace Hawes gave the women an empty lot in the then-remote area bounded by Van Ness, Geary, Franklin, and Post streets.[23] The SFPOA likewise received gifts of stocks, bonds, gold bullion, and property. When the Sansome Hook and Ladder Company gave the SFPOA the firehouse at Montgomery and Jackson in 1860, James Lick donated the land on which it stood. Conflict between Catholics and Protestants occasionally flared up, as will be seen, but San Franciscans generally gave across denominational lines. In the 1860s James Donahue, a prominent Irish Catholic businessman, gave the Protestant orphans twenty years' dividend income from stock in his gas company.[24]

The personal and political connections of women leaders had an obvious bearing on the success of their charities. As was true elsewhere, the state's most respected citizens served as trustees and honorary members of the city's woman-led philanthropies. For example, the wives of San Francisco's first Protestant clergymen formed the original board of the SFPOA. Over the years, SFPOA trustees included Darius Ogden Mills, a pioneer banker; David Shattuck and Royal Waller, superior court judges; San Francisco Supervisor and Mayor James Otis; and Henry Haight, supervisor and future governor.[25]

Given their intimate connections to elite men, the success with which local women raised money is not surprising.[26] However, blue- and white-collar workers gave cheerfully as well. When the Catholic Laborers Union Association donated five hundred dollars to the Roman Catholic Orphan Asylum in 1854, a group of Protestant laborers donated two hundred dollars for "their" orphans a few days later.[27] When two SFPOA managers made a walking canvass of the business district in 1854, they found even the clerks begging to give them money: "We visited every place of business in town, offices, banks and stores, asking always for the head of the firm, who not only responded liberally, but other gentlemen happening to be present, and men and clerks, would say, 'Are you not going to ask me to give?' or, 'Won't you allow me to contribute?'"[28]

Material assistance was not limited to cash. Over a three-year period, one merchant supplied the SFPOA with roughly three thousand dollars in groceries.[29] Swain Bakeries gave the SFLP&RS free bread, cakes, and crackers. A local druggist donated medicines, another merchant supplied free groceries, and a third contributed wood for cooking and heating.[30] Businessmen also donated their professional services. Every year the SFPOA and SFLP&RS publicly thanked the newspaper editors who printed their annual reports without charge, published flattering articles about their activities, and encouraged the community to give generously to their causes.

Public officials were equally generous. In 1855 the California legislature appropriated five thousand dollars each to the Protestant and Catholic women's orphanages.[31] That same year, the City of San Francisco allocated $125 per month in city funds to the SFPOA and an equal sum to the Sisters of Mercy, a Roman Catholic nursing and teaching order, for their orphanage. City supervisors also gave local women a small slice of the public treasury when they decreed that proceeds from certain fines would be donated to the SFPOA.[32] Strapped city administrators found non-monetary ways to assist the women as well. In the 1850s Mayor C. K. Garrison more or less gave two city-owned lots to the SFPOA by arranging to have the land sold at a public auction. Garrison limited announcement of the auction to Asylum trustees, which allowed them to purchase both lots for only one hundred dollars. Officials then donated materials from the city-owned stone quarry to build the orphanage.[33] When the women discovered that construction could not begin until the side streets had been surveyed, Supervisor Henry Haight arranged the surveys and then, as a bonus, had two streets named after Elizabeth Waller and Anna Haight, both lady managers.[34]

With such generous support available, some local women's organizations realized their objectives in short order. By 1853 the women of the SFPOA could point to a substantial orphanage built entirely by private donations.[35] The SFLP&RS quickly proved its worth as well. Managers organized an "Intelligence Office," which routinely solicited Protestant and Catholic congregations for housing, employment, and cash donations. The office found work for women as domestics and oversaw the distribution of funds raised for the poor. In 1857 the SFLP&RS expanded its services by opening a "Home" for poor women and children. The Home accepted both paying and non-paying boarders, some of whom were allowed to earn their keep by serving the Home as cooks and laundresses. The SFLP&RS

2. Farms and drifting sand dunes defined the neighborhood at Buchanan and Haight streets when the San Francisco Protestant Orphan Asylum was completed in 1853. San Francisco History Center, San Francisco Public Library. AAD-5947, S.F. Orphanages-Protestant.

also boarded local children, including those with families, regardless of whether or not they could pay.[36]

Poor families were quick to take advantage of the services offered by women's benevolent societies. The SFPOA opened with twenty-six children in 1853, but that number doubled within three years.[37] By 1869 the Home was caring for 173 children between the ages of eight months and twelve years; by 1884 the facility was full beyond capacity, with 212 children.[38] The SFLP&RS also aided scores of women and children living outside the Home. Between 1863 and 1873 the SFLP&RS paid rents, bought provisions, and provided nurses, medical attention, clothing, and fuel for fifty-one families.[39] Periodic economic crises increased demand for SFLP&RS services. During the depression years of 1876 and 1877, the Home distributed money, fuel, and provisions; housed and fed a monthly average of 196 women and children; found homes for 17 orphans; and schooled an average of 272 children per month.[40]

To win support for their charitable enterprises, the leaders of the SFPOA and SFLP&RS drew upon religious and gender ideology—and, no doubt, the loneliness of the city's many bachelors. But Christian ideals, separate-spheres ideology, and loneliness did not automatically guarantee the success of San Francisco women's organizations. Although civic leaders were often generous toward woman-led charities, they usually withheld support from more controversial organizations. The tiny Woman's State Suffrage Association, for example, received little public or private funding for the cause of women's rights.[41] Because women's benevolent organizations focused almost exclusively on service to the sick and dependent—areas traditionally within the feminine sphere—charity leaders were able to walk the fine line between acceptable female activism and intolerable feminist stridency. Gender ideology promoted some women's entry into the public sphere at the same time that it limited the entry of those who hoped to expand women's political and economic opportunities.[42]

But even charitable organizations could face political, economic, and moral opposition. In those instances, the essentially political nature of women's benevolence becomes apparent. Charity leaders were compelled to overcome resistance in the same way as leaders of the perennially unpopular women's temperance and suffrage movements. Sometimes charity leaders chose to ignore their detractors and proceed despite public objections. In other instances, women leaders neutralized the opposition by rethinking their goals and tactics.

Founders of the San Francisco Female Hospital (SFFH) provide an example of the first approach. In 1867 the wives of several prominent businessmen opened a hospital specializing in gynecology and obstetrics. Because they believed that all women deserved competent medical care, the founders vowed to accept all applicants, regardless of nativity, race, religion, or marital status. Despite these benign aims, SFFH founders encountered resistance, perhaps over the promise to treat all women—even unwed mothers—humanely. In their second annual report, C. T. Deane, a surgeon, admitted that, in the beginning, "there were not wanting prophets of evil, who foretold the failure and misrepresented the object for which the charity was inaugurated."[43] Founders proceeded with their hospital despite the murmurings. They collected $13,037 in private donations and netted another $230 in a fundraising fair. With this

3. Surrounded by sand dunes and modest homes, this is how the San Francisco Ladies' Protection & Relief Society Home looked in 1865. Given as a gift, this valuable real estate at Van Ness, Geary, Franklin, and Post streets is now known as Cathedral Hill. San Francisco History Center, San Francisco Public Library. AAC-9987, Ladies' Protection & Relief Society, Franklin and Geary streets, T. E. Hecht Collection.

sum, they rented two large houses, purchased furnishings and bedding, hired a physician, matron, nurses, and servants, and began providing free medicines, medical care, food, and accommodations to needy women.[44] In its first year the SFFH served 198 women, a record that simultaneously proved San Francisco needed a maternity hospital and silenced those who had predicted failure. By the end of its second year, SFFH had treated 384 sick and pregnant women and delivered 214 babies. SFFH not only provided a high volume of medical care, it also provided high-quality care—in the same two years, only five babies were lost and not one mother died.[45]

Even the much-admired SFLP&RS sometimes faced public opposition. In 1860 SFLP&RS leaders decided they needed a larger building. Convinced that they were providing a vital public service, the women turned to the state for funds. As was customary among nineteenth-century women's charities, the leaders approached a prominent local man and asked him to draft a petition on their behalf. To their surprise, Frederick Billings, an attorney, who championed women as charity leaders above, refused to draft their petition. Worse still, Billings advised SFLP&RS leaders to abandon their plans altogether. Dismayed but not defeated, the women adopted a new approach. They prepared a precise statement of their future financial needs in addition to a statistical analysis of the women and children served to date. The leaders then deviated even further from protocol. Rather than proceeding through a male proxy to the legislature, the SFLP&RS presented its petition directly to the governor, and women leaders met personally with the governor themselves. The new strategy worked. The governor approved an allocation of six thousand dollars to the SFLP&RS, and the women began looking for a parcel on which to build their new Home.[46]

Compared to the SFPOA and the SFLP&RS, the Ladies' Seamen's Friend Society of the Port of San Francisco (the "Society") was a singularly unsuccessful women's charity. Like its female counterparts, the Society had been founded to aid the sick and dependent. Unlike its peers, however, the Society intended to aid adult men—specifically, San Francisco's large and notoriously rowdy population of sailors. The Society's founders endured twenty years of disappointment before they achieved their long-cherished goal—a permanent Sailors' Home.

Local women founded the Society in 1857, after a male-led seaman's association dissolved. The Society's leaders vowed to provide the comforts of home to San Francisco's "ship wrecked and destitute seamen," and an alternative to the gambling dens, gin-shops, and brothels they considered injurious to the sailor's spiritual condition. The women rented a large waterfront building and were soon providing nutritious meals, clean sheets, and homey surroundings to aged, destitute, sick, and injured sailors. As the founders had promised, the Sailors' Home protected residents from "pernicious influences" through a library stocked with wholesome books. In the evenings the Society's volunteers gave stimulating lectures geared toward boarders' "moral and intellectual improvement."[47] A resident (male) missionary conducted a regular "family worship" and, with a small group of women volunteers, carried religious tracts to ships at anchor. Once a week a committee of women visited the U.S. Marine Hospital and "by kind acts and words...comfort[ed] and cheer[ed] the hearts of those lone wanderers."[48]

Many San Franciscans expressed doubt that seamen actually wanted to be spared pernicious influences or desired an alternative to the city's gambling dens, gin-shops, and brothels. Yet the Sailors' Home proved surprisingly popular. In its second year the Sailors' Home housed more than twelve hundred sailors, and many more had to be turned away for lack of room.[49] With more patrons than space, the Society's first annual report noted gleefully that founders had "proved conclusively that a portion at least of Seamen appreciate a comfortable boarding house, while on shore."[50] By its ninth year the Sailors' Home had sheltered 10,871 paying and non-paying boarders and provided many more with medical care, emergency financial aid, and transportation home.[51]

With proof positive that seamen wanted what the Society had to offer, leaders made plans to move out of their cramped rented quarters and purchase a building of their own. Thus began a twenty-year odyssey of frustration and failure. Unlike the SFPOA or SFLP&RS, the Society's leaders failed to inspire much enthusiasm for their cause. For some San Franciscans, the problem may have been one of appearances. By nineteenth-century standards, it was unseemly for "ladies" to fraternize with sailors, even for charitable purposes. A more likely explanation, however, was a conflict of interests. Located in the working-class South-of-Market district, which held nearly a third of the city's boarding houses, a third of its restaurants, a quarter of its hotels, and half of its lodging houses, the proposed Sailors' Home threatened the hostelries, restaurants, taverns, brothels, and low dives that depended on the seamen's trade.[52]

The Society attempted to neutralize waterfront opposition by aligning elite business and political leaders against the dockside interests. Lady managers argued that their opponents were illegitimate entrepreneurs who exploited the poor seaman. They decried the prostitutes who degraded his morals; the corrupt tavern- and boardinghouse keepers who took his money for dirty quarters and unhealthful fare; and the "crimps" who exploited unwary sailors and worked with shipping companies to coerce or manipulate men into accepting undesirable jobs. The Society reminded San Franciscans that the city's economy depended on its port, which in turn rested upon the health and happiness of the long-suffering seaman.[53]

Although the women's arguments were well chosen, their funding campaign flopped. The Society's leaders could not convince the city's business elite that a permanent Sailors' Home was in its best interests. Indeed, civic leaders might have felt their interests were best served by corrupt hostelries, taverns, and brothels. A disorganized waterfront may have appealed to the legion of seasonal workers who returned each year to San Francisco, lured by its reputation as the cheapest town on the coast, and its array of public and private welfare services, thriving vice districts that were known worldwide, and a generally lax moral attitude.[54]

Unable to raise the money they needed at home, the Ladies' Seaman's Friend Society turned to state leaders. In February 1861 the Society crafted a memorial to the legislature. "Could a history of the Sailor's wrongs and sufferings be written," the petition began, "it would furnish a picture that would cause the heart of humanity to turn with horror from the scene." Their Sailors' Home would right these wrongs: "Thousands of our wisest and best men, in all parts of the civilized world, have decided long since that the first step towards the moral, physical, and intellectual elevation of seamen is to provide a place of refuge, where they will be surrounded by salutary influences, and mingle in respectable society."[55]

Although the Society wrapped its appeal in the powerful image of the home as refuge, it also attempted a bit of subtle leverage. The reference to the "wisest and best men" in the "civilized world" gently goaded state leaders, reminding them that Americans east of the Mississippi River still viewed San Francisco as an uncouth frontier outpost.

Their campaign for state funding also showed that women of the Society appreciated the intricacies of state and local politics. On the one hand, local businessmen were more likely to throw the women their support if they didn't have to provide the funds. On the other, the legislature was more likely to grant the women's request if San Francisco's business community—which exercised great influence in Sacramento—appeared to favor it. Thus, the Society's volunteers distributed their petition to dozens of prominent local men, asking them to sign the petition and then forward it to the legislature. Although quite a few local men signed, the legislature refused to allocate the funds.

With the collapse of the state campaign, the Society's lady managers redoubled their efforts to raise funds at home. In 1867 they turned over day-to-day operation of the Sailors' Home to a retired seaman and began an earnest campaign that blanketed San Francisco with female volunteers. By 1869 the women had raised more than six thousand dollars; it was a sizable sum but still not enough to purchase a new building.[56] During San Francisco's 1874 Industrial Fair, the Society rented a large building near the fairgrounds for a "New England Kitchen." With the combined forces of several local churches, the New England Kitchen cooked and served meals to hundreds of fair-goers every day for eight weeks. The work was arduous and, for some volunteers, unusual. Leaders noted that many elite women worked for the seamen's cause "more earnestly than [they] were accustomed to doing in their own homes."[57]

By such labor-intensive efforts, the Society amassed a tidy little nest egg of ten thousand dollars. The following year, the women invested in commercial real estate, hoping to collect enough in rental income to purchase a suitable building. But two years later they found they were no closer to their goal. The women again reconsidered their strategy, this time turning to the federal government for aid. In 1877 the women of the Society petitioned Congress to give them the abandoned U.S. Marine Hospital in San Francisco. Built in 1853 at the corners of Harrison and Spear streets, the U.S. Marine Hospital was built to care for sick and injured seamen. When the building was badly damaged in the earthquake of 1868, the structure was abandoned.[58] Despite the damage, the building's interior design and spacious grounds fit the women's needs, and they believed their nest egg could be stretched to cover the costs of renovation.

For San Francisco's business community, the primary virtue of the women's plan was economic. If the women could convince Congress to turn over the building, the Society would have a Sailors' Home at no further cost to the city or the state. A well-respected businessman, Joseph W. Stow, agreed to carry a new petition to members of San Francisco's Chamber of Commerce and to the state legislature.[59]

It is worth noting that the scope of the federal campaign far exceeded the Society's original vision. In addition to asking for the crumbling hospital building and grounds, the women also asked Congress to regulate maritime working conditions, including uniform rates of pay for seamen, enforceable contracts of employment, and abolition of the most notorious abuses of seamen. Furthermore, the petition pressed national leaders for legislation with teeth, punishing employers that failed to comply. This new tactic entered upon explicitly political terrain and traveled far beyond the provincial focus characteristic of San Francisco women's charities. And yet it was the federal campaign that ultimately succeeded. In 1877 Congress voted to give the U.S. Marine Hospital to the Society.[60]

Victorious at last, the women were able to sell their commercial property and apply the proceeds, along with their laboriously collected nest egg, to renovating the Marine Hospital and reopening it as their Sailors' Home. Ironically, although the Society's lady managers had raised thousands of dollars, guided legislation through state and national assemblies, and displayed considerable political acumen, they could not sign any of the contracts needed to complete the work. Final authority for all legal matters rested with the Society's male trustees.[61]

The Society's hard-won battle is instructive. Like the Female Hospital, SFPOA, and SFLP&RS, the Society necessarily evolved into a political lobbying group. Like the leaders of the hundreds of woman-led associations that dotted the American landscape, the Society's leaders learned the "masculine" political skills they needed in order to achieve their "feminine" objectives. However, the Society's leaders ran into difficulty when they tested the limits of Christian thought and separate-sphere ideology, focusing their efforts on adult men instead of the more traditional women and children. At the same time, the Society's leaders waged an explicit assault on local business interests, specifically the waterfront businesses that catered to seamen. Where the women failed in their 1865 campaign, they succeeded in their federal campaign twelve years later, largely because they struck upon a solution that met the Society's needs with no out-of-pocket expense for state and local businessmen. Not unlike California's perennially unsuccessful woman suffrage movement, which achieved success only when progressive men saw the advantage of teaming up with their female counterparts to achieve shared reform goals, the Ladies' Seaman's Friend Society succeeded only when leaders finally found the correct balance between altruism and self-interest.[62]

As these founding stories make clear, local women used charitable organizations to exercise a particularly feminine version of political participation. By exploiting their cultural and religious claims upon community support, benevolent women's societies were able to raise large sums of money for the social welfare projects they deemed vital to the well-being of the community. Beyond revealing how charity work offered substantial influence to some nineteenth-century women, the evolution of woman-led benevolent associations also illustrates how public social welfare systems evolved.

In San Francisco, women's charities succeeded because they provided badly needed services. The city's rapid growth combined with weak bureaucratic development, on the one hand, and voter opposition to expansion of public welfare spending, on the other, to make private charity a practical necessity. Elected officials gratefully integrated San Francisco women's organizations into the city's patchwork of public and private social welfare agencies. San Francisco's continued reliance on private charities for social welfare services illustrates how women entered local politics and remained there to shape municipal welfare policies and programs.

Organizations like the SFPOA and SFLP&RS significantly expanded the range of services available to the city's working poor. But elected officials also took advantage of women's charities, incorporating them into San Francisco's public welfare system. The administrators of public institutions, for example, routinely transferred their inmates to women's shelters.[63] In the depression of 1876–1877, when fifty-five children aged eleven months to nine years were found in the city's Alms House, administrators transferred them to the SFPOA, SFLP&RS, and other private facilities.[64]

Other public agencies likewise preferred woman-run institutions to their own. In the 1870s when Elizabeth Armer began an informal day-care center in a working-class neighborhood, the police and criminal courts lost no time in sending the children of defendants, witnesses, and others "up to Miss Armer's to be looked after."[65] After the U.S. Marine Hospital mentioned above was damaged in the earthquake of 1868, hospital administrators moved their patients to Mercy Hospital, a private hospital managed by the Roman Catholic Sisters of Mercy.[66]

Private citizens shared public officials' preference for woman-run institutions. When the California Society for the Prevention of Cruelty to Children (CSPCC) was founded in 1876, its leaders devoted much of their energies to retrieving children from public facilities—a fate volunteers evidently equated with cruelty. Public officials seemed to agree: In May 1877 the CSPCC was allowed to remove thirteen-year-old William Reagan from the city jail; Reagan was transferred to St. Vincent's Orphan Asylum, a Roman Catholic institution operated by the Brothers of the Order of St. Dominic. That same month, the CSPCC found Mary Walker and her child Lizzie in the city jail, "where they had applied for lodging, perfectly destitute." CSPCC records are silent on Mary's fate but report that Lizzie was promptly transferred to the SFLP&RS Home.[67]

State officials also preferred the city's private facilities to its public institutions. In 1877 the probate court placed a total of fifty-eight abandoned, abused, or neglected children under CSPCC jurisdiction. Of these, twelve children were placed in families, five were returned to their parents, and one was sent to the Alms House. The remaining children were divided among private institutions. Eighteen children were placed in male-led facilities: thirteen were sent to the Roman Catholic St. Joseph's Youth Directory, and five went to St. Vincent's Orphan Asylum. Twenty-two youths were placed in woman-run shelters: twelve went to the SFLP&RS Home, and ten were sent to the Home of Friendless Children.[68]

Two years later the state again followed CSPCC recommendations in placing the majority of probate court wards in private institutions. Among children for whom adoptive families could not be found, only six were sent to public institutions (one to the City Hospital, four to the Industrial School, and one to the Alms House). Of the remaining thirty-eight children, all were placed in facilities managed by women—sixteen were sent to the SFLP&RS Home, eleven to Mt. St. Joseph's Infant Asylum, ten to the Roman Catholic Orphan Asylum, one to the Presbyterian (Chinese) Mission Home, and three to the private, woman-run Children's Hospital and Training School for Nurses.[69]

These transfers from public to private institutions suggest widespread agreement that women's facilities came closer than public institutions to replicating the ideal situation for children—that is, the family home. Of course, administrators had a very practical reason for transferring public charges to women's institutions, where they would be supported by private donations rather than tax dollars.

But public officials preferred woman-run facilities even when they had to pay for the women's services, and even when the city offered identical services. This was the case with the San Francisco Industrial School. The Industrial School was opened in 1865 to house the city's growing population of delinquent and dependent youth. But the school quickly became a source of controversy and criticism. Before the end of its first year, the *California Police Gazette* complained that the Industrial School virtually ensured that female graduates would end up as prostitutes. The school's entire program of "rehabilitation" consisted of dumping all of the institution's cooking, cleaning, and laundry chores on female inmates.[70]

Worse still, local officials had to admit that children were not safe in the Industrial School. In 1868 Sheriff P. J. White advised against committing young women to the Industrial School, where they would be vulnerable to sexual assaults by inmates and even school personnel.[71] White unsuccessfully urged the city to transfer Industrial School girls to either the SFLP&RS Home or to the Magdalene Asylum, a private facility operated by the Sisters of Mercy.[72]

A year of unrelenting criticism finally convinced city officials to transfer Industrial School girls to the Magdalene Asylum.[73] In 1869 the city appropriated a five-thousand-dollar payment to the Sisters of Mercy, which allowed the Sisters to expand their facility to take in the Industrial School girls. Thereafter, San Francisco paid the Sisters fifteen dollars per girl, per month.[74]

Starting in 1869, local courts also began to send all dependent and delinquent female juveniles to the Magdalene Asylum. Citizens and elected officials were quite satisfied with this arrangement until July 1875, when a San Francisco grand jury recommended that the courts once again send female juveniles to the Industrial School. The editors of the *San Francisco Post* immediately objected: "The Magdalene Asylum is as yet the only reform School in this City, and to send the girls back to the Industrial School would be simply to take them from a place where they may be made better to a place where they are certain to be made worse."[75] Officials voted to leave the girls where they were, tacitly acknowledging that the Sisters' care was superior to that provided by the city.[76]

The City Hospital provides another example of San Francisco's reliance on women for social welfare services. In the summer of 1850, on the heels of a series of public health crises, San Franciscans voted to establish a City Hospital. As was typical of the era, the city turned operation of the hospital over to a private contractor, Dr. Peter Smith. Smith agreed to pay all the operating expenses of the hospital in exchange for a flat rate of four dollars per patient, per day. As the city was temporarily short on cash, Smith agreed to accept city scrip backed by municipal property.[77]

For the next seven months, Smith received only scrip for his services. Unfortunately, the city's cash flow did not improve. When the debt to Smith reached sixty-five thousand dollars, rumors began to circulate that Smith had ceased to provide medical care or even food for his patients.[78] Smith resigned and successfully sued San Francisco for his fees. City leaders

Table 1: Annual Costs of Operation, San Francisco City Hospital, 1853–1857

Administrator	Year	Total Cost
Private contractor	1853–1854	$213,364
Private contractor	1854–1855	$278,328
Sisters of Mercy	1855–1856	$ 89,478
Sisters of Mercy	1856–1857	$ 43,880

Source: San Francisco Board of Supervisors, Municipal Reports, 1853–1857.

sold a number of valuable municipal properties at fire-sale prices to satisfy Smith's liens. The press then excoriated both Smith and elected officials for this fiasco, and continued to do so for years to come.[79]

Despite the obvious flaws of the contract system, officials continued to hire private physicians to run the City Hospital. This changed when the Sisters of Mercy arrived in San Francisco in 1854. The city had recently experienced a devastating cholera epidemic, followed by an outbreak of smallpox. The Sisters offered their services on the heels of these disasters, and in 1855 officials turned the City Hospital over to them.[80]

The financial benefits of private care were soon apparent. As table 1 shows, operating costs for the City Hospital fell immediately.[81]

Over the next two years, all but the most intolerant Protestant critics agreed that the Sisters of Mercy gave economical and high-quality service to City Hospital patients. Yet in 1857, responding to mounting complaints that the Sisters were proselytizing among their patients, officials fired the Sisters.[82] When the city began contracting with private physicians again, the cost of operating the hospital began to rise. By 1863 the cost of operating the City Hospital was nearly double that charged by the Sisters in their last year.[83]

Religious rivalry between Protestants and Catholics could sometimes overpower city officials' good sense, as management of the City Hospital makes clear. As religious fervor often inspired men and women to engage in charity work in the first place, these flares of religious prejudice between competing denominations should not be surprising. However, as strong a motivator as religious thought was, the gendered division of communal life into private and public spheres was equally influential in shaping local welfare.

The line between the supposedly public sphere of men and the private sphere of women was, of course, illusory. The metaphor of separate spheres was a social construction, not an accurate description of reality. San Francisco women often crossed the line into public activism, and local men frequently displayed the qualities of sympathy and selflessness attributed to women.[84] But because care for the sick and dependent fell within the traditional boundaries of the women's sphere, woman-led social welfare organizations fell into the vague frontier that divided "public" and "private" in nineteenth-century America. Thus, local women could assume highly visible public roles, successfully raising funds, writing petitions, and button-holing legislators, all without jeopardizing their middle-class claims to gentility, domesticity, and femininity.

At the same time, however, men and women did in fact operate in separate political spheres. It was the different modes of political participation that were open to men and women that underlay the very real differences between public and private welfare provision in San Francisco. The most obvious difference between public and private welfare was in the kind of services provided, especially the differences between "indoor" and "outdoor" relief. Indoor relief meant custodial care of the poor in institutions, while outdoor relief was noncustodial assistance, in the form of cash, goods, or services. Like many cities of the period, San Francisco provided only indoor relief.[85] From 1850 to 1880—and, in fact, well into the next century—public welfare in San Francisco meant institutionalization in the jail, City Hospital, Industrial School, or Alms House. There were two possible alternatives. In 1870 the city began donating half of all fines received to the male-led San Francisco Benevolent Society (SFBS). A "charity organization society," the SFBS collected and distributed funds as outdoor relief.[86] Thereafter, the SFBS received a maximum of five thousand dollars a year to distribute to the city's poor. The only other public outdoor relief in this era was the Robinson Bequest. In 1881 a wealthy citizen left forty thousand dollars to the city with the request that the annual interest be given to poor women and children. Like the SFBS allocation, this sum was small—in 1893 interest on the Robinson Bequest totaled only $2,395.80. From 1850 to 1906, the city made no other allocations for outdoor relief.[87]

Private charities, on the other hand, provided both indoor and outdoor relief. As mentioned above, between 1863 and 1873, the SFLP&RS paid rents, bought provisions, and provided nurses, medical attention, clothing, and fuel for fifty-one families living outside the SFLP&RS Home.[88] The availability of outdoor relief was critically important to poor mothers and fathers. Outdoor relief allowed families to stay together, while institutionalization meant separation, with adult men, women, and children divided among facilities.

The gap between public and private welfare spending could also be quite dramatic. In 1893, the only year for which relatively complete figures exist, the city expended $7,395.80 for outdoor relief. In contrast, private charities distributed more than $308,500 in outdoor relief—forty-one times as much as the city. When sums spent on indoor and outdoor relief are combined, the gap is still substantial. In 1893 San Francisco spent $57,601 on poor relief, while private charities expended $503,622—nearly nine times as much.[89]

One of the most obvious differences between private and public welfare was the care with which managers shepherded their financial resources. Comparison of male- and female-led institutions is difficult but not impossible. One public institution—the City Hospital—operated under both male and female leadership. As we saw above, the Sisters of Mercy operated the City Hospital with unsurpassed economy. The same economy is observed when public facilities are compared with private institutions. The closest parallels are between the SFLP&RS Home and the city's Industrial School and Alms House. The institutions were not entirely analogous, in that they catered to different clientele. The SFLP&RS Home accepted infants, children, and women, whereas the Industrial School served only male juveniles, and the Alms House accepted children and adults of both sexes and all ages. The three institutions were similar, in that each provided custodial care of varying lengths to a shifting population. Moreover, each operated in the same political and social climate and spent dollars of equal value. As table 2 demonstrates, in each of the years examined, the cost of maintaining an inmate in the Alms House or Industrial School was two to three times higher than in the SFLP&RS Home.[90]

The superior economy of the SFLP&RS over public facilities reflects the charity's different status in the community. Whereas the city was compelled to purchase everything its institutions required, the SFLP&RS and other woman-run entities regularly reaped the benefits of community

Table 2: Approximate Cost of Maintenance, per Inmate, per Month, SFLP&RS Home, Alms House, and Industrial School, 1872–1879

Year	SFLP&RS Home	(N)*	Alms House	(N)	Industrial School	(N)
1872–1873	$7.80	(170.5)	$21.92	(290)	$13.09	(258.5)
1873–1874	6.68	(169)	22.11	(319.5)	19.22	(249.5)
1874–1875	8.56	(170)	19.63	(363)	13.23	(231)
1875–1876	7.33	(186.5)	14.36	(370.5)	14.51	(394)
1876–1877	7.82	(196)	21.79	(395)	12.79	(202.5)
1877–1878	6.10	(206.5)	20.95	(437)	13.03	(221.5)
1878–1879	6.60	(212.5)	20.73	(472)	10.51	(205.5)

(N)* = Average number of residents per month.
Source: San Francisco Ladies' Protection and Relief Society, "Minutes," 1872–1879; San Francisco Board of Supervisors, "Alms House Reports" and "Industrial School Reports," in Municipal Reports, 1872–1879.

support. As seen above, the dollar value of community support could be substantial. But the primary reason that women's charities operated with greater efficiency than their public counterparts was the voluntary labor of the lady managers themselves. Like the Sisters of Mercy, SFLP&RS volunteers received no salaries. Free labor, in fact, accounts almost entirely for the significant cost difference between private charities and public institutions. Charities could operate their institutions less expensively than public facilities because managers were not paid for their labor, typically the most expensive item in the budgets of public institutions. Over its first eleven years of operation, for example, the greatest expense for the Industrial School was always salaries. In all but two years of the period 1872 to 1880, the city spent more on Industrial School salaries than it did on food and provisions for inmates.[91] Thus, a larger percentage of public funds earmarked for the poor went to those providing aid, rather than to those needing it.

One might argue that the difference between public welfare and women's charities derived from the differences between men and women. However, local evidence suggests that the main difference was not due to gender per se. Private charities led by men could also operate with greater efficiency than public programs, for the same reason—lower overhead meant that more private charity dollars earmarked for the poor were actually spent on the poor. The key distinction between women's benevolence and public welfare derived from the sexual division of labor dictated by nineteenth-century gender ideology. Private charities relied upon volunteers for their services, often women, whereas public institutions paid their workers, usually men.

The distinctions observed between public and private institutions also derived from their differing modes of operation. In managing their facilities, lady managers drew upon the model with which they were most familiar—that is, their own homes. The well-ordered homes of the white, middle-class, Christian women described here provided both blueprint and creed for their charitable institutions. Leaders of the SFPOA and SFLP&RS consistently referred to their facilities as "homes" and to the residents as "family." Managers of San Francisco's Female Hospital likewise described their maternity hospital as "a quiet and comfortable home."[92] The Women's Christian Association blended domesticity and Protestantism, envisioning their institution as "not only a home but a 'Christian Home,'" where volunteers did "all that was necessary to make the Home in every respect a happy Christian family."[93]

Because benevolent women's political activism was shaped by the values of piety and domesticity, the institutions they created seemed to rise above self-interested partisanship. The political ethic that motivated San Francisco's lady managers was based, as one historian put it, "on responsibility rather than cupidity."[94] By comparison, public welfare institutions seemed incapable of offering their inmates either comfort or economy. The poor showing of public welfare institutions may have been inherent in the nature of nineteenth-century public administration. As demonstrated by San Francisco's City Hospital, nineteenth-century municipal government blended public service with private economic aspirations. Municipal strategies for meeting such urban needs as medical care, public transit, garbage collection, and poor relief—namely, the contract system and the almshouse—provided public figures with opportunities for private gain.[95]

San Francisco's public welfare system was just as prone to corruption as those in the East. Local welfare administrators manipulated supply contracts for personal profit, for example, and the coffers of public facilities were sometimes raided for graft and political patronage. In the 1850s, members of the city's Democratic machine diverted $166,000 earmarked for the State Marine Hospital for patronage and gifts to prostitutes and mistresses. On election day, reports one historian, the entire medical staff and all the hospital's movable patients were required to get out and "vote 'the ticket'—as many times as they could."[96] A study of City Hospital records for the period 1849–1936 showed that food contractors routinely defrauded the city, with the result that patients sometimes went hungry. In 1872 San Francisco Alms House Superintendent M. J. Keating admitted that unscrupulous businessmen were supplying rotten meat and short-weighted goods to the facility; as a result, Alms House inmates were slowly starving to death.[97]

Women's charities, in contrast, operated outside the system of patronage and "public service for profit." It is no wonder that San Franciscans were so willing to entrust welfare services to local women. Citizens must have felt themselves fortunate indeed to possess a supplemental welfare system managed by individuals apparently immune to the evils of greed and corruption. From the citizen's perspective, women's charities were superior because women were excluded from formal politics. Giving funds, goods, and political support to women's organizations allowed local men to meet the obligations of Christian charity. At the same time, citizens avoided expansion of the public sector, with its associated risks of waste, fraud, higher taxes, and corruption. Any discomfort local leaders might have felt in supporting women's excursion into the political sphere was outweighed by the benefit of retaining financial control over the city's social welfare system.

The availability and efficiency of local woman-run entities may actually have retarded the development of some forms of public welfare. The city resisted demands for outdoor relief until the earthquake and fire of 1906. Because surviving institutions could not meet the overwhelming demand for housing, officials agreed to board children in private homes at city expense. When officials realized that those funds could be used to keep children in their own homes, the city began paying small pensions to widowed mothers to care for their own children. These payments became the precedent for California's mother's pension program, which was implemented in 1913. Another thirty years were to pass, however, before the cataclysm of the Great Depression compelled local officials to revise their policies and support outdoor relief for adults.[98]

The power that San Francisco's lady managers exercised was that of the lobbyist, fundraiser, and resource distributor. Women collected and expended large sums of public and private money to meet what they perceived as vital community needs. In the process, local women were redistributing local wealth and resources according to their own, particularly feminine vision of personal and communal responsibility. Thus, women's charities were central to San Francisco's social and political development.

San Francisco developed key public services only when women stepped in to fill the gaps. As a result of their prodding, public officials provided support for women and children. Women activists inaugurated other community services that we now take for granted, such as kindergartens, playgrounds, and free libraries. As pioneers in local welfare provision, San Francisco women were the essential force that shaped San Francisco's evolution from crude frontier outpost to modern municipality.

Notes

This chapter is based on Mary Ann Irwin, "'Going About and Doing Good': The Lady Managers of San Francisco" (Master's thesis, San Francisco State University, 1995). A version of this thesis was published as "'Going About and Doing Good': The Politics of Benevolence, Welfare, and Gender in San Francisco, 1850–1880," *Pacific Historical Review* 68, no. 3 (August 1999), which won the Coalition for Western Women's History Jensen-Miller Prize for the best article published on western women's history in 1999.

1. Frederick Billings, *An Address Delivered at the Fifth Anniversary of the Orphan Asylum Society of San Francisco at Musical Hall, Tuesday Evening, February 5, 1856* (San Francisco: Whitton, Towne, 1856), Bancroft Library, University of California, Berkeley (hereafter "Bancroft").

2. For examples of the use of "Lady Manager" by local organizations, see San

Francisco Lying-In Hospital and Foundling Asylum, *First Printed Report of the Secretary* (San Francisco: Alta Printing House, 1872); Protestant Episcopal Church Home Association, *Langley's San Francisco Directory, 1877* (San Francisco: Francis, Valentine, 1877) (hereafter "Langley's," followed by the year); San Francisco Orphan Asylum Society, *Fifth Annual Report of the San Francisco Orphan Asylum Society* (San Francisco: Whitton, Towne, 1856).

3. Paula Baker, "The Domestication of Politics: Women and American Political Society, 1780–1920," *American Historical Review* 89 (1984): 620–47.

4. Ruth Shackelford, "To Shield Them from Temptation: 'Child-Saving' Institutions and the Children of the Underclass in San Francisco, 1850–1910" (PhD dissertation, Harvard University, 1991), 289.

5. Gunther Barth, *Instant Cities: Urbanization and the Rise of San Francisco and Denver* (New York: Oxford University Press, 1975).

6. Shackelford, "To Shield Them," 306; Sophia Eastman to "Sister," July 18, 1850, Sophia Eastman Papers, Bancroft. San Francisco had two other medical facilities, neither of which were of much use to the general public. The State Marine Hospital opened in 1850 and closed in 1855; it accepted non-mariners if they were wealthy enough to post bond. The U.S. Marine Hospital opened in 1854 and was abandoned after the earthquake of 1868; it served only seamen. Frances Cahn and Valeska Bary, *Welfare Activities of Federal, State, and Local Governments in California, 1850–1934*, Publications of the Bureau of Public Administration, University of California (Berkeley: University of California Press, 1936), 139; Roger W. Lotchin, *San Francisco, 1846–1856: From Hamlet to City* (Lincoln: University of Nebraska Press, 1974), 87, 185, 221; Shackelford, "To Shield Them," 361. Beginning in 1875, mariners could take advantage of a new U.S. Marine Hospital, located on the southern edge of the Presidio, where it is still visible today. Norman E. Tutorow, "A Tale of Two Hospitals: U.S. Marine Hospital No. 19 and the U.S. Public Health Service Hospital on the Presidio of San Francisco," *California History* 75, no. 2 (Summer 1996): 154–69; Presidio Trust, "Public Health Service Hospital District," August 2009, at http://www.presidio.gov/trust/projects/phsh, accessed February 12, 2010. After 1877, of course, seamen could also avail themselves of the Ladies' Seamen's Friend Society Home, discussed in this chapter.

7. Shackelford, "To Shield Them," 287–301.

8. Sam Bass Warner Jr., *The Private City: Philadelphia in Three Periods of Its Growth* (Philadelphia, 1987), 175–76; Mary P. Ryan, *Civic Wars: Democracy and Public Life in the American City during the Nineteenth Century* (Berkeley: University of California Press, 1997), 163–64; Maureen A. Flanagan, *Charter Reform in Chicago* (Carbondale: Southern Illinois University Press, 1987), 35.

9. *San Francisco Bulletin*, October 15, 1861, October 13, 1860, quoted in Terrence J. McDonald, *The Parameters of Urban Fiscal Policy: Socioeconomic Change and Political Culture in San Francisco, 1860–1906* (Berkeley: University of California Press, 1986), 122.

10. McDonald, *Parameters of Urban Fiscal Policy*, 49, 18.

11. See Bradford Luckingham, "Associational Life on the Urban Frontier: San Francisco, 1848–1856" (PhD dissertation, University of California, Davis, 1968); Cahn and Bary, *Welfare Activities*, 46, 137; Peter R. Decker, *Fortunes and Failures: White-Collar Mobility in Nineteenth-Century San Francisco* (Cambridge MA: Harvard University Press, 1978); Robert A. Burchell, *The San Francisco Irish, 1848–1880* (Berkeley: University of California Press, 1980); Douglas Henry Daniels, *Pioneer Urbanites: A Social and Cultural History of Blacks in San Francisco* (Berkeley: University of California Press, 1991).

12. See Merle Stewart Jaque, "The Origins of Private Benevolence in California, 1769–1869" (Master's thesis, San Diego State College, 1966) for pre–Gold Rush benevolence.

13. Luckingham, "Associational Life," 28, 79, 31; Jaque, "Origins of Private Benevolence," 21–22; Mitchel Roth, "Cholera, Community, and Public Health in Gold Rush Sacramento and San Francisco," *Pacific Historical Review* 66 (1997), 527–51.

14. Roth, "Cholera, Community," 534. Bruce Dorsey discusses the intersections of nineteenth-century notions of masculinity and benevolence in Bruce Dorsey, *Reforming Men and Women: Gender in the Antebellum City* (Ithaca NY: Cornell University Press, 2002).

15. San Franciscans created at least 103 benevolent and reform organizations between 1848 and 1879. Of these, sixty were led by men and thirty-eight were led by women, four had mixed boards, and one had identical but separate same-sex boards. Information on charity organizations was gathered from city directories for the period 1850–1880.

16. Cahn and Bary, *Welfare Activities*, 142. San Francisco's City Hospital treated women but not children; its first children's ward opened in the 1890s. Leontina Murphy, "Public Care of the Dependent Sick in San Francisco, 1847–1936" (Master's thesis, University of California, Berkeley, 1938), 72–74; Rickey Hendricks, "Feminism and Maternalism in Early Hospitals for Children: San Francisco and Denver, 1875–1915," *Journal of the West* 32 (1993), 61–69; Rickey Hendricks and Mark S. Foster, *For a Child's Sake: History of the Children's Hospital, Denver, Colorado, 1910–1990* (Niwot: University Press of Colorado, 1994); Joan E. Lynaugh, *The Community Hospitals of Kansas City, Missouri, 1870–1915* (New York: Garland, 1989); Clement A. Smith, *The Children's Hospital of Boston: Built Better Than They Knew* (Boston: Little, Brown, 1983).

17. Peter Decker and Philip Ethington disagree on whether San Francisco had a political "machine" during this period. See Decker, *Fortunes and Failures*, 127; Philip J. Ethington, *The Public City: The Political Construction of Urban Life in San Francisco, 1850–1900* (New York: Cambridge University Press, 1994), 289–90. Cahn and Bary found that, when California began allocating public funds for outdoor

relief in the 1880s, officials gave significantly more aid to men of voting age than they gave to women and children (it is not clear if Cahn and Bary factored in the state's unequal gender ratio). Cahn and Bary, *Welfare Activities*, 171–72, 175.

18. Shackelford, "To Shield Them," 290, 294, 296.

19. Carol Green Wilson, *A History of the Heritage, 1853–1970* (San Francisco: Ladies' Protection & Relief Society, 1970), 3–5; San Francisco Ladies' Protection and Relief Society (SFLP&RS), *Articles of Incorporation* (San Francisco: n.p., 1855); SFLP&RS Records, 1854–1969, California Historical Society, San Francisco, California (hereafter "CHS").

20. *San Francisco Alta*, July 12, 1853, 7–2.

21. SFLP&RS, Articles; Rowena Beans, *Inasmuch . . . The One Hundred Year History of the San Francisco Ladies Protection and Relief Society, 1853–1953* (Berkeley CA: James J. Gillick, 1953), 3.

22. Barth, *Instant City*, ix.

23. Joseph Torchia, "Our Greatest Tradition Is One of Love," *San Francisco Chronicle*, May 1, 1978, 16–17; Russ Cone, "The Asylum Where Babies Were Deposited Like Books," *San Francisco Examiner*, August 25, 1982.

24. Nellie Stow, *Tower of Strength in the City's Building: A Reminiscence by Nellie Stow, Secretary of the San Francisco Protestant Orphanage* (San Francisco: San Francisco Protestant Orphanage Society, 1941), 3–4, Bancroft; Anna Bissell [Mrs. W. A.] Haight, *Some Reminiscences of the San Francisco Protestant Orphan Asylum* (SFPOA) (San Francisco: n.p., 1900), CHS, 8, 10–12.

25. The clergymen were Albert Williams, Jesse Boring, Samuel H. Willey, and O. C. Wheeler. SFPOA, *Constitution and Bylaws*; *Fifth Annual Report of the San Francisco Orphan Asylum Society* (San Francisco: Whitton, Towne, 1856), Bancroft, 21.

26. Lori Ginzberg found a correlation between class standing and women's voluntarism; elite women, for example, were more likely to join charitable associations than woman suffrage groups. Lori D. Ginzberg, *Women and the Work of Benevolence: Morality, Politics, and Class in the Nineteenth-Century United States* (New Haven CT: Yale University Press, 1990), 6.

27. Luckingham, "Associational Life," 29.

28. Haight, *Some Reminiscences*, 7.

29. Haight, *Some Reminiscences*, 8.

30. SFLP&RS, *Meeting Minutes*, August 10, 1859.

31. Shackelford, "To Shield Them," 321.

32. Shackelford, "To Shield Them," 9.

33. Haight, *Some Reminiscences*, 8; Shackelford, "To Shield Them," 330.

34. Haight, *Some Reminiscences*, 6. Of course, "Haight" was his own name as well.

35. SFPOA, *Constitution and By-Laws*, 21–22.

36. Shackelford, "To Shield Them," 326–27.

37. Haight, *Some Reminiscences*; SFPOA, *Constitution and By-Laws*, 21–22.

38. Shackelford, "To Shield Them," 326.

39. Wilson, *A History*, 23. According to its 1877 report, the SFLP&RS also gave outdoor relief in 1859, 1860, and 1869. Unfortunately, reports from those years are not available. SFLP&RS, *Twenty-Third and Twenty-Fourth Annual Reports of the Managers and Trustees of the San Francisco Ladies' Protection and Relief Society for the Two Years Ending September 1, 1877* (San Francisco: n.p., 1877), CHS, 6–7.

40. SFLP&RS, *Twenty-Third and Twenty-Fourth Annual Reports*, 6–7.

41. Elizabeth Cady Stanton, Susan B. Anthony, and Matilda Joslyn Gage, *History of Woman Suffrage* (6 vols., New York: Fowler & Wells, 1881–1922), vol. 2, 749–68.

42. Peggy Pascoe, *Relations of Rescue: The Search for Female Moral Authority in the American West, 1874–1939* (New York: Oxford University Press, 1990), 15–17; Linda K. Kerber, "Separate Spheres, Female Worlds, Woman's Place: The Rhetoric of Women's History," *Journal of American History* 75 (1988): 9–39, 26. I found very few local women who belonged to both charitable associations and the state woman suffrage organization. The notable exception was Marietta Stow; see Donna C. Schuele, "In Her Own Way: Marietta Stow's Crusade for Probate Law Reform within the Nineteenth-Century Woman's Rights Movement," *Yale Journal of Law and Feminism* 7 (1995): 279–306.

43. San Francisco Female Hospital of the State of California (SFFH), *Report* (San Francisco: Edward Bosqui, 1874), 6–9, 11. Neither local newspapers nor surviving SFFH reports explain the opposition hinted at by Dr. Deane. My suspicion is that it related to the admission of unwed mothers; this assumption is based on the hospital's annual tally of illegitimate births, followed by the assertion that, without the SFFH, these infants would have "shared the fate of so many thousands of innocents murdered in their mothers' womb." SFFH, *Report*, 6; *Langley's*, 1871, p. 883.

44. SFFH, *Report*, 5.

45. SFFH, *Report*, 11–12.

46. SFLP&RS, *Meeting Minutes*, June 13, 1860.

47. Ladies' Seamen's Friend Society of the Port of San Francisco (LSFSPSF), *Second Annual Report* (San Francisco: C. A. Calhoun, 1858), 5, Bancroft; Jaque, "Origins of Private Benevolence," 37. The LSFSPSF records referenced here are located at Bancroft.

48. LSFSPSF, *Second Annual Report*, 4.

49. LSFSPSF, *Second Annual Report*, 4.

50. LSFSPSF, *Second Annual Report*, 5 (emphasis in original).

51. LSFSPSF, *Thirty-Sixth Annual Report* (San Francisco: George Spaulding, 1892).

52. Alvin Averback, "San Francisco's South of Market District, 1858–1958: The Emergence of a Skid Row," *California Historical Quarterly* 52, no. 3 (Fall 1973), 200–202.

53. LSFSPSF, *Ninth Annual Report* (San Francisco: Mining & Scientific Press, 1865), 5.

54. Averback, "South of Market," 206.

55. LSFSPSF, letter "To the Honorable Senate and Assembly of the State of California" (n.p., n.d.).

56. LSFSPSF, *Report, 1869–1870* (San Francisco: Spaulding & Barto, 1870).

57. LSFSPSF, *Report of 1874, 1875, and 1876 of the Ladies' Seamen's Friend Society* (San Francisco: Spaulding & Barto, 1876), 4–5.

58. John W. Blackett, "San Francisco Cemeteries," at http://www.sanfrancisco cemeteries.com/usmarinemap1.html, accessed May 25, 2008; see also Cahn and Bary, *Welfare Activities*, 139.

59. LSFSPSF, *Report, 1869–1870*.

60. LSFSPSF, *Twenty-First Annual Report of the Ladies' Seamen's Friend Society of the Port of San Francisco for the Year Ending August 8, 1877* (San Francisco: Spaulding & Barto, 1877), 3.

61. LSFSPSF, *Twenty-First Annual Report*.

62. See Gilman M. Ostrander, *The Prohibition Movement in California, 1848–1933* (Berkeley: University of California Press, 1957).

63. Board of Supervisors, City and County of San Francisco, *Municipal Reports for Fiscal Year Ending 1868* (San Francisco: John H. Carmany, 1868) (hereafter "Municipal Reports," followed by the year), 392.

64. *Municipal Reports, 1876–1880*. On the growth of institutions in the nineteenth century, see Cahn and Bary, *Welfare Activities*, 141–42; Ginzberg, *Women and the Work of Benevolence*, 119; Theda Skocpol, *Protecting Soldiers and Mothers: The Political Origins of Social Policy in the United States* (Cambridge MA: Harvard University Press, 1992), 93; Nathan I. Huggins, *Protestants against Poverty: Boston's Charities, 1870–1900* (Westport CT: Greenwood, 1971), 83–93; and David J. Rothman, *The Discovery of the Asylum: Social Order and Disorder in the New Republic* (Boston: Little, Brown, 1971).

65. Rev. Dennis John Kavanaugh, S.J., *The Holy Family Sisters of San Francisco: A Sketch of Their First Fifty Years* (San Francisco: Gilmartin, 1922), 27–53.

66. John W. Blackett, "San Francisco Cemeteries"; see also Cahn and Bary, *Welfare Activities*, 139.

67. California Society for the Prevention of Cruelty to Children (CSPCC), *First Annual Report for the Year Ending December 31, 1877* (San Francisco: n.p., 1877), 16. Records for the CSPCC referenced here are located at Bancroft.

68. CSPCC, *First Annual Report...1877*, 19; Shackelford, "To Shield Them," 312–14; Charles K. Jenness, *The Charities of San Francisco: A Directory of the Benevolent and Correctional Agencies: Together with a Digest of Those Laws Most Directly Affecting Their Work* (Stanford CA: Leland Stanford Jr. University, 1894), 41.

69. CSPCC, *Third Annual Report for the Year Ending December 31, 1879* (San Francisco:

n.p., 1879). The Roman Catholic Orphan Asylum and Mt. St. Joseph's Infant Asylum were managed by the Sisters of Mercy and the Sisters of Charity, respectively. Ruth Shackelford provides an invaluable study of children's work by San Francisco's Catholic women's orders in "To Shield Them from Temptation," 287–428.

70. *California Police Gazette*, quoted in Jacqueline Barnhart Baker, *The Fair but Frail: Prostitution in San Francisco, 1849–1900* (Reno: University of Nevada Press, 1986), 115n39; "The Industrial School of San Francisco," *Hutchings' California Magazine* 4 (1859), 58–61.

71. Charles Loring Brace, *The New West; or, California in 1867–1868* (New York: G. P. Putnam, 1869), 72; Shackelford, "To Shield Them," 355; Capt. Joseph C. Morrill, *The Industrial School Investigation with a Glance at the Great Reformation and Its Results* (San Francisco: n.p., 1872), 2, Bancroft.

72. Municipal Reports, 1867–1868, 392.

73. Shackelford, "To Shield Them," 361–83.

74. Shackelford, "To Shield Them," 379.

75. Shackelford, "To Shield Them," 379.

76. The city sent female juveniles to the Magdalene Asylum even after completion of the State Reform School at Whittier in 1891. Shackelford, "To Shield Them," 379.

77. JoAnn Levy, *They Saw the Elephant: Women in the California Gold Rush* (Hamden CT: Archon Books, 1990), 117.

78. Lotchin, *Hamlet to City*, 186, 222.

79. Frank Soule et al., *The Annals of San Francisco* (New York: O. Appleton, 1855), 370–76; Cahn and Bary, *Welfare Activities*, 138.

80. Shackelford, "To Shield Them," 314–15.

81. Municipal Reports, 1861–1862, 260.

82. Shackelford, "To Shield Them," 315n60; Municipal Reports, 1864–1865, 260.

83. Municipal Reports, 1863–1864.

84. Kerber, "Separate Spheres," 9–39, 26.

85. Michael B. Katz, *Poverty and Policy in American History* (New York: Academic Press, 1983), 132; Rothman, *Discovery of the Asylum*, 28, 166–67, 183.

86. Municipal Reports, 1871–1872.

87. Jenness, *Charities of San Francisco*, ii, iv.

88. Wilson, *A History*, 23. The SFLP&RS also gave outdoor relief in 1859, 1860, and 1869. SFLP&RS, *Twenty-Third and Twenty-Fourth Annual Reports*, 6–7.

89. Jenness, *Charities of San Francisco*, ii, iv.

90. The SFLP&RS provided monthly inmate figures, but public institutions reported the number of inmates only at the beginning and end of each report year. I derived a monthly average for public institutions by averaging beginning and ending populations in each facility. Both public and private facilities provided

annual expenditures. To arrive at the average cost per inmate per month for public and private institutions, I multiplied the average number of inmates per month by twelve, and divided total expenditures by this figure.

91. For the period 1872–1880, the city spent $33,000 more on Industrial School salaries ($146,056.37) than on food and provisions ($112,711.31). Municipal Reports, 1872–1880.

92. SFFH, Report, 8.

93. Women's Christian Association of San Francisco, Constitution, By-Laws (n.p., n.d.), 5, Bancroft.

94. James T. Kloppenburg quoted in Skocpol, Protecting Soldiers, 318–24.

95. Kloppenburg in Skocpol, Protecting Soldiers, 72; Warner, Private City, xiii, 99, 175–76, 202; Ryan, Civic Wars, 101; Michael B. Katz, In the Shadow of the Poorhouse: A Social History of Welfare in America (New York: Basic Books, 1996), 26–27; Katz, Poverty and Policy, 11–12; Steven Mintz, Moralists and Modernizers: America's Pre–Civil War Reformers (Baltimore: Johns Hopkins University Press, 1995), 85; Priscilla Ferguson Clement, Welfare and the Poor in the Nineteenth-Century City: Philadelphia, 1800–1854 (Cranbury NJ: Fairleigh Dickinson University Press, 1985), 43, 59; Stephen J. Leonard and Thomas J. Noel, Denver: Mining Camp to Metropolis (Niwot: University Press of Colorado, 1994), 68–69.

96. Lotchin, Hamlet to City, 186, 222.

97. Murphy, "Public Care," 70–72, 75; Municipal Reports, 1874–1875, 380–81.

98. Shackelford, "To Shield Them," 412n69; Cahn and Bary, Welfare Activities, 174–75.

3. "WOMAN IS EVERYWHERE THE PURIFIER"

The Politics of Temperance, 1878–1900

JOSHUA PADDISON

"Governments have forgotten the requirements of morality in the hot pursuit of emoluments of fame and fortune, until the degradation and criminal tendencies of the masses are something appalling," complained an anonymous editorialist in the June 1, 1893, edition of the *Pacific Ensign*, the state newspaper of the Woman's Christian Temperance Union (WCTU) of California. Ostensibly condemning the proliferation of barrooms in San Francisco, the writer devoted most of her attention to a cause that, for the WCTU, increasingly seemed a panacea for all of California's ills: woman suffrage. "Woman is everywhere the purifier," noted the editorialist, "and as she makes brighter and purer the home life, so will she elevate and cleanse the moral atmosphere of State and nation. In the crusade against wrong her hour has come."[1] The editorial—with its Protestant moral righteousness, its maternalist mix of disgust and concern for the "masses," its characterization of women as "purifiers," and its endorsement of woman suffrage—encapsulated the intertwined values of the WCTU of California, a state branch of the largest women's organization in the United States during the Gilded Age.[2]

One of the few organizations active in all parts of the country after the Civil War, the national WCTU held its first nationwide convention in Cleveland in 1874. By working to stamp out drinking, WCTU reformers sought to extend the feminine values of the private sphere into the public sphere. In the process, the organization used prevailing gender expectations to secure a degree of political power for women. Under the ambitious direction of Frances Willard, president of the national body, the WCTU expanded its agenda far beyond temperance during the 1880s and 1890s to include the promotion of the humane treatment of prisoners, an eight-hour work day, women's vocational education, child labor reform, kindergartens, urban boardinghouses for young women, "pure" newspapers and novels, and much more.[3] After 1881 the WCTU joined feminist organizations in support of woman suffrage. However, the group assured men that it sought the ballot "for no selfish ends," but merely to guard "the home, which has been and is woman's divinely appointed province."[4] Willard's motto, "Woman will bless and brighten every place she enters, and she will enter every place," epitomized how the WCTU's wide-reaching activism both sprang from and helped change traditional conceptions of femininity.[5] More than any other group, the WCTU helped convert ordinary American women to the suffrage cause by insisting that a woman's social responsibility did not stop when she exited her home or church. In the words of Dorcas J. Spencer, a longtime officer of the WCTU of California: "The temperance cause has created a thirst for franchise that will not be appeased without it."[6]

Following the example of Willard, the state WCTU strove to end the sale and consumption of alcohol in California and to enact a wide set of political and social reforms. Under the twin banners of domesticity and purity, the WCTU endeavored to give "poor, neglected, debased politics a good mothering" and to improve society by making the world "more home-like."[7] For its overwhelmingly white, middle-class, Protestant membership, the WCTU of California provided opportunities for personal growth and organized political action. The California women of the WCTU, who increasingly worked for suffrage in the 1880s and 1890s, paradoxically expanded their power beyond the private sphere by championing the feminine values that had helped confine women to that sphere throughout the nineteenth century. As their vision of "womanly" benevolence became more and more aggressive, WCTU leaders at times embraced nativism, racism, and religious bigotry. Ultimately, temperance activism helped transform popular notions of middle-class white femininity, paving the way for women's suffrage and Prohibition in the twentieth century.

The most popular and persistent reform movement in nineteenth-century America, temperance attracted thousands of California men and women of various socioeconomic classes. The Gold Rush made California famous for its unruly insobriety, a reputation supported by both anecdotal and statistical evidence.[8] A series of temperance organizations emerged after 1849 to combat California's frontier bibulousness. The Order of the Sons of Temperance, a secret fraternal organization with strong ties to evangelical Protestant congregations, managed to put a prohibitory "Maine law" on the California ballot in 1855.[9] The measure lost, but the surprisingly close margin of support (55.6 percent to 44.4 percent) revealed widespread sympathy for temperance goals.[10] The San Francisco–based Dashaway Association, active from 1859 to 1865, eschewed legal coercion for moral suasion—the winning of drinkers' hearts and minds through outreach, dialogue, and peer pressure. The Dashaways literally removed drunkards from saloon floors, sobered them up in their San Francisco Home for the Care of the Inebriate, and then, appealing to their manhood, asked them to exercise "manly self-control" to "dash away the intoxicating bowl."[11] Women had been involved at the periphery of California temperance activism since the 1850s, but men continued to dominate the movement until the emergence of the WCTU in 1878. The transformation of temperance from a man's issue to a woman's concern reflected changes in middle-class gender roles, as accelerating industrialization prompted fears that white men were becoming over-civilized, and as a new masculine ideal emphasizing passion and sexuality increasingly eclipsed the older ideal of "manly self-control."[12] California women embraced the WCTU, using it to extend the state's tradition of anti-alcohol activism with a new attempt to regulate and remake public life.

The WCTU of California experienced steady growth throughout the late nineteenth century. The organization established its first chapter in Petaluma in December 1878. It held its first statewide convention less than a year later in September 1879, counting six chapters and around two hundred members.[13] A decade later the organization had grown so large that it had split into northern and southern divisions, with 3,687 members in 117 chapters in the north, and 1,481 more members in the south.[14] Its newspaper boasted a paid subscription of twenty-six hundred in 1889, making it the largest WCTU state paper in the nation.[15]

Modeled after the national organization, the WCTU of California created a series of departments devoted to separate causes. In 1879 the group had eleven such departments, including "Enquiry and Statistics of Liquor Traffic," "Influencing the Press," and a section with a particularly unwieldy title: "Inducing Corporations and Employers to Require Total Abstinence in their Employees, also to Banish Liquor from Boats and Cars."[16] By 1889 the number of departments had grown to thirty, two of which—"Song" and "Viticulture"—were unique to California.[17]

Who were the women of the WCTU of California? Of the 214 officers' names listed in the annual convention minutes for 1885, 170 (or 79 percent) bore the honorific "Mrs.," indicating that the majority of officers were married or widowed.[18] In a study of the Riverside chapter in southern California, the historians Marie L. Kreider and Michael R. Wells characterize WCTU women as "primarily white, well-educated, economically prosperous, native-born Protestants of Anglo-Saxon ancestry."[19] Cross-checking the Riverside County WCTU directory against the 1910 federal census, Kreider and Wells found that only 8 percent of WCTU households were those of unskilled laborers, and concluded that "almost all of these women lived in middle-class households and enjoyed some degree of prosperity."[20] San Francisco's branches (which numbered ten in 1889) were the most ethnically diverse, including German, Swedish, and Russian chapters.[21] By and large, however, most WCTU of California members were middle-class, married, Protestant women of western European heritage.

Interrelated discourses of domesticity, purity, and California "exceptionalism" both fueled and justified the WCTU of California's participation in the public sphere. Responsibility and devotion to children and home were central components of most white middle-class American women's self-identity. Accordingly, the WCTU of California endeavored to ensure the warmth, coziness, and comfortableness of its surroundings. Its literature dictated that WCTU boardinghouses should include a "pleasant parlor, warmed and lighted, and supplied with newspapers, books, and a piano," for "many beautiful girls are driven out by the cold, cheerless aspect" of such public rooms.[22] The California president Mary Frank (Mrs. P. D.) Browne exhorted, "Let us hold Parlor meetings with beautiful baskets of roses, sweet peas, etc., throughout the room. Let us have our young girls in pretty light gowns, wearing flowers of pink for one entertainment, yellow for another, etc."[23] The women also took care to ensure that WCTU reading rooms were "well warmed and brightly lighted."[24]

Far from limiting women to the home, however, the WCTU's vision of domesticity spurred California members into public action. "'Women should be homekeepers, silent in public life,' was the old-time cry, and the first proposition is as true and as acceptable today as it has ever been," declared the president Mrs. S. J. Churchill in 1888. "But through woman's demand, and a better appreciation by man of her capabilities, she is coming more and more into public life."[25] The WCTU intended to protect the home by improving the wider world. "Let us see that justice is done the thousands of poor women with drunken husbands who have no one to care for them," urged Mary Browne in 1881.[26] The WCTU placed special emphasis on saving "helpless" children: "Many so-called Christian mothers have set too long with folded hands and closed eyes," lamented one WCTU woman, "while their children were passing through the fire to Moloch. The work of child-saving devolves upon the nation's consecrated motherhood."[27] In short, the WCTU of California expanded the notion of domesticity to include not simply members' own homes and children, but all homes and all children.

A second WCTU of California theme was purity—personal, sexual, national, political, religious, and racial.[28] Purity proved to be an especially flexible concept, fitting well with the WCTU of California's arguments for woman suffrage, political reform, social censorship, and nativism, all the while drawing strength from the evocation of a recognizably feminine goal. At the 1887 state convention, the body adopted a resolution supporting "stringent laws in the interest of social purity" to accompany its newly created Department of Social Purity.[29] "In enlightened nations—nations whose laws are founded on God's laws—it is thought of man that woman should be pure," reported one supervisor of Social Purity, who added, "If she [is to] have his respect she must be pure. Her life must be beautiful in its purity and modesty." California's Social Purity supervisor challenged the double standard that allowed men greater sexual freedom than women: "Let us, as Christian mothers, teach our boys that their virginity is as priceless as their sisters'!"[30] Another speaker complained that newspapers "cater too much to the lower stratum of society, to those who love the coarse jest and the appetizing scandal." She demanded that journalists reflect: "I am sending out a message into ten thousand homes, shall its influence there be pure and elevating or pernicious?"[31] In the name of purity, the WCTU also criticized male-dominated politics, calling politicians "mossback tools of corrupt rings" in a government dominated by "great monopolies, of which the liquor traffic is chief."[32] Extending this logic, the WCTU insisted that "the purification of our governmental affairs" depended on the granting of woman suffrage.[33]

In response to the era's surging levels of urban poverty and immigration, the WCTU of California employed xenophobic concepts of social purity that mingled religious and racial prejudice.³⁴ "Generations of paupers, criminals, lunatics and idiots are constantly coming into the world," complained Mary Browne in 1881, employing language her audience would have understood as referring to Catholic and Jewish immigrants, seen by many nineteenth-century Americans as less than fully white. "Impure influences cannot emanate from the lowliest American home without ultimately, and perhaps speedily, affecting the entire body politic," she added.³⁵ An anonymous editorial in the *Pacific Ensign* in 1892 contrasted "old" immigrants from western Europe, who had been "educated, industrious, and frugal," with the new Catholic and Jewish immigrants, and "Hungarians, Italians, Russians and Poles, the most ignorant and degraded," who were said to "live like pigs." Echoing the logic of the wider nativist movement that surged in late nineteenth-century California, the editorialist called for a halt to open immigration "until those who [had already come] had time to become civilized and Christianized."³⁶ (We can only wonder what the Russian chapter of the WCTU's San Francisco branch thought of such rhetoric.) Moreover, it infuriated WCTU leaders that these male newcomers could vote while white native-born Protestant women could not. "Our nation sees fit to withhold the ballot from its loyal, intelligent, and Christian sisters, wives, and mothers and put it into the hands of the ignorant, vicious, and disloyal foreigners," complained Mrs. R. R. Johnson in 1888.³⁷

The WCTU viewed Asian immigrants, who did not enjoy more rights than white women, in a more positive light. Union leaders expressed "burning shame" at the treatment Chinese immigrants received in California, and established an "Oriental Work" department in 1895, which focused on "uplifting" Chinese and Japanese Americans.³⁸ Much like children, prostitutes, and Indians, Asian Americans' vulnerable position aroused a sense of maternalism in WCTU women, rather than a hostility such as that with which the organization spoke of European immigrants.

Throughout the nineteenth century, Americans of all kinds envisioned California as a place akin to John Winthrop's "city on a hill," bountiful in natural resources and ripe with promise.³⁹ For the women of the WCTU, California's untapped potential meant great responsibility. "We are all proud of our Golden State," Mrs. Ella S. Pringle noted in 1887. "Then comes the solemn thought: 'Unto whomsoever much is given much is required.'

4. Mrs. Dorcas J. Spencer, tireless officer for the WCTU of California, sits at her desk. She estimated that she wrote more than a thousand letters per year in the service of her temperance work. Huntington Library, San Marino, California.

Are we, a Christian people, rendering an equivalent for so many blessings and prosperity? There should go out from California the greatest religious and temperance influences in all our country."[40] Other WCTU members spoke of having been "placed where our responsibility is great," and predicted that California was "destined to be in the future years a second Garden of Eden, if we, the Christian women arouse ourselves to our individual responsibilities."[41] Accordingly, the WCTU of California shaped its activities to the particulars of the state's economy and geography. California departments included sections devoted to "Railroad Rates," "Work among Lumbermen," "Oriental Work," and "Indian Work." The WCTU gave special emphasis to California's famous wine industry by creating the country's only WCTU Department of Viticulture, which vowed to "encourage the culture of the raisin against the wine grape."[42] They also urged winemakers to consider cultivating olives or mulberry trees instead of grapes.[43] For the women of the WCTU, California's seemingly boundless resources and spiritual potential provided unique opportunities for reform efforts outside the home.

In an era when American women had few chances to gain experience in finance or public speaking, the WCTU of California gave its members opportunities for activism in the public sphere. The WCTU's first president, Mary Browne, initially refused to speak in front of an audience or even to sit on a raised platform. However, over time, she became "a most successful presiding officer and a fine platform speaker," recalled a WCTU historian, "distinguished for her fluency and readiness of speech."[44] All WCTU officers and superintendents necessarily gained experience in business correspondence, public speaking, and speech writing.

Dorcas J. Spencer reported in October 1888 that, during the previous year, she had traveled 4,502 miles, given seventy-nine lectures, presided over an equal number of afternoon meetings, helped organize twenty-one new WCTU branches, attended seven conventions, and addressed ten Sunday schools, thirty public schools, and fourteen boards of public health.[45] Other members helped run WCTU coffee houses and reading rooms, such as the two on Sacramento Street in San Francisco; in the early 1880s these facilities served more than five hundred customers per day.[46] WCTU members also staffed booths at local fairs, organized annual conferences, and contributed letters, editorials, and articles to WCTU newspapers and pamphlets. Members flocked to hear internationally famous speakers, such as Frances Willard, the national president, who toured California in 1883, and India's Pundita Ramabai, who visited the state in 1888 on behalf of the World WCTU.[47]

The state WCTU also met members' social needs by providing camaraderie, friendship, and intellectual stimulation, plus a missionary's sense of contributing to a movement larger than oneself. In the words of one California member, "We are but a small part of a great host of Christian workers—not 'a company of silly women,' as a weak brother in a neighboring city has been pleased to call us, but a people of one idea."[48] With its many reforms, the WCTU of California gave its members an outlet for evangelical outreach, an obligation that many Protestant, middle-class women of the nineteenth century saw as their moral and social duty. The WCTU of California often used evangelical language to describe the battle against alcohol. Members identified saloons as the "strong holds of Satan" and referred to the individual's conversion to temperance as his "saving moment."[49] WCTU members described themselves as "earnest and devoted Christian women . . . glad to work, even in an unpopular cause, and in the face of great discouragements, 'if by any means they [might]

COMPARATIVE COST OF LIQUOR.

The following diagram is a comparison of the annual expenditure in the United States for intoxicating liquors, with various other of the largest items of expenditure. It is based on the census of 1880 and other reliable authorities. Scale: Each three-fourths of an inch represents an expenditure of $100,000,000. The liquor bill represents the cash paid for it by consumers, and is, in our opinion, not an exaggeration of the facts. We consider it just about the actual amount.

We, all of us, even those who never buy liquor, are obliged to help pay this bill. It comes to us in the shape of taxes and high rents, jury duty, public and private benevolence, and much of the cost of hospitals and asylums; fires, collisions, shipwrecks, and other accidents; incompetence in public and private service; failure to meet obligations of all sorts; besides the more terrible and direct visitations by which it takes away friends, health, happiness, and even life itself. We cannot get away from it. We must extinguish it, or it will extinguish us, as it has the Indians in our very presence. It would probably have been our ruin before this time but for the Temperance Reform which has checked its rapid growth, but which cannot conquer it unless we all "come up to the help of the Lord, against the mighty." Dear reader, what are *you* doing about it?

- Liquor, $900,000,000.
- Tobacco, $600,000,000.
- Bread, $505,000,000.
- Meat, $303,000,000.
- Iron and Steel, $290,000,000.
- Woolen Goods, $237,000,000.
- Sawed Lumber, $233,000,000.
- Cotton Goods, $210,000,000.
- Boots and Shoes, $196,000,000.
- Sugar & Molasses, $155,000,000.
- Public Education, $85,000,000.
- Christian Missions, home and foreign, $5,500,000.

5. The San Francisco branch of the WCTU of California published this "Comparative Cost of Liquor" chart in its 1885 annual report; the chart contrasts the amount Americans annually spent on alcohol to what they spent on other products. Huntington Library, San Marino, California.

save some.'"⁵⁰ Their goal was to reach at least "one soul," to lift at least "one household from darkness into light."⁵¹

The WCTU's zealous quest to "save" California began with its children, which leaders proclaimed to be "the foundation stone of the great temperance temple we are striving to rear."⁵² In 1881 the WCTU sponsored a "Twin Evils, Intemperance and Tobacco" essay contest for California grammar and high school students, who responded with twenty thousand entries.⁵³ By 1887 the organization had created seventeen Loyal Temperance Unions for northern California children, designed to "train boys and girls from a moral and scientific standpoint in the principles of total abstinence, purity, and self-control."⁵⁴ WCTU activists established WCTU kindergartens and produced anti-alcohol pamphlets for children. The *Temperance Arithmetic*, published in 1885, offered didactic word problems such as: "California consumes about 10,000,000 gallons of wine annually. Allowing 50 gallons of wine to each drinker, how many can be supplied?"⁵⁵

The WCTU of California scored a major political victory in 1887, when the state legislature succumbed to WCTU campaigning and passed the Scientific Temperance Instruction Law. The law mandated education about "the nature of alcoholic drinks and narcotics and their effects upon the human system" in California's public schools.⁵⁶

The WCTU also gave members opportunities to behave charitably, another practice that many nineteenth-century middle-class women saw as central to their identity (see chapter 2 in this volume). The organization extended maternalist altruism to disadvantaged groups: sailors, working-class women, Indians, Asian Americans, prisoners, and ex-convicts. WCTU members worked to establish boardinghouses for the "working girls of San Francisco," and affordable coffee houses for the "hundreds of honest young men and virtuous girls, in workshop and factory, struggling to keep respectability, honor, and virtue."⁵⁷ In 1888 California's superintendent of prison work reported, "I wend my lone way once a week to the prison. Oh, such sights! Cells filled with women, some cursing, some smoking, others so far stupid from a late debauch as to be really unable to receive the truth."⁵⁸ Accordingly, the WCTU provided Sabbath services and temperance reading materials for prisoners, and jobs, clothing, and "Christian homes" for ex-prisoners.⁵⁹ The plight of sailors likewise stirred the WCTU's "pity and indignation."⁶⁰ WCTU women donated books to ships, knitted "wristlets" for the "man at the wheel," cosponsored gospel temperance meetings with the Sailors' Union, publicly condemned cruel treatment of sailors at sea, and even considered buying a boat to meet sailors "yet in the stream" to prevent them from becoming "demoralized"—that is, inebriated—while onshore.[61]

The members of the WCTU of California did not hesitate to attempt to use the law to carry out their reforms. In so doing, they gained political experience and power. Prohibiting the sale and distribution of alcohol was, of course, the WCTU's first and most enduring objective. Members used education and moral suasion to win over hearts and minds. They asked churches to stop using wine for communion, requested that the Southern Pacific Railroad remove liquor from their buffet cars, and placed temperance tracts in streetcars and other public places.[62] However, given the entrenchment of alcohol in the state's society and economy, the WCTU recognized that "prayer alone would cure no evil"—legal coercion was also required.[63] "Let us see that temptation is removed from the weak," urged Mrs. S. J. Churchill in 1885. "Who will save them from themselves, their own worse foe?"[64] Although they failed in their repeated attempts to gain a statewide prohibition referendum, the WCTU successfully appealed to the regents of the University of California in 1880 to enforce a law outlawing the sale of liquor within two miles of campus.[65] Eleven years later, WCTU members managed to pass an ordinance in Sutter County making unlawful "any tippling-house, dram-shop, cellar, saloon, bar, barroom, sample-room or other place where spirituous, vinous, malt, mixed, or intoxicating liquors" would be "sold or given away."[66]

Success with the university regents, officials in Sutter County, and Scientific Temperance Instruction Law encouraged the WCTU to launch new petition campaigns through the late 1880s and 1890s. Members petitioned city supervisors and the state legislature for laws requiring the establishment of police matrons, and the prohibition of child labor, prostitution, Sabbath nonobservance, employment of women in saloons (discussed in chapter 12 in this volume), and sale of tobacco.[67] Spencer reported that she wrote "more than one thousand letters" in 1887 alone.[68] The WCTU encouraged members to work behind the scenes and thus affect politics in less visible ways. "We can influence the votes of our friends, we can hold public meetings, we can be at the polls with the ballots that contain the names of those we desire elected," noted Mrs. M. E. Congdon. (Congdon was referring to the nineteenth-century practice of allowing political parties to print and distribute their own ballots at polling places. It was not until 1891 that, at the urging of the WCTU and other reform groups, California adopted the standardized, secret instrument known as the "Australian" ballot.) "We can circulate temperance literature," Mrs. Congdon continued, and "we can furnish on election days hot lunches and help remove the temptation of the open back door of the saloon."[69]

The WCTU's commitment to woman suffrage increased during the 1880s and 1890s, culminating in their involvement in the statewide referendum campaign of 1896. California members were initially slow to support suffrage, although Willard's national WCTU officially supported woman suffrage in 1881. At the 1883 convention, President Browne forbade discussion of the franchise. However, as Dorcas J. Spencer later recalled, when one speaker defied the mandate, "the silent audience felt the thrill it produced ... as she gave utterance to thought so radical."[70] Finally, in 1887, the state WCTU resolved, "Loyalty to our National society and justice to ourselves demand that we seek the ballot, for by the ballot alone can political evils be overcome."[71] This cautious wording belied the ferocity with which the group soon took up the cause. Outspoken proponents of woman suffrage, such as Sarah M. Severance, the longtime superintendent of the franchise department, soon convinced the WCTU's more conservative members that voting was the key to realizing all of the organization's goals. "More is involved in this [franchise] department than all the others combined, for the ballot box is the armory in which is locked the weapons needed to conduct our bloodless campaign," argued Severance in 1892.[72] Many activists justified the radical cause by invoking domesticity: "She who keeps the home fires burning and cares for the children, can see as clearly what measures are best for the home interests and the city's welfare, as he who ... goes out to battle with the world."[73] Other speakers used racialized arguments, proclaiming that, without the right to vote, America's white women were "upon the same level with Indians, Chinese, idiots and criminals."[74] This sort of rhetoric was hardly unique to California: similar appeals to white solidarity across gender lines were frequently advanced by national women's rights organizations and had helped activists win suffrage for white women in Wyoming in 1869.[75]

By 1893 the WCTU of California was able to deliver a legislative petition with twenty thousand names calling for woman suffrage.[76] Although a suffrage bill passed the legislature, the governor vetoed it. In 1896, however, members of California's self-styled "organized womanhood"—a coalition of suffrage organizations, women's clubs, and the WCTU—persuaded the legislature to place a referendum for woman suffrage on a statewide ballot.[77] The WCTU's Beaumelle Sturtevant-Peet and Sarah M. Severance had collected thousands of signatures and sent its leaders to Sacramento to lobby for the ballot measure. Representing the conservative arm of the coalition, the WCTU contributed grassroots organizational skills, well honed from earlier activism, in the campaign that followed.[78] Despite furious campaigning, California voters voted down the measure, in major part because the urban centers of San Francisco and Oakland justifiably feared that women's suffrage would mean prohibition.[79] The WCTU must still look forward to a day "when men and women shall walk side by side to the polls, to the court-room, to the assembly hall, and possibly to Congress."[80]

The twentieth century not only brought woman suffrage to California but also further weakened the ideology of separate spheres for men and women, as voting rights, greater opportunities for women's education and employment, and reliable methods of birth control gradually increased the freedom of American women. In 1919 the Eighteenth Amendment began Prohibition, the culmination of more than a century of U.S. temperance activism. The efforts of the WCTU of California during the Gilded Age had contributed to these changes. By insisting that women must enter the public sphere to protect the private sphere, the WCTU of California made an argument that was simultaneously conservative and radical. The feminine values of domesticity and purity, together with a belief in the exceptionalism of California, became justifications for public activism.

Through temperance work, thousands of white middle-class California women became engaged in politics for the first time. They debated the path of their organization; wrote hundreds of articles, editorials, and letters to the editor; organized conventions; delivered lectures and speeches; petitioned legislators, universities, and businesses; helped pass county and state laws; attempted to sway elections; and sent lobbyists to Sacramento. Temperance women involved themselves in every aspect of state politics short of voting and holding elected office. This activism not only transformed the lives of California women but profoundly influenced statewide debates on education, public health, urban problems, industrial capitalism, child care, ballot reform, immigration, and women's rights. By the time of Prohibition, for example, many if not most adult Californians had been exposed to temperance ideas because of the Scientific Temperance Instruction Law of 1887.[81] The white California women of the WCTU used nativist and racist arguments to further their crusade, and, compared to twentieth-century feminists, defined womanhood in stiflingly narrow terms. Yet their actions helped redefine and democratize American gender roles, a process that continued throughout the twentieth century and beyond.

Notes

This chapter is adapted from a chapter in Joshua Paddison, "Temperance and Gender in Northern California, 1850–1900" (Master's thesis, San Francisco State University, 2001).

1. *San Francisco Pacific Ensign*, June 1, 1893, p. 4.
2. Ruth Bordin, *Woman and Temperance: The Quest for Power and Liberty, 1873–1900* (Philadelphia: Temple University Press, 1981), 3.
3. Bordin, *Woman and Temperance*; Barbara Leslie Epstein, *The Politics of Domesticity: Women, Evangelism, and Temperance in Nineteenth-Century America* (Middletown CT: Wesleyan University Press, 1981), 115–37; Lori D. Ginzberg, *Women and the Work of Benevolence: Morality, Politics, and Class in the 19th-Century United States* (New Haven CT: Yale University Press, 1990), 202–6; Rebecca Edwards, *Angels in the Machinery: Gender in American Party Politics from the Civil War to the Progressive Era* (New York: Oxford University Press, 1997), 42–55; Catherine Gilbert Murdock, *Domesticating Drink: Women, Men, and Alcohol in America, 1870–1940* (Baltimore: Johns Hopkins University Press, 1998), 20–34; Dale E. Soden, "The Woman's Christian Temperance Union in the Pacific Northwest: The Battle for Cultural Control," *Pacific Northwest Quarterly* 94 (2003): 197–207.
4. Quoted in Bordin, *Woman and Temperance*, 119.
5. Quoted in Carolyn DeSwarte Gifford, "Frances Willard and the Woman Christian Temperance Union's Conversion to Woman Suffrage," in *One Woman, One Vote: Rediscovering the Woman Suffrage Movement*, ed. Marjorie Spruill Wheeler (Troutdale OR: NewSage, 1995), 119.
6. Dorcas J. Spencer, "Woman's Christian Temperance Union," *Californian Illustrated Magazine* 3 (January 1893): 170.
7. *Minutes of the Annual Convention of the WCTU of California*, 1888: 149 (hereafter, "Minutes").

8. See, e.g., Hinton Helper, *The Land of Gold: Reality versus Fiction* (Baltimore: Henry Taylor, 1855), 67; and J. S. Holliday, *The World Rushed In: The California Gold Rush Experience* (New York: Simon & Schuster, 1981), 454.

9. See Paddison, "Temperance and Gender," 27–55.

10. Gilman M. Ostrander, *The Prohibition Movement in California, 1848–1933* (Berkeley: University of California Press, 1957), 20.

11. Paddison, "Temperance and Gender," 56–78; James Andrew Baumohl, "Dashaways and Doctors: The Treatment of Habitual Drunkards in San Francisco from the Gold Rush to Prohibition" (PhD dissertation, University of California, Berkeley, 1986).

12. Gail Bederman, *Manliness and Civilization: A Cultural History of Gender and Race in the United States, 1880–1917* (Chicago: University of Chicago Press, 1995); E. Anthony Rotundo, *American Manhood: Transformations in Masculinity from the Revolution to the Modern Era* (New York: Basic Books, 1993).

13. Minutes, 1883; Mrs. Dorcas James Spencer, *A History of the Woman's Christian Temperance Union of Northern and Central California* (Oakland CA: West Coast Printing, 1911), 17; Ostrander, *The Prohibition Movement*, 58.

14. Minutes of the Annual Convention of the Woman's Christian Temperance Union of California, 1889; Marie L. Kreider and Michael R. Wells, "White Ribbon Women: The Woman's Christian Temperance Movement in Riverside, California," *Southern California Quarterly* 81 (1999), 119. For the WCTU's activities in southern California, see Mary Alderman Garbutt, *Victories of Four Decades: A History of the Woman's Christian Temperance Union of Southern California, 1883–1924* (Los Angeles: Woman's Christian Temperance Union of Southern California, 1924); Betty Jane Woods, "An Historical Survey of the Woman's Christian Temperance Union of Southern California: As It Reflects the Significance of the National WCTU in the Woman's Movement of the Nineteenth Century" (Master's thesis, Occidental College, 1950); and Michael E. James, "The City on the Hill: Temperance, Race, and Class in Turn-of-the-Century Pasadena," *California History* 80 (2001–2002): 186–203.

15. Minutes, 1889, p. 153. The state newspaper of the WCTU of California was called the *Bulletin* from 1885 to 1888, the *Pharos* from 1888 to 1891, and the *Pacific Ensign* from 1891 to 1906.

16. Minutes, 1881.

17. Minutes, 1889; Spencer, *A History*, 30.

18. Minutes, 1885.

19. Kreider and Wells, "White Ribbon Women," 117.

20. Kreider and Wells, "White Ribbon Women," 120–21.

21. Minutes, 1888, p. 143; Minutes, 1889.

22. Minutes, 1882, pp. 6–7.

23. *San Francisco Pacific Ensign*, May 5, 1892, p. 3.

24. Minutes, 1882, p. 5.

25. Minutes, 1888, pp. 46–47.

26. Minutes, 1881, p. 14.

27. Minutes, 1889, p. 52; see also Kyle E. Ciani, "The Power of Maternal Love: Negotiating a Child's Care in Progressive-Era San Diego," *Journal of the West* 41, no. 4 (2002): 71–79.

28. The national WCTU's concern with social purity has been well studied; see David J. Pivar, *Purity Crusade: Sexual Morality and Social Control, 1868–1900* (Westport CT: Greenwood, 1973); Megan Hailey-Dunsheath, "'Save Them before They Fall': Cordelia Throop Cole and the WCTU's Social Purity Movement," *Iowa Heritage Illustrated* 77, no. 3 (1996): 98–115; Alison M. Parker, *Purifying America: Women, Cultural Reform, and Pro-Censorship Activism, 1873–1933* (Urbana: University of Illinois Press, 1997); Alison M. Parker, "'Hearts Uplifted and Minds Refreshed': The Woman's Christian Temperance Union and the Production of Pure Culture in the United States, 1880–1930," *Journal of Women's History* 11 (1999): 135–58; Sharon Anne Cook, "'Do Not... Do Anything That You Cannot Unblushingly Tell Your Mother': Gender and Social Purity in Canada," *Social History* 30 (1997): 215–38; and Ann R. Gabbert, "Prostitution and Moral Reform in the Borderlands: El Paso, 1890–1920," *Journal of the History of Sexuality* 12 (2003): 575–604.

29. Minutes, 1887, p. 27; Spencer, *A History*, 38.

30. Minutes, 1887, p. 122.

31. Minutes, 1889, pp. 136, 138.

32. *San Francisco Pacific Ensign*, March 9, 1893, p. 4; November 10, 1892, p. 2.

33. Minutes, 1888, p. 49.

34. On the WCTU and race, see the differing positions of Edward J. Blum, *Reforging the White Republic: Race, Religion, and American Nationalism, 1865–1898* (Baton Rouge: Louisiana State University Press, 2005), 179; Glenda Elizabeth Gilmore, "'A Melting Time': Black Women, White Women, and the WCTU in North Carolina, 1880–1900," in *Hidden Histories of Women in the New South*, ed. Virginia Bernhard, Betty Brandon, Elizabeth Fox-Genovese, Theda Perdue, and Elizabeth H. Turner (Columbia: University of Missouri Press, 1994), 153–72; and Glenda Elizabeth Gilmore, *Gender and Jim Crow: Women and the Politics of White Supremacy in North Carolina, 1896–1920* (Chapel Hill: University of North Carolina Press, 1996), 45–59.

35. Minutes, 1881, p. 13.

36. *San Francisco Pacific Ensign*, October 13, 1892, p. 4; Priscilla Frances Knuth, "Nativism in California, 1886–1897" (Master's thesis, University of California, Berkeley, 1947); Brenda D. Frink, "'God Give Us Men!': Manliness, the American Protective Association, and Catholicism in San Francisco, 1893–1896," *Ex Post Facto: Journal of the History Students at San Francisco State University* 11 (2002): 49–64.

37. Minutes, 1888, pp. 45–46.

38. Rumi Yasutake, "Transnational Women's Activism: The Woman's Christian Temperance Union in Japan and the United States," in *Women and Twentieth-Century Protestantism*, ed. Margaret Lamberts Bendroth and Virginia Lieson Brereton

(Urbana: University of Illinois Press, 2002), 93–112. The WCTU did not similarly target California's African American population for "uplift," either due to racism or to the population's small size; Lawrence B. de Graaf, "Race, Sex, and Region: Black Women in the American West, 1850–1920," *Pacific Historical Review* 49 (1980): 310.

39. Kevin Starr, *Americans and the California Dream, 1850–1915* (New York: Oxford University Press, 1973).
40. Minutes, 1887, p. 34.
41. Minutes, 1889, p. 153; 1881, p. 24.
42. Minutes, 1885, p. 93.
43. Minutes, 1887, p. 27; 1883, pp. 43–45.
44. Spencer, *A History*, 23–24.
45. Minutes, 1888, p. 4.
46. Minutes, 1881, p. 48; Minutes, 1882, pp. 10–11; *San Francisco Pacific Ensign*, October 13, 1892, p. 4.
47. "Miss Frances E. Willard" broadside, May 16, 1883, Scrapbook #24, 1882–1884, 34, California Historical Society, San Francisco (hereafter "CHS"); Spencer, *A History*, 27; Minutes, 1888.
48. Minutes, 1888, p. 45.
49. Minutes, 1881, p. 24; 1888, p. 124.
50. Minutes, 1882, p. 4.
51. Minutes, 1883, p. 32.
52. Minutes, 1887, p. 104.
53. Minutes, 1881, pp. 40–42; Spencer, *A History*, 25.
54. Minutes, 1887, p, 101; 1888, p. 154.
55. "Grand Concert for the Benefit of Kindergartens," September 28, 1886, San Francisco Miscellaneous, Kindergartens, 1880–1889, CHS; *Temperance Arithmetic* (Oakland: The Union, 1885).
56. Spencer, *A History*, 43–45; Ostrander, *Prohibition Movement*, 60–61; Wendell E. Harmon, "A History of the Prohibition Movement in California" (PhD dissertation, University of California, Los Angeles, 1955), 73. For a national study, see Jonathan Zimmerman, *Distilling Democracy: Alcohol Education in America's Public Schools, 1880–1925* (Lawrence: University of Kansas Press, 1999).
57. Minutes, 1882, p. 11; 1888, p. 124.
58. Minutes, 1888, pp. 112–13.
59. Minutes, 1885, p. 98.
60. Minutes, 1888, p. 135.
61. Minutes, 1888, pp. 135–37; 1889, pp. 130–33. See also the documentary *The Odyssey of Captain Healy*, video recording, produced, written, and directed by Maria Brooks (1998; San Jose CA: Waterfront Soundings Production and KTEH, San Jose Public Television).

62. Minutes, 1883, p. 34; 1888, pp. 102, 132. They "set afloat" 900,000 pages of temperance literature in 1887 alone.

63. Minutes, 1885, p. 24

64. Minutes, 1885, p. 37.

65. Spencer, A History, 23.

66. Spencer, A History, 55–56.

67. Minutes, 1888, p. 35; Spencer, A History.

68. Minutes, 1887, p. 111.

69. Minutes, 1889, pp. 114–15.

70. Spencer, A History, 27.

71. Minutes, 1887, p. 27.

72. San Francisco Pacific Ensign, December 8, 1892.

73. Minutes, 1888, p. 49.

74. Minutes, 1889, p. 58.

75. Ellen Carol DuBois, Feminism and Suffrage: The Emergence of an Independent Women's Movement in America, 1848–1869 (Ithaca NY: Cornell University Press, 1978), 53–104; Suzanne M. Marilley, Woman Suffrage and the Origins of Liberal Feminism in the United States, 1820–1920 (Cambridge MA: Harvard University Press, 1996), 159–86; Louise Michele Newman, White Women's Rights: The Racial Origins of Feminism in the United States (New York: Oxford University Press, 1999); Virginia Scharff, Twenty Thousand Roads: Women, Movement, and the West (Berkeley: University of California Press, 2003), 68–92; Rebecca J. Mead, How the Vote Was Won: Woman Suffrage in the Western United States, 1868–1914 (New York: New York University Press, 2004), 35–52.

76. San Francisco Pacific Ensign, February 23, 1893, p. 2.

77. Donald G. Cooper, "The California Suffrage Campaign of 1896: Its Origin, Strategies, Defeat," Southern California Quarterly 71 (1989): 311–25; Gayle Gullett, Becoming Citizens: The Emergence and Development of the California Women's Movement, 1880–1911 (Urbana: University of Illinois Press, 2000), 11–23; Mead, How the Vote Was Won, 73–96.

78. Gayle Gullett, "Constructing the Woman Citizen and Struggling for the Vote in California, 1896–1911," Pacific Historical Review 69 (2000): 573–93; Gullett, Becoming Citizens, 23, 79–81.

79. The final vote was 137,099 (55.4 percent) to 110,355 (44.6 percent), a result almost identical to that of the Sons' failed prohibition referendum of 1855; Gullett, Becoming Citizens, 95–96.

80. Minutes, 1888, p. 47.

81. Ostrander, Prohibition Movement, 61.

4. "Continually Doing Good"
The Philanthropy of Phoebe Apperson Hearst, 1862–1919

MILDRED NICHOLS HAMILTON

When Phoebe Apperson Hearst wrote to the regents of the University of California at Berkeley on September 28, 1891, offering the first scholarships to "worthy young women" of "high character and noble aims," she could have been describing herself thirty-five years earlier as a Missouri farm girl hungering for a decent education.[1] Born to a modest frontier family in 1842, Phoebe Apperson, like most young women of her community, seemed to have slight opportunity to do more than duplicate the life of her mother as a hardworking and efficient housewife. Yet, by her death in 1919, she had become a major force in education and philanthropy, donating millions inherited from her mining-tycoon husband, George Hearst, to promote the causes of progressive-era reform. Although she shared her husband's wealth with a wide variety of organizations and institutions—from women's clubs and kindergartens to libraries and suffrage groups—Phoebe Hearst was most devoted to education, particularly in California and particularly in the interests of women. Her financial assistance provided a lifeline for reformers in San Francisco and around the country, and she did much to expand opportunities for women in higher education and the professions. At the same time, her vast wealth afforded her a degree of political power that was highly unusual for women of her generation. Hearst reached the pinnacle of this power in 1897, when Governor James H. Budd appointed her the first female regent of the University of California. In that role she became one of the highest-ranking female public officials in the United States—and one of the first to direct public policy on a statewide scale.

Phoebe Apperson Hearst led a singular and remarkable life, but her philanthropic career grew out of a larger reform tradition among wealthy women of the late nineteenth century. Like Mary Rozet Smith and Louise deKoven Bowen, two of the most important backers of Hull House, and like Mary Garrett, who offered Johns Hopkins University sixty thousand dollars if it would admit women to its medical school, Phoebe Hearst gave away her money in order to promote the interests of women and children and to meet social needs that were too often overlooked by government. By donating funds to institutions large and small, women like Phoebe Hearst helped steer the course of progressive reform.[2]

Tracing the philanthropic career of Phoebe Apperson Hearst sheds light on a path to power taken by certain wealthy women during the nineteenth century. Like other philanthropic women, Hearst targeted much of her giving to serve the needs of women and children, donating thousands of dollars to kindergartens, teacher-training programs, university scholarships, women's clubs, and mothers' associations. In this respect, she used her wealth to improve people's lives and to create new opportunities for women as professional teachers, social workers, and reformers. At the same time, Phoebe's philanthropic work taught her important skills that served her as her career became more public. After the death of her husband in 1891, she increased the scale of her giving and built a close, ongoing relationship with the University of California, where she served as regent from 1897 until her death in 1919. In addition to serving the needs and expanding the opportunities of others, Phoebe Apperson Hearst wielded her impressive economic power in order to improve her own ability to direct government policy and affect social change. In the end, the combination of immense wealth and intense philanthropic devotion allowed Phoebe to carve out a unique political role for herself that would have been unimaginable to the young girl who grew up on a modest frontier farm.

Little in Phoebe Hearst's background or upbringing prepared her for a life of wealth, comfort, or influence. She was born on December 3, 1842, in a Franklin County settlement some forty-five miles south of St. Louis. Her father, Randolph Walker Apperson, farmed, raised livestock, and was a respected elder in the evangelical Cumberland Presbyterian Church. He never provided more than a modest living for his family.[3] Phoebe's mother, Drucilla Whitemire, arrived in Franklin County as a toddler in a migration from South Carolina. Randolph and Drucilla married in 1841, and Phoebe was their first child; a brother, Elbert, followed eight years later.[4]

Phoebe's recorded reminiscences of her childhood center on religious observances and, especially, on strict and constant training by her mother, who emphasized efficiency and the importance of completing household tasks. She spent much of her leisure time with her father, whose expert riding lessons permitted her to venture over rough mountain trails in later trips to mines with her husband. She divided the rest of her time between assisting her mother and going to school. Phoebe attended the one-room Salem District Public School and spent a year at the Steelville Academy, operated in a neighboring county by the Cumberland Presbyterian Church.[5] This brief education helped her secure teaching positions that augmented her family's income and gave her a degree of independence. But as Adele Brooks, her friend and biographer, later noted, Phoebe always yearned for a broader education than her early environment afforded her. Brooks also wrote, "Easily and eagerly she had absorbed all that the meager curriculum of town and district schools of that day could give her. But higher education for which she longed was unavailable to girls."[6] This longing disciplined her and, later, when she had resources at her command, fueled Phoebe's desire to help other young women attain solid educations.

Phoebe's life took a fateful turn in 1860, when the Apperson's former neighbor, George Hearst, returned from California at the request of his ailing mother. The son of a prominent local family, Hearst had already made a healthy sum of money in the mining camps of California and Nevada, where he developed the expertise that later enabled him to amass many millions.[7] Their courtship raised eyebrows, as Hearst, at age forty-one, was twenty-two years her senior. But the headstrong Phoebe welcomed his advances. On June 15, 1862, the couple was married. Five months later, George and Phoebe were on their way to San Francisco.[8]

The Hearsts alighted at Stevenson House, an apartment-hotel at California and Montgomery streets, where on April 29, 1863, their son William Randolph was born. Not long after, George bought a comfortable brick house on fashionable Rincon Hill, settled his family, and set out for his mines.[9] With her husband away much of the time, Phoebe devoted herself to caring for her son and developing her artistic and literary interests. She resumed her French lessons, aiming to become "a thorough French scholar." Her library swelled with books on history, art, and architecture as she investigated the varied cultural offerings of the city. "We have been going out a great deal," she wrote to William's nurse. "There was a splendid opera troupe at the Academy of Music. We went six or eight nights. . . . I enjoyed it very much."[10] The young matron also entertained with growing ease and enthusiasm, cultivating connections with local artists and literary figures, many of whom came to rely on the Hearsts as patrons. A biographer noted that George Hearst, a consummate miner for whom museums and theater held no attraction, was a "fond husband who gave her everything she wanted but the thing she wanted most—an interest in the arts." Phoebe solved this problem by "letting him grub in the dirt and become involved in Democratic politics while she embarked on a cultural career of her own."[11] George gave her carte blanche for such activities. "Spend as much money as is necessary for your pleasure and not think of it," he wrote once, "for if you feel you are doing wrong you lose all your pleasure. . . . So do not write me that you are feeling bad about the costs. You will get all you want for your pleasure and comfort and it only makes me happy for you to have the money to use in that way."[12]

Phoebe used her husband's money to finance elaborate European tours for herself and the young William Randolph, who was a precocious ten-year-old when they made their first culture-laden trip abroad in 1873. Mother and son traveled together for eighteen months, enjoying a socially acceptable excursion that was also a status symbol for many wealthy families of the Gilded Age. Kathleen D. McCarthy has linked grand tours like these to philanthropists' later good works. Well-to-do women, in particular, found a badge of acceptability as they "took time to investigate the workings of the Continent's great museums, operas, civic monuments, and symphonies, and on their return . . . did their best to reproduce cultural bastions of the Old World on American soil." Anne Firor Scott has also noted the benefits of European travel for leisure-class women as they encountered other cultures and discovered new perspectives on intellectual and moral issues.[13] Phoebe Hearst followed a similar pattern. During her early years in San Francisco, she gave away small amounts of money on an individual basis, providing help to needy friends and struggling students of art and music.[14] However, by the 1880s, after returning from her early European tours, she began to practice philanthropy on a more systematic basis. Her gifts were varied and numerous. She continued to support individual artists and musicians, but she also began to give large amounts to orphan asylums, hospitals, an infant shelter, a convalescent home, and a training school for women physicians.[15]

Some of Hearst's most important and best-known contributions were in service to San Francisco kindergartens. In 1879 Sarah B. Cooper, an American pioneer in the educational movement founded by Friedrich Frobel, opened her first free school for poor children in the city's South-of-Market district. Its popularity led to a second and then a third school. By 1883 Cooper had recruited Hearst to provide substantial financial backing. Phoebe financed an entire kindergarten, and then another, renting a large building that accommodated seven classes and Cooper's Golden Gate Kindergarten Association, for which Hearst served as honorary president. Her levels of support grew by leaps and bounds. By 1888 she had purchased a building to house kindergartens for children in North Beach, Telegraph Hill, and the Barbary Coast, and by 1891 she had constructed the Hearst Free Kindergarten Building for both children's classes and a teacher-training school.[16] In the meantime, she continued her travels in Europe, where she studied educational philosophy. Writing to her husband from Berlin in 1889, Phoebe indicated that she was "anxious to obtain all information possible about the Froebel system of kindergartens." From Vienna she wrote, "I have been most carefully studying the care and training of little children among the poorer classes. There is so much that can aid us in America for the experience here is surely worth something to us, and there is much work to be done among our cosmopolitan population."[17] Like other well-traveled women of her generation, Phoebe applied lessons learned abroad to the social issues she encountered at home.

Hearst was not alone in donating money to San Francisco kindergartens. Jane Lathrop Stanford, the wife of the railroad mogul Leland Stanford and cofounder of Stanford University, also gave generously, as did Mary Crocker, the wife of the Southern Pacific Railroad partner Charles Crocker, and Miranda Lux, the wife of the cattle king Charles Lux.[18] According to Carol Roland, a historian of the California kindergarten movement, educational giving was a means by which wealthy women like Hearst could "affirm their newly acquired social position and define their civic leadership and sense of responsibility." These women, she suggested, hoped to instill "in the children of the poor a commitment to work and morality which would make them productive citizens rather than a threat to society." Roland credits Hearst and her counterparts with San Francisco's "charities' explosion" of the late 1870s and 1880s, portraying them as models of philanthropic involvement whose leadership and generosity "reinforced the idea that wealth carried with it responsibility to promote social and civic betterment."[19] Alexandra Nickliss adds that Hearst's early philanthropy "provided career opportunities for women and gave middle- and working-class women and the poor a chance to get a proper education so that they could lift themselves out of poverty."[20] This dual-edged pattern of helping both poor people and aspiring professional women persisted for the rest of Phoebe Hearst's philanthropic career.

Having established herself as an important patron and donor in San Francisco, Phoebe continued her good works when her husband's political ambitions brought the couple to Washington DC, in 1886. That year, the California senator John Miller died. The governor, George Stoneman, was a Democrat who had received support from George Hearst's *Examiner* when he had sought election. Stoneman appointed Hearst to the vacant Senate seat, and, a year later, the legislature elected Hearst to a full term.[21] Now a senator's wife, Phoebe found herself chatting with First Lady Frances Cleveland, attending White House parties, and captivating Washington society with her own elaborate entertainments. She continued her European travels, returning home with luxurious draperies, tapestries, paintings, furniture, chandeliers, and art objects—all collected to furnish her family's thirty-room mansion. National newspapers commented on the opulence of the Hearst home and the extravagance of the Hearsts' parties, sometimes inviting rebukes from Phoebe, who informed a *Chicago Herald* writer that the cost of a recent bash "was not unduly great and not nearly as much as the sum mentioned in your paper."[22] More sympathetic journalists noted the "quiet modest way" in which Phoebe had become "the arbiter of unsullied elegance at the capital" and a "recognized friend and helper of struggling artists."[23]

Like the clubwomen described by Karen Blair in her study of women and amateur arts associations, Phoebe Hearst's embrace of progressive reform was linked to her perception of culture as a tool to civic betterment.[24] While she filled her home with privately collected European treasures, Phoebe also worked to protect public treasures to which all Americans could lay claim. After moving to Washington, Phoebe joined the Mount Vernon Ladies' Association, a group founded in 1858 to protect the integrity of George Washington's historic home. She served the organization for twenty-nine years, devoting time and money to every improvement, from building a new visitors' pavilion and sea wall to searching out and restoring original furnishings.[25] Phoebe also continued her work in the kindergarten movement, founding the Columbia Kindergarten Association, a group that played a role in congressional legislation to bring kindergartens into the public schools of the District of Columbia. Serving as president from 1893 to 1895, Phoebe financed the tuition of both black and white children and established a school that supplied most of the district's kindergarten teachers for years to come. After serving her term, she established three independent kindergartens in the city—two for white children and one for black children—and founded a training program for African American teachers.[26] Phoebe also brought the kindergarten gospel to Lead, South Dakota, the site of George Hearst's Homestake Mine, where she established a free library.[27]

If Phoebe Hearst's life changed dramatically when she married her husband in 1862, her life took another drastic turn when George died of cancer on February 28, 1891. Memorial services in Washington and a special funeral train bearing his body to final rites in San Francisco honored the man whose career "from illiterate, penniless gold hunter to a popular member of the national legislature and a millionaire" was called "phenomenal" by the *New York Times*.[28] His will left everything to his wife, making her sole executor of an estate worth more than twenty million dollars—a bequest to be forfeited only in the event that Phoebe remarried. The will had been signed ten years earlier, and his son, to whom George Hearst had advanced some two million dollars, now had to turn to his mother.[29] Reeling from her husband's death, Phoebe retreated to rural Sonoma County to recuperate both physically and emotionally, and to begin her rapid education in managing her late husband's business affairs.[30] The experience taught her a further lesson in the importance of education and independence for women.

Phoebe Hearst's philanthropic work increased substantially after her husband's death, and providing educational help for women became a primary interest. Always an advocate of education for women, Phoebe placed special emphasis on training that would permit a woman to be self-supporting. She set out her strong views in a letter to a friend who opposed her own daughter's studies:

> In regard to your letter of August 6th, we must like good friends 'agree to disagree,' for truly my convictions lead me to an entirely different conclusion about Ada's desire to do something. I believe that, leaving out any consideration as to the motives that prompt one to work, the training and influence coming from a well-directed effort to learn a business are calculated to strengthen the character, ennoble the life, and benefit society as well as the individual. The best life results come from training young people in the direction of their tastes and worthy predilections, and it seems to me that if a daughter greatly desired to fit herself for a special vocation, it would be an indication of how I should plan for her.[31]

Phoebe argued to the mother, in vain, that the uncertainties of life made it a parent's duty to help his or her children become self-supporting, and she stressed her sympathy for Ada's desire to study for a profession. Phoebe later financed three years of Ada Butterfield's musical studies in Europe; in return, she received several letters of appreciation from the grateful young woman.[32]

Phoebe did much more than finance the educational pursuits of individual women. In 1893 the chance to establish a school for young women in Washington DC drew her into a campaign by the National Cathedral Foundation to add an educational facility. When the bishop asked her if she would be one of five donors to raise $100,000 to found the program, Phoebe replied, "One person can do this work better than five," and offered the more "sufficient" amount of $175,000. Phoebe took an active part in finding a suitable location, increased her gift to two hundred thousand dollars to meet the mounting cost estimates, and remained steadfast during the six-year effort to get the school built.[33] Phoebe gave another ten thousand dollars to Washington's American University as a memorial to George Hearst's mother, providing the funds that built the university's College of History Building. Other gifts made in the years after George's death included five thousand dollars each to San Francisco's Boys' and Girls' Aid Society, Emanu-El Sisterhood Polyclinic, Girls' Union, Old Peoples' Home, Mercantile Library, Children's Hospital, Ladies Protection and Relief Society, and Young Men's Christian Association—all California institutions that received the money "in Mr. Hearst's name and in accordance with his wish."[34]

Another major project to which Phoebe devoted time and energy began in her living room and evolved through the years into the influential Parent Teacher Association, a national organization. From her own pleasure in teaching her son and from her earliest work in the kindergarten movement, Phoebe had always sought to link education to the home. Alice Birney, a Washington socialite and mother of nine, first introduced Phoebe to the idea of community mothers' meetings to share information on parenting and on improving the schools through an organization Birney called the National Congress of Mothers. Phoebe was so impressed that she offered to bankroll the endeavor—as long as fathers and teachers were also involved. Preliminary planning took place in Phoebe's Washington mansion. She provided a secretary and supplies, furnished transportation for committee members with her carriages, and invited some out-of-town members to be houseguests during early meetings. Despite some opposition to the "radical" idea that parents needed some education in childrearing and in working with teachers, the concept spread rapidly. By the time the first national session met in the capital on February 17, 1897, the expected attendance of fifty had swelled to more than two thousand. Phoebe helped arrange housing in private homes, found auditoriums to accommodate the crowds, and even persuaded her friend, First Lady Frances Cleveland, to host the opening luncheon in the White House.[35]

Phoebe's enthusiastic backing brought considerable attention. "The project owes its success to Mrs. Hearst more than any other person," wrote a reporter for the *New York Tribune*. "From the first, she has been in warm sympathy with the idea and has been most generous in advancing funds for prosecution of the work."[36] The expenses for the organization's founding and the first convention exceeded thirty-two thousand dollars. Phoebe wrote a check for that amount and continued to support the organization for several years as it became established. "She stands before the world as godmother for this plan for a National Congress of Mothers," Alice Birney wrote. When the first international congress of the organization met in Washington DC in March 1908, a report listed Phoebe as first honorary vice president and called her "the energizing spirit of the whole enterprise," adding, "To her munificence, the success of the great meeting must be largely attributed." Three thousand supporters attended, and President Theodore Roosevelt addressed the gathering.[37]

In California, Phoebe became best known for her generous support of the University of California. In 1900, after donating considerable funds to the University of Pennsylvania's Department of Archaeology and Paleontology (she had developed an interest in anthropology and archaeology while being treated by a doctor who was also a professor in that department), Phoebe informed the school: "[My] purpose now is to turn my every effort to giving the people of California every educational advantage in my power to secure."[38] Thereafter, Phoebe embarked on a giving campaign that was to exceed ten million dollars in her lifetime. She literally adopted the university, its faculty, and its student body, devoting enthusiastic attention that earned her a tribute as "the best friend the University of California ever had."[39]

Phoebe Hearst's contributions to the University of California fell into two categories: the promotion of women's education, and the structural development of the campus. Her support began in 1891 with a telling gift: the creation of the university's first scholarship for women—a program that continues today through a trust fund established by her will. Remembering her own struggle to attain an education during her youth, Phoebe pledged to contribute fifteen hundred dollars annually to fund five scholarships of three hundred dollars each for "worthy young women" of "noble character and high aims." At the regents' meeting of September 19, 1892, the acting president announced that Mrs. Hearst had increased the number of scholarships from five to eight. In acknowledging her action, the regents wrote her, "It seems peculiarly fit and pleasing in this instance that, as the University of California was one of the first to throw open its doors to women, a woman is the first to give the University a benefaction for the encouragement of undergraduates." However, when the committee on scholarships received sixty applications in 1895 and asked for permission to reduce the annual value of each scholarship from three hundred dollars to two hundred dollars to further increase the number of scholarships, Phoebe Hearst refused. She argued that three hundred dollars was already "quite little enough to pay for a girl's living expenses." Early recipients came to be known as "Phoebes," and today they number in the thousands.[40]

Phoebe expanded her financial support of female students in 1900. Inspired by some of the programs she had observed in Europe, she formed

Hearst Domestic Industries (HDI), an economic cooperative. Here, women students who needed outside work to meet school expenses were paid while they received instruction in several forms of needlework. Their projects were then sold.[41] Hundreds of young women benefited from HDI, although, as Alexandra Nickliss points out, the program's success reduced the Berkeley dressmaker trade by half. In this case, Phoebe's generosity in favor of one group of women worked against the interests of another.[42]

Hearst recognized that tuition assistance alone was insufficient to improve women's experiences in higher education. Concern over inadequate housing prompted her to purchase and furnish two residential buildings near the campus, the Enewah and Pie del Monte lodges, which were early forerunners of sororities. She also noted the deplorable lack of social facilities for women and asked the renowned architect Bernard Maybeck to design a redwood entertainment pavilion next to her rented Berkeley home. For years, "Hearst Hall," with its tapestry-hung walls and elegant furnishings, was the lively scene of Saturday afternoon receptions, musicales on Sundays, "at home" Wednesdays, dinners three evenings a week, and every kind of social gathering. Because women students also lacked physical education facilities, Phoebe directed Maybeck to design an addition to Hearst Hall that included an outdoor basketball court with tanbark flooring and seating for six hundred. In addition to these structural improvements, Phoebe paid attention to the small details of women's experiences on campus. Young women students greatly appreciated the little luxuries she provided. Her purchase of flowers for women to wear to a big game brought this freshman girl's reaction: "Just look at me with a corsage at lunch at Hearst Hall. You know, I never could have afforded to buy one."[43]

As Phoebe turned more and more of her attention to the school, its many deficiencies began to bother her. In 1891 the campus consisted of a small cluster of structures on a bleak, dirt path, unlit at night. Phoebe presented a typically practical gift in February 1896, when she spent twenty-seven hundred dollars to install lighting for campus walks and at the Bacon Library and the art gallery.[44] A few months later she made a dramatic, magnanimous proposal to the regents: Phoebe suggested and offered to pay all expenses for an international competition to produce a comprehensive and permanent building plan for the university.[45] Her offer, which ultimately amounted to more than two hundred thousand dollars, received immediate, enthusiastic acceptance. The competition itself was a huge success, attracting international attention and more than one hundred architectural submissions. It also helped nudge the California legislature to pass a tax increase to help support the university. Martin Kellogg, the university president, wrote to Phoebe:

> Doubtless others will inform you of the good turn the Legislature has just done in adding another cent to the fractional tax in support of the State University. I wish to express my own great satisfaction in this result and at the very handsome way in which it has come about. The vote in our favor was unanimous in both Houses—a remarkable fact when we take into consideration the comparative newness and heterogeneous character of our population, the sectarian jealousies so easy to be aroused, and the hard times which have borne so heavily upon the State. It gives us especial pleasure to note that your generosity has contributed to this fortunate result. In the arguments before the Committees, the Hearst benefactions proved an effective challenge to the State's liberality. I wish you to know how timely was your recent proposal to help us. I feel that our University has the brightest prospects, for these we are greatly indebted to you.[46]

Phoebe Hearst was now reaching the pinnacle of her power as a philanthropist and reformer. By lavishing support on the University of California, she achieved several goals. By funding scholarships and providing for new facilities, she promoted women's access to higher education. By contributing the funds for buildings such as the Hearst Memorial Mining Building and other structures, she created a tribute to the memory of her late husband. Finally, Phoebe's strategic generosity legitimized her own authority as a prominent decision-maker. As Kellogg noted with appreciation, she was now influencing social policy on a statewide scale. Governor James H. Budd, a Democrat, recognized as much when he appointed Phoebe the first female regent of the University of California on July 28, 1897.[47] Fourteen years before California women gained the right to vote, Phoebe Hearst became one of the highest-ranking female public officials in the nation. The position brought her many new opportunities, and it delivered an important victory to the Pacific Coast Branch of the

6. Benjamin Ide Wheeler, president of the University of California, conferring with Phoebe Apperson Hearst. By 1912, the date of this photograph, Mrs. Hearst had served on the university board of regents for fifteen years and was widely acknowledged as the most significant member of that board. San Francisco History Center, San Francisco Public Library.

Association of Collegiate Alumnae, which had been heartily lobbying for a female regent to be appointed.[48]

Repeatedly reappointed, although by Republican governors after her initial appointment, Phoebe Hearst conscientiously served on the university's Board of Regents for the rest of her life. One of her protégés, Donald H. McLaughlin, who became a mining executive and later served on the board himself, commented on her power: "She must have been very forceful on the regents. I saw old minutes in which President Wheeler said, 'We must consult Mrs. Hearst about this,' or 'This would be subject to Mrs. Hearst's approval.'"⁴⁹ When named to replace President Kellogg, Benjamin Ide Wheeler, a Cornell professor, delayed his acceptance until Phoebe returned from a European trip. He wanted to be sure that she approved of his appointment and could discuss with him her further plans regarding the "endowment and equipment of the institution."⁵⁰ Backed by the power of her wealth and her astuteness in applying it, Phoebe was no ornamental appointee.

Over the course of her career, Phoebe became more comfortable with her varied public roles, just as she began to understand—and to defend—the importance of public life for all women. As a young matron in San Francisco, her interest in education and the arts led her into work with the Century Club, a group described by the *New York Tribune* as "the first women's club started on the Pacific Coast, an organization of San Francisco elite through which aid and support could be given to women struggling for recognition in order to obtain work."⁵¹ A founding member, Phoebe became the club's first president, serving from 1888 to 1890. In that post she helped numerous young artists and arranged frequent lectures and educational events, often hosting meetings in her own home. During her tenure the club also became involved in local politics, financing a slate of women reform candidates for the 1888 San Francisco School Board elections. The women were not elected, but their campaign was competitive, and it lent new legitimacy to women's demands for public officeholding in California. It also gave Phoebe Hearst, as Century Club president, increased visibility as a reformer and political leader. In 1889 she was the club's delegate to the meeting in New York of the newly formed General Federation of Women's Clubs. Elected treasurer of the new body, Phoebe was still uncomfortable with the spotlight. "I could not make a speech," she wrote, "but I could keep accounts."⁵² Nevertheless, the role contributed to her growing prominence on the national stage.

Phoebe's early discomfort with public life derived from her tacit belief that women should leave the more bumptious side of party politics to the men. Although she had been strong and independent in many ways beginning in her girlhood, and although she had always attached great importance to equal education for women, Phoebe inched her way only slowly into the growing suffrage movement. Many suffrage leaders emerged from the club movement; knowing her, they often sought Phoebe's participation. She, however, considered their demonstrations distasteful. When Susan B. Anthony met with her during the 1896 California woman suffrage campaign, Phoebe insisted that she had never been an advocate of votes for women. Nevertheless, she admitted that she viewed "with deep respect your heroic life and entire devotion to the cause." She quietly donated a thousand dollars to the campaign but did not join the National American Woman Suffrage Association and did not become publicly involved in the campaign. To another suffragist she wrote, "I feel that the day when women will vote is sure to come, but I have always held myself apart from the organizations that were working for suffrage because the methods did not appeal to me."[53] Phoebe's reticence about a public statement in support of suffrage may well have been what Anthony had in mind when she wrote to Jane Stanford, in the midst of the 1896 campaign, "It is cruel for the women of position and power in California not to let the people know they stand with us—do you not think so?"[54]

As Phoebe grew older, however, her opinion changed—perhaps as a result of her own growing experience in state politics. In October 1911, just days before the special state election on suffrage, Phoebe permitted herself to be cited as a supporter of the state constitutional amendment that gave the vote to the women of California.[55] "Mrs. Hearst Is for Suffrage," declared a newspaper headline. She clearly expressed her change of heart in a letter to a friend:

> In reply to your inquiry, I will say that I was not in favor of suffrage until the campaign in California was well on, and then certain information had come to me which convinced me that the time had come—here, at any rate—when women should have the right to vote. I felt convinced then that women would unite in favoring certain work tending towards the betterment of conditions affecting women and children particularly, which men heretofore could never be relied upon to favor when it came to the test of the ballot.[56]

Hearst's reasoning reflected a common attitude among supporters of woman suffrage: that women needed and deserved the vote because of their unique interest and ability in identifying and protecting the interests of women and children. As Nancy Cott argues in *The Grounding of*

Modern Feminism, this belief in women's uniqueness coexisted with a parallel demand for suffrage based on women's similarity to men—that is, women needed and deserved the vote because they were equal citizens.[57] Phoebe's support grew out of the former tradition, but her experience as a philanthropist, and especially as a member of the board of regents, taught her that her womanhood did not detract from her ability to take a part in the public affairs of men. Certainly, she had needed to become adept at negotiating the Victorian demand for proper female decorum while undertaking the public activities required to achieve her social agenda—hardly a small task. But as Phoebe mastered that negotiation, she provided a valuable model for other ambitious women. At the same time, Phoebe increased her support for a growing suffrage movement that would enable both her and her sisters to move even more forthrightly into the public sphere.

Phoebe Hearst died at her Pleasanton home on April 13, 1919, from complications resulting from influenza, which she contracted during the worldwide epidemic. During the final years of her life, she continued her philanthropic pursuits, playing a major supporting role in the San Francisco Young Women's Christian Association and at Mills College, a women's college in Oakland, California. Phoebe also served as honorary president of the Women's Board for the San Francisco Panama–Pacific International Exposition of 1915.[58] All three projects continued her tradition of promoting the interests of women. Following her death, national newspaper coverage hailed her work. The *New York Times* reported on her national reputation for charity, the *Oakland Enquirer* called her "one of the most prominent, useful, and blessed personalities in this State, not only, but in the country," and her son's paper, the *San Francisco Examiner*, named Phoebe "the greatest woman California has ever known."[59] Two thousand mourners thronged the sidewalks outside of San Francisco's Grace Cathedral for her funeral services. Honorary pallbearers included the governor, both of California's senators, the president of the University of California, and the city's mayor. Federal flags flew at half-mast, the university closed, and the state legislature and local courts all adjourned for the funeral.[60]

The mining fortune that George Hearst left to Phoebe had grown to thirty million dollars by 1915, when the *Boston Herald* listed her worth and identified her as the tenth wealthiest woman in America. By the time of her death in 1919, she had given away more than twenty-one million dollars. Phoebe Hearst was a one-woman foundation long before foundations were commonplace. Her background and intellect made her, first, an enthusiastic champion of women's education, and, eventually, a defender of their other civil rights. Backed by the power of her wealth, Hearst carved out a role for herself as a reformer, a philanthropist, and a director of social policy. At the same time, she helped pave the way for other women to take on public and professional roles of their own.

Notes

This essay is based on Mildred Nichols Hamilton, "'Continually Doing Good': The Philanthropic Career of Phoebe Apperson Hearst" (Master's thesis, San Francisco State University, 1995). It was edited and condensed for this volume by Ann Marie Wilson.

1. University of California Regents, 1891 Minutes, Bancroft Library, University of California, Berkeley (hereafter "Bancroft").

2. See Kathryn Kish Sklar, *Florence Kelley and the Nation's Work: The Rise of Women's Political Culture, 1830–1900* (New Haven CT: Yale University Press, 1995); Robyn Muncy, *Creating a Female Dominion in American Reform, 1890–1935* (New York: Oxford University Press, 1991). For more on Mary Rozet Smith, see Kathryn Kish Sklar, "Hull House in the 1890s: A Community of Women Reformers," in *American Vistas: 1877 to the Present*, ed. Leonard Dinnerstein and Kenneth T. Jackson, 108–27 (New York: Oxford University Press, 1995). For Mary Garrett, see Kathleen D. McCarthy, *Noblesse Oblige: Charity and Cultural Philanthropy in Chicago, 1849–1929* (Chicago: University of Chicago Press, 1982), 19.

3. Judith Robinson, *The Hearsts: An American Dynasty* (Newark: University of Delaware Press, 1991), 28–29. See also Phoebe Apperson Hearst Historical Society, St. Clair, Missouri, Papers (hereafter "PAH"); reprints in Hearst Foundation Archives (hereafter "HFA"), San Francisco.

4. Ann H. Hatton Lewis, "The Whitmires of South Carolina," *Atlanta Sunday American*, December 22, 1935, clipping in HFA; Robinson, *The Hearsts*, 28.

5. Winifred Black Bonfils, *The Life and Personality of Phoebe Apperson Hearst* (San Francisco: John Henry Nash, 1928), 4; Robinson, *The Hearsts*, 31.

6. Adele S. Brooks, "Phoebe Apperson Hearst: A Life and Some Papers," PAH, carton 5.

7. Cora Older and Fremont Older, *George Hearst: California Pioneer* (San Francisco: John Henry Nash, 1933); Lois Elaine Mahoney, "California's Forgotten Triumvirate: Haggin, Tevis, and Hearst," (Master's thesis, San Francisco State University, 1977), 53.

8. W. A. Swanberg, *Citizen Hearst* (New York: Collier Books, 1961), 7; Bonfils, *Life and Personality*, 11; Robinson, *The Hearsts*, 56.

9. Cora [Mrs. Fremont] Older, *William Randolph Hearst, American* (New York: D. Appleton-Century, 1936), 7; Robinson, *The Hearsts*, 60, 62; Milicent Wilson [Mrs. William Randolph] Hearst, *The Horses of San Simeon* (San Simeon CA: San Simeon, 1985), 84.

10. Phoebe Apperson Hearst to Eliza Pike, 1864–66, PAH, Box 60.

11. Swanberg, *Citizen Hearst*, 9.

12. George Hearst to Phoebe, July 17 (year not given), PAH, Box 24.

13. Kathleen D. McCarthy, *Noblesse Oblige: Charity and Cultural Philanthropy in Chicago, 1849–1929* (Chicago: University of Chicago Press, 1982), 32; Anne Firor Scott, *Natural Allies: Women's Associations in American History* (Urbana: University of Illinois Press, 1993), 81.

14. PAH, carton 5.

15. Bonfils, *Life and Personality*, 55–58; PAH.

16. Richard H. Peterson, "Philanthropic Phoebe: The Educational Charity of Phoebe Apperson Hearst," *California History* 64, no. 4 (Fall 1985), 284; Bonfils, *Life and Personality*, 57; Carol Roland, "The California Kindergarten Movement: A Study in Class and Social Feminism" (PhD dissertation, University of California, Riverside, 1980), 97; Robinson, *The Hearsts*, 171; Alexandra M. Nickliss, "Phoebe Apperson Hearst's 'Gospel of Wealth,' 1883–1901," *Pacific Historical Review* 71, no. 4 (2002), 582.

17. Phoebe Apperson Hearst to George Hearst, August 2, 1889, and September 16, 1889, PAH, Box 63.

18. Nickliss, "Gospel of Wealth," 581. See also Alexandra M. Nickliss, "Phoebe Apperson Hearst: The Most Powerful Woman in California" (PhD dissertation, University of California, Davis, 1994).

19. Roland, "California Kindergarten Movement," ix, 13.

20. Nickliss, "Gospel of Wealth," 582.

21. Swanberg, *Citizen Hearst*, 26, 42; Bonfils, *Life and Personality*, 61; William Randolph Hearst Jr., *The Hearsts: Father and Son* (Niwot CO: Roberts Rinehart, 1991), 21.

22. Phoebe Apperson Hearst to Editor, *Chicago Herald*, April 1, 1895, Hearst Foundation Archives. See also *Washington Post*, February 20, 1889, PAH, carton 17.

23. Undated clippings from Washington newspapers, PAH, carton 18.

24. Karen J. Blair, *The Torchbearers: Women and Their Amateur Arts Associations in America, 1890–1930* (Bloomington: Indiana University Press, 1994), 56.

25. Bonfils, *Life and Personality*, 81–82; PAH, Box 35.

26. PAH, carton 5; Nickliss, "Gospel of Wealth," 584.

27. PAH, carton 9; Peterson, "Philanthropic Phoebe," 287.

28. *New York Times*, March 1, 1891, p. 1.

29. Copy of will, filed April 29, 1880, in PAH, carton 5.

30. Notes of June and July 1891 retreat at "Camp Sesame," Valley of the Moon, PAH, carton 7.

31. Phoebe Apperson Hearst to Mrs. Butterfield, August 17, 1886, PAH, Box 60.

32. Ada Butterfield to Phoebe Apperson Hearst, PAH, Box 28.

33. Mary Kay Lewis, *Polished Corners: A History of the National Cathedral School for Girls* (Washington DC: Mount Saint Alban, 1971), 3, 5, 7, 33, 40; Robinson, *The Hearsts*, 315–18; Bonfils, *Life and Personality*, 12, 77–79; Phoebe Apperson Hearst to Dr. McKim June 3, 1895, PAH, Box 60; Richard H. Peterson, "The Philanthropist and the Artist," *California History* 66, no. 4 (December 1987): 278–285.

34. Brooks, "Phoebe Apperson Hearst," PAH, carton 5.

35. Vocille McCord Eastham, "PAH and the PTA," *Missouri Parent-Teacher* (February 1973), 18–20; Robinson, *The Hearsts*, 313; Bonfils, *Life and Personality*, 18.

36. *New York Tribune*, January 17, 1897, PAH, carton 17.

37. Eastham, "PAH and the PTA," 20; PAH, carton 9.

38. Original letter in Philadelphia Museum Archives; copies in HFA and University of California Phoebe Apperson Hearst Museum of Anthropology.

39. President William Wallace Campell, 1925, quoted by J. R. K. Kantor, "She Was the Best Friend the University Ever Had," *Seminar Quarterly* 17 (March 1973): 30.

40. Regents, 1891 Minutes.

41. PAH, carton 1, carton 5, Box 8; Bonfils, *Life and Personality*, 111.

42. Nickliss, "Gospel of Wealth," 599.

43. PAH, Box 8; Bonfils, *Life and Personality*, 110; James R. K. Kantor, *The Best Friend the University Ever Had* (San Francisco: n.p., 1972), 29; Sally B. Woodbridge, *Bernard Maybeck, Visionary Architect* (New York: Abbeville, 1992), 77–79; Gifts for Lands and Buildings, University of California Archives, 16.

44. Kantor, "She Was the Best Friend," 28–29.

45. Phoebe Apperson Hearst to Regents, October 22, 1896, PAH, Box 60, carton 5.

46. Martin Kellogg to Phoebe Apperson Hearst, February 1897; Bonfils, *Life and Personality*, 100–101.

47. PAH, Box 60.

48. Nickliss, "Gospel of Wealth," 595.

49. PAH, carton 5; Bonfils, *Life and Personality*, 104.

50. Bonfils, *Life and Personality*, 104.

51. *New York Tribune*, July 3, 1898, PAH, carton 17.

52. PAH, carton 5; Nickliss, "Gospel of Wealth," 583–84.

53. PAH, carton 5; Robinson, *The Hearsts*, 375.

54. Anthony to Stanford, August 23, 1896, folder 5, box 3, series 1, Jane Stanford Papers, Special Collections, Stanford University Library.

55. Selina Solomons, *How We Won the Vote in California: A True Story of the Campaign of 1911* (San Francisco: The New Woman, 1912), 56, 60.

56. Phoebe Apperson Hearst to Mrs. Stearns, PAH, carton 18.

57. Nancy F. Cott, *The Grounding of Modern Feminism* (New Haven CT: Yale University Press, 1987), 50.

58. PAH, carton 5; Bonfils, *Life and Personality*, 117–20; Susan Mills to PAH, April 27, 1908, PAH, Box 35; Aurelia A. Reinhartdt to Phoebe Apperson Hearst, December 14, 1917, PAH, Box 43; PAH, cartons 5 and 17.

59. *New York Times*, April 14, 1919; *Oakland Enquirer*, April 14, 1919; *San Francisco Chronicle*, April 14, 1919.

60. *San Francisco Examiner*, April 15, 1919 and April 17, 1919; Older, *William Randolph Hearst*, 530.

5. "Neutral Territory"

The Politics of Settlement Work in San Francisco, 1894–1906

ANN MARIE WILSON

In 1902 the *Labor Clarion*, the house organ of the San Francisco Labor Council and the State Federation of Labor, presented a biting report on the "eight thousand wealthy women" convening in Los Angeles for the national convention of the General Federation of Women's Clubs. Invoking the clubwomen's "earnest wish to . . . make this world a better place in which to live," the unnamed author remarked,

> The laboring woman knows that if you would stand for one thing, just one . . . the greatest crime of this age would be removed and abolished. This is child labor. . . . Insist that all goods that are brought into your home, from a broom to a beefsteak, from a shoe to a bonnet, [be] the product of a shop where the union label is in evidence. That is all. The way is simple. The duty plain. It does not require either oratory or spasms of ethics. Simply ask for the union label on everything, [and] the child will be set free.

Although it acknowledged the value of retaining organized womanhood as an ally, the *Labor Clarion* insisted that labor organizations would lead the way in bettering society. In closing, the author challenged clubwomen: "Help in the cause of humanity, where the battle is waging . . . and where victory will come without you, but infinitely easier and quicker with you."[1]

A year later, the same newspaper turned its attention to the "publicists, educators, and other professional and business men who undertake to speak and write on labor union topics." This time, however, it expressed unabashed enthusiasm for the "many intelligent and fair-minded men and women" of the social settlement movement who had "earnestly and unostentatiously tried to establish cordially sympathetic relations with working men, women, and children," and had "succeeded in accomplishing vast good." The writer praised the San Francisco Settlement Association's South Park Settlement, and especially its head worker, Lucile Eaves, for establishing closer relations between middle-class reformers and labor leaders than had been the case elsewhere. According to the *Labor Clarion*, the "practical assistance" of Eaves and people like her "resulted in a better understanding of the movement by a class which does much to form public opinion."[2]

This chapter tells the story of how a San Francisco settlement house transformed itself from a relatively quiet neighborhood gathering place into an important locus of social reform, one that ultimately helped win an important legislative victory for organized labor during the first years of the twentieth century. Founded by men and women who believed that poverty in their western city was neither dramatic nor inevitable, the San Francisco Settlement Association initially veered away from direct political action, focusing instead on providing wholesome entertainment and uplifting instruction for local children and adults. With the arrival of Lucile Eaves as the head worker in 1901, however, this cautious orientation quickly changed. A budding sociologist in the early stages of her career, Eaves joined the very battle the *Labor Clarion* assigned to women of the middle class: she committed herself to abolishing child labor. But instead of taking up the consumer activism associated with the union label, Eaves channeled the resources of the South Park Settlement into a campaign led by San Francisco labor leaders to restrict children under fourteen from California factories, stores, and workshops. In doing so, she remade the South Park Settlement into a lively, reform-oriented institution where men and women of different class backgrounds could work together toward a common political goal. Thanks in large part to her efforts, Californians won a new child labor bill in 1905.

Yet if Lucile Eaves and the San Francisco Settlement Association offered "practical assistance" to the California labor movement, the South Park Settlement gave Eaves much-needed help in return. Like many other academic women of her generation, Eaves used her settlement experience as a stepping-stone in her career as a professional social scientist. When she became the head worker in 1901, she recently had left a teaching post at Stanford University, forced out in the wake of an academic freedom scandal concerning her controversial colleague and mentor, Edward A. Ross. Bereft of other professional options, Eaves took up "practical social work" at the South Park Settlement, where she used her position to carry out social scientific study of contemporary labor issues.[3] In the end, this work not only contributed to the passage of a new child labor law in 1905; it also provided the basis for Eaves's doctoral dissertation on the history of California labor legislation. She completed her work at Columbia University, and the University of California Press published it in 1910.[4]

The early history of the San Francisco Settlement Association therefore reveals how Lucile Eaves took advantage of a unique institutional space—what some historians have called a "politicized woman's sphere"—in order to achieve a set of class-bridging political goals and, at the same time, to further her career.[5] Like many of its better-known counterparts in Boston, New York, and Chicago, the South Park Settlement served as an important incubator for activist and professional networks, while helping launch women like Eaves into political and professional life.[6]

The San Francisco Settlement Association was founded in the spring of 1894, following Jane Addams's visit to California earlier that year. With the country in the grips of an economic depression, Addams traveled to Palo Alto and Berkeley, meeting with faculty and students of the recently established Leland Stanford, Jr., University and the University of California.[7] A detailed record of her stay does not survive, but it is likely that Addams delivered some version of her 1892 paper, "The Subjective Necessity of Social Settlements," in which she outlined her philosophy of social democracy.[8] Addams also may have spoken about her work on *Hull House Maps and Papers*, a sociological study of Chicago's nineteenth ward that was published the following year.[9] Whatever her topic, she left a strong impression. According to the San Francisco Settlement Association's *First Annual Report*, a local committee formed "as a result of the interest aroused by her," and soon met to discuss establishing a settlement house in San Francisco. On April 14, 1894, after a series of planning meetings, the San Francisco Settlement Association was officially born.[10]

The men and women who founded the Settlement Association were prominent figures in local intellectual and charitable circles. The association's first president, Bernard Moses, was a University of California professor who lectured in history, economics, political science, and jurisprudence; he later served on the Philippine Commission under William Howard Taft, the future U.S. president.[11] Other members included Fred

E. Haynes, a recent Harvard PhD; Frank Angell, a professor of psychology at Stanford University; and Jessica Peixotto, a University of California graduate student and member of a prominent San Francisco Jewish family, whose brother belonged to the elite Bohemian Club. Peixotto later became the university's first female full professor, serving in the Department of Economics.[12] Some association members, including Haynes and Fannie W. McLean, a Berkeley schoolteacher, had spent time in the settlements of Boston and New York.[13] Others were active on the boards of local charitable groups including the Harrison Street Boys' Club, the Buford Kitchengarten, and the Associated Charities of San Francisco, an organization that provided the San Francisco Settlement Association with "constant advice" during its first year.[14] Many council members and early assistants were college educated, and a large number were listed in the city's exclusive *Social Directory*, lending support to the historian Carol Roland's suggestion that participation in charitable activities was held in high esteem by San Francisco elites.[15]

The organizations that contributed members to the San Francisco Settlement Association cultivated a belief that poverty in San Francisco was less drastic and more easily avoidable than poverty in the nation's industrial centers. In its 1895 annual report the Associated Charities of San Francisco claimed that "for climatic reasons, the poverty and distress in our city can never be so severe as in the Eastern cities," even though it acknowledged that the depression of 1893 had caused widespread hardship.[16] Three years later, Millicent Shinn, the editor of the *Overland Monthly* and a member of the California branch of the Association of Collegiate Alumnae (another organization that contributed members to the San Francisco Settlement Association), published a study of San Francisco charities in which she concurred that "no really honest, industrious, capable person need lack work or seek charity." Shinn further suggested that "drunkenness and laziness are the real causes of all poverty in San Francisco," especially "among foreigners."[17] This perception was shared by such visitors as Katherine Coman, the president of the College Settlement Association and a professor of economics at Wellesley College, who commented in 1903 that "the metropolis of the Pacific Coast is the paradise of the workingman." In Coman's estimation, San Francisco presented "little need of relief work except for the ne'er-do-well and the incapacitated."[18]

Despite their optimism about San Francisco's seemingly exceptional social environment, association workers believed that special effort was required in San Francisco to bring the disparate social classes into mutual understanding. Accordingly, they established the South Park Settlement with two goals in mind. On the one hand, settlement workers hoped to "serve as a medium among the different social elements of the city," leading all to "a more intelligent and systematic understanding of their mutual obligations." This effort would be facilitated by residence in a working-class neighborhood and cooperation with local religious, educational, charitable, and labor organizations. In a related fashion, the members of the Settlement Association wished to arouse citizens to a "healthy interest in social problems" and hoped to gain the community's assistance "in the efforts for their solution" by sponsoring public discussions led by "impartial" experts.[19] Though developed in a western context, both goals adhered to the example set by Jane Addams's Hull House.

A monthly contribution of fifty dollars from Phoebe Apperson Hearst (see chapter 4) made it possible for the association's leaders to secure appropriate headquarters in August 1894. They chose for their residence a large home at 15 South Park, located in the southeast corner of San Francisco's South-of-Market district. South Park ran between Second Street and Third Street, and in its center stood the park for which it was named—an elongated hexagon of grass and trees. By their own description, the neighborhood was "one specially suited for the work that a Settlement undertakes to do," as it situated the settlement workers among families of diverse social classes. The association noted that South Park, once the "residence quarter of the local aristocracy," was now "occupied by families varying very greatly in circumstances," including "a few families who are well-to-do, . . . a great many families of workingmen, who earn good wages," and a smaller number of "families in need of assistance." Third Street Nearby, the association's report continued, was home to "small stores of every description, among which saloons, restaurants, bakeries, and pawnshops are the most numerous," while to the east and south stretched warehouses and the waterfront, which "constitut[ed] an important part of the life of the neighborhood."[20] Other local businesses included wine vaults, flour mills, marble works, gas and electric works, lumberyards, and furniture factories, all of which dotted the map along with single-family homes, subdivided flats, and densely constructed rear tenement buildings.[21]

Set apart from these bustling surroundings on its quiet, tree-filled park, the South Park Settlement, as it came to be known, provided a welcoming setting for cautious middle-class settlement workers acquainting themselves with the exigencies of urban, working-class life. The settlement workers must have found added reassurance in the fact that many other charitable institutions shared their environs. The Silver Street Kindergarten, the Episcopal Mission of the Good Samaritan, St. Mary's Hospital, Our Lady's Home for Old and Infirm Women, and a branch of the San Francisco Free Public Library were all within walking distance.[22]

The demographic characteristics of the South-of-Market neighborhood influenced the course of settlement life. After Chinatown, South of Market was San Francisco's most densely populated district; it was also the largest and most important area served by the Associated Charities.[23] But San Francisco's grittiest neighborhoods could not top the extreme poverty endemic to a place like Chicago's nineteenth ward, with its dense tenement buildings and overlapping immigrant communities.[24] Having witnessed the scene around Hull House, many visitors found South Park to be "surprisingly pleasant" with "little to suggest the need of settlement work."[25] This favorable impression derived in large part from the fact that most area residents spoke English, a factor that rendered "easy and natural the many social gatherings, lectures, concerts, and entertainments which form so important a part of the South Park Settlement life."[26] Even though half of the population living south of Market Street in 1900 was foreign-born, the Irish and German immigrants who passed through South Park likely seemed less "foreign" to settlement workers than the non-English-speaking Italian and Latin American immigrants who lived near the city's northern waterfront—let alone the Chinese immigrants who also lived above Market Street.[27]

During its first five years of operation, the South Park Settlement quietly went about the work of encouraging friendly relations among its neighbors. Despite their early and perhaps overly sanguine expectations, settlement workers soon found themselves "confronted on every side [by] sickness, poverty, ignorance, viciousness, [and] lack of work." Nonetheless they resolved that "sympathetic friendship is more valued than material aid, and . . . we can and do give [it] with joy."[28] The bulk of this friendship was delivered in the form of clubs and classes for boys and girls. The San Francisco Boys' Club Association, which organized its clubs through the Settlement, charged itself with the "moral elevation of boys in San Francisco." To that end the Boys' Club offered "as many channels as possible for the overflow of energy hitherto wasted, or worse, in this locality."[29] Boys between the ages of twelve and sixteen gathered for athletic activities, model-government practice, and training in basket-weaving, chair caning, and book covering, while older boys met weekly to discuss "municipal questions" of the day.[30] Girls were similarly targeted for moral uplift, organized into classes that taught skills in sewing and cooking and lessons in art and literature.[31]

Neighborhood women, for their part, met regularly for coffee, sewing, and lectures with such titles as "Clara Barton," "The Women of India," and "Colonel Waring's Street Cleaning Brigade"—in other words, the same kinds of topics that interested elite women's clubs.[32] And on Tuesday evenings the Political Economy Club met for "discussions of practical value in this time of social ferment." These gatherings brought workingmen into contact with university professors, including Bernard Moses, Carl Plehn, Clive Day, and Edward A. Ross, who delivered talks on a range of political and economic matters, from Ross's "Signs and Causes of Social Discontent" and Day's "The Industrial Revolution of the Nineteenth Century" to Plehn's "Evils of Taxation in California." Other speakers included C. E. Hawkes, the president of the San Francisco Typographical Union; Reverend W. D. P. Bliss, a well-traveled Christian Socialist; and Frederick W. Dohrman, a prominent local businessman and civic leader.[33]

Although it represented only a small part of the South Park Settlement's activities, the Political Economy Club embodied the Settlement Association's mission to ease social upheavals by bringing diverse social elements into mutual understanding. This objective led Philip J. Ethington to argue that the Settlement endeavored "to make the public sphere more rational, more open to dispassionate, scientific ideas, and more democratic: more accessible for the working people of the neighborhood." But Ethington suggests that, despite its best efforts, the Settlement "could carve out only a small segment of the political sphere," as it was overpowered by a "sea of mass-media produced on an industrial scale by [William Randolph] Hearst and his competitors."[34] However, as the South Park Settlement gradually devoted more energy to fostering cross-class goodwill, and especially as it entered into coalitions with working-class leaders, it claimed a much greater ability to intervene in public life. In time the South Park Settlement became a potent agent of reform.

The first steps in this transformation were guided by Dr. Dorothea Moore, a Boston-trained physician who joined the Settlement as the head worker in 1898. After the end of her marriage to Los Angeles newspaperman Charles Fletcher Lummis in 1888, Moore spent time at the University Settlement in New York and then at Hull House, where she met and married her second husband, Ernest Carroll Moore. In 1898 the couple relocated to northern California, where Ernest joined the faculty at the University of California and Dorothea took charge of the Settlement.[35]

Under Moore's leadership, the South Park Settlement began to resemble its more politically inclined counterparts in the East and Midwest. Moore conceded that in San Francisco "a certain bounteousness of physical life, the abundance of sun and salty winds, a certain ease of the hard side of struggle, together with a tang of the Western spirit . . . have here so concurred as to make living take on its less tragic, its simpler aspects." Nevertheless, as a veteran of Hull House, she insisted on the need for "enlarged civic action."[36] Moore began by appealing to the San Francisco Merchants' Association to help fund scholarships for the study of social conditions by local college students. Together with the California Club, a local women's organization to which she belonged, she also won their assistance in improving nearby streets and establishing a public playground.[37] In addition, Moore facilitated the research projects of a number of visiting scholars. Frank Fetter, a Stanford economist, led a group of students in the "first systematic study of the Settlement district," and Meyer Jaffa, a nutritionist from the University of California Agricultural Experiment Station, embarked on studies of infant-feeding practices in North Beach and the dietary habits of Chinatown. Moore even sent a resident to work in a local laundry to gain knowledge "of conditions both good and bad," although it is unclear what action, if any, was taken as a result of the findings.[38]

Despite these efforts at "enlarged civic action," the South Park Settlement refrained from direct participation in local politics. Moore herself was intimately involved in movements among clubwomen, leading the California Club and the California Federation of Women's Clubs in a campaign to establish a statewide juvenile court system. But she did not involve the Settlement in this work.[39] Indeed, there seems to have existed a clear separation between the academic studies conducted through the South Park Settlement and the practice of direct political action. Social scientific investigation may have contributed to a more intelligent understanding of municipal issues among professionals and scholars, but, aside from their participation in community lectures, researchers did not develop practical application for the results of their work.

This equation changed dramatically with the arrival of Lucile Eaves in 1901. Eaves brought with her a new determination to apply the work of the Settlement to concrete political ends, but her commitment to her position—at least at first—was reluctant at best. Eaves's dream, after all, was not to become a settlement worker, but to establish herself as an academic social scientist. Born in Leavenworth, Kansas, in 1869, she taught in an industrial school for the Nez Percé Indians in Idaho and then in the public schools of Portland, Oregon, before obtaining her bachelor's degree from Stanford in 1894, just three years after the university opened its doors. After graduation Eaves directed the history department at San Diego High School in southern California, but she had set her sights on a career in academia. In 1898 she began studies in sociology, economics, and philosophy at the University of Chicago.[40]

In Chicago, Eaves encountered an unusually close-knit community of women studying the social sciences under the tutelage of John Dewey, Albion Small, J. Laurence Laughlin, and Thorstein Veblen. Thanks in part to the unflagging support of Marion Talbot, the university's dean of women, many of the female students in Eaves's cohort—including Sophonisba Breckinridge, Frances Kellor, Katherine Bement Davis, and Annie M. MacLean—successfully completed their studies and went on to make names for themselves as professionals. But Eaves's sojourn in Chicago did not last long. Though she returned to the city to continue her studies during the summers, Eaves went west in 1899 to Stanford University to become a lecturer in "Pacific Slope" history. By accepting a full-time position, Eaves was able to financially support both herself and her sister Anna Ruth, with whom she lived for most of her life.[41]

Fortunately for Eaves, the intellectual climate at Stanford was just as exciting as the one she'd left behind. In Palo Alto she worked closely with a dynamic group of scholars actively probing questions of social and political reform. Her colleagues included the charities experts Amos G. Warner and Mary Roberts Smith (later Coolidge), the economists Franklin Fetter and E. Dana Durand, and the sociologists Edward A. Ross and George Howard, both of whom became Eaves's mentors and friends. The student body was equally dynamic, sprouting a crop of graduates that included the reformer and journalist Franklin Hichborn, the suffragists Ida Husted Harper and Ann Martin, and the future U.S. president Herbert Hoover.[42]

These were happy times for Eaves, but they came to an abrupt end in late 1900. That autumn, Jane Stanford, the university's sole trustee, dismissed Ross when he publicly condemned Chinese immigration before a group of San Francisco labor leaders. Eaves was not alone when she resigned in protest, but as a woman—and one without a PhD—she found it difficult to locate alternative academic employment. Thus, with apparently few other options in the summer of 1901, Eaves accepted the post of head worker when the San Francisco Settlement Association offered it.[43]

In relocating herself to 84 South Park, Eaves was succumbing to the bifurcated development of early twentieth-century social science. The path that Eaves had hoped to follow was predominantly male and ensconced in the academy. The path that welcomed her, by contrast, was largely female and rooted in social settlements, voluntary associations, and, to an increasing degree, government.[44] Yet despite her initial misgivings about taking on a position that was not "exactly university work," Eaves soon discovered that the South Park Settlement presented an excellent opportunity to learn "a very good deal about social and economic conditions," and she quickly developed a strong commitment to what she defined as popular education.[45]

Political developments in San Francisco gave Eaves's work added urgency. In the aftermath of a violent 1901 strike in which police defended strikebreakers, city voters swept mainstream political figures aside and elected as mayor Eugene E. Schmitz, the president of the Musician's Union and a representative of the nascent Union Labor Party.[46] This remarkable election made San Francisco the largest U.S. city to be governed by a labor party, a situation Eaves regarded with cautious enthusiasm.[47] Though a strong supporter of trade unions, she shared Jane Addams's conviction that it was the duty of intellectuals to hold the labor movement to its "highest ideal." Eaves felt that the South Park Settlement could carry out that responsibility by working to ensure the "intelligent use of the great political power which these great organizations will wield." Presenting her thoughts to the readers of the Settlement Association's 1903 annual report, Eaves argued that close cooperation with trade unionists would earn settlement workers "the right to criticize more radical measures which might prove injurious." She further suggested that the Settlement had an important role to play in promoting the "the strongly educational tendencies" of the labor movement and in lending support to legislation needed to protect the "weaker members of the community."[48] Making the most of her new situation, and determined to connect her abstract intellectual interests to meaningful work in the public sphere, Eaves led the Settlement into partnership with California labor leaders.

Lucile Eaves worked most closely with the San Francisco Labor Council (SFLC), a central body for nearly all of the city's unions, most of which represented skilled and semi-skilled workers. The SFLC and most of its member unions espoused a brand of "business unionism" that meshed well with the Settlement's outlook.[49] Eaves declared its leaders to be "practical sociologists" of "unusual natural ability," but she lamented their lack of free time to devote to social scientific study. To help ensure the intelligent development of what she called a "scientific" labor movement, Eaves offered to share with the SFLC her distillations of "the world's latest thought on economic questions."[50] To that end, she contributed more than sixty articles to the SFLC newspaper, the *Labor Clarion*, between 1902 and 1906.

Covering a wide range of topics, Eaves's "Reviews of Labor Literature" presented the latest thought on economic questions, drawing material from popular magazines and academic journals alike. A typical review summarized the findings of U.S. Labor Commissioner Carroll D. Wright's *Sixteenth Annual Report*, a tome Eaves called "indispensable as a reference book for every student of the labor movement."[51] Eaves held Wright in the highest regard, insisting that "no one" "possessed "a fuller knowledge of labor conditions in this country than our Commissioner."[52] Eaves

7. Lucile Eaves as she appeared in the Labor Clarion in 1910.
Courtesy Labor Archives and Research Center, San Francisco State University.

lavished further praise on the "dignified forbearance" of the United Mine Workers president, John Mitchell, who had played a prominent role in the Anthracite Coal Strike of 1902.[53] Other articles offered historical analyses of European and American trade unions, explanations of contemporary labor law, and commentary on the danger of machine politics. Interestingly, Eaves never addressed the issue of woman suffrage—whether or not she was an advocate remains unclear—but she did touch upon the unique needs of working women.[54] No matter her subject, however, Eaves used straightforward language and carefully constructed arguments to narrow the divide between academic social science and what she perceived as the practical concerns of hard-working labor organizers.

On a personal level, Eaves's contributions to the *Labor Clarion* helped develop her scholarly thinking about the successes and failures of California labor unions. In March 1903, she wrote: "Few students of San Francisco conditions have recognized the fact that the strength of the local labor movement is largely due to race conditions." Commenting on two aspects of local demography, Eaves wrote approvingly: "The classes of European immigrants that are most difficult of organization and assimilation rarely come to California." The general knowledge of English and the "superior intelligence" of Irish, German, and native-born American workers, she argued, contributed to a greater unity of action than was possible in polyglot Eastern cities.[55] On the other hand, she stressed the powerful influence of Chinese labor. While Eaves recognized and distanced herself from the "race prejudice" of white workingmen, she never challenged exclusionary views. Indeed, like the unionists she sought to educate—and like her mentor, Edward A. Ross—she believed that the presence of Chinese workers unfairly lowered the wages of American-born craftsmen. From a scholarly perspective, however, she gave much thought to the effect of Chinese immigration on the development of the California labor movement. In her 1910 history of California labor legislation, Eaves astutely observed that the long campaign against the "common enemy" of Chinese labor had "contributed more than any other factor to the strength of the California labor movement"—an assertion that anticipated arguments made by historians Alexander Saxton and Michael Kazin more than six decades later.[56]

In addition to her voluminous work for the *Labor Clarion*, Eaves opened the doors of the Settlement to greater participation by organized labor. In a September 1902 cover story entitled "University Settlements and Trade Unions," Eaves outlined the many ways an institution like the South Park Settlement could be of use to working people. Not only could it "secure the attention and support of those prominent members of the community who do the most to mould public opinion," but it could also furnish "neutral territory" where contending forces could meet for "frank discussion." Eaves pledged that the Settlement would make a special effort to accomplish both of these goals, announcing a new series of "regular lectures and discussions on topics of particular interest to working men and women."[57] She inaugurated the program herself with two meticulously researched presentations on "Injunctions on Labor Disputes" and "The History of the Typographical Union." The *Labor Clarion* voiced its enthusiastic approval, reporting that the latter event was attended by a "good-sized audience of the craft, with their wives and friends."[58] A subsequent talk given by

Katherine Coman on labor problems in the Hawaiian Islands instigated a lively discussion on Japanese immigration. Walter Macarthur, editor of the *Coast Seamen's Journal*, the newspaper of the Sailors' Union of the Pacific, served as moderator. In addition to sponsoring such lectures as these, Eaves opened the Settlement gymnasium once a month for meetings organized by trade unionists themselves.[59]

Whereas Dorothea Moore entered politics mainly through her work with women's clubs, Eaves—who belonged to the Association of Collegiate Alumnae but not the influential California Club—derived authority from her qualifications as a university-trained settlement worker.[60] Her most prominent public role came in 1903 when the San Francisco Labor Council's Law and Legislative Committee invited her to assist in the drafting of legislation to raise the state's age limit of employment from twelve to fourteen years.[61] Eaves readily agreed, drawing the Settlement into a statewide, labor-led campaign that was to last for more than two years. With financial assistance from local branches of the Consumers' League and the Association of Collegiate Alumnae, she prepared literature in support of the bill and joined the Legislative Committee in lobbying for it in Sacramento.[62] Their efforts were thwarted, however, by the vigorous opposition of San Francisco fruit-canning companies, who feared that the loss of child labor at canning season would result in diminished profits. Canners mailed hundreds of postcards to rural precincts warning farmers that the law would jeopardize the next year's fruit crop by banning children from work in the fields. The proposed legislation exempted agricultural labor, but the canners' deceptive tactics proved successful. Representatives in the state senate weakened the bill so thoroughly with amendments that it provided even fewer restrictions than the law already in effect. Accepting defeat, the Labor Council's Legislative Committee withdrew its proposal and vowed to return in 1905.[63]

For the next two years, Eaves continued to fight against child labor by helping ensure strenuous enforcement of the compulsory education law, a measure that did make it through the 1903 legislature. As a first step, Eaves briefly took on a position at the California Bureau of Labor Statistics, where she conducted a study on women and children wage-earners in San Francisco and Oakland. In a survey of over two hundred businesses, she concluded that far too many children had been permanently withdrawn from school.⁶⁴ Next, Eaves directed a private study carried out by members of the Settlement Association. Using the records of San Francisco's Twenty-First School District, which encompassed the South Park neighborhood, Eaves and a team of settlement workers investigated the whereabouts of several hundred children between the ages of five and seventeen who were listed as having attended neither public nor private schools during the school year ending in June 1902. In a report published in the *Western Journal of Education*, Eaves publicized her findings. First, she found that of the 436 children investigated, 141 had moved or could not be found, suggesting a high number of "transient residents" in the district. Of the children aged eight to fourteen who were covered by the existing law, "all but eight were in school or started at the beginning of the next term." Eaves concluded that "the actual number of children on the streets has been grossly exaggerated," but she insisted that there still remained "an unquestionable need for the present vigorous effort to enforce the compulsory education law."⁶⁵

Blurring the line between disinterested investigation and engaged political intervention, Eaves took the matter of enforcement into her own hands. Throughout her research she remained "on the lookout for children of school age playing on the streets," and she included in her report several disparaging comments about "dirty faced" girls and gangs of "little criminals" whose parents allowed them to stay home for the "most trivial reasons." Eaves referred at least three young boys to juvenile detention homes and made five visits to a single family in order to persuade them to return their daughter to school.⁶⁶ Though she admitted that families often put their children to work because of "stern economic necessity," she pointed to instances of "carelessness or indolence on the part of the parents," and she was not afraid to intervene where she found parental guidance to be lacking.⁶⁷ At the close of her report, she defended her actions by calling for increased intervention by truant officers and "other interested neighborhood workers." Like many reform-minded women of the settlement movement, Eaves confidently believed that she was acting in the children's best interests—even though her actions likely caused hardship to families dependent upon children's wages in order to make ends meet.⁶⁸

In 1905 the San Francisco Labor Council and the San Francisco Settlement

Association returned to Sacramento to win passage of a revamped child labor law. This time, however, they organized on a much grander scale. Both settlement workers and union officials helped draft revisions that made the bill more palatable to canning companies, but members of the Settlement Association took the lead in obtaining the support of business interests throughout the state—making good on Lucile Eaves's promise that the Settlement would influence "those prominent members of the community who do the most to mould public opinion."[69] J. P. Chamberlain, a San Francisco lawyer and a member of the Settlement Association's governing council, secured the endorsement of the San Francisco Merchants' Association and the Los Angeles and Santa Barbara chambers of commerce. He also made arguments on behalf of the bill before the joint senate and assembly committee. Settlement workers joined him in interviewing every member of the legislature, and together they watched carefully to prevent the bill from coming to the floor while its friends were absent. Settlement workers also arranged for the publication of supportive editorials in San Francisco newspapers, and they sent arguments in favor of the measure to nearly every paper in the state. Finally, they won Governor George Pardee's consent to be quoted as being "heartily in sympathy with such legislation." Thanks in part to Eaves's efforts to bring her middle-class peers into collaboration with the leaders of the SFLC, the measure passed, the governor signed it into law, and the state labor commissioner energetically took up the cause of enforcement. In 1906 the California State Supreme Court sealed the victory by declaring the law constitutional.[70]

The coalition between the San Francisco Settlement Association and the San Francisco Labor Council stands out in the history of relations between working-class and middle-class reformers in early twentieth-century San Francisco. The *Labor Clarion* remarked on the uniqueness of the partnership, praising Lucile Eaves for establishing closer relations with the labor movement than other middle-class groups had managed to create. The significance of the *Labor Clarion*'s unique affection for Eaves is underscored by the relative absence of California clubwomen from contemporary reports about the legislative campaign. Although Dorothea Moore briefly mentions child labor reform as a concern in a 1906 report on the work of women's clubs in California, Mary Gibson's *Record of Twenty-Five*

Years of the California Federation of Women's Clubs elides the issue altogether, focusing instead on the concurrent battle to establish a statewide juvenile court system. A yearbook of the California Club from the same period is similarly silent on child labor, and contemporary newspaper articles consistently name the SFLC and the San Francisco Settlement Association as campaign leaders but give no mention of allied women's groups.[71] Though they considered children's issues paramount, organized women at this time apparently were more likely to assume political leadership when addressing problems relating to juvenile delinquency, public education, and the dearth of urban playgrounds. To the extent that middle-class women outside the Settlement did get involved in the campaign for child labor reform—the Collegiate Alumnae provided financial assistance, after all—they appear to have done so via their association with Lucile Eaves. Her presence helped bridge the divide between potentially contentious groups.

Historians have noted the difficult challenges posed by class-bridging activism in early twentieth-century San Francisco. Rebecca Mead's analysis of San Francisco trade union women and California's legislated minimum wage (see chapter 11) shows how middle-class and working-class women came to loggerheads between 1913 and 1915 over legislation purporting to protect the interests of female workers.[72] Conflict between middle-class and working-class activists in the woman suffrage movement has also been well documented, notably by Susan Englander (chapter 9).[73] What, then, contributed to the successful partnership between the San Francisco Settlement Association and the San Francisco Labor Council? What made this coalition different?

Although the South Park Settlement was founded with the goal of bringing disparate classes together in mutual understanding, this aim was not fully realized until Lucile Eaves led the Settlement into political collaboration with the San Francisco Labor Council. Several factors made the partnership stick—at least for a time. First, Eaves earned the respect and trust of working-class leaders by placing her scholarly abilities at their disposal. Her contributions to the *Labor Clarion*, together with her willingness to dedicate the Settlement's resources toward investigations designed to improve enforcement of the compulsory education law, established her commitment to labor's cause—even though her efforts clearly spoke to her own goals as well. This trust was further bolstered by Eaves's insistence on opening the doors of the Settlement to greater use by local trade unions.

Second, Eaves and her cohorts willingly fell into step behind SFLC leadership, rather than attempting to wrest control of the campaign for themselves, as clubwomen sought to do in the campaign for the legislative minimum wage. Third, the need for child labor reform was a topic on which all parties could easily agree. Although they may have approached the issue from different perspectives, trade unionists, settlement workers, and civic-minded merchants all agreed that the state should intervene to restrict children from the workplace. Finally, the Settlement itself provided shared institutional space—or "neutral territory," to use Eaves's phrase—where all these groups could come together to work toward their common goal.

The victory on child labor closed a chapter in the history of the South Park Settlement. In August 1905, six months after the law was signed into effect by Governor Pardee, Lucile Eaves wrote to Edward A. Ross expressing her desire to pursue doctoral study in sociology with Franklin Giddings at Columbia University. After four years of hard work, she felt she was ready for a change, and she admitted to fears that her settlement responsibilities—which entailed entertaining neighborhood children in addition to spearheading political reforms—tended toward "provincialism." She fully intended to return to California with her degree, however, believing that it would afford her greater effectiveness in leading the "new social movements" of the Pacific Coast.[74] Before she left, Eaves turned her post at the Settlement over to Mary Roberts Coolidge who, having lost her job at Stanford as a result of a breakdown she suffered after her divorce, found herself in a position similar to the one Eaves had been in four years earlier.[75] By September, Eaves had moved to New York City.[76]

The ensuing years brought unexpected challenges for the San Francisco Settlement Association. The earthquake and fire of April 1906 destroyed the South Park Settlement and left its neighborhood in ruins. Settlement workers relocated to the Mission District, where they reestablished themselves as the San Francisco Settlement. The few records that remain from the years after 1906 suggest that the organization's reform impulse lessened during this period in favor of neighborhood relief and a continued emphasis on social clubs for boys and girls. A 1912 fundraising piece, for example, describes the Settlement as a "great Club-House, a Social Gathering Place and a Center for Neighborhood Relief in the Mission," adding that it "does not give money to the poor because it has no money to give."[77] Newspaper coverage from the same period similarly notes frequent social events but does not suggest any sustained political activity.[78] And when the reform-minded National Association of Settlements was founded in 1911, the San Francisco Settlement did not become a member. Instead, San Francisco was represented in that group by Elizabeth Ashe of the Telegraph Hill Neighborhood Center.[79] If the San Francisco Settlement Association indeed participated in reform campaigns after 1906, the traces are difficult to find.

For her part, Eaves went on to build a successful career as a professional sociologist. After the 1906 earthquake, she immediately left her studies to participate in the relief effort.[80] By 1910 she had published her book about California labor legislation and completed her PhD, thanks in part to fellowships from the University of California and the Carnegie Foundation. Although she had intended to participate further in the social movements of the Pacific Coast, Eaves took advantage of new professional opportunities to teach applied sociology at the university level, first at the University of Nebraska, alongside her former Stanford colleague, George Howard, and then at Simmons College in Boston, where she also served as the director of the Women's Educational and Industrial Union. In 1925 she finally achieved her goal of becoming a full professor.[81]

Despite her academic placement, however, Eaves continued to apply the fruits of her research to concrete political ends, conducting numerous studies on working women and children in order to inform the practice of social workers and policymakers. In this sense, she held on to the model of social scientific practice she had developed as the head worker of the San Francisco Settlement Association. The South Park Settlement therefore had an important effect on Eaves personally, just as it held public significance for the leaders of the San Francisco Labor Council.

Notes

An earlier version of this essay appeared as "Settlement Work in a Union Town: Lucile Eaves, the San Francisco Settlement Association, and Organized Labor, 1894–1906," *Ex Post Facto: Journal of the History Students at San Francisco State University* 11 (Spring 2002): 79–98.

1. *San Francisco Labor Clarion*, May 9, 1902.
2. *Labor Clarion*, August 28, 1903.
3. Lucile Eaves, "My Sociological Life History" [1928], *Sociological Origins* 2, no. 2 (2000): 65–70.
4. Lucile Eaves, *A History of California Labor Legislation, with an Introductory Sketch of the San Francisco Labor Movement* (Berkeley: University of California Publications in Economics, 1910). For biographical information on Eaves, see Mary Jo Deegan, "Lucile Eaves," in *Women in Sociology: A Bio-Bibliographical Sourcebook*, ed. Mary Jo Deegan(New York: Greenwood, 1991), 140–41; and Ann Mari May and Robert W. Diamand, "Trouble in the Inaugural Issue of the *American Economic Review*: The Cross/Eaves Controversy," *Journal of Economic Perspectives* 23, no. 2 (2009): 1–16.
5. A rich literature exists on women in the social settlement movement. See Estelle Freedman, "Separatism as Strategy: Female Institution Building and American Feminism, 1870–1930," *Feminist Studies* 5, no. 3 (1979): 512–29; Kathryn Kish Sklar, "Hull House in the 1890s: A Community of Women Reformers," *Signs* 10, no. 4 (1985): 658–77; Sklar, *Florence Kelley and the Nation's Work: The Rise of Women's Political Culture, 1830–1900* (New Haven CT: Yale University Press, 1995); Linda Kerber, "Separate Spheres, Female Worlds, Woman's Place: The Rhetoric of Women's History" *Journal of American History* 75 (1988–89): 9–39; John P. Rousmaniere, "Cultural Hybrid in the Slums: The College Woman and the Settlement House, 1889–1894," *American Quarterly* 22, no. 1 (1970): 45–66; and Mary Jo Deegan, *Jane Addams and the Men of the Chicago School, 1892–1918* (New Brunswick NJ: Transaction Books, 1988). The most comprehensive study of the settlement movement remains Allen F. Davis, *Spearheads for Reform: The Social Settlements and the Progressive Movement, 1890–1914* (New Brunswick NJ: Rutgers University Press, 1994). For somewhat more critical revisions, see Mina Carson, *Settlement Folk: Social Thought and the American Settlement Movement, 1885–1930* (Chicago: University of Chicago Press, 1990); Ruth Hutchinson Crocker, *Social Work and Social Order: The Settlement Movement in Two Industrial Cities, 1889–1930* (Urbana: University of Illinois Press, 1992); Rivka Shpak Lissak, *Pluralism and Progressivism: Hull House and the New Immigrants, 1890–1919* (Chicago: University of Chicago Press, 1989); Judith Ann Trolander, *Professionalism and Social Change: From the Settlement House Movement to Neighborhood Centers, 1886 to the Present* (New York: Columbia University Press, 1984); Elizabeth Lasch-Quinn, *Black Neighbors: Race and the Limits of Reform in the American Settlement House Movement, 1896–1945* (Chapel Hill: University of North Carolina Press, 1993); and Howard Jacob Karger, *The Sentinels of Order: A Study of Social Control and the Minneapolis Settlement House Movement, 1915–1950* (New York: University Press of America, 1987). Also valuable are Maureen A. Flanagan, *Seeing with Their Hearts: Chicago Women and the Vision of the Good City, 1871–1933* (Princeton:

Princeton University Press, 2002), and Sarah Deutsch, *Women and the City: Gender, Space, and Power in Boston, 1870–1940* (New York: Oxford University Press, 2000).

6. The Russell Sage Foundation's 1911 *Handbook of Settlements* lists sixty-one active settlements west of the Mississippi, with twenty-one located in California alone. See Robert A. Woods and Albert J. Kennedy, eds., *Handbook of Settlements* (New York: Arno, 1970). While western settlement houses have yet to receive in-depth treatment from historians, literature is available on women's mission homes in California, Colorado, and Nebraska. See Peggy Pascoe, *Relations of Rescue: The Search for Female Moral Authority in the American West, 1874–1939* (New York: Oxford University Press, 1990). For an architectural exploration of the West Oakland Settlement, see Marta Gutman, "Inside the Institution: The Art and Craft of Settlement Work at the Oakland New Century Club, 1895–1923," in *People, Power, Places: Perspectives in Vernacular Architecture*, ed. Sally McMurry and Annmarie Adams (Knoxville: University of Tennessee Press, 2000), 248–79.

7. Jane Addams to Sarah Anderson, February 20, 1894, Jane Addams Papers (Ann Arbor: University Microfilms International, 1984).

8. Jane Addams, *Philanthropy and Social Progress* (New York: Thomas Y. Crowell, 1893), 1–23.

9. *Hull House Maps and Papers* (New York: Thomas Y. Crowell, 1895). See also Kathryn Kish Sklar, "Hull House Maps and Papers: Social Science as Women's Work in the 1890s," in *Gender and American Social Science: The Formative Years*, ed. Helene Silverberg (Princeton: Princeton University Press, 1998), 127–55.

10. San Francisco Settlement Association (SFSA), *First Annual Report*, 1895, Bancroft Library, University of California, Berkeley (hereafter "Bancroft").

11. Eric C. Bellquist to Robert Scalapino, June 14, 1961, Autobiography of Bernard Moses, Bernard Moses Papers, Bancroft; James E. Watson, "Bernard Moses: Pioneer in Latin American Scholarship," *The Hispanic American Historical Review* 42, no. 2 (1962): 212–16.

12. SFSA, *First Annual Report*. "Jessica Peixotto," in *Notable American Women, 1607–1950, Volume II*, ed. Edward T. James (Cambridge MA: Belknap, 1971), 42–43.

13. Fannie W. McLean to Jane Addams, September 26, 1893, Jane Addams Papers; Philip Ethington, *The Public City: The Political Construction of Urban Life in San Francisco, 1850–1900* (Berkeley: University of California Press, 1994), 353.

14. Fred E. Haynes to Jane Addams, January 19, 1895, Jane Addams Papers; SFSA, *First Annual Report*, 1895. San Francisco (Harrison Street) Boys' Club, *First Annual Report*, 1894, Bancroft. Associated Charities of San Francisco, *Annual Report*, 1895, Bancroft. The Buford Kitchengarten offered classes in housekeeping, sewing, and cooking to neighborhood girls. See C. K. Jenness, *The Charities of San Francisco* (Palo Alto: Published for the Department of Economics and Social Science, Leland Stanford Jr. University, 1894). For the Kitchengarten movement, see Dolores Hayden, *The Grand Domestic Revolution* (Cambridge MA: MIT Press, 1995), 125–26.

15. *Our Society Blue Book* (San Francisco: Hoag & Irving, 1895); Carol Roland, "The California Kindergarten Movement: A Study in Class and Social Feminism" (PhD dissertation, University of California Riverside, 1980), 13.

16. Associated Charities of San Francisco, *Annual Report*, 1895.

17. Millicent Shinn, "Poverty and Charity in San Francisco," *Overland Monthly* 14 (November 1889): 541, 543.

18. Katherine Coman, "The South Park Settlement, San Francisco," *The Commons* 8 (August 1903): 8.

19. Coman, "South Park Settlement," 8; SFSA, *First Annual Report*.

20. SFSA, *First Annual Report*.

21. Sanborn Insurance Maps, 1899, microfilm, University of California, Berkeley.

22. Sanborn Insurance Maps, 1899. SFSA, *First Annual Report*, 1895. For more information on the South-of-Market district, see William Issel and Robert W. Cherny, *San Francisco 1865–1932: Politics, Power, and Urban Development* (Berkeley: University of California Press, 1986), 58–63; and Jules Tygiel, *Workingmen in San Francisco, 1880–1901* (New York: Garland, 1992), 233–73. The South-of-Market neighborhood is also described by Jack London in his short story, "South of the Slot." For more on San Francisco charities, see Mary Ann Irwin, "'Going About and Doing Good': The Lady Managers of San Francisco" (Master's thesis, San Francisco State University, 1995), and Roland, "The California Kindergarten Movement."

23. Issel and Cherny, *Politics, Power*, 59; Associated Charities of San Francisco, *Annual Report*, 1895.

24. For a particularly unfavorable portrait, see Ray Ginger, *Altgeld's America: The Lincoln Ideal versus Changing Realities* (New York: Funk & Wagnalls, 1958), 15–34.

25. Coman, "South Park Settlement," 7.

26. Fannie McLean, "South Park Settlement: Characteristic Work in a San Francisco Neighborhood," *The Commons* 14 (June 1897): 2.

27. McLean, "South Park Settlement," 2; Issel and Cherny, *Politics, Power*, 59. For missions to the Chinese in San Francisco, see Pascoe, *Relations of Rescue*.

28. SFSA, *Fourth Annual Report*, 1898, Bancroft.

29. San Francisco Boys' Club Association, *Second Annual Report*, 1895, Bancroft.

30. SFSA, *Second Annual Report*, 1896, Bancroft. SFSA, *Fifth Annual Report*, 1899, Bancroft.

31. SFSA, *Second Annual Report*.

32. SFSA, *Third Annual Report*; SFSA, *Fourth Annual Report*. See also, Karen Blair, *The Clubwoman as Feminist* (New York: Holmes & Meier, 1980).

33. SFSA, *Fourth Annual Report*.

34. Ethington, *Public City*, 353–54.

35. Dorothea Moore deserves further attention from historians. See Mark Thompson, *American Character: The Curious Life of Charles Fletcher Lummis and the Rediscovery of the Southwest* (New York: Arcade, 2001), 15–16, 122–26, 135–39; Gayle Gullett, *Becoming Citizens: The Emergence and Development of the California Women's Movement, 1880–1911* (Urbana: University of Illinois Press, 2000), 141–42; Jane Addams to Anita McCormick Blaine, January 8, 1896, Jane Addams Papers; Rockwell Dennis Hunt, *California and Californians* (New York: Lewis, 1926), 475–76.

36. SFSA, *Fifth Annual Report*.

37. SFSA, *Fifth Annual Report*; Dorothea Moore, "San Francisco Settlement Association," *Merchants Association Review* (February 1900): 3; California Club, *Yearbook*, 1905, Bancroft; Gullett, *Becoming Citizens*, 139–40.

38. SFSA, *Fifth Annual Report*; Ethington, *Public City*, 352.

39. Gullett, *Becoming Citizens*, 141–42; Mary Gibson, *A Record of Twenty-Five Years of the California Federation of Women's Clubs, 1900–1925* (California Federation of Women's Clubs, 1927), 34–36.

40. Eaves, "My Sociological Life History," 65–67.

41. Mary Jo Deegan, "Lucile Eaves," 140–41; J. Graham Morgan, "Women in American Sociology in the 19th Century," *Journal of the History of Sociology* 2, no. 2 (Spring 1980): 29. See also Ellen Fitzgerald, *Endless Crusade: Women Social Scientists and Progressive Reform* (New York: Oxford University Press, 1990).

42. For a discussion of intellectual currents at Stanford during this period, see Ethington, *Public City*, 349–52.

43. James C. Mohr, "Academic Turmoil and Public Opinion: The Ross Case at Stanford," *Pacific Historical Review* 39 (1970): 39–61; Mary O. Furner, *Advocacy and Objectivity: A Crisis in the Professionalization of American Social Science, 1865–1905* (Lexington: University of Kentucky Press, 1975), 229–59; Deegan, "Lucile Eaves," 141.

44. Nancy Folbre, "The 'Sphere of Women' in Early Twentieth-Century Economics," in *Gender and American Social Science*, ed. Silverberg, 35–60; Robin Muncy, *Creating a Female Dominion in American Reform, 1890–1935* (New York: Oxford University Press, 1991).

45. Lucile Eaves to E. A. Ross, November 20, 1901, Edward A. Ross Papers, Wisconsin Historical Society, Madison, Wisconsin (hereafter "Ross Papers").

46. Jules Tygiel, "Where Unionism Holds Undisputed Sway: A Reappraisal of San Francisco's Union Labor Party," *California History* 63 (Fall 1983): 196–215.

47. Lucile Eaves to E. A. Ross, November 20, 1901, Ross Papers.

48. SFSA, *Ninth Annual Report*, 1903, Bancroft.

49. Mary Ann Mason, "Neither Friends nor Foes: Organized Labor and the California Progressives," in *California Progressivism Revisited*, ed. William Deverell and Tom Sitton (Berkeley: University of California Press, 1994), 60. The SFLC took the lead in forming the California State Federation of Labor. See Philip Taft, *Labor*

Politics American Style: The California State Federation of Labor (Cambridge: Harvard University Press, 1968).

50. Lewis L. Gould, The Presidency of Theodore Roosevelt (Lawrence KS: University Press of Kansas, 1991), 70–71. SFSA, Ninth Annual Report.

51. Labor Clarion, September 26, 1902.

52. Labor Clarion, January 23, 1903.

53. Labor Clarion, December 5, 1902.

54. For representative articles, see Labor Clarion, October 31, 1902; March 27, 1903; May 1, 1903; January 15, 1904; March 11, 1904; November 11, 1904; April 28, 1905; May 5, 1905; January 19, 1906.

55. Labor Clarion, March 25, 1903, and April 24, 1903.

56. Lucile Eaves, A History of California Labor Legislation (Berkeley: University of California Publications in Economics, 1910), 5–6. Both Saxton and Kazin cite Eaves in their work. See Alexander Saxton, The Indispensable Enemy: Labor and the Anti-Chinese Movement in California (Berkeley: University of California Press, 1971), and Michael Kazin, "The Great Exception Revisited: Organized Labor and Politics in San Francisco and Los Angeles, 1870–1940," Pacific Historical Review 55 (August 1986): 371–402.

57. Labor Clarion, September 19, 1902.

58. Labor Clarion, November 14, 1902, November 7, 1902.

59. Labor Clarion, December 26, 1902; Coman, "South Park Settlement," 9.

60. Association of Collegiate Alumnae, Register, December, 1903. In the Labor Clarion, Eaves emphasized her university background. Labor Clarion, September 19, 1902.

61. Eaves, History of California Labor Legislation, 299.

62. Eaves, History of California Labor Legislation; Labor Clarion, August 28, 1901; SFSA, Ninth Annual Report.

63. Eaves, History of California Labor Legislation, 299–300; Labor Clarion, March 27, 1903.

64. Eleventh Biennial Report of the Bureau of Labor Statistics for the State of California (Sacramento: Superintendent State Printing, 1904), 11–17.

65. Lucile Eaves, "School Attendance in the 21st District School of San Francisco," Western Journal of Education, October 1904, 717–20.

66. Eaves, "School Attendance."

67. Labor Clarion, August 21, 1903.

68. Eaves, "School Attendance," 720. Eaves's experience is reminiscent of that of Florence Kelley in Illinois; see Sklar, Florence Kelley and the Nation's Work, 280–85, and Sklar, "Community of Women Reformers," 671–73.

69. Labor Clarion, November 14, 1902.

70. Eaves, History of California Labor Legislation, 301–4.

71. Dorothea Moore, "The Work of the Women's Clubs in California," Annals of the American Academy of Political and Social Science 28 (Summer 1906): 257–60; Gibson,

A Record of Twenty-Five Years, 34–36; California Club, Yearbook, 1905; San Francisco Call, January 21, 1905; Merchants Association Review (February 1905), 4.

72. See also Rebecca J. Mead, "'Let the Women Get Their Wages as Men Do': Trade Union Women and the Legislated Minimum Wage in California," Pacific Historical Review 67 (1998): 317–47.

73. See also Susan Englander, "The San Francisco Wage Earners' Suffrage League: Class Conflict and Class Coalition in the California Woman Suffrage Movement, 1907–1912" (Master's thesis, San Francisco State University, 1989); Gullett, Becoming Citizens. For other cities, see Sherry Katz, "Frances Nacke Noel and 'Sister Movements': Socialism, Feminism and Trade Unionism in Los Angeles, 1909–1916," California History 67 (September 1988): 181–89; Nancy Schrom Dye, As Equals and as Sisters: Feminism, the Labor Movement, and the Women's Trade Union League of New York (Columbia: University of Missouri Press, 1980), and Meredith Tax, The Rising of the Women: Feminist Solidarity and Class Conflict, 1880–1917 (New York: Monthly Review, 1980).

74. Lucile Eaves to E. A. Ross, August 8, 1905, Ross.

75. Deegan, "Lucile Eaves," 141; Deegan, "Mary Elizabeth Burroughs Roberts Smith Coolidge (1860–1945)," in Women in Sociology: A Bio-Bibliographical Sourcebook, ed. Mary Jo Deegan (New York: Greenwood, 1991), 100–109.

76. Lucile Eaves to E. A. Ross, September 28, 1905, Ross.

77. SFSA, "Dollar Campaign," San Francisco Settlement Vertical File, California Historical Society, San Francisco. See also Phoebe A. Hearst Papers, San Francisco Settlement Folder, Container 10, Bancroft.

78. Call, September 29, 1910; May 2, 1912; and June 5, 1912.

79. "Settlement Bible," Archive of the National Federation of Settlements, 1899–1958 (Woodbridge CT: Research Publications, 1989–1990), text-fiche. Telegraph Hill Neighborhood Center, Annual Report, 1911, Bancroft.

80. Eaves, "Where San Francisco Was Sorest Stricken," Charities and the Commons 16 (May 1906): 161–63; James Rogers, "Social Settlements in the San Francisco Disaster," Charities and the Commons 16, no. 9 (June 2, 1906): 311–13.

81. Deegan, "Lucile Eaves," 142. As WEIU director, Eaves authored several reports related to working women and children: The Food of Working Women in Boston (1917); Training for Store Service: The Vocational Experiences and Training of Juvenile Employees of Retail Department, Dry Goods and Clothing Stores in Boston (1920); Old-Age Support of Women Teachers: Provisions for Old Age Made by Women Teachers in the Public Schools of Massachusetts (1921); Gainful Employment of Handicapped Women (1921); Children in Need of Special Care: Studies Based on Two Thousand Case Records of Social Agencies (1923); A Legacy to Wage Earning Women: A Survey of Gainfully Employed Women in Brattleboro, Vermont, and of Relief Which They Have Received from the Thomas Thompson Trust (1925).

6. "CITIZEN BIRD"

California Women and Bird Protection, 1890–1920

MICHELLE KLEEHAMMER

At the turn of the twentieth century, a nationwide movement emerged to protect a variety of wild bird species, many of them in urgent danger of extinction due to overhunting. At the heart of this effort was the organizing power of middle- and upper-middle-class white women across the country whose political activism has come to typify a broad swath of progressive era reform. Though years away from formal suffrage, granted in California in 1911 and nationally in 1920, these women used their vast social networks and extraordinary civic organizing skills to challenge what they perceived to be a system of complacency and negligent stewardship of the nation's resources by male policymakers, businessmen, and scientists.

Clubwomen in particular spearheaded a national campaign that secured the legal protection of several species of birds, and the women of California's bird-conservation movement came to exemplify this confluence of progressive efficiency, environmental activism, and moral imperative. By 1920, California women had succeeded in initiating and offering educational programs for schoolchildren, authoring and circulating informational materials throughout their communities, creating and enforcing hunting and commercial restrictions, establishing bird refuges, and securing the passage of significant protective legislation.

The organizing power demonstrated by California women committed to bird protection offers a unique window into the nature of women's political culture at this time. Without the grassroots work and conservation ideology of local Audubon societies and women's clubs, it is unlikely that the protective legislation would even have been introduced, much less passed, as quickly as it was. Such women as Alice L. Park, Catherine Hittell, and Mary McHenry Keith of San Francisco's prominent California Club used their social influence and networks to agitate for legislative reforms in many aspects of wildlife and habitat conservation. Local Audubon leaders throughout California, including Harriet Williams Myers, Anna Head,

8. Harriet Williams Myers, California Audubon Society Secretary, checking on a recovering bird in the rescue station she built and maintained. Thomas Gilbert Pearson, The Bird Study Book (1917), illustrated by Will Simmons. Garden City NY: Doubleday, Page, 1917.

and Josephine McCracken, waged parallel lobbying and educational campaigns to promote community-wide and statewide interest in protecting birds through social and legal means.

California clubwomen authored legislation and lobbied state and county governments, but these activities served as only a piece of their overarching agenda and, on their own, do not reveal the women's broader commitment to progressive goals. In addition to overtly political work, these women consciously participated in a campaign of "organized womanhood" that blended women's traditionally defined domestic and nurturing roles with a progressive era interest in social improvement and a broad understanding of conservation. Their concern for birds emerged not only from the growing popularity of amateur ornithology and an appreciation for nature study, but also out of an interest among progressive women to advocate for creatures with whom they were often connected in the popular discourse. Middle- and upper-class white women fighting for suffrage and political influence frequently found their contributions devalued or dismissed because they were reputed to prefer triviality, fashion, beauty, and decoration, which paralleled much of the contemporary rhetoric about birds. For

California women the bird-protection cause mirrored late nineteenth-century gender ideologies in surprising ways.

The reformers who became involved in the bird-protection movement, and the Audubon movement in particular, had many motivations. They responded to a wide array of concerns, such as the effects of urbanization and industrialization on the natural environment, the professionalization of the natural sciences, and a specific interest in popular ornithology and "citizen science" that emerged in the late nineteenth century. Foremost among these concerns was the fear that in the United States and internationally bird populations suffered dramatically due to human destruction. Sport and commercial hunting of birds came under attack, as did the professional fields of ornithology (bird study) and oölogy (egg study) for encouraging the collection of numerous specimens. Hunting at this time was generally unregulated. The U.S. Department of Agriculture did not officially define "game" birds or regulate hunting until 1916, despite estimates that there were three million active hunters in 1912 and six million in 1920.[1] In the end, however, the millinery trade's ruthless harvesting of birds most captured the imagination of the public and catalyzed the reform impulse of the majority of bird-protection advocates at this time.

High-fashion magazines in Paris, London, and New York reflected a vast upsurge in decorative plumage. Jennifer Price notes that hats held the most prominent place among late nineteenth- and early twentieth-century fashion accessories and often signified a woman's status in society.[2] In her history of the millinery industry, Wendy Gamber argues that although women thought of hats as high class, and many preferred ornate custom-designed hats, by 1900 the ready-to-wear hat covered in fashionable plumage "was within reach of all but the most destitute."[3] Egrets, herons, ostriches, peacocks, birds of paradise, grebes, terns, and blackbirds produced some of the most coveted feathers, but the millinery industry also commonly used wings, breasts, heads, and even entire birds, such as hummingbirds, on hats.[4] In an effort to dramatize the devastation and frivolity of the entire trade, the ornithologist and *Bird-Lore* publisher Frank Chapman took a tally of the hats worn by women in New York's fashion district over two days in 1886. Chapman counted seven hundred hats, three-quarters of which contained bird parts, totaling 173 birds from forty species.[5] Joel A. Allen, another ornithologist, asserted in *Science* magazine the same year that hunters slaughtered five million birds annually—even then a conservative estimate—and scholars have recently surmised that the number could have been three or even four times higher.[6]

In addition to the urgency caused by the exploits of the millinery trade, hunting, and scientific study, progressive era conservationists had cultural reasons for seeking to protect birds. The pioneering environmental historians Samuel Hays and Roderick Nash have demonstrated that the early twentieth century ushered in a surge in both conservation activism and awareness of the limitations of natural resources that for the first time seemed to be seriously threatened by the effects of industrialization, urbanization, and the rapid development of the West.[7] Bird protection paralleled and in some ways foreshadowed the larger "back to nature" campaign that sought to counteract with exposure to the natural world what reformers viewed as physical and psychological degeneration brought on by the rapid pace of modernization at the turn of the century.[8] According to Robin W. Doughty, birds in particular "[struck] a responsive chord in the minds and hearts of many people."[9] Mark V. Barrow Jr., a historian of American ornithology, similarly argues that these reformers "viewed nature as an important means to ameliorate many of the problems plaguing modern America." He adds that they "touted the benefits of getting 'back to nature,' and the bird protection cause both benefited from and promoted this new sensibility."[10]

At the turn of the century, writing about nature, in general, and about birds, in particular, attracted many women to amateur nature study, which both encouraged and reflected the growing popularity of bird-lore. In his study of nineteenth-century birding field guides, Thomas Dunlap, an environmental historian, has found that these publications "mixed science and sentiment," making them accessible and interesting to a broad range of Americans. Guides written by women "used narrative prose, the familiar frame of home life, and the decorative illustrations of popular natural history to introduce a largely female audience to birds around the home."[11] Bird studies, natural histories, juvenile literature about birds, and fiction about birds became extremely popular, undergoing several editions and re-printings between the 1880s and the 1920s.[12] By the 1930s the circulation of magazines affiliated with local Audubon societies numbered 18,867, and those of the ornithological clubs 3,520.[13]

Not only did birds serve as the objects of great scientific and popular interest at the turn of the century, but they also became vessels through which Americans both challenged and reinforced their ideas about domesticity and proper gender roles.[14] Women and children could become "citizen-scientists," engaging in their own study of wildlife in the natural world. But their projects and writing served primarily sentimental and educational purposes, areas considered traditionally "feminine." Anna Head, a Berkeley educator, clubwoman, and frequent contributor to nature publications, exemplified this tactic when she lovingly described her objects of study as "busy little parents . . . less inclined to fight with all the world."[15] When writing about a bird-watching trip she had taken to Lake Tahoe, Head explained that the birds "showed great affection and solicitude for their young" despite "a good deal of flutter and scolding."[16]

Mabel Osgood Wright's nationally popular *Citizen Bird: Scenes from Bird-Life in Plain English for Beginners* (1897) also reinforced idealized domestic roles: "The mother [meadowlark] tends the eggs and nestlings, the father always keeping near to help her, and continually singing at his daily toil of providing for his family as charmingly as if he were still a gay bachelor."[17] As Kevin C. Armitage argues in his study of the origins of Bird Day, "advocates attempted to imbue students with the moral sentiment to save vanishing birds and at the same time provide them with scientifically grounded information about birds' lives and habitats."[18] Nature writers, both amateur and scientific, anthropomorphized birds by imbuing them with contemporary gender and family values in an attempt both to better understand the species and to make sense of their own increasingly complicated modern lives.

By humanizing birds, female nature writers also revealed interesting ambiguities about their own status in U.S. civic life. In *Citizen Bird*, Wright portrayed birds as underappreciated members of society that exhibit valuable talents in their song, beauty, industry, and feeding habits.[19] In one of Head's essays, she described a kinglet that "effectually policed the whole bird city."[20] Harriet Williams Myers, a longtime activist in California's bird-protection movement and a future president of the California Audubon Society, wrote of birds as civic or political figures in a parallel but fictional world. In *The Birds' Convention* (1913), the birds take on professional personas, holding each other to parliamentary procedures and a proper reverence for social decorum.[21] Myers illustrates the close connection between birds and women by mockingly reenacting the structure of a typical club meeting: "After the morning chorus... we will have breakfast, followed by an experience meeting. We are all anxious to know what has happened to our various families over the past winter. We shall also discuss many subjects that will interest the ladies, such as 'The Difficulties of Nest-Building,' 'Trials of Young Mothers,' 'The Audubon Society,' etc."[22] The concept of birds as "citizens" in turn-of-the-century America emerges again and again in these writings, perhaps as a way for women to explore parallels in their own struggle to define their status in an increasingly complex, contested, and hierarchical society, even as the most obvious defining quality of citizenship—the vote—eluded them.[23]

In the late nineteenth century, ornithologists founded several clubs, reflecting the scientific community's efforts to standardize and professionalize. The American Ornithologists' Union (1883) in the Northeast, the Wilson Ornithological Club (1888) in the Midwest, and the Cooper Ornithological Club (1893) in the West were the most prominent examples.[24] In contrast to these scientific professional organizations, the Audubon clubs focused on appealing to and organizing the widest possible membership from all parts of society.

The current incarnation of the Audubon Society, named after the esteemed illustrator and naturalist John James Audubon, began in 1896 among a group of Boston's society women disgusted with millinery practices and the mass slaughter of birds, as described in popular magazines.[25] They organized with the express purpose of appealing to other women "to discourage the buying and wearing, for ornamental purposes, of feathers of wild birds, and to otherwise further the protection of native birds."[26] Unlike the first attempt at an Audubon Society, organized in New York City in 1886 by George Bird Grinnell, the women's efforts enjoyed long-term success, and chapters quickly formed in sixteen other states by the turn of the century and in an additional twenty states by the end of 1903.[27] In 1905 the state chapters collaborated to form the National Association of Audubon Societies (NAAS).

Where the earlier one had failed, this Audubon movement succeeded, in large part due to the enthusiastic reform climate of the progressive era. The vast female membership, their informal networking ability,

9. "Frank Chapman and His Legion of Women," Condor 3 (March 1901): 55.

and the organizing impulse of the era, along with its coalition of female ornithologists, amateur bird-watchers, schoolchildren, and clubwomen, all played crucial roles in the success of the Audubon movement. Unlike ornithology clubs, whose leadership was exclusively male, the state and local Audubon chapters' leadership split almost evenly between men and women.[28] The typical pattern was that women—already organized through a civic women's club—founded a chapter, then asked men to join the executive committee to provide professional ornithological expertise, or perhaps to lend their names to the cause for the extra prestige that male endorsement could provide. In California, as elsewhere, this often meant that a woman served as chapter secretary, performing the time-consuming grassroots organizing work, while a man took the honorific position of president.[29]

Women also appear to have comprised a notably high proportion of the membership rolls both in California and nationwide, sometimes close to 80 percent.[30] This model of male leadership and mass female participation was apparently so typical that it was spoofed in a cartoon in the California-based Cooper Ornithological Club's *Condor* magazine in 1901, entitled "Frank Chapman and His Legion of Women."[31] In the cartoon, the ornithologist Frank Chapman is depicted carrying several reference books and a large camera, and is followed by a phalanx of marching women chanting, holding conservation signs, and reprimanding young hunters. Here the distinction that conservationists drew between the male role of scientific expert and leader and the female role of sentimental follower, advocate, and moral guardian is made quite explicit.

The women's club influence was particularly important in organizing and staffing California's Audubon movement. For example, the Los Angeles Audubon Society, founded in 1910, branched out of local activities within the California Federation of Women's Clubs (CFWC) and maintained an all-female governing board, though their membership included men as well.[32] Many state and local women's clubs, along with the General Federation of Women's Clubs (GFWC), created committees devoted to protecting birds and other wildlife. The size of the GFWC, and its potential for conservation organizing, made it tremendously influential. According to the proceedings of the National Conservation Congress, in 1909 the GFWC claimed 800,000 members, and its membership grew to 2.5 million in 1917.[33] GFWC conservation committees and Audubon clubs advocated for bird protection through extensive direct action, such as civic work and public school outreach. In 1910 the GFWC reported 250 clubs nationwide performing bird-conservation work. California's entire public school system, and nearly a thousand cities and towns nationwide, celebrated Bird Day along with Arbor Day—a day on which citizens, especially children, paid special attention to the diversity and value of local birds and their habitats.[34]

One of the most active women's clubs in California, San Francisco's California Club, boasted members of considerable social and civic prominence, including Phoebe Hearst, Dr. Dorothea Moore, Mary McHenry Keith, Alice L. Park, and Catherine Hittell.[35] Keith, Park, and Hittell, in particular, combined their interests in wildlife protection with their club's political and social activities. These California Club members, ardent suffragists, expressed sentiments similar to those of the female nature writers whose anthropomorphization of birds revealed uncertainties about women's political status. In 1905, the year after the founding of the California Audubon Society, the California Club numbered almost five hundred members and created the position of an Audubon liaison.[36] These women explicitly linked their belief in women's social and political equality with an interest in animal rights and a commitment to work toward legislative victory even as they continued to agitate for their own right to vote. A brief look at their activities highlights the fluid dynamic between women's political culture and conservation during the progressive era.

Mary McHenry Keith, a Berkeley attorney and wife of the renowned California artist William Keith, remained active in both women's rights organizations and animal-protection groups throughout her life. Having received a law degree from the University of California, Mary Keith became one of California's first female attorneys. She was very active in political reform for women, including as a member of the California Woman Suffrage Association.[37] Beginning in 1900 she was also president of the Berkeley Political Equality Society, the California Equal Suffrage Association, and the Berkeley Women's City Club, in addition to being a member of the National American Women's Suffrage Association.[38] Along with holding these impressive suffrage credentials, Keith also devoted a large part of her public life to animal rights, particularly under the auspices of local chapters of the Humane Society, regarding which she kept an extensive scrapbook.[39] Keith made reference to the debates over "Women's Heartlessness" and the millinery trade in her scrapbook, writing, "my sympathies are aroused in behalf of that loveliest and most innocent part of creation. The Birds." She continued, "it is a question of some interest to social philosophers whether women are essentially cruel and heartless, or whether those qualities have been acquired in the struggle for beauty." Keith's humane work grew to include an affiliation with the California Audubon Society, once it was established in 1904; after seeing the Santa Cruz Audubon leader Josephine McCracken deliver a lecture entitled "Audubon Work," Keith encouraged the California Club to become extensively involved in the bird-protection cause.[40]

Alice L. Park was a prominent suffragist, pacifist, and reformer in California. She served as the recording secretary of the California Equal Suffrage Association, in which Keith was involved, and she maintained a decades-long involvement in the movement for women's political equality. As an active member of the California Club, Park, too, used her connections and reform impulse to aid in wildlife conservation. She attended the first meetings of Anna Head's Audubon Society in Berkeley, and promoted California's Bird and Arbor Day in local newspapers.[41] She brought these ideas back to the California Club in her committee position, and along with Catherine Hittell drafted protective legislation and organized a California Federation of Women's Clubs (CFWC) lobby of the state legislature on behalf of birds.[42]

Catherine H. Hittell was an especially well-connected figure in California society in the early twentieth century. The daughter of Theodore Henry Hittell, a famous Berkeley attorney and historian, she grew up in a San Francisco house that was a meeting place for a number of Bay Area artists, writers, feminists, politicians, conservationists, and reformers.[43] Hittell was one of the University of California's earliest female graduates, and described herself in her yearbook as "devoted to the emancipation of women."[44] Like Alice Park and Mary Keith, Hittell was active in Audubon work through her membership in the California Club and the CFWC. Hittell worked to gain statewide protection for the meadowlark and corresponded with John Muir, the famous California naturalist, about securing that bird's protection.[45] In the spring of 1895, the *San Francisco Examiner* interviewed her about her interest in bird conservation. She responded with a sensible appeal to the people of California to protect their natural treasures: "Why, apart from sentiment, it is a plain question of mathematics. . . . A meadow lark, cooked, gives one person pleasure for, at most, ten minutes. A living one gives pleasure to a whole community all its life long. It's a clear case of the greatest good to the greatest number."[46] Like women's efforts to preserve California's redwoods (discussed in chapter 7), women's activism in bird protection was motivated by the belief that birds served as a communal resource that required protection to ensure their future vitality. Hittell, like other members of the California Club, used her privileged position in Bay Area society to influence protective legislation and popular support.

The organized Audubon movement in California, as in much of the West, had a slow start as Audubon chapters and legislative activism spread from the northeastern core, mainly Massachusetts and New York, where state Audubon Societies had been organizing as early as the 1890s.[47] After a false start for a society in Redlands, a Santa Cruz Ladies' Forest and Songbird Protective Association formed in December 1900. In 1903 their leader, Josephine McCracken, contacted *Bird-Lore*, the official publication of the national Audubon organization, about their "project to organize bird-protective associations in different counties, with one state president," which they believed would be the best method of allying various groups across California.[48] Further, McCracken described the group's goal to awaken interest in nature education in public schools, exemplified by her work in writing individually to all 109 teachers in the vicinity of Santa Cruz. The initial response to her efforts was disappointing, however. She reported in the ornithology publication, *The Auk*, "the public schools evaded and avoided [our club], giving as a reason that the teachers were already overburdened with studies." It turned out, however, that the public school administrators had prevented the letters from reaching their teachers; knowing that many of the teachers were members of her Songbird Protective Association, McCracken reported that they would have been willing accomplices had they been notified. Her response was to initiate several alliances with local women's clubs, particularly in Santa Clara County, and work toward establishing a statewide Audubon organization the following year.[49]

The California Audubon Society (CAS) was established in Pasadena in 1904, under the leadership of Dr. Garrett Newkirk as president, W. Scott Way as secretary, and Josephine McCracken as their assistant.[50] Within its first couple years, the presidency of the CAS passed to David Starr Jordan, the president of Stanford University and a nationally prominent biologist.[51] Despite its late start, in only a few short months the California Audubon Society was a success and an exemplar to other states' societies. *Bird-Lore* indicated an initial membership of six hundred, with a strong showing at the first annual meeting.[52] The first issue for the CAS was the protection of the mourning dove, then a seriously endangered species in California, and this single-interest policy aided immensely the growth and success of the organization. By the end of 1904, the CAS had won passage of a series of laws, including an ordinance preventing the shooting of birds on public roads in Los Angeles County, the mandatory posting of hundreds of game law notices across the state, convictions of those violating existing local game laws, and a lobbying plan for stricter protective measures.[53] Such successes led the *Bird-Lore* editor Olive Thorne Miller to praise California for having "an active, aggressive and progressive society." Miller wrote, "such work is commended to some of the other [state] societies who seem somewhat lethargic."[54]

The CAS grew steadily through the early twentieth century. At the end of 1905, the second year of its organization, the CAS's adult membership exceeded eight hundred, and junior membership included more than five hundred; total membership had grown to more than three thousand by 1911.[55] In 1910 Harriet Williams Myers replaced W. Scott Way when he resigned his position as secretary; in this capacity Myers guided the CAS through a dynamic period of societal growth and legislative victories into the early 1920s. Furthermore, she encouraged the formation of local Audubon clubs in communities throughout California, including Pasadena, Garvanza, Berkeley, and Fresno.[56] The Ladies' Songbird Protective Society in Santa Cruz was still strong and under the leadership of Josephine McCracken. Humane Society chapters in San Diego and Corona listed Audubon secretaries affiliated with the CAS, and San Francisco and San Diego had each formed their own Audubon chapters by 1917.[57] A farmers' club in Glendora with a devotion to bird protection also joined the society, and the CAS indicated an interest in soliciting the support of more farm families. Fourteen chapters of the Junior Audubon Society reported an affiliation with municipal public schools, including seven in Pasadena and one each in Berkeley, Los Angeles, Chico, Glendora, San Pedro, Ranchito, and Montecito.[58] Throughout California, and nationally, organizers recruited teachers to Audubon work by inviting them to regional training facilities during summers. The State Normal School in Chico served as one such training site for Audubon teachers in California, and some educators spent part of their summer vacations meeting other conservationists and collecting curriculum materials from the CAS.[59]

Its female membership played a special role in strengthening the CAS and achieving many of its objectives. The 1907 *California Audubon Society Annual Report* demonstrated that, consistent with the national pattern, most of the leadership of the CAS was male, whereas the membership, in terms of affiliated societies, local chapters, and Junior Audubon Society organizers, was overwhelmingly female, including three all-female Audubon clubs out of ten statewide.[60] In addition, the San Bernardino Woman's Club and the California Club formally affiliated themselves with the CAS.[61] The California Federation of Women's Clubs, which claimed a membership of more than ten thousand women, officially joined the CAS after a lecture by Myers, the Audubon secretary, at their 1911 state convention.[62] The following year the CFWC began an "Audubon Page" in its official magazine, the *Federated Courier*, which circulated among California, Utah, and Nevada clubwomen and reported that "in this way the work of the [Audubon] Society reached thousands of women who otherwise would know nothing of it."[63] Myers's connection to the CFWC was especially productive and "brought [her] in close touch with the various clubs of the state and extended the bird-protective work." In 1915 she was appointed as the Federation's Commissioner of Birds and Wildlife, an office through which she lectured, dispersed educational materials, and organized legislative lobby groups.[64]

Due to their various efforts, California's Audubon activists achieved significant legislative victories throughout the progressive era and gained wide support among both politicians and the general public. The women who participated in these lobbying efforts engaged directly in the political arena both before and after the adoption of suffrage in California and nationally. Of course, gaining the vote in 1911 provided California women a degree of recognition and access to state government that had previously been denied to them, but the bird-protection movement did not depend upon enfranchisement to build or maintain its momentum. Progressive-era activists generally relied on methods outside of suffrage to enact reform. Consistent with these broader patterns, female conservationists sought to expand federal and state authority through a combination of public education, lobbying for legislation, and both unofficial and official enforcement. The passage of several laws protecting birds became the most obvious gauge of the tangible successes of the Audubon movement.

At the federal level the 1900 Lacey Act was the first significant piece of bird-protection legislation. This act curbed commercial hunting by prohibiting illegally acquired game and plumage from being shipped across state lines.⁶⁵ In 1913 the Weeks-McLean Act passed, making the federal government responsible for the protection of migratory birds that crossed state and international boundaries.⁶⁶ This act was bolstered in 1916 by the Migratory Bird Treaty between the United States and Canada, which, according to Kurk Dorsey, a diplomatic historian, "still ranks as one of the greatest triumphs of international wildlife protection" for any species and set an important precedent for government intervention into wildlife conservation.⁶⁷ In the critical years between the Lacey Act and the Migratory Bird Treaty, the Audubon clubs in California—spearheaded by California women—introduced myriad bills and molded a wide range of reform initiatives into state legislation that helped pave the way for these important national victories. In 1913 alone the Bureau of the Biological Survey reported that state governments had between four hundred and five hundred game bills under consideration nationwide; in California, the busiest of all states, advocates introduced ninety-three such bills.⁶⁸ Across the country, legislators enacted nearly two hundred of these bills, and Californians made several important gains.⁶⁹

The first piece of protective legislation in California was the 1901 Meadowlark Preservation Act, which made it illegal to kill meadowlarks. This bill was drafted by Catherine Hittell and Alice Park of the California Club. The historian of the CFWC claimed that this act marked the first time that a bill drafted by a women's club had become a state law in California.⁷⁰ Though it passed, this law faced significant opposition among farmers, particularly vintners, who complained that meadowlarks often sabotaged their crops, an accusation that the Audubon members contested. In each legislative session from 1901 to 1919, Audubon lobbyists defended the act against efforts to repeal it.⁷¹ The 1907 CAS *Annual Report* described the struggle to salvage this law: "When this movement [to repeal the act] was sprung in the Legislature, the Audubon Society issued a large edition of a special leaflet on the *food habits* and indisputable benefits of these birds to the farmer for circulation at Sacramento and for the information of farmers' organizations throughout the State."⁷² In preparation for the 1919 legislative session, California Audubon Society representatives spent two years collecting testimonials from farmers and ranchers as to the benefits of meadowlarks, blackbirds, and flickers to present to politicians and rural constituents. Due to the women's persistence, the Meadowlark

Preservation Act was never repealed in California, and in 1919, for the first time in nearly two decades, it did not face a serious challenge.[73]

Other non-game birds received particular attention in California. In 1905 the mourning dove gained legal protection, and in the same year California adopted the American Ornithologists' Union "Model Law," which prohibited the trapping or slaughter of wild non-game birds.[74] In response the CAS sent five thousand educational leaflets explaining the new law to teachers, game wardens, and farmers.[75] Unfortunately, the version of the Model Law enacted in California exempted shore birds, because plume hunters had lobbied for the economic importance of this feather trade. In 1913 the state legislature passed a bill to protect thirty-eight species of shore birds, but Governor Hiram Johnson vetoed the measure. Harriet Myers, the secretary of the CAS, reflected in *Bird-Lore*: "Just why the man posing as a conservationist should have vetoed so splendid a bill is still a mystery."[76] But in 1915 Audubon lobbyists overcame this obstacle with the Protection of Wading Birds Act.[77]

The California Audubon Society achieved a number of other important legislative victories before the end of World War I. In 1908 a law was passed that required permits for the scientific collection of birds and eggs, enforced by the State Fish and Game Commission.[78] Bird Day was officially established in California in 1909, in conjunction with the existing Arbor Day, and was observed at many public schools.[79] In 1912 a law established smaller, more enforceable game districts and created a schedule of open seasons based on nesting times as a way of making hunting less destructive to bird populations.[80] That same year, the Los Angeles Museum of Ornithology opened, revealing the extent of public interest and support that had developed around bird conservation.[81] Finally, in 1917 the state legislature passed the Baldwin Bird Law, making it a misdemeanor in California to possess or sell within the state the plumes or feathers of some of the most endangered birds, such as egrets, ospreys, and birds of paradise.[82] These legislative successes boosted the morale of Audubon members and protected California's bird population in tangible ways. In 1920 Harriet Myers wrote to *Bird-Lore*: "This past winter many rare bird visitants came freely into the village and visited our dooryards. May we [the CAS] not take some credit for this increase and familiarity of the birds?"[83]

These legislative victories demonstrated the strength of the Audubon activists' lobbying strategies and their seizure of an opportune political and cultural moment to enact both federal and state conservation legislation. After gaining the vote in California in 1911, female Audubon members continued their local activism, networking and lobbying in much the same ways that they had when building their movement from its inception. Without the years of local organizing that laid the foundation for public interest in bird protection, such political victories would not have been possible. Though often lost in the historical account and overshadowed by the more conspicuous legislative record, it was at the local club level—the Santa Cruz Ladies' Forest and Songbird Protection Association and San Francisco's California Club—that the majority of grassroots activity occurred. Through this nexus of women's networking and their gender and conservation ideologies, the strength of women's political culture in the progressive era becomes most apparent.

Carolyn Merchant, an environmental and gender historian, was one of the first scholars to recognize the centrality of women's role in early twentieth-century conservation, as demonstrated in her 1984 article, "Women of the Progressive Conservation Movement, 1900–1916." According to Merchant progressive women viewed environmental work as a natural outgrowth of their Victorian role as nurturers and protectors of the family. She provides a framework for understanding women's environmental ideology through "a trilogy of slogans—conservation of womanhood, the home, and the child."[84] The CAS and the NAAS consistently advocated strategies that exemplified this trilogy of conservation and illustrated women's broad understanding of environmental protection at this time. These women crafted a wide-ranging definition of conservation, combining their interest in bird protection with their political agendas, domestic lives, and children's welfare.[85] Yet, at the same time, a paradox developed around women's devotion to environmental activities; though their interest in bird protection mirrored contemporary gender roles, devotion to conservation brought clubwomen into local, state, and even international politics through their attempts to regulate and protect birdlife.

The appeal to an idealized notion of womanhood was logical, given the nature of the problem. In California, as elsewhere, birds were being slaughtered in alarming and increasing numbers due in largest part to the millinery trade, in which women were the most obvious consumers, producers (as milliners), and supporters. Early Audubon members and nature writers recognized this connection and appealed to women to exercise their "natural" tendency toward mercy, virtue, and good taste in essays such as "Woman's Heartlessness" and "Murderous Millinery."[86] The 1906 Audubon report also focused on women in their pleas for bird protection: "For women, birds were killed, that their plumage might be worn as an ornament—not a necessary article of clothing, but something entirely superfluous."[87]

The NAAS appealed to women in their role as consumers by issuing a "Milliner's White List," which was a list of "firms prepared to forgo feather trim entirely."[88] The tactic of the white list was borrowed from another female-dominated progressive organization, the Consumers' League, which introduced its list of labor law–compliant factories in 1891 in New York City, even before the league became a national organization. The NAAS used this strategy as a positive alternative to the blacklist, researching and rewarding milliners who adhered to the Audubon Society's moratorium on feather decorations.[89] In addition, the Audubon Society enticed its female members with the design of its own feather-free hat, decorated with ribbons and artificial flowers rather than plumage. The hat became affectionately known as the "Audu-bonnet."[90] In California such benign hat decorations were advocated as early as the 1890s to prevent women from striving toward what the *Examiner* called "the utmost limits of their barbaric instincts."[91]

Women involved in Audubon work also made economy-driven arguments and used the ideology of domesticity and women's homemaking responsibilities to bolster support for the protection of birds. They argued, as did many male ornithologists at the time, that birds ate harmful insects that would otherwise destroy precious crops and wreak havoc on the incomes of farm families. Pamphlets used in Audubon education in California emphasized this pragmatic relationship between birds and people: "A reasonable way of viewing the relation of birds to the farmer is to consider the birds as servants, employed to destroy weeds and insects. In return for this service, they should be protected, and such as need it should receive a fair equivalent in the shape of fruit and small grain."[92] Such pamphlets directed at California farm families attempted to stop farmers from agitating against protective legislation by arguing that such sentiments went against their own self-interest.

Conservationists in California capitalized on the advantages of preserving insectivorous birds to win important support from rural families, and this tactic became especially effective during the mobilization for World War I. According to Kurk Dorsey, "with American entry into World War I, bird protection became a war measure; conservationists claimed that the 'winged squads of workmen' deserved protection while guarding crops from insect hordes."[93] The CAS, in association with the CFWC, issued a wartime bulletin to its members, with articles connecting the work of birds to the war effort, such as "Birds and Food Conservation." Audubon members also worried that the "spirit of the war" might encourage boys to start shooting birds, regardless of new legal restrictions, emulating the soldiers fighting abroad. The CAS acted immediately to educate youth and display posters in public areas warning against shooting birds illegally.[94] At the same time, the Los Angeles chapter, under the direction of Carrie Elizabeth Fargo (Mrs. F. T.) Bicknell and an entirely female executive board, asserted its patriotism and support for the war by creating a war committee with ten-dollar lifetime membership dues and using this income to purchase Liberty Bonds.[95] While the CAS indicated that its social activities suffered during the war, its educational work remained in full force.[96] Even after the war had ended, the CAS used the same rhetoric of patriotism to advocate for the utility of birds. In an essay entitled "How the Birds Helped Win the War," the author credited the birds for helping "save food for the Allies." This essay taught students in California's public schools that by 1920 the battle was no longer against women's vanity but more pressingly against the Germans and the Bolsheviks, including such domestic labor radicals as the Industrial Workers of the World.[97]

Finally, the NAAS and CAS both spent considerable resources and energy to involve children, and this became the area of greatest achievement for the Audubon clubs in California. To encourage children to join, adult Audubon members produced educational leaflets, children's books, and school activities to engage young people in the study of birds.[98] Women's work with children took on a primary importance because it was believed that if children became bird lovers at a young age, they would not mistreat birds as adults, and the problems of endangerment would gradually disappear.

William Dutcher, an ornithologist, articulated this philosophy in 1896 when he stated, "When we have educated our children, laws will become unnecessary."[99] The NAAS also regarded the involvement of children as "a subject ranking with legislation, reservations, or the [game] warden system" and strove to organize millions of young people into Bird Clubs or Junior Audubon Societies.[100]

In California various CAS chapters actively recruited junior members. The Berkeley chapter was especially engaged in work with schoolchildren. Anna Head, a clubwoman and educator, organized the Berkeley chapter in 1905, then quickly organized and led a junior branch at "Miss Anna Head's School."[101] Another successful chapter was the Los Angeles Audubon Society, established in March 1910 and affiliated from its inception with the CFWC.[102] This chapter, led by Carrie Bicknell, grew to more than one hundred members in 1919 and exerted a large influence citywide. Focusing on children's education through library work and field trips, it organized a bird-protection exhibit at the public library that attracted two thousand attendees.[103] Most strikingly, the CAS created the position of a full-time Audubon school secretary and hired Gretchen Libby, who spent her time visiting schools around California, where she lectured teachers on how to include bird study in their curricula and engage students in bird-related activities.[104] Activities for young people included field trips and the hands-on scientific observation of birdlife, in addition to nature writing and art projects.[105] Libby was a dedicated and productive worker: within her first seven months, she gave 230 bird talks at seventy-two schools, reaching twelve thousand children and seventeen hundred adults. Because of her efforts, forty-six new chapters of the Junior Audubon Society were formed in 1911 alone.[106]

In 1910 California established Bird Day in conjunction with the quarter-century-old tradition of Arbor Day as an annual celebration in public schools on March 7. As the CAS secretary Harriet Myers explained, Bird Day was to be observed "not as a holiday, but by including in the school work suitable exercises and instruction of the value of birds and trees, and the promotion of the spirit of protection toward them."[107] In honor of Bird and Arbor Day (sometimes called Conservation Day), the superintendent of California's public schools, Edward Hyatt, issued a series of booklets to be handed out in classrooms to facilitate the study of birds and forests. These publications contained such didactic stories as "The Bird Is Our Brother," "The Balance of Nature," and "Why We Have State Laws Protecting Birds and Animals."[108] Teachers instructed children to recite these essays in class, taught them to make birdhouses and feeders, took them on outings on school grounds, and engaged them in other nature-based activities. Most importantly, the booklets attempted to convince children that birds should be enjoyed and protected rather than killed for sport. They taught children to have compassion for birds and to see the intrinsic value of preserving wildlife. These booklets listed several reasons birds should be protected, including their beauty, interesting behavior, and significance in "the fundamental laws of nature," in addition to their economic value to the farmer and their spiritual value to the urban worker.[109] Through women's work, Audubon teachers and the public school system demonstrated a commitment to bird protection and invoked a progressive rhetoric of conservation, efficiency, the common good, and a back-to-nature campaign in their appeals to children and their families.

The history of conservation in the late nineteenth- and early twentieth-century United States typically emphasizes the accomplishments and ideologies of such leaders as Theodore Roosevelt, Gifford Pinchot, and John Muir. This view obscures the years of grassroots activism occurring at the local level, often generated by women reformers. Organized bird protection, both nationally and in California, illuminates these hidden layers of progressive era conservation history. Viewing themselves as particularly sensitive to the plight of the less fortunate, progressive club-women positioned themselves at the community level of the conservation movement, just as they did with urban reform, peace, suffrage, and other contemporary social issues. At the same time, a movement to embrace the natural world as an antidote to the modern, industrialized urban landscape made wildlife protection a central concern for progressives in general. It was this confluence of the massive organizational structure of women's clubs, the simultaneous popularization of amateur ornithology, and contemporary conservation ideologies that enabled the prominence and success of the bird-protection cause. Women's voluntary associations provided the infrastructure for the outreach and education necessary to achieve legislative victories—well before suffrage offered an additional formalized method for women to assert their political beliefs. Through their extensive networks, clubwomen could circumvent such initially resistant institutional bureaucracies as the public school system and the state legislature.

Although the Audubon movement in California had a late start compared to that of the Northeast, it scored an impressive series of successes between the turn of the century and World War I, just at the time when the suffrage movement was reaching its fullest development and various reform efforts were drawing women more deeply into public life. Audubon women communicated with government representatives, arranged public speakers, circulated informational pamphlets to politicians and the general public, posted and vigorously enforced hunting regulations in their communities, and attempted in other ways to educate the public about local and statewide protective laws won through their exhaustive lobbying efforts. California women also wrote popular literature about birds, initiated education programs in schools, and organized Junior Audubon clubs to ensure that future generations would be knowledgeable about and sympathetic to bird protection. In these and other ways, California women engaged deeply in all kinds of civic activities, demonstrating truly broad definitions of conservation and of women's political culture at this time.

The bird-protection movement could not have emerged without the expertise and leadership of male scientists, administrators, and legislators, but women's work was crucial to its success. Margaret T. Olmstead, a prominent clubwoman, expressed the centrality of female activism when she referred to "the law and the lady . . . 'standing with locked hands to form a twentieth century alliance in the cause of bird protection as they have so often done.'"[110] As the historian Carolyn Merchant has demonstrated, women stood at the center of progressive environmental reform, shaping policies with an eye toward the power and responsibilities of organized womanhood. The bird-protection movement demanded a broad understanding of local activism that women used in tandem with their civic organizations to redefine California's and the nation's environmental policies. As Americans entered the twentieth century, such activism permanently linked conservation with grassroots mobilization and progressive political reform, leaving a rich and complicated legacy for modern environmentalists.

Notes

1. Peter J. Schmitt, *Back To Nature: The Arcadian Myth in Urban America* (New York: Oxford University Press, 1969), 41. On tensions between hunting and conservation, see also Louis S. Warren, *The Hunter's Game: Poachers and Conservationists in Twentieth Century America* (New Haven CT: Yale University Press, 1997); and Karl Jacoby, *Crimes Against Nature: Squatters, Poachers, Thieves, and the Hidden History of American Conservation* (Berkeley: University of California Press, 2001).

2. Jennifer Price, "When Women Were Women, Men Were Men, and Birds Were Hats," in *Flight Maps: Adventures with Nature in Modern America* (New York: Basic Books, 1999), 75–76.

3. Wendy Gamber, *The Female Economy: The Millinery and Dressmaking Trades, 1860–1930* (Urbana: University of Illinois Press, 1997), 97, 105.

4. Robin W. Doughty, *Feather Fashions and Bird Preservation: A Study in Nature Protection* (Berkeley: University of California Press, 1975), 20–22.

5. Deborah Strom, ed., *Birdwatching with American Women: A Selection of Nature Writings* (New York: W. W. Norton, 1986), xi–xii; and Price, "When Women Were Women," 57–58.

6. Joel A. Allen, "The Present Wholesale Destruction of Bird-Life in the United States," *Science* (Supplement), February 26, 1886, 194. For a more recent estimate, see Joseph Kastner, "Long before Furs, It Was Feathers That Stirred Reformist Ire," *Smithsonian*, July 1994, 97.

7. Samuel P. Hays, *Conservation and the Gospel of Efficiency: The Progressive Conservation Movement, 1890–1920* (Cambridge MA: Harvard University Press, 1959); Roderick Frazier Nash, *Wilderness and the American Mind* (New Haven CT: Yale University Press, 1967). See also, for example, Donald Worster, ed., *American Environmentalism: The Formative Period, 1860–1915* (New York: Wiley, 1973); Carolyn Merchant, "Women of the Progressive Conservation Movement, 1900–1916," *Environmental Review* 8 (Spring 1984): 57–83; Stephen Fox, *The American Conservation Movement: John Muir and His Legacy* (Madison: University of Wisconsin Press, 1985); and Richard A. Walker, *The Country in the City: The Greening of the San Francisco Bay Area* (Seattle: University of Washington Press, 2007).

8. Schmitt, *Back to Nature*. See also Paul S. Boyer, *Urban Masses and Moral Order in America, 1820–1930* (Cambridge MA: Harvard University Press, 1978); T. J. Jackson Lears, *No Place of Grace: Antimodernism and the Transformation of American Culture, 1880–1920* (Chicago: University of Chicago Press, 1981); and Roy Rosenzweig and Elizabeth Blackmar, *The Park and the People: A History of Central Park* (Ithaca NY: Cornell University Press, 1992).

9. Doughty, *Feather Fashions*, 40.

10. Mark V. Barrow Jr., *A Passion for Birds; American Ornithology after Audubon* (Princeton NJ: Princeton University Press, 1988), 127. See also "Report of the National Association of Audubon Societies," *Bird-Lore* 7, no. 1 (1905): 45–46.

11. "Tom Dunlap on Early Bird Guides," *Environmental History* 10, no. 1 (January 2005): 110.

12. Ralph H. Lutts, *The Nature Fakers: Wildlife, Science, and Sentiment* (Golden CO: Fulcrum, 1990), 31; and Paul Brooks, "Birds and Women," *Audubon* 82, no. 5 (September 1980): 88–97.

13. T. Gilbert Pearson, "Fifty Years of Bird Protection in the United States," in *Fifty Years' Progress of American Ornithology, 1883–1933* (Lancaster PA: American Ornithologists' Union, 1939), 204.

14. Elizabeth Donaldson, "The Egg and the Nest: Gender Politics, John Burroughs, and Popular Ornithology," in *Sharp Eyes: John Burroughs and American Nature Writing*, ed. Charlotte Zoë Walker (Syracuse NY: Syracuse University Press, 2000), 178–91; and Schmitt, *Back to Nature*, 36–37.

15. Anna Head, "Nesting of the Ruby-Crowned Kinglet," *Bird-Lore* 5, no. 2 (1903): 53.

16. Anna Head, "Nesting Habits of Two Flycatchers at Lake Tahoe," *Bird-Lore* 5, no. 5 (1903): 154–55.

17. Mabel Osgood Wright and Elliott Coues, illus. Louis Aggasiz Fuertes, *Citizen Bird: Scenes from Bird-Life in Plain English for Beginners* (New York: Macmillan, 1897), 272.

18. Kevin C. Armitage, "Bird Day for Kids: Progressive Conservation in Theory and Practice," *Environmental History* 12, no. 3 (July 2007): 530–31.

19. Wright and Coues, *Citizen Bird*.

20. Head, "Ruby-Crowned Kinglet," 53.

21. Harriet Williams Myers, *The Birds' Convention* (Los Angeles: Western Publishing, 1913), 69–70.

22. Myers, *Birds' Convention*, 7.

23. See, e.g., Olive Thorne Miller, *Little Folks in Feathers and Fur, and Others in Neither* (New York: E. P. Dutton, 1879); Florence A. Merriam, *Birds through an Opera-Glass* (Boston: Houghton Mifflin, 1889); Florence Merriam Bailey, *Handbook of Birds of the Western United States* (Boston: Houghton Mifflin, 1902); Olive Thorne Miller, *The Bird Our Brother: A Contribution to the Study of the Bird as He Is in Life* (New York: Houghton, Mifflin, 1908); Mabel Osgood Wright, *Gray Lady and the Birds: Stories of the Bird Year for Home and School* (New York: MacMillan, 1914); Neltje Blanchan, *Birds Worth Knowing* (Garden City NY: Doubleday, Page, 1917); Gene Stratton Porter, *Homing with the Birds* (Garden City NY: Doubleday, Page, 1919); and Florence Merriam Bailey, *Birds of New Mexico* (New Mexico Department of Fish and Game, 1928).

24. See Theodore S. Palmer, "A Brief History of the American Ornithologists' Union," in *Fifty Years' Progress*, 7; and Barrow, *Passion for Birds*, 46, 69–70. For an

analysis of the exclusion of women from scientific organizations in this period, see Margaret W. Rossiter, "'Women's Work' in Science, 1880–1910" *Isis* 71, no. 258 (1980): 287–304.

25. "History of the Audubon Movement," *Bird-Lore* 7, no. 1 (1905): 45–57. See also John H. Mitchell, "The Mothers of Conservation," *Sanctuary* (January-February, 1996), 3–5; and Kathy S. Mason, "Out of Fashion: Harriet Hemenway and the Audubon Society, 1896–1905," *Historian* 65, no. 1 (2002): 1–14.

26. Quoted in Barrow, *A Passion for Birds*, 127.

27. "Annual Report of the National Association of Audubon Societies for 1905," *Bird-Lore* 7, no. 6 (1906): 297. On the founding of the first Audubon Society in 1886, see *Audubon Magazine* 1, no. 1 (1887). It attracted a large membership, but dissolved in 1895 along with the *Audubon Magazine* due to a lack of organizational structure. See "Report of the National Association of Audubon Societies," *Bird-Lore* 7, no. 1 (1905): 55–56.

28. Price, "When Women Were Women," 63–64; and Kastner, "Long before Furs," 100.

29. Price, "When Women Were Women," 64.

30. Price, "When Women Were Women," 62–64.

31. "Frank Chapman and His Legion of Women," cartoon, *Condor* 3 (March 1901): 55.

32. "Report of the State Societies and Bird Clubs: Los Angeles Audubon Society," *Bird-Lore* 18, no. 6 (1916): 471; and *Bird-Lore* 20, no. 6 (1918): 494.

33. Mrs. Overton G. Ellis, "The General Federation of Women's Clubs in Conservation Work," *Address and Proceedings of the National Conservation Congress Held in Seattle, Washington, August 26–28, 1909* (Washington DC: National Conservation Congress, 1910), 157; and Mrs. John Dickinson [Mary K.] Sherman, "Women's Part in National Parks Development," *Proceedings of the National Parks Conference*, vol. 4 (Washington DC: Government Printing Office, 1917), 45.

34. Lydia Adams-Williams, "Woman's Work for Conservation: Notes from the Biennial of the General Federation of Women's Clubs," *American Forestry* 16 (June 1910): 344; and Edward Hyatt, *Bird and Arbor Day for 1911 in the Schools of California* (Sacramento CA: W. W. Shannon, 1911). For a historical analysis of the ways Bird Day typified progressive era reform, see Armitage, "Bird Day for Kids."

35. *Club Women of California: Official Directory and Register*, 1907 (San Francisco: California Federation of Women's Clubs, 1907), 17–23.

36. "State Reports: California," *Bird-Lore* 7, no. 1 (1905): 76.

37. Program, Annual Convention of the California Woman Suffrage Association, October 24–25, 1902. Keith-McHenry-Pond Family Papers, container 3, Bancroft Library, University of California, Berkeley (hereafter "KMP Papers").

38. Letters and Membership Certificates, n.d., KMP Papers, container 3.

39. Scrapbook, n.d., KMP Papers, Container 3. Regarding the Keith family,

including Mary's life, activities, and suffrage work, see Brother Cornelius, Keith: Old Master of California (New York: G. P. Putnam's, 1942).

40. Scrapbook, n.d., KMP Papers, Container 3.

41. Clipping, The Upland News, October 11, 1946; and Notecard, n.d., KMP Papers, Container 3.

42. Mary S. Gibson, A Record of Twenty-Five Years of the California Federation of Women's Clubs (Los Angeles: California Federation of Women's Clubs, 1927), 173.

43. Edan M. Hughes, Artists in California, 1786–1940 (San Francisco: Hughes, 1986), 216.

44. Junior Class of the University of California at Berkeley, The Blue and Gold 1886 (Berkeley: Pacific Press, 1886), 132. For more on Hittell and her connections to the Keiths, suffrage work, and the art world, see Cornelius, Keith: Old Master of California.

45. Letters, John Muir to Catherine Hittell, April 1895, reprinted in "Victorians and Meadowlarks: Two Muir Letters Rediscovered," John Muir Newsletter 1, no. 4 (Fall 1991): 3–4.

46. Clipping, San Francisco Examiner, 1895, reprinted in "Victorians and Meadowlarks," 3.

47. "Report of the National Association of Audubon Societies," Bird-Lore 7, no. 1 (1905): 47, 56–57.

48. "Report of Societies: California," Bird-Lore 5, no. 5 (1903): 173.

49. "Report of Committee on Bird Protection," The Auk 21 (January 1904): 112–13.

50. "Upon the Necessity of Accuracy," Bird-Lore 6, no. 3 (1904): 104, 108.

51. See "Well-Known Men Organize a State Audubon Society," San Francisco Call, June 2, 1906, 8; and "Notes and News," Condor 6 (September-October 1904): 141.

52. "National Committee Notes," Bird-Lore 6, no. 5 (1904): 175; and "First Annual Meeting of the California Audubon Society," Bird-Lore 6, no. 6 (1904): 214.

53. "First Annual Meeting," Bird-Lore, 214.

54. "National Committee Notes," Bird-Lore 6, no. 5 (1904): 175.

55. "State Audubon Reports: California," Bird-Lore 10, no. 6 (1908): 296–97; and "State Audubon Reports: California," Bird-Lore 12, no. 6 (1911): 284.

56. California Audubon Society Annual Report, 1907 (Sacramento CA: California Audubon Society, 1907). Daniel E. Koshland History Center, San Francisco Public Library (hereafter cited as CAS Annual Report, 1907).

57. "Reports of State Societies: California Audubon Society," Bird-Lore 19, no. 6 (1917): 437.

58. CAS Annual Report, 1907, 5.

59. See "Open Letter to Teachers," n.d., C. Hart Merriam Papers, Reel 167, Bancroft Library, University of California, Berkeley.

60. CAS Annual Report, 1907, 4–7.
61. CAS Annual Report, 1907, 5–6.
62. "State Audubon Reports: California," Bird-Lore 12, no. 6 (1911): 284. Regarding the CFWC membership, see Gayle Gullett, *Becoming Citizens: The Emergence and Development of the California Women's Movement, 1880–1911* (Urbana: University of Illinois Press, 2000), 117.
63. "Reports of State Societies: California," Bird-Lore 14, no. 6 (1912): 428.
64. "Reports of State Societies, and of Bird Clubs: California," Bird-Lore 17, no. 6 (1915): 510.
65. *Congressional Record: Containing the Proceedings and Debates of the Fifty-Sixth Congress, First Session*, vol. 33 (Washington DC: Government Printing Office, 1900), 3603. For a legal and diplomatic history of bird protection, see Kurk Dorsey, "Scientists, Citizens, and Statesmen: U.S.–Canadian Wildlife Protection Treaties in the Progressive Era," *Diplomatic History* 19, no. 3 (Summer 1995): 423. See also Clarence M. Weed and Ned Dearborn, *Birds in Their Relation to Man: A Manual of Economic Ornithology for the United States and Canada*, 3rd ed. (Philadelphia: J. B. Lippincott, 1924), 341–43; and Barrow, *Passion for Birds*, 133.
66. *United States Statutes at Large*, vol. 38, part 1, chap. 16 (Washington DC: Government Printing Office, 1913), 148. See also Dorsey, "Scientists, Citizens, and Statesmen," 423; and "Migratory Bird Laws Are Now in Effect," *San Francisco Examiner*, October 5, 1913, p. 41.
67. Dorsey, "Scientists, Citizens, and Statesmen," 422, 427. See also "Migratory Bird Law in Effect," *San Francisco Examiner*, September 15, 1916, p. 17; "Water Fowl to Be Protected," *San Francisco Chronicle*, October 14, 1917, p. 3; and "Sweeping Changes in Game Laws Are Made," *San Francisco Examiner*, August 9, 1918, p. 6.
68. "Notes and News," *The Auk* 30 (April 1913): 321.
69. "Notes and News," *The Auk* 31 (January 1914): 143, 145.
70. Gibson, *Record of Twenty-Five Years*, 12, 173.
71. "Reports of Affiliated State Societies and of Bird Clubs: California Audubon Societies," Bird-Lore 19, no. 6 (1917): 436; "Reports of Affiliated State Societies and of Bird Clubs: California Audubon Societies," Bird-Lore 21, no. 6 (1919): 420; and "The Meadowlark," *San Francisco Chronicle*, February 13, 1909, p. 18.
72. CAS Annual Report, 1907, 12.
73. "Reports of Affiliated State Societies and of Bird Clubs: California Audubon Societies," Bird-Lore 21, no. 6 (1919): 420.
74. "State Reports: California," Bird-Lore 7, no. 1 (1906): 76; and "State Reports: California," Bird-Lore 7, no. 6 (1906): 311.
75. "State Reports: California," Bird-Lore, 311.
76. "State Reports: California," Bird-Lore 15, no. 6 (1913): 441–42.
77. "Reports of State Societies, and of Bird Clubs: California," Bird-Lore 17, no. 6 (1915): 510.

78. "State Audubon Reports: California," *Bird-Lore* 10, no. 6 (1909): 296.

79. "State Audubon Reports: California," *Bird-Lore* 11, no. 6 (1910): 308; and Gibson, *Record of Twenty-Five Years*, 173.

80. "State Audubon Reports: California," *Bird-Lore* 13, no. 6 (1912): 363.

81. "Reports of State Societies: California," *Bird-Lore* 14, no. 6 (1912): 427.

82. "Baldwin Bird Law in Effect Tomorrow," *San Francisco Chronicle*, October 31, 1917, 4.

83. "Reports of Affiliated State Societies and Bird Clubs: California," *Bird-Lore* 22, no. 6 (1920): 400.

84. Merchant, "Women of the Progressive Conservation Movement," 73.

85. See, for example, "Audubon Club Reports Work," *San Francisco Examiner*, February 3, 1918, N9.

86. See Celia Thaxter, "Woman's Heartlessness," *Audubon Magazine* 1, no. 1 (1887): 13–14; and "Murderous Millinery," *Living Age* 251 (December 8, 1906): 636.

87. "Annual Report of the National Association of Audubon Societies for 1905," *Bird-Lore* 7, no. 6 (1906): 308.

88. "An Addition to the White List," *Bird-Lore* 4, no. 1 (1902): 40; and Doughty, *Feather Fashions*, 149.

89. For more on the origins of the white list as a strategy, see Kathryn Kish Sklar, "The Consumers' White Label Campaign of the National Consumers' League, 1898–1918," in *Getting and Spending: European and American Consumer Societies in the Twentieth Century*, ed. Susan Strasser, Charles McGovern, and Matthias Judt (Washington DC: Cambridge University Press, 1988), 17–35.

90. Margaret T. Olmstead, "The Preservation of Birds," *The Club Woman* 8 (August 1901): 155.

91. Clipping, *San Francisco Examiner*, 1895, reprinted in "Victorians and Meadowlarks," 3.

92. Hyatt, *Bird and Arbor Day for 1911*, 6. See also *Bird-Lore* 21, no. 6 (1919), 420.

93. Dorsey, "Scientists, Citizens, and Statesmen," 426.

94. "Reports of Affiliated State Societies and of Bird Clubs: California," *Bird-Lore* 20, no. 6 (1918): 472.

95. "Reports of Affiliated State Societies," 494–95.

96. "Reports of Affiliated State Societies," 472.

97. M. M. Reynolds, "How the Birds Helped Win the War," in *Conservation, Bird, and Arbor Day in California, 1920* (Sacramento CA: W. W. Shannon, 1920), 15–16.

98. Pearson, "Fifty Years of Bird Protection," 206.

99. William Dutcher quoted in Barrow, *A Passion for Birds*, 130.

100. "Annual Report of the National Association of Audubon Societies for 1905," *Bird-Lore* 7, no. 6 (1906): 308.

101. CAS *Annual Report*, 1907, 5, 7; and "State Reports: California," *Bird-Lore* 7, no. 1 (1905): 75.

102. "Reports of State Societies and Bird Clubs: Los Angeles Audubon Society," *Bird-Lore* 18, no. 6 (1916): 471. See also "Reports of Affiliated State Societies and of Bird Clubs: California," *Bird-Lore* 20, no. 6 (1918): 472.

103. "Reports of Affiliated State Societies and of Bird Clubs: Los Angeles Audubon Society," *Bird-Lore* 20, no. 6 (1918): 493–95; and "Reports of Affiliated State Societies and of Bird Clubs: Los Angeles Audubon Society," *Bird-Lore* 21, no. 6 (1919): 439.

104. "State Audubon Reports: California," *Bird-Lore* 12, no. 6 (1911): 284.

105. Barrow, *A Passion for Birds*, 130.

106. "State Audubon Reports: California," *Bird-Lore* 12, no. 6 (1911): 284.

107. "State Audubon Reports: California," *Bird-Lore* 11, no. 6 (1910): 307–8.

108. Edward Hyatt, *Arbor Day in California*, 1914 (Sacramento CA: W. W. Shannon, 1914), 8; and Edward Hyatt, *Conservation, Bird, and Arbor Day in California*, 1916 (Sacramento CA: W. W. Shannon, 1916), 5, 13. On the tensions between the scientific and sentimental messages of Bird Day literature, see Armitage, "Bird Day for Kids," 534–39.

109. Hyatt, *Conservation, Bird, and Arbor Day in California*, 1916, 13.

110. Olmstead, "Preservation of Birds," 156.

7. SAVING REDWOODS
Clubwomen and Conservation, 1900–1925

CAMERON BINKLEY

On January 17, 1900, delegates from women's civic associations from around California converged at the Ebell clubhouse in Los Angeles. Their meeting was organized by the prominent women's club leader, Clara Bradley Burdette, and on that date they founded the California Federation of Women's Clubs (CFWC). Since assuming the presidency of the Ebell club in 1898, the ambitious Burdette had worked tirelessly to bring together a union of the state's growing list of women's clubs.[1] As she retold it, the event was brought about by "progressive, thoughtful women, who had come into the fullness of life through the one law of greatness—'greatness by service and greatness for service.'"[2] Be that as it may, the delegates to Burdette's meeting were drawn together by specific concerns, common cause, and a deep intent to promote their views and effect change. Burdette offered two immediate projects that the new federation would facilitate. First, she called upon women to improve children's welfare through educational reform. Second, and no less important, she appealed to women to cooperate to help protect "our world famous Sequoias" from "men whose souls are gang-saws." In other words, she sought to mobilize women by harnessing their desire to improve their children's potential and by urging women to cooperate in restraining the excesses of an industry that was turning the state's great redwood trees "into planks and fencing worth so many dollars."[3]

Burdette was persuasive. The gathered clubs unanimously adopted her agenda, elected her to be the CFWC's first president, elected other statewide officers, drafted a charter and bylaws, and resolved immediately to ally themselves with the national General Federation of Women's Clubs (GFWC). By the end of the year, the CFWC represented one of the national organization's largest affiliates, with sixty-one associated clubs of some six thousand members.[4]

Burdette was an astute observer of politics. She later contended with Sarah Platt Decker of Colorado for the presidency of the GFWC and served with distinction in several high-level positions in that organization. During World War I she managed California's food-conservation program, which brought her to the attention of Herbert Hoover, who later asked her to run his presidential campaign in California. Certainly, Burdette understood the utility of coordinating women's efforts through linked associations or federations. Numerous other states in the East and the West had already been federated, but two previous attempts had failed to organize the women of California on a similar basis. Sheer geographic breadth was a major reason for the delay, a challenge Burdette met by grouping the state's women into districts, each of which elected its own vice-president.[5]

The main reason Burdette succeeded in organizing the CFWC, however, was that she understood her constituents. Burdette had toured the state to sound out issues of common concern and had shrewdly allied herself with influential northerners—most importantly, Laura White, the wife of a wealthy San Francisco financier. White had founded the California Club, the largest and probably most influential women's civic society in the San Francisco Bay Area. It was a trendsetter in championing children's causes and also in espousing the desire, as early as 1898, to cooperate with others to protect California's redwoods from logging.[6] After Burdette was elected CFWC president, it was not a coincidence that White was next elected to the CFWC's second-highest post, vice-president at large. Hence, by including children and redwoods in her plans to federate the state, Burdette secured the support of the California Club, which helped bind the state's northern and southern clubs, and she found two statewide issues that middle- and upper-class clubwomen could generally support with unproblematic passion.

The creation of the CFWC in 1900 was a benchmark for the rising political power of California's women. Nature preservation, known to early proponents as "forestry" and later as "conservation," was a major factor that aided women's mobilization. To understand why, one must consider the basis of club values and how these related to conservation. First, women were attracted to the club movement because its leaders—Clara Burdette, Laura White, and others—espoused a commitment to one of the major social constructions of the era—the notion that men and women belonged in separate spheres and that respectable middle- and upper-class ladies restricted their role in society to that of mothers and homemakers. This domestic ideal was not the end of the story, however. In fact, by tailoring their public rhetoric and civic activities to conform with the strictures of domesticity, clubwomen expanded women's influence far beyond the home. As Burdette said, "Home must always be the center, not the limit, of woman's life."[7] This fundamental viewpoint brought women together for a common cause. It allowed them to advance their interests in the public sphere by claiming a special right to speak and act on issues that related to areas of women's expertise, especially children, but also on more general issues where community or family life were concerned. Second, clubwomen explicitly disavowed an interest in politics, in commercial activities, and in suffrage advocacy (until suffrage became a mainstream issue). They purposely sought to avoid controversy or to invade areas, namely politics and commerce, widely considered male-only domains. Third, nineteenth-century society encouraged women's interest in art, literature, music, and nature appreciation (which focused upon such things as gardening but which permitted the study of landscape architecture and amateur botany). Indeed, many women's civic clubs first arose from women's literary associations, which marked them as institutions of the middle and upper classes, that is, educated women who had some time for leisure.[8]

Conservation related well to these values, because it was a term that held various shades of meaning. Gifford Pinchot, the famous American forester, had tried to limit the meaning of conservation to something like the efficient management of natural resources in order to obtain a maximum value for their use. Pinchot's formulation was largely an economic argument of interest to scientists and government bureaucrats who hoped to promote the nation's commercial growth.[9] Clubwomen, however, interpreted conservation through a domestic lens.[10] They argued that homes and communities were threatened by the reckless destruction of forests. Development in the arid West was tied closely to the availability of water. Forests protected watersheds by absorbing and storing moisture and preventing the erosion of topsoil. Thus, conservation was about protecting homes, farms, and community life. Society granted women permission to be concerned with community health, if not business activity per se. Moreover, women downplayed their interest in the economics of conservation and generally deferred to men on either side of the issue to debate the tourist potential of nature parks or the commercial harm imposed by logging restrictions. Instead, clubwomen focused upon the aesthetics of saving beautiful natural settings, the avarice of unrestricted logging, and what was good for the community overall. Clubwomen were well acquainted with the Romantic nature literature of Henry David Thoreau, Ralph Waldo Emerson, John Muir, and others. They exploited their society's encouraging attitude toward women's interest in literature and nature, the expectation of feminine nurturing, and a deferential attitude toward men. Thus, when women couched their nature leanings in terms of the need to provide opportunities for healthy, morally uplifting, clean-cut outdoor recreation to benefit (and educate) children and future generations of children, or as a tonic for the harried urban dweller, it resonated with mainstream values. Certainly, that was the approach of Laura White, who once begged off a query about her involvement in public policy-making by denying it: "I'd much rather confine myself to making the world more beautiful," she said. "The creation of a park or playground does as much good to the world as the study of a difficult problem."[11]

None of this is to say that clubwomen had no self-interest in conservation. Certainly, many members' husbands stood to gain from park tourism. More subtly, clubwomen hoped to use conservation and appeals to the protection of forests and beauty to reduce class conflict and the disaffection of the urban poor. They also hoped that it would attract the involvement of women in club work from all social levels. These intentions were made clear in 1902 when the national GFWC elected to hold its Sixth Biennial Convention in Los Angeles. California was chosen as the site of the convention as a direct result of Clara Burdette's success in organizing the CFWC in 1900. Californians were well represented at the event, which brought more than one thousand women delegates from across the nation, and conservation, under the guise of forestry and reclamation, was a major theme under discussion. Governor Henry T. Gage welcomed the opening session of women delegates. He declared that "woman's sphere" had been far too circumscribed by culture and law for a modern society and that "this industrial and mechanical age requires the refining and educating work of woman." The aid of women, he said, was needed in the "solving of the sociological problems that vex and perplex the statesmen of the times."[12] Gage's Republican Party was hardly ready to endorse suffrage, of course. That would have to await the arrival of the progressives in 1910, but his remarks are a good measure of how even conservative politicians viewed clubwomen's work.

If Gage had stayed for the session on reclamation, he would have been pleased to hear the talk given by Mrs. Lou V. Chapin. Chapin argued that "the foundation of the nation rests upon the individual home." She intoned that "the American workman longs for the individual home, and cannot be content in the crowded tenements of the great city." It was thus essential, she reasoned, for government to reclaim arid lands to increase the available living room for the poor and lower classes and to enable the West to blossom into a society with populated settlement and commercial opportunity as great as that existing in the East. Chapin's sentiments were reflected in GFWC-passed resolutions affirming the importance of forestry and endorsing water conservation through reservoirs and irrigation works. Any reclaimed lands, Chapin pointed out, were not intended for speculators but for "actual settlers only," the type of folk who would build homes and create new communities. Like many men, clubwomen clearly hoped that their advocacy of conservation would help address major social problems and would lead their communities to greater prosperity.[13]

If there was any doubt about the role that conservation and the promotion of nature preservation played in the rise of women's influence, it was soon displaced by the high visibility of women in major campaigns to save redwoods that began the very year that Clara Burdette founded the CFWC. The brief sketch of three major campaigns in which women participated that follows is intended to indicate both the extent of women's involvement in early conservation in California and how the values detailed above were expressed in actuality.

The California Club worked for many years to save the Calaveras "Big Trees," two groves of giant sequoia (larger cousins of the coast redwood) located in the Sierra near Yosemite. In January 1900 Robert P. Whiteside, a lumberman from Minnesota, purchased these trees, which included the Mammoth Grove Hotel and thousands of acres of nearby forest land. For decades the area had served as a tourist destination where guests could rest in comfort at one of the largest resort hotels in California.

Alarmed, the San Joaquin Valley Commercial Association soon passed a resolution asking Congress to establish a Calaveras Big Trees national park.¹⁴ The association was concerned that Whiteside would build mills, log the trees, and then abandon the area, a standard nineteenth-century lumbering practice, which would briefly fuel a boom and then a major bust in local towns.

The California Club immediately recognized both the threat to the famous resort and the opportunity for women's action. Taking up where the commercial association had left off, Laura White inaugurated a national campaign to entice Congress to purchase the Big Trees to preserve them as a public park "for the pleasure and benefit of the people for all time."¹⁵ The club sent a resolution to numerous state and national organizations and government bodies, requesting congressional action. Members collected thousands of signatures, launched a letter-writing campaign, met with California's congressional representatives, and even secured a meeting with President William McKinley.¹⁶

Over the years, White traveled several times to Washington DC to lobby congressional and government officials. She testified before committee hearings and even sparred with those opposed to congressional action, including "Uncle" Joe Cannon after he became Speaker of the House in 1903. Cannon felt California wealthy enough to afford the trees on its own behalf. In spite of such opposition, the California Club succeeded in convincing other congressmen to act. A joint resolution, sponsored by Senator George C. Perkins and Representative Marion de Vries (in whose district the trees were located), was introduced in Congress calling for the purchase of the two main Calaveras groves. The bill passed both houses and was signed by President William McKinley on March 8, 1900. After he signed the bill, McKinley expressed admiration for the women's legislative achievement.¹⁷

The act authorized negotiation to buy the property from Whiteside, but he stubbornly refused to sell. The women urged condemnation, but Congress proved unwilling to act against the owner's will. However, the opprobrium generated by the California Club must have convinced Whiteside to continue managing the groves as an attraction, for that is what he did. If nothing else, the attention demonstrated the property's speculative value. Indeed, Whiteside infuriated Californians by stating that he would only willingly sell the groves for one million dollars, ten times what he had paid.[18]

In 1904 White consulted with Senator Perkins about how to proceed and then launched a national petition drive that capitalized upon the California Club's ties with the CFWC and the GFWC. Through such means the California Club registered more than 1,400,000 names on a petition that was delivered to President Theodore Roosevelt. Upon its receipt the president forwarded the petition to Congress, adding his own plea: "The Calaveras Big Tree Groves are not only a Californian but a National inheritance and all that can be done by the Government to insure its preservation should be done." White stated that it was unprecedented that the president should take such a step on behalf of an organization run by women. Whiteside, however, remained intransigent, and Congress would not force the issue.[19]

In December 1907 the California Club switched tactics. It lobbied Senator Perkins to submit a bill to Congress empowering the Department of Agriculture to exchange portions of land held in federal forest reserves for the Calaveras Big Trees.[20] Perkins acted upon this request, and by 1909 such a measure had passed into law. By then Whiteside had for nine years faced persistent criticism and attempts to separate him from possession of the Big Trees. This was due in large part to the agitation of White and her clubwomen. Still, Whiteside gained a grudging respect for White, to whom he often referred as "Mrs. Lovely White."[21]

The California Club remained involved with the Calaveras issue for several more years.[22] Whiteside still refused to sell the groves, but he did not cut them. The struggle continued for decades, but all the trees in both groves were finally saved. Had the California Club not acted to convince Congress to purchase the trees, thereby inadvertently demonstrating their long-term speculative value, Whiteside might well have logged the groves instead of keeping them intact in the hope of an eventual windfall.

John Muir was amazed by the California Club's success in saving the Calaveras trees, since he had himself failed to interest the state legislature in their purchase in 1877.[23] One reason the club succeeded was that the relationship between forest cover, erosion, and the supply of water to agricultural and urban areas was better understood in 1900. Another reason was that the Big Trees had gained status through heavy visitation and publicity and had become, in effect, a public forest, a monument enhancing to the state's reputation. More importantly, the growth of civic-minded associations, including those of the women's club movement, had made it possible for citizens to voice concern on issues that traditional party politics eschewed. Such activism may even have helped induce the Republicans in 1904 to become the first party in California to adopt an interest in conservation by supporting national expenditures to preserve forests and reclaim arid lands.

In 1900, a few months after the creation of the CFWC, logging threatened a superb stand of coast redwoods in a rugged portion of the Santa Cruz Mountains known as Big Basin. Andrew P. Hill, a prominent artist and photographer, started a movement to save the trees and got the support of two colleagues, John E. Richards, a San Jose attorney, and Josephine McCracken, a Santa Cruz writer. Both soon published articles in local papers. As a result, on March 17 the *Santa Cruz Surf* lamented that the preservation of Big Basin seemed to be "nobody's business." Pining for a dedicated group to take up the cause, the editor extolled the California Club, which had only recently been able "to stay the hand of the destroyer in the Calaveras grove." He wondered if perhaps there was "work here and now for women to do" in Big Basin.[24]

There was. Hill asked the San Jose Woman's Club (SJWC) and the San Jose and Santa Cruz trade boards to urge Congress to purchase the trees for a national park. They were happy to make that request. Hill probably especially appreciated the women's participation because it helped offset criticism that the movement was intended to benefit local commercial interests. Whether that was true or not, the SJWC did bring greater respectability to the movement, because clubwomen were known for supporting projects that benefited women, children, and communities in general. At least, it was known that the SJWC garnered no direct commercial advantage from its work. Next, the San Jose Board of Trade appointed Richards, Hill, and another writer, Carrie Stephens Walter, an SJWC member, to a standing redwood committee. Hill sought to widen the movement further and solicited the aid of Stanford's president, David Starr Jordan, and other academics. After an encouraging meeting at Stanford University, Hill and Walter were chosen to lead an investigative committee to tour Big Basin. The party also included two Santa Cruz city supervisors, a San

10. Louise C. Jones and Carrie Stephens Walter, San Jose Woman's Club, inspect Big Basin with the Sempervirens Club (1900). Courtesy, History San José.

Francisco city supervisor, two sportsmen from San Jose, and Louise C. Jones, the SJWC president.[25]

A few days later, the group assembled by Hill and Walter gathered for an extended camping tour of the remote but threatened area. One night around the campfire, wrote Jones, the group discussed "the best way to begin in the matter of trying to preserve this forest, to preserve it not only for ourselves and our friends, but for the State, for the world, for future ages." On the spot the party founded the Sempervirens Club, an organization whose explicit purpose was to lobby for an appropriation to purchase Big Basin for protection as a public park. That task was later made easier when members secured the cooperation of the property owner, who, unlike Whiteside, agreed to sell his holdings.[26]

On May 12, 1900, immediately after Walter and Jones reported upon their redwoods tour, the SJWC unanimously resolved to endorse the campaign to set aside Big Basin as a redwood park. On May 26—again voting unanimously—the club joined the Sempervirens as a body, the first group to do so, and so began a whole-hearted effort to aid the movement. Eventually, numerous newspapers, educators, other women's clubs, the Pioneers' Society, and the Native Sons (and Daughters) of the Golden West supported the Sempervirens.[27]

SJWC members, especially Walter and Jones, wrote widely in local papers and other publications about their impressions and experiences working to save trees. Walter described the wastefulness of logging as "the criminally extravagant system—or lack of system, of forestry" that had to that point "cursed California." She later claimed that the cutting of the redwood forest would have destroyed, or greatly weakened, the streams that fed several counties, bringing "disaster to one of the most fertile and populous sections of the State." Jones wrote eloquently about how the forest was a place of beauty, not utility, a "holy" sanctuary where "nature distills a balm for our hurts, a subtle essence that heals and soothes."[28]

The campaign of the "Sempervirens Association" met significant opposition. In August 1900, anticipating insufficient national support, the group altered its fundraising strategy and sought state aid instead of federal funds. This move avoided a conflict with those seeking funds for the Calaveras Big Trees from a Congress whose support for even one park, though achieved, proved difficult to get. The club thus sent representatives to the state conventions of both political parties in a fruitless attempt to persuade at least one to include the purchase of Big Basin in their political platforms.[29]

Despite opposition, the Sempervirens Club was not without support. While Sempervirens's men employed high-level connections to lobby for their cause, its women relied on grassroots politicking. They wrote letters, gathered signatures, and networked among themselves. They supported the efforts of the California Club to save the Calaveras trees, and the reverse was also true. Indeed, after achieving national prominence for her work on the issue, Laura White assumed the presidency of the Sempervirens Club in 1902. Through such means, clubwomen secured the aid of Phoebe Apperson Hearst, the wealthy heiress and mother of the publisher William Randolph Hearst (see chapter 4). A clubwoman and major patron of the women's movement, Hearst decided to bankroll the drive to save Big Basin by covering expenses of several thousand dollars.[30]

Early in 1901 SJWC President Mrs. E. O. Smith, along with Carrie Walter and other Sempervirens Club members, especially Andrew Hill, took the fight for the park to Sacramento. Finally, a bill was passed and signed by Governor Gage, who appointed a commission to survey and negotiate the purchase of thirty-eight hundred acres. Park status did not bring full protection to Big Basin, however. The California legislature soon abolished the park commission, ceding control to corrupt managers who allowed a private contractor to engage in logging under the pretext of removing fallen timber. The Sempervirens raised an outcry, but their pleas went unheard for a decade, until the progressive administration of Governor Hiram Johnson restored the commission and dismissed those connected with the scandal.[31]

In March 1901 the SJWC held a reception to honor Hill for his leadership in the movement to save Big Basin. President Smith noted, "San Jose should be proud that she has raised up a man to do this great work, to protect this wonder of the world from the car of progress known as commerce which would ruthlessly pluck the stars from the heavens to make headlights for its engines were they not hung beyond its reach."[32] It was a typical display of the understated practices and overblown rhetoric that so ingratiated clubwomen with progressive-era men.

A third group of women sought to save redwoods in the heavily logged forests of Humboldt County. In February 1907 the Humboldt Times ran an editorial calling for women to organize a club that would "undertake agitation looking to the beautification of [Eureka]" and "the preservation of those natural beauty spots in and around the city that have been spared by the woodsman." The paper remarked further, "The uncouth hand of man scars and gnashes the beautiful face of nature in Humboldt, oft-times, but the smooth and gentle hand of woman can touch the wound and heal them."[33] Humboldt's clubwomen took their gentle hands seriously, but the involvement of many husbands in the lumber industry dampened their initial enthusiasm for saving redwoods. At first, county clubwomen focused their efforts upon creating playgrounds and city parks, beautifying local towns by planting trees and flowers and cleaning up refuse, and organizing social events for themselves and their families in "those natural beauty spots" amid the redwoods. Humboldt clubwomen became involved in campaigns to save redwoods when the Eureka Chamber of Commerce and the Sons of the Golden West (SGW), a men's civic club, began to promote the notion of a public redwood park. The chamber and SGW hoped to build sympathy for the construction of a railroad linking the city to San Francisco.[34]

George Burchard and George B. Albee, SGW members and son and husband, respectively, of women's club members, spoke to the Humboldt County Federation of Women's Clubs (HCFWC) on November 8, 1909. Burchard also edited the *Humboldt Standard* and sat on the chamber.[35] The men explained to the HCFWC the need to mount a movement to create a Humboldt redwood park. They asked the women to pass a resolution backing their effort "to preserve a representative forest of these trees for future generations to see in all their pristine beauty." The resolution was adopted.[36]

The SGW was glad to have the women's support. Despite the commercial angle, in 1910 saving redwoods was not yet a popular idea. Indeed, those who made such a proposition complained they were often "laughed at." Nevertheless, by 1912, park backers had convinced their congressman, John Raker, to sponsor a bill calling for a commission to investigate the possibility of establishing a redwood national park in Humboldt County. Two HCFWC members, Annie Murray and Edith S. Albee, attended the CFWC's Eleventh Annual Convention to support this effort. Conveniently posted to its Committee on Resolutions, with Murray as state chairman, the clubwomen were instrumental in crafting several conservation measures. As a result, the CFWC resolved to support Raker's bill. Other resolutions followed, as did several petitions gathered by the clubs and sent to Congress. The clubs also lobbied the county's supervisors to appoint a forestry board to supervise the conservation of trees along public grounds and highways, and they created a county-wide women's "Redwood Park Committee." One clubwoman, Laura Mahan, whose husband was an attorney, was elected to visit sites that could be considered for purchase as a redwood park. She obtained acreage figures and the price for which tracts could be bought.[37] Later, the HCFWC even hired its own Washington lobbyist, Hester Hosford, whom Mahan had escorted on a tour of the redwoods in 1912. Mahan wrote to Hosford, a specialist on Woodrow Wilson, to ask for help. Hosford was so saddened by the logged-over lands that she agreed to lobby President Wilson on behalf of the park effort. Funding for the lobbyist came from the Humboldt Chamber of Commerce, which supported the women's initiative.[38]

So much attention was being drawn to the redwood park movement that it attracted the attention of the independent congressman William Kent. Kent became well known in California when he purchased a significant stand of redwoods in Marin County near San Francisco. He donated this holding to the federal government, which made possible the creation of Muir Woods National Monument in January 1908. Kent used the acclaim from his Muir Woods donation to help secure his election to Congress in 1910 and also to promote his reformist agenda. In 1914 Kent's First Congressional District was reapportioned to include Humboldt County. This gave Kent a similar political opportunity, allowing him to woo friends among his new constituents and to reestablish his credentials as a conservationist and reformer in the wake of the bruising public debate surrounding the Hetch-Hetchy issue. (Kent had supported damming the canyon in Yosemite National Park to benefit San Francisco, to the horror of John Muir, which ended their friendship and divided the conservation movement.) No doubt with this in mind, Kent offered to donate twenty-five thousand dollars to help create another redwood park in Humboldt County.[39]

Despite these efforts and others, advocates lacked the support to create a redwood park until 1917, when a major highway was built through the heart of the redwood area. The road traversed some of the finest old-growth stands just south of Eureka. Private owners held much of this forest but had not been able to initiate logging because of restricted access. The new road gave this access, thereby creating a logging frenzy. According to Madison Grant, a gentlemen scientist and friend of Theodore Roosevelt, at one area along the South Fork, the landscape presents "a scene comparable only to the [war-]devastated regions of France."[40]

Grant began to investigate the situation in 1917. He joined John C. Merriam, a University of California paleontologist, and Henry Fairfield Osborne, the curator of the American Museum of Natural History, on a trip through Humboldt's redwoods. Shocked by the carnage that logging had produced along the roadway, they decided to create the Save the Redwoods League, a national organization that would raise funds to purchase and preserve redwoods. According to one source, Merriam first became concerned about the situation in Humboldt after his help was solicited by members of Humboldt's women's clubs.[41]

The men who founded the league chose Newton B. Drury, a bright young entrepreneur and a future director of the National Park Service, to manage the day-to-day effort of fundraising. William Kent soon urged Drury to enlist the aid of the women's clubs, which he lost no time in doing. If nothing else, the clubs knew how to generate publicity.[42]

During the summer of 1919, Secretary of Agriculture David Houston, Chief Forester Henry Graves, and Park Service Director Stephen Mather visited Humboldt to promote the commercial benefits of parks. The visit reinvigorated the chamber of commerce's park committee just as cutting along the roadway began to hasten.[43] Mather joined with the league in touring Humboldt and was well received. The immediate aim of the league was to halt the disastrous cutting along the highway. Its secondary aim was to encourage the local enthusiasm that was vital to soliciting outside attention and aid. Grant emphasized the potential tourist revenue of parks, while Mather urged the creation of a local branch of the Save the Redwoods League.[44]

Working with timber owners, the league gained the larger firms' promises to refrain from cutting along the highway. Except for Pacific Lumber Company, most owners seemed willing to support a limited national park. Additional measures were needed to stop the smaller operators. Being wealthy men with political fortunes tied to conservation, Kent and Mather pledged fifteen thousand dollars apiece, if the county provided matching funds, to buy lands along the roadway held by the small timber companies. This gesture revitalized the preservation movement in Humboldt, especially among local clubwomen.[45]

On August 9, 1919, Humboldt women came together to form a unique woman's club, one dedicated solely to the effort of saving redwoods. Laura Mahan was elected president of some thirty-five women who formed the group's core, the typical woman's civic club arrangement.[46] Mahan quickly gathered subscriptions from several hundred other locals. Fourteen clubwomen were elected as vice-presidents to represent each town in the county. Through a school competition, the club acquired a suitably feminine logo to grace its stationary. On it was emblazoned the slogan "Save the Redwoods League as Organized by the Women of Humboldt County" above a sentimental fine ink drawing of a road through a redwood grove where on one side of the road only stumps remained.[47]

The women's redwood club immediately began to lobby. In one project the club even produced a short Save-the-Redwoods film, to be played along with two popular silent films made in Humboldt. In 1920 they offered the trailer to Save the Redwoods's John Merriam, after learning that the league had organized a "Save the Redwoods Day" at a major auto show in San Francisco.[48]

Throughout the long struggle, the main organizations involved in the early Humboldt campaign to save redwoods were separate entities. The Women's Save the Redwoods League was an adjunct of neither the national Save the Redwoods League or the local chamber of commerce. It was an independent entity run to serve the women's own purposes. The three groups certainly cooperated, but they did not necessarily coordinate their efforts. Occasionally, the women even had differences with their male counterparts. This fact became obvious when Pacific Lumber—which owned several important tracts of park-suitable land at an area called Bull Creek—adamantly refused to sell. When the company offered to hand over three hundred acres of forest at another location, Dyerville Flat, in exchange for the county renouncing its power of eminent domain over the rest of the company's lands, the chamber proved sympathetic. The women's redwood club, however, strenuously objected, because the deal would have severely stunted any potential park and left the much-loved Bull Creek unprotected. The chamber abandoned the offer after Mahan embarrassed it by publicizing the issue.[49]

Eventually, the Save the Redwoods League was able to capitalize upon the grassroots popularity of saving trees and convinced Governor William Stephens to support a three-hundred-thousand-dollar league-backed state appropriation for purchasing redwoods along the Humboldt highway. Redwoods were, after all, good for the tourist industry. Nevertheless, facing a budget shortfall in 1921, the governor remained reluctant until his wife, an active clubwoman and GFWC member, talked him into it.[50] The climax of the early redwood park movement in Humboldt occurred three years later. On November 10, 1924, frustrated after several failed maneuvers to block park supporters, Pacific Lumber began clandestine logging on Dyerville Flat. The company had promised not to log the trees until the park issue was resolved. Its action was clearly intended to destroy any chance of creating a park in that vicinity. Fortunately, Laura Mahan was suspicious. Accompanied by her husband, she visited the area and discovered the subterfuge; the two alerted the press. With the alarm sounded, public condemnation swiftly ensued and Pacific Lumber was forced, begrudgingly, to negotiate the sale of its land. Years later, on the Mahan Trail at Dyerville Flat, grateful citizens erected a bronze plaque to mark the spot near where Laura Mahan first saw loggers beginning to fell the trees that are today a part of Humboldt Redwoods State Park.

As clubwomen participated in the various conservation campaigns sketched above, they worked to affect the scope and direction of public policy. Clubwomen's success is indicated in how public officials and public agencies, in addition to private entities, including industrial corporations and wealthy philanthropists, adapted their attitudes and procedures in response to women's demands for reform.

For example, Laura White and other women associated with the various efforts of the California Club lobbied consistently over many years to induce congressional action to save the Calaveras Big Trees from being logged. In the process, their concerns were taken seriously by the state's congressional representatives, who introduced several pieces of legislation that ultimately became law. The women's efforts also elicited specific public backing from two presidents. The California Club was only the first of many organizations that lobbied to save the Big Trees over the course of several decades. The early public attention that clubwomen focused upon the issue, however, convinced the trees' owner not to log them in the short term, and that was the key to the trees' survival.

In the case of Andrew Hill's efforts to save Big Basin, the photographer knew at once that the San Jose Woman's Club would be an important ally. Clubwomen brought the appearance of impartiality to a movement that was strongly backed by the tourist-minded trade boards of local towns. The trade boards' prospects could only be furthered by the inclusion of women whose motives were not as likely to be impugned, especially when these emphasized community vitality and spiritual aestheticism. On top of this contribution, the SJWC also joined the Sempervirens Club as a body, committing its own resources wholeheartedly. When clubwomen joined the Sempervirens Club, they greatly expanded the latter's grassroots lobbying capacity. This contribution was not idle: SJWC members were prominent in the community and local officials were willing to hear them out, if for no other reason than that their prominent husbands, at a minimum, were likely to remember their wives' causes at the polls. Of course, although SJWC members lacked the vote themselves, they published their opinions widely, networked with other men's and women's associations, and acquired the financial support of Phoebe Apperson Hearst, activities that unquestionably helped put pressure on elected officials.

Similarly, the clubwomen of Humboldt County influenced their elected officials. After 1911, Humboldt women could express their views through the ballot, of course, and they did. It was more important, however, that the county's women were effectively organized at the local level, were integrated into state and nationwide networks, and had even created their own redwood park club. Humboldt women could thus lobby elected officials by using resolutions, petitions, mail and advertising campaigns (including motion pictures), and by turning out in numbers at important meetings. Clubwomen were so effective that when the Save the Redwoods League's Newton Drury set out to build support, he turned to them immediately. Drury contacted all fourteen vice-presidents to distribute league information, solicited their advice on how to start similar women's leagues in other counties, and curried their favor for many years.[51] In 1921 the league elected three women to sit on its council of advisors. These were Mrs. Aaron Schloss, the president of the CFWC; Mrs. F. G. Law, the president of the California Civic League; and Mrs. Charles H. Toll, the president of Clara Burdette's old Ebell Club in Los Angeles.[52]

When these club members were elected to the Council of the Save the Redwoods League, few women in the United States could have gained high standing on such an august body on the basis of their own professional merit. It was still a rarity for a woman to enter and to succeed in male-dominated professions. That women reached such a level within the league testifies to the success of Clara Burdette's plan to mobilize women's influence by means of conservation. This influence was demonstrated in 1924, when Laura Mahan brought Mary Sherman, the GFWC president, to visit Humboldt. Drury soon wrote to congratulate Mahan for having interested one of the most prominent women in the United States in their cause. He then proceeded to cover Sherman's expenses on a trip to see the redwoods.[53] In February 1925, in the wake of Pacific Lumber's clandestine logging, the Humboldt County Board of Supervisors met in a special session to consider a proposal from the Save the Redwoods League to acquire both the Dyerville and the Bull Creek flats. The league brought to the meeting the telegrams of the prominent San Francisco banks that had pledged sufficient funds to back the league's proposal. Mahan arrived at the meeting bearing her own "sheath of telegrams" from clubwomen across the country, including one from Mary Sherman, whose endorsement brought Drury the support of the GFWC's nearly three million members.[54] The board adopted the proposal because of the league's adroit politicking and the willingness of league men to curry the favor and aid of women conservationists.

All of this is to say that the CFWC, the SJWC, the California Club, and the women's Save the Redwoods club were special interest groups. In the early twentieth century, politicians found it increasingly necessary to respond to such groups, which exerted influence through increasingly sophisticated campaigns that coordinated the efforts of a diverse membership, obtained media attention, circulated petitions, mounted letter-writing and personal lobbying campaigns, and educated the public and supporters about issues. California's clubwomen were able to take advantage of this opportunity because they were organized and represented mainstream values. They did so on a number of fronts, promoting their interests in conservation and everything else, from the need for a juvenile justice system to the placement of female physicians in the women's wards of hospitals for the insane.

Conservation was a defining feature of progressivism—and particularly important in the arid West, where it was simultaneously an instrument of political, social, and economic reform. Such club leaders as Clara Burdette, Laura White, and Laura Mahan recognized the advantages that conservation had in enabling them to garner women's support for increased involvement in public life. Moreover, by embracing conservation from a domestic perspective, clubwomen gained a voice in debates about major public policy issues—issues of political economy, a man's exclusive domain. Clubwomen's willingness to defer to prevailing social custom may have frustrated the suffragists among their ranks. Over the long term, however, this prudent and "responsible" strategy drew the respect and appreciation of male sympathizers and the acceptance of male opponents, who at least had to recognize the legitimacy of women's involvement in the making of public policy. Many men probably directly transferred an increased regard for the "woman's work" of saving trees (and civic work in general) to an increased willingness to accept the legitimacy of suffrage. Thus, clubwomen's domestic approach to conservation, and their numerous successes, may be counted among the reasons that western women gained the right to vote sooner than their eastern sisters. Regardless, faced with the inherent inertia of entrenched viewpoints, reform-mind politicians proved pragmatic in their willingness to accept women as allies, both before and after suffrage.

To understand progressivism, therefore, is to understand the importance of conservation and the role that women played in helping make conservation a progressive issue. This is nowhere more true than in the West, where the conflict between special interests over the disposition of water, land, trees, and beauty gained the greatest salience and made it possible for progressive-era women to make genuine and long-lasting contributions to political and social reform.

Ironically, although some women turned to club life after the failure of the California suffrage campaign of 1896, when suffrage was finally achieved in California in 1911 it had little immediate effect on women's civic work. Clubwomen widely understood that the key to their influence was organized action based upon a distinct separatist strategy—a strategy that was erected around the notion of women's special concerns as mothers and homemakers. Consequently, the right of an individual woman to vote was far less important. In the long term, the achievement of suffrage, which emphasized essential similarities between men and women instead of supposed differences, inevitably helped dilute the strong nineteenth-century attitude regarding gendered spheres.

Nevertheless, the women's clubs of California have remained active in public life. The CFWC and numerous individual women's clubs continue to support municipal improvement and environmental protection, as they have done since the days of Clara Burdette and her call eleven decades ago for women to unite by saving trees.

Notes

This chapter is based on Cameron Binkley, "What We Did for Trees: Women's Clubs and Conservation in California during the Progressive Era" (Master's thesis, San Francisco State University, 1999). Binkley's work on conservation and women's clubs has also appeared in *Western Historical Quarterly* and *California History*. Formerly with the National Park Service, Binkley is currently serving as deputy command historian at the Defense Language Institute Foreign Language School and Presidio of Monterey, California. His views do not necessarily reflect any position of the U.S. government.

1. Clara Burdette, "General Federation of Women's Clubs" (hereafter "GFWC"), Box 135, Clara Bradley Burdette Papers, Huntington Library, San Marino, California.

2. Clara (Mrs. Robert J.) Burdette, "California Women's Clubs and Their Work," *Sunset Magazine* 8, no. 4 (1902): 175.

3. Clara (Mrs. Robert J.) Burdette, "Address of Welcome to the Women's Clubs of California Assembled for the State Federation," address delivered at Los Angeles, January 16, 1900, 12–13 (copy in author's possession). See also excerpts in *A Record of Twenty-five Years of the California Federation of Women's Clubs, 1900–1925*, comp. Mary S. Gibson, (Pasadena: CFWC, 1927), 9–10.

4. Burdette, "California Women's Clubs," 175.

5. "Women's Clubs Now United," *San Francisco Call*, January 19, 1900.

6. California Club, *The California Club, 1898–1899* (San Francisco: California Club of California, 1899), 8; unless otherwise noted, the California Club records referenced here are located at the California Club offices.

7. Clara Burdette, "Club Woman's Creed," a widely published GFWC flyer (ca. 1902). See insert in CFWC, *Clubwomen of California* (San Francisco: CFWC, 1907), an official CFWC directory and register located in the Bancroft Library, University of California, Berkeley (hereafter "Bancroft").

8. See Karen Blair, *The Club Woman as Feminist: True Womanhood Redefined, 1868–1914* (New York: Holmes & Meier, 1980) for more detailed discussion of clubwomen's "domestic feminism." Note, many clubwomen who supported suffrage—and many did not—accepted that suffrage activism had no role in club work.

9. This classic argument is found in Samuel P. Hays, *Conservation and the Gospel of Efficiency: The Progressive Conservation Movement, 1890–1920* (Cambridge: Harvard University Press, 1959).

10. See Carolyn Merchant, "Women of the Progressive Conservation Movement, 1900–1916," *Environmental Review* 8 (Spring 1984): 57–85.

11. Edward F. O'Day, *Varied Types* (San Francisco: Town Talk, 1915), 320.

12. *Los Angeles Daily Times*, May 9, 1902, Section IV.

13. "To Reclaim Arid Land, Federal Irrigation Indorsed [sic]," *Los Angeles Daily Times*, May 9, 1902, p. 2. Reclamation was an important component of early conservation in the arid and sparsely populated West, especially because the destructive effects of damming were not yet well understood. Tension, however, was growing between the branches of conservation, becoming notably divisive in the battle to dam Yosemite's Hetch-Hetchy Valley.

14. "Lumbermen Threaten Calaveras Big Trees," *San Francisco Chronicle*, January 19, 1900.

15. Sempervirens Club, "Resolution in support of the California Club," n.d., Miscellaneous Resolutions and Petitions, Box 2, Sempervirens Club Papers, San Jose Historical Museum, San Jose (hereafter "Sempervirens Club Papers").

16. Gibson, *A Record*, 175.

17. "Big-Tree Bill Is Signed by the President," *San Francisco Call*, March 19, 1900, p. 1; Joseph H. Engbeck Jr., *The Giant Sequoias* (Berkeley: University of California,

1973), 95–96; Gibson, *A Record*, 175. For her dealings with Congressman Cannon, see Frona Eunice Wait Colburn, "Mrs. Lovell White—As I Knew Her," *Overland Monthly* 81, no. 6 (1923): 4.

18. Engbeck, *Giant Sequoias*, 95–96; and Gibson, *A Record*, 176.

19. Colburn, "Mrs. Lovell White," 4; Gibson, *A Record*, 176; and Dorothea Moore, *The Work of Women's Clubs in California* (1906; reprint, Philadelphia: American Academy of Political and Social Science, Annals, 1906), 257–60.

20. California Club, *Year-Book of the California Club of California, 1906–1907* (San Francisco: California Club, 1908), 35.

21. According to Colburn, "Mrs. Lovell White," 3.

22. "Mrs. Lovell White Is Claimed by Death: Activities on Behalf of Public are Recalled," *San Francisco Chronicle*, January 19, 1916.

23. Engbeck, *Giant Sequoias*, 92.

24. *Santa Cruz Surf*, March 17, 1900, quoted in Arthur A. Taylor, *California Redwood Park* (Sacramento: Superintendent of State Printing, 1912), 23–25.

25. Gibson, *A Record*, 13; and Carolyn de Vries, *Grand and Ancient Forest: The Story of Andrew P. Hill and Big Basin Redwood State Park* (Fresno: Valley Publishers, 1978), 20–23.

26. Gibson, *A Record*, 16; Frank E. Hill, *The Acquisition of California Redwood Park* (San Jose: Florence W. Hill, 1927), 18; and De Vries, *Grand and Ancient Forest*, 22–24, 26. Charles W. Reed was elected president. Walter became club secretary.

27. "Big Basin Exploration," *Santa Cruz Sentinel*, May 19, 1900, p. 1; San Jose Woman's Club (SJWC), "General Records Book of the SJWC" (1898–1901) (hereafter "SJWC General Records"), May 12, 1900, SJWC, San Jose (records of the SJWC referenced here are located at the SJWC offices unless otherwise noted); Gibson, *A Record*, 13, 16–17.

28. Carrie Stevens Walter, "The Preservation of Big Basin," *Overland Monthly* (October 1902): 355–57; Mrs. Stephen A. Jones quoted in Taylor, *California Redwood Park*, 29.

29. De Vries, *Grand and Ancient Forest*, 29; "The Big Basin," *Santa Cruz Surf*, August 4, 1900, and "Sempervirens Club Meeting," *Santa Cruz Surf*, August 8, 1900, both reprinted in Jennie and Denzil Verardo, *The Mountain Echo* (San Jose: Sourisseau Academy, San Jose State University, 1973).

30. Sempervirens Club Minutes, December 17, 1902, Sempervirens Club Papers; Arthur A. Taylor, *California Redwood Park* (Sacramento: Superintendent of State Printing, 1912), 25, which, incidentally, is dedicated to Phoebe Hearst.

31. Gibson, *A Record*, 16–18; Alexander Lowry and Denzil Verardo, *Big Basin* (Los Altos: Sempervirens Fund, 1973), 44; and De Vries, *Grand and Ancient Forest*, 47–50.

32. "Honored by Reception," unidentified newspaper clipping, March 26, 1901, SJWC General Records.

33. "Work for Eureka's Women," *Humboldt Times*, February 26 1907, p. 4.

34. Cameron Binkley, "No Better Heritage than Living Trees," *Western Historical Quarterly* 33 (2002): 189.

35. Susan Schrepfer, "A Conservative Reform: Saving the Redwoods, 1917 to 1940" (PhD dissertation, University of California, Irvine, 1971), 54; "Will Work to Secure Redwood Park: Movement Again Started to Get a Grove of Representative Trees for Humboldt," *Humboldt Standard*, November 6, 1909, pp. 1, 4.

36. "Federated Clubs in Session Here," *Humboldt Standard*, November 8, 1909, p. 8; Humboldt County Federation of Women's Clubs (HCFWC), "Minutes" (hereafter "HCFWC Minutes"), 43–46.

37. HCFWC *Yearbook*, 1909–1911, 73; HCFWC Minutes, 90–93, 101; F. W. Georgeson to Robert G. Sproul (March 25, 1920), Save the Redwoods League (SRL) Papers, "History of the SRL: 1911–1966," SRL offices, San Francisco, California (all SRL records referenced here are located at the SRL offices unless otherwise noted); "Plan to Save Giant Trees," *Humboldt Times*, February 17, 1912, p. 1; "Raker Has Prepared Bill on Redwood Park," *Humboldt Standard*, March 19, 1912, p. 1; "Redwood Park Resolutions Adopted by Women's Club," *Humboldt Standard*, October 20, 1913, p. 2; and "Will Ask for a Committee to Look at Park," *Humboldt Times*, February 7, 1912, p. 6.

38. HCFWC Minutes, pp. 122, 133–34; Margaret Scott, "Save Redwoods Movement Wins Strength," *Eureka California Standard*, December 25, 1923, pp. 4, 6. Hosford saw Wilson and gained the American Forestry Association's support, but to no avail.

39. "Raker Helps Redwood Park in Congress," 1913 (month and day not given), press clipping in Laura P. Mahan scrapbook, SRL offices (hereafter "Mahan scrapbook").

40. Madison Grant, "Saving the Redwoods," *New York Zoological Society Bulletin* (September 1919), excerpted in *Literary Digest* (March 27, 1920): 102–5.

41. John DeWitt, Executive Secretary, SRL San Francisco, personal interview with John Amodio, November 25, 1980, in John Amodio, "Save the Redwoods, 1919–1925: Humboldt County Redwood Movement" (BA thesis, Humboldt State University, 1980), 8.

42. SRL, "Reply of the SRL to William Kent," April 30, 1920, Box 1, William Kent folder (1920–1924), SRL Papers (hereafter "League Papers,") Bancroft.

43. Amodio, "Save the Redwoods," 14–16.

44. Joseph H. Engbeck Jr., *State Parks of California, from 1864 to the Present* (Portland: Graphic Arts Publishing Center, 1980), 42; press clipping, 1918 (month and day not given), Mahan scrapbook; and Amodio, "Save the Redwoods," 16.

45. Engbeck, *State Parks*, 43; "Humboldt County Aroused to Action," *Ferndale Enterprise*, February 27, 1920.

46. "Ladies Back of Redwood Park Plan" *Humboldt Times*, August 7, 1919, Mahan

scrapbook; Lillian Ross, "Women's Save the Redwoods League Organized in 1919," *Humboldt Standard*, January 15, 1932, p. 7.

47. Amodio, "Save the Redwoods," 20; "Humboldt Women Aided Work for Redwood Park," *Humboldt Standard*, September 6, 1919, p. 2; "Women's Save the Redwoods League Organized in 1919," *Humboldt Standard*, January 15, 1932, p. 7; "Women Speed Work to Save Big Redwoods," and "High School Students Asked to Design Letterhead for Women's League to Preserve Redwoods," unidentified newspaper clippings, August 1919 (no day given), Mahan scrapbook.

48. "Committee with Photographer Goes This Morning to Make Trailer for 'Giant of the Redwoods' Production," unidentified newspaper clipping, probably August or September 1919, Mahan scrapbook; Mrs. J. A. Putnam to John C. Merriam, February 19, 1920, in League Papers, Correspondence folder: 1919–1920, Bancroft.

49. Amodio, "Save the Redwoods," 12, 22, 28; "Redwood League Says Chamber's Memory Is Short," unidentified newspaper clipping, February 1925 (no day given), Mahan scrapbook.

50. Newton B. Drury to Mrs. J. A. Putnam, October 22, 1920, Box 7, League Papers, Bancroft. (Correspondence of the league with various women's groups is found in Box 7, League Papers.) Both Schrefper, *Fight to Save the Redwoods*, 99, 128 and Stephen Fox, *John Muir and His Legacy: The American Conservation Movement* (Boston: Little, Brown, 1981), 345, note the influence of Stephens's wife.

51. Newton B. Drury to Mrs. J. A. Putnam, October 22, 1920, Box 7, League Papers, Bancroft.

52. Councilors of the SRL are listed on its stationary, examples of which can be found in Box 7, League Papers, Bancroft.

53. Newton B. Drury to Mrs. J. P. Mahan, June 17, June 18, 1924; July 2, 1924, and Drury to Mrs. John G. Sherman, June 16, 1924, in Box 7, League Papers. Incidentally, Drury wrote to Sherman in care of Clara Burdette, who was hosting Sherman in Los Angeles.

54. Amodio, "Save the Redwoods," 25–26; Myra Nye, "Redwood Fight Success Told," *Los Angeles Times*, February 18, 1925, pp. 1–2.

8. THE *CIVITAS* OF WOMEN'S POLITICAL CULTURE
The Twentieth Century Club of Berkeley, 1904–1929

SANDRA L. HENDERSON

The Twentieth Century Club of Berkeley (TCC) offers a microhistory that uncovers several important lessons regarding women's political culture in early twentieth-century California, illustrating the complexities of women's political activism as it emerged through urban voluntary associations. The history of Berkeley's TCC reveals that California enfranchisement did not politicize organized women; they had been fighting for the vote since the 1880s, and by 1911 they had already crafted sophisticated political identities as more than just suffragists. Likewise, organized women's activism did not cease after the vote was won, contrary to traditional accounts of women's political quiescence after suffrage and activist dormancy until second-wave feminism in the 1960s.

The declared lacuna in women's activism after suffrage was won exposes how the significance of women's political culture was obscured by narrow definitions of politics, and conventional measurements that took masculine political practices as the normative standard. Women's activism in such voluntary organizations as the TCC changed the very definition of what counted as politics during the progressive era and the interwar years. Women enlarged not only their own citizenship but the entire realm of political engagement.

The TCC's activism demonstrates the fluidity of politics and our need for expanded definitions of political culture and the functions of community during the early twentieth century. As Paula Baker first observed, historians need to define politics more broadly "to include any action, formal or informal, taken to affect the course or behavior of government or the community."[1] The activism of the women of the Twentieth Century Club of Berkeley during the opening decades of the 1900s fits well within this definition of politics, and the culture that they developed invites closer examination.

As citizens without ballots, California women before 1911 actively debated what governments should do, and how women could effect social change. They invented ways to apply pressure to politicians and policymakers, shape public opinion, and leverage reforms. California women thus transformed what constituted local politics, as well as state-level politics (particularly through their federated women's club networks), and they inaugurated this new political world with an innovative, gendered playbook.

TCC women epitomize the progressive-era creation of a political culture grounded in a *civitas*. The Latin term denotes a range of relational meanings—citizenship, a union of citizens, the inhabitants of a city, townsfolk. In U.S. political practice, it encompasses qualities that the women of the TCC exemplified: "(1) The body of citizens who constitute a state, especially a city-state, commonwealth, or the like; (2) Citizenship, especially as imparting shared responsibility, a common purpose, and sense of community."[2] TCC women founded their club at the ground level of their city-state, and it molded their sense of citizenship, their public identities, their consciousness shifts, their urban activism, and their political culture generally. Furthermore, their embodied civitas took a trajectory from urban to international politics, sometimes even sidestepping nationalism to engage directly in globalism.

TCC women offer a prime example of the contradictions within progressivism, which could be simultaneously liberal and conservative in its impulses. They were liberal on such issues as labor protection and reforming the juvenile justice and mental health systems, yet conservative regarding others—film censorship, alcohol prohibition, and racial segregation. These tendencies continued well beyond the progressive era.

The TCC also demonstrates activist women's resistance to partisanship in California prior to the New Deal realignment. Although they played a critical role in shaping state politics in the early twentieth century, and generally supported progressive Republican candidates as the best reformers, California clubwomen did not view party allegiance as the means to reform. Newly enfranchised women resisted being taken for granted by any party, and at the national level the fight for suffrage employed a strategy of opposition to incumbent parties until the vote was won.

The TCC influenced women's political culture and California's legislative agenda years before equal suffrage, through organized legislative lobbying, civic forums, voter education, candidate support or opposition, petitioning, letter-writing campaigns, and publicity. These well-honed tools subsequently enhanced their voting power. Organized women thus accrued significant political power prior to California's equal suffrage amendment in 1911, and continued their wide-ranging activities beyond World War I. The vote renewed opportunities and reinvigorated agendas of civic and state reform that had been evolving since the club's 1904 inception. After 1911, TCC women used suffrage as a critical tool that enabled them to expand and continue their work reforming public policy at city, county, state, national, and even global levels.

The women of the TCC remained true to their 1904 mission statement by emphasizing the dualism of personal improvement and communal good. The key to this activism was their practice of a civitas that placed the roots of their citizenship in the city. For Berkeley clubwomen, their city was a laboratory for civic activism that not only enhanced their citizen status but also improved living standards throughout their community.

The Twentieth Century Club (1904–1989) was organized by two veterans of women's clubs in Pasadena and San Francisco. Both had been active in the Woman's Christian Temperance Union (WCTU) (discussed in chapter 2), which a later president of the TCC referred to as "that mother of all women's clubs."[3] Founders of the TCC felt excluded by Town and Gown, the sole women's club in Berkeley, which they perceived to be academic and elitist.[4] (In 1916 Town and Gown membership included Phoebe Apperson Hearst, discussed in chapter 4; Mrs. Benjamin Ide Wheeler; and women whose names echo the geography of Berkeley: Addison, Barrows, Blake, Colby, Kaiser, Le Conte, McDuffie, and Woolsey, place names that reflect both the elite status of the city's founding families and the esteem enjoyed by faculty wives and daughters.)

The TCC grew quickly from fifty members at the 1904 induction meeting to nearly three hundred by 1917. Members were drawn largely from upper-middle-class women not directly linked to the University of California, the town's dominant institution.[5] The club's mission statement emphasized personal growth and community service: "The object of the Twentieth Century Club of Berkeley shall be the discussion of current events, the mutual improvement of the members in literature, art, and social culture, and the creation of a greater interest in whatever is for the good of the community."[6]

From the TCC's 1904 genesis its members developed political power from an array of internal practices. One of the club's most important tools was homogeneity of membership—exclusively white and upper-middle class—which fostered unity, cohesiveness, and prestige. Although TCC records are silent regarding race, contemporary statewide events offer some context for discrimination by clubs. The General Federation of Women's Clubs (GFWC) held its national convention in Los Angeles in 1902 and, although a few clubwomen vehemently protested (notably Jane Addams and Mabel Craft), the national federation voted to allow member clubs to exclude African American women.[7] The California Federation of Women's Clubs (CFWC) followed suit, making their corrupt bargain for fear that desegregation might fracture the state federation. As Gayle Gullett observes, "California women did not break up their federation; they reinforced the color line."[8] Black California clubwomen responded to segregation by establishing their own clubs, forming a State Federation of Colored Women's Clubs in 1906.[9]

If the question of admitting women of color ever arose within the TCC, there is no evidence of it. There is, however, a tantalizing trace at the state level of one member's racial politics. In 1909, black clubwomen in Oakland established a "Woman's Exchange" and invited Bay Area clubwomen to the opening. Mrs. James B. Hume, a member of the TCC and the CFWC president, and her secretary were the only white clubwomen to attend.[10]

The black population of Berkeley remained relatively small before World War II. In 1900 there were only 66 black residents out of a total population of 13,214, or less than 0.5 percent; by 1910, blacks were 0.6 percent of the city's population, 247 out of 40,434 total residents. Berkeley's 1910 census also enumerated 710 Japanese, 451 Chinese, 2 Indians, and 20 "others." In 1910, white women in Berkeley numbered 20,545, and black women 145. With approximately 200 members, the TCC most likely would have encountered Berkeley's female population of color as domestics, and their relatively small numbers probably allowed white Berkeley clubwomen to avoid consciousness of their own racism.[11]

Despite its reputation for relative tolerance, Berkeley was still an informally segregated town, as Mary Frances Albrier, a pioneer black civil rights activist, recalled:

> During... the twenties and the thirties, there were no black women in any of the white clubs that were interested in communities and activities of people, because it was a pattern of segregation... in the biggest institution in the United States, and that's the church. Naturally, these clubs came down with the same pattern. They were clubs for white people, white women only. They didn't open their doors up to black women. I think the reason was that they felt that the black people were not yet educated enough to participate in the clubs. Out West, they never saw a black institution like Tuskegee or Howard University, or Hampton University, or Fisk University.[12]

Through demographics, segregation, and the exclusive political culture they created for themselves, TCC women sidestepped the complicated and potentially divisive issues of class and race, leaving them free to strategize and develop consensus in a homogeneous setting.

The TCC employed several other tactics to build cohesion. Club federation amplified their political influence and connected small-town members to statewide political organizations and agendas. TCC sociability fostered the affinity, unity, and networks essential to political lobbying and reform. Club culture for women also entailed mastering fundamental political skills, including parliamentary procedure and the ballot process. These cornerstones enabled the TCC to develop an effective political culture that the organization used to reshape public policy in California between 1904 and the Great Depression. The 1913 construction of a clubhouse edified the TCC as a civic institution in Berkeley; it both provided a locus for the women's activities and illustrated their emergent stature in the city's geography of power.

Clubwomen participated in an enormous variety of political activities at many levels. TCC members were integral to shaping the successful "Women's Legislative Agenda" at the 1913 California state legislature (see chapter 10). They campaigned for peace and internationalism in the first two decades of the twentieth century, lobbied for social welfare reforms, and engaged in boosterism for San Francisco's bid for the 1915 Panama–Pacific International Exposition (PPIE). The TCC worked in 1918 to send a member, Anna L. Saylor, to the California State Assembly, where she served from 1919 to 1926. One of the first four women to serve in the state legislature, Saylor led successful campaigns to abolish the death penalty for minors, reduce juvenile crime, establish psychiatric clinics in prisons, secure new child labor legislation, create mental health assistance, and increase aid for the elderly.

Although TCC members participated diligently in the mobilization for World War I, they resumed their pacifist activism after the war. The club lobbied for U.S. membership in the League of Nations and for participation in the Kellogg-Briand Pact of 1928. That same year, the TCC organized an international conference on peace and global relations, which they hosted at their Berkeley clubhouse. Despite their support for U.S. troops, clubwomen's involvement in "the war to end all wars" was actually in keeping with their pacifism, which found new avenues in the postwar international world.

The TCC effectively served the varied interests of its many members through a combination of intellectual and social enrichment. "Blue stockings and butterflies have lived contentedly side by side in our flower garden of Club ladies, making it a place of delight for all," lauded the 1908–1909 President's Report.[13] This comment corresponds to a 1915 handbook for women's clubs, which identified three types of members: first, those who had been absorbed in homemaking and child-rearing, without any opportunity for self-development, and who were now eager to study art and culture; second, younger, college-educated women, impatient with study clubs and "devoted to the good of the community, to the 'larger housekeeping,' to preparation for citizenship"; and third, homemakers who had "kept up their reading" despite responsibilities, and who wanted to engage in work outside the home but lacked the public-speaking skills and self-confidence of the college women.[14] Judging from TCC activities, it appears that the club contained all three types of members and that leaders tried to balance the desires of a diverse polity with a mixture of sociability, culture, and political activism.

For the women who inhabited the TCC, the issue of diversity was complicated because they viewed unity and cohesiveness as essential to the club's effectiveness. The 1908–1909 President's Report thanked the membership committee for using "wise discrimination" to keep the TCC "homogeneous and united."[15] This evinces the prevailing philosophy of women's clubs, which viewed restricted membership as empowering; a Los Angeles journalist observed in 1902 that clubs were "willing to risk much that no objectionable element might be introduced."[16] This dynamic manifests the "impulse toward social cohesiveness and homogeneity" that Eric Foner has ascribed to progressivism.[17] For middle- and upper-middle-class white clubwomen, race and class were important factors in their claims to the powers of citizenship. This was especially true prior to enfranchisement, since clubwomen possessed more social privileges than they did political rights. This philosophy was clearly reflected in the CFWC's motto, "Strength United Is Stronger," adopted in 1902 at the suggestion of the TCC's cofounder Annie Little Barry.[18] Over-inclusiveness would threaten the power the women derived from their racial and economic advantages. For activist clubwomen, race and class homogeneity and gender separatism formed a complex dynamic, subtly yet clearly conveyed by the term "ladies," which served as cultural shorthand for the position of social and political standing claimed by organized women.

Upon the TCC's founding, its members quickly realized the importance of federation, establishing ties to county, state, and national networks of women's clubs to enhance their power. In May 1905, only six months after organizing, the women voted to join both the CFWC and the Alameda District Federation of Women's Clubs (ADFWC). Seven years later, in March 1912, the TCC joined the national network, the GFWC.[19] This sequence raises the question of priorities, with allegiance to local and state federations preceding national federation by several years. It also suggests a western pattern of urban, state, and regional loyalties that superseded national alliance. This interpretation is supported by club events: the 1905 annual breakfast theme, "California—dear land by the blue western sea," for example; a 1909 presentation on historic landmarks in California; and the 1911 annual breakfast address: "The Vision of California Women."[20]

Linkages between the TCC and the CFWC were key to Berkeley women's activism. In a typical example, the January 1916 TCC *Bulletin* announced the appointment of three TCC members to CFWC offices.[21] TCC leaders steered members toward civic issues within Berkeley and at the state level and worked on the Women's Legislative Council through the CFWC. TCC leaders relayed CFWC policy positions to their members; in January 1920, for example, they called for "the early ratification of the Peace Treaty and the League of Nations." In October they urged "support of the Community

Property measure" before the state assembly.²² A local newspaper noted that the TCC "unanimously endorsed the immediate ratification of the League of Nations without reservation, at their meeting of yesterday afternoon, and last night telegraphed their wishes." It continued, "The club also joined the League to Enforce Peace at the same meeting, a petition from the State Women's committee . . . being circulated and receiving a majority signing."²³ By branching out through federation, the TCC influenced California politics on a much wider scale than might be supposed for a small women's club organized at the turn of the century in a bucolic land-grant university town.

Rituals of sociability were central to the TCC and served vital purposes. Social events—luncheons, teas, special programs, afternoon receptions, "Federation Days," lectures, Christmas dinners, annual breakfasts, pageants, plays, and cultural performances—were integral to the structure and function of the club. In 1912, members unanimously approved when the Tea Committee declared that the true purpose of hospitality was community service.²⁴ A brief history of the club reports that the 129 charter members reiterated that spirit when each "gave a cup and saucer to the club."²⁵ The taking of tea together was an important ritual that bordered on sacrament. Open to members only, teas were performed in the clubhouse with vessels bestowed by the club's founding generation. The ceremony fostered familiarity, camaraderie, and unity that could then be channeled toward external causes. The mingling of political activism and rituals of sociability by progressive-era clubwomen recalls the pattern that Julie Roy Jeffrey has found among abolitionist women.²⁶ This attention to the nurturance of bonds among activist women is also reflected in a contemporary statement Charlotte Perkins Gilman made before a woman's club: "Clubwomen learn more than to improve the mind; they learn to love each other."²⁷ TCC women placed great importance upon unifying rituals, and it is within this context that their gestures of companionability must be approached.

The importance of homosocial bonds was clearly marked following the San Francisco earthquake and fire of April 18, 1906. President Annie Little Barry exhorted TCC members to seek out and comfort displaced San Francisco clubwomen: "This is an opportunity to show the kindness we must all feel toward other women."²⁸ TCC women saw themselves

11. The TCC clubhouse at 2716 Derby Street in Berkeley, ca. 1922. From Louis S. Lyons and Josephine Wilson, eds., Who's Who among the Women of California (San Francisco: Security, 1922), 58.

as part of a wide network of female affection, hospitality, and service, declaring in 1909, "Our social relations with the clubs about the bay and the increasing Federated Clubs of Berkeley have been most cordial and delightful."[29] Their power as organized women was relational, rooted at the city level but branching into wider networks that joined women across the state.

The TCC's response to the 1906 calamity also demonstrates civitas. "Within three days," club leaders reported to the CFWC, "the women of Berkeley, Oakland and Alameda were at work, in an organized manner, relieving the distress of the thousands thrust so suddenly in their midst. Two hundred children were fed, clothed and housed for many weeks ... the sick and destitute by the thousands were fed, clothed and healed by clubwomen of Berkeley."[30] The earthquake reveals the clubwomen's intersection of service and social impulses.

The TCC's emphasis on hospitality led to the conviction that they needed a structural home. The importance of attaining such a structure can hardly be overestimated. The club's first Year Book, printed in 1906, contained a "President's Report" with a gendered rationale for a clubhouse: "In every human heart is the longing for a home; particularly is this true of woman. We believe the Twentieth Century Club should have her own home."[31]

Years of fundraising ensued, and completion of the clubhouse in 1913 was an important advancement for the club.

The TCC clubhouse provided a space for women that was separate, autonomous, and gendered—a hybrid between public and private, both an institutional and a residential space. The TCC sought to blend the quiet decorum of the domestic domain with its desire for a public forum that could accommodate large events. The first-floor entrance was somewhat domestic, formal yet modest, with its wide steps and triple-arched entrance. The first floor contained sitting rooms, a large formal banquet hall, a kitchen, committee meeting rooms, and an auditorium to seat five hundred.[32] A grand staircase led to a second story that proclaimed the building's public stature, with five arched doorways opening onto a balcony, a flagpole and medallion above, with "TCC" inscribed on a shield. The second floor held a ballroom and a second auditorium, banked by windows across the rear wall, designed for public lectures and performances, the perfect complement to the women's civitas. The clubhouse thus provided a gendered bridge between private and public realms, creating an atmosphere at once domestic and formal. It was a controlled environment, with the advantages of members-only admittance when women wanted to practice public speaking in a hospitable atmosphere, while also being sufficiently capacious for public lectures and conferences. Building the clubhouse made the Twentieth Century Club an institution in the community, literally and figuratively. It advertised the group's ability to raise money, manage its finances, acquire land, charter the design and construction of a specialized structure, and operate it across the century.

TCC women were conscious of the need to find their voices and train themselves in public speaking. Closed meetings provided a sanctuary for reticent members who might otherwise have been sidelined by professional speakers. TCC president Mrs. Stephen E. Kieffer expressed this awareness in 1913: "The closed meetings have met with favor . . . [and] have been among the best of the year. . . . In this way new talent has been developed and we have learned to know our own resources."[33] The clubhouse thus provided a space for women to find their voices, buffered from intimidation by experts, dominant personalities, and professional speakers.

Because public life required public speaking, the importance of parliamentary procedure was constantly emphasized within the TCC. This in turn suggests the tactical process by which clubwomen entered the realm of public discourse and political activism. Most women in the early twentieth century were entirely ignorant of procedures for conducting public meetings and had to tutor themselves with copies of *Robert's Rules of Order*. Women's clubs viewed parliamentary process as a model of efficiency, and contemporary handbooks extolled the virtues of acquiring the skills needed to conduct meetings and debates according to precise rules.[34] Club minutes and press releases invariably emphasized TCC debates as inclusive, participatory, orderly, harmonious, and cordial.

In her 1927 history of the CFWC, Mary Gibson suggests the context behind clubwomen's interest in mastering the mechanics of public procedures. Gibson quoted approvingly a 1914 essay entitled "The Unparliamentary Woman," which lamented the fact that many clubwomen resisted parliamentary usage as "a troublesome formality" that was not naturally "womanly." The essayist deflected this criticism, countering, "It is undeniably true that the person who is familiar with parliamentary practice has an advantage in any deliberate assembly over one who does not possess such knowledge." President Annie Little Barry, a TCC founder, strongly agreed. An accomplished parliamentarian, Barry established the practice of opening TCC meetings with parliamentary procedure drills, in which all members were encouraged to participate.

The importance to women of learning basic political procedures is again glimpsed in the farewell address of the 1903–1904 CFWC president, who related that in the early years delegates experienced difficulty electing officers because they did not know formal voting procedures: "There was a heated discussion over the question of ballots, many not knowing how to use them until Mrs. Kinney, the parliamentarian, was called. This was thought very important, since the question of Equal Suffrage was imminent."[35] TCC history offers several poignant moments of realization, when members recognized that women were so excluded from full political citizenship and the democratic process that they did not know how to speak in public, conduct a meeting, or cast a ballot. TCC women were acutely aware of their procedural deficiencies and sought to overcome them in the refuge of their clubhouse.

For the TCC, sociability and activism were seamless components of club life. Internal practices fostered greater awareness of political issues and gave members the confidence to address them publicly. Civic consciousness in the TCC continued to unfold during the years between the club's December 1904 founding and April 1917, when the United States entered World War I. The earliest extant club bulletin, dated December 1905, lists a "Current Events" section.[36] Monthly club bulletins from 1906 through the Great Depression are filled with programs devoted to contemporary political events, social problems, and civic issues, reflecting sustained activism spanning the first half of the twentieth century.

In 1913 the TCC president reported that "the programs throughout the year have been prepared to meet the desires of the Club members" in the areas of "readings, music, literature, and drama." Nonetheless, she challenged members to do more. "The success of our Civic meetings," she wrote, demonstrates "the fact that the Twentieth Century Club has grown along civic lines and is ready to identify itself with others in efforts for the betterment of city and country."[37] This call for a more ambitious agenda evokes Frances Willard's WCTU motto, "Do Everything," and the TCC's civic activism did indeed expand during the progressive era. The topic of a 1914 club program, "The Awakening of a Civic Conscience," is suggestive of the trend.[38]

TCC pre-suffrage activism was extensive and not only focused on gaining the vote. From its founding, the club fostered an expanded sense of women's citizenship through civic altruism, and its Current Events, Parliamentary, and Civic sections led members directly into municipal activism. The campaigns waged by section leaders indicate that they were more activist than the term "study group" implied. In November 1906, for example, the club considered "Child Labor and the Juvenile Court." The clubwomen expressed dismay at the 75 percent recidivism rate among ex-convicts from San Quentin and Folsom prisons, and the example of a man sentenced to ten years in San Quentin for stealing a length of rope. The TCC decided to support prison rehabilitation programs, the probation system, the juvenile court system, and child labor protection laws.[39]

In anticipation of a vote to reform local government, in April 1909 the TCC held a "Civic Afternoon" and invited William Carey Jones, a University of California law professor, to deliver an address on "The Working of the New Charter."[40] The July 1909 election brought approval of the new Berkeley City Charter that contained several elements Berkeley clubwomen had worked for, including a public charities board, a playground board, and a civic art commission.[41] The balloting also delivered the first woman elected to the Berkeley Board of Education, Elinor Carlisle.[42] The historian Gayle Gullet reports that Carlisle, a clubwoman, teacher, and suffragist, "campaigned with the active support of the city's women's movement."[43] The TCC provided Carlisle a venue for such pre-election addresses as "The Mother's Attitude towards Civics," and members campaigned for her Good Government platform.[44] It was a significant victory for women who did not yet possess suffrage. TCC records from 1909 show determination to make the most of the new political tools created by the city charter.[45]

The TCC did not generally fall into partisan politicking. Issues dominated 1910 — county public health, the success of women at Mills College, and the National Playground Congress. In February the Current Events section discussed state issues at the forefront in 1910: "During the session of our State Legislature our discussions were both lively and edifying, and the engrossing subject of equal suffrage was debated in a thoughtful and earnest spirit, the section as well as the Club desiring to throw the weight of its influence with all that looks toward the betterment of the home."[46] The women defined their legislative agenda in terms of their urban and domestic civitas, and anticipated that suffrage would expand their activities for the commonweal.

Although women's municipal suffrage was denied by the 1909 Berkeley Town Charter vote, the TCC published a "Women's Edition" of the *Berkeley Daily Gazette* in December 1910 that proclaimed, "The Clubwomen of Berkeley Have Arrived, and an Amendment to the Charter will no Doubt allow them to Vote in the Near Future."[47] By 1911, as the focus overtly turned to state suffrage, the women were already political veterans debating legislative issues.

In tandem with their local activism, TCC members were also instrumental in the passage of state suffrage. At the annual CFWC convention at Long Beach in May 1911, the California Equal Suffrage Amendment was hotly debated. It had been placed on the state ballot in February in response to concerted lobbying by California women, especially clubwomen. The Political Equality League and the suffrage association had been pressuring the CFWC to endorse the amendment, but the CFWC was noncommittal. In her history of the CFWC, Mary Gibson notes, "Nothing now remained but an endorsement of the amendment by the California Federation of Women's Clubs, the largest and most conservative body of organized women in the State. Of these women the strong leaders were suffragists, but there was an unknown quantity of skeptics and timid souls."[48] The TCC took up "the stirring question of equal suffrage" in its Current Events section prior to the convention and voted its support: "The Club went on record in favor of the extension of the right to suffrage to women by instructing our delegates to the State Convention to vote in favor of the resolution of indorsement [sic]."[49] When the issue finally made it to the floor of the CFWC convention, the TCC member Mrs. James B. Hume (née Lida Munson) was one of five delegates allowed to make "strong speeches in its favor . . . and when the vote was taken there was an overwhelming majority in its favor, nearly five to one."[50] TCC women were thus instrumental in lobbying the CFWC to endorse suffrage, support that ultimately facilitated passage of the measure in the California assembly.

Statewide, California clubwomen clearly gained with the vote a strong sense of their own political efficacy, as well as a remarkable degree of partisan independence. In the October 1911 election, Berkeley voters chose J. Stitt Wilson, a Socialist, as mayor. While San Francisco and Oakland voted against women's suffrage, Berkeley Mayor Stitt had publicly campaigned for it. Berkeley was the only municipality in Alameda County to vote for women's suffrage by a substantial majority, which was crucial to the narrow statewide victory.[51] Members of the TCC must have concluded that their work in maintaining a high public profile, shaping public opinion through education and debate, and engaging in nonpartisan civic altruism had been rewarded by the election results.

Although women reformers in Berkeley tended toward the progressive wing of the Republican Party, the TCC and the California suffrage movement rejected partisan alliances. Sara Bard Field, a San Francisco poet and feminist, summed up their strategy toward partisanship while recalling lobbying efforts in 1915 for national women's suffrage at the PPIE in San Francisco:

> The Republicans were just as adamant on the question of it being a states' rights matter as the Democrats were. There wasn't any great division of opinion among them. Indeed, as I went on deeper and deeper into the work of the Woman's Party I was forced to realize

that in political life men are influenced only and solely by the hope of political backing, and that all the pleading and the urging and the brilliance of the delegations of Eastern women that had gone [before] had just evaporated because they were helpless; they couldn't deliver the votes. Being so convinced, I could not say to Senator Phelan ... that we would promise never to go out against Democrats; if they failed to give us the amendment in the next election, in fact, we would go out against them regardless of their personal support, because it was the party we wanted to defeat.[52]

Acquisition of suffrage in California had involved opposition from and alliances with men of various parties, so women were cautious about ceding their autonomy to any male-dominated party.

Political engagement by the women of the TCC grew stronger with the passage of equal suffrage. This corresponds with Nancy Cott's thesis of continuity in women's activism after gaining the vote.[53] TCC women were acutely conscious of their new expanded political opportunities. Just three months after the 1911 election, the club's "Civic Affairs" section set an ambitious agenda, declaring, "This is in line with the broader field of work planned by the women's clubs, now that the ballot is an assured thing. The one object which stands paramount among the women at present is the proper exercising of the long-coveted franchise."[54] The club's leadership laid out a path for the members: "May a keener sense of our larger responsibilities outside immediate club interest cause us to turn our activities more and more to civic work and social service."[55] No longer required to split their labors between suffrage and civic reforms, TCC women redoubled their commitment to civitas.

The TCC played a key role in the creation of California's Women's Legislative Council (WLC) in 1912 at the CFWC conference in San Francisco. The WLC declared itself "non-partisan" with the aim "to secure better laws for women and children, public welfare measures and laws that make for better moral, economic and social conditions."[56] The WLC viewed its power in "its ability to focus as well as enlighten public opinion," which it did very successfully during its first year of lobbying.[57] The WLC campaign was a huge success, with fifteen of the seventeen bills from the clubwomen's platform enacted by the 1913 state legislature (discussed at greater length in chapter 10). This achievement convinced women activists to create a permanent WLC in the fall of 1913. The standing WLC was drawn from fifty-three women's associations and contingents from labor and socialist organizations, but the CFWC was recognized as the "largest and most actively interested" body in the WLC. The TCC elected its Civic Section leader, Mrs. William Colby, to the CFWC and the WLC.[58] Thus, when Colby addressed sister members in Berkeley on legislative measures, she did so not as an observer but as a prime operative in California politics.

In February 1913 the local press reported on a talk given by the TCC's legislative chair on "a number of bills introduced in the state legislature which are of especial interest to women. Among them are the mothers' pension, red-light injunction, equal guardianship and property rights bills."[59] In other words, the TCC agenda closely paralleled the 1913 CFWC state legislative agenda. During the spring of 1913 the club also discussed pure-foods reforms and the prevention of war, demonstrating that their range of interests spanned both local and global issues.[60]

On March 4, 1913, the club held a "Civic Afternoon," which featured a "discussion of legislative measures." The event was led by Mrs. William Colby (née Rachel Vrooman), TCC member, WLC delegate, and newly elected president of the Alameda District Federation of Women's Clubs.[61] The local press entitled their report "Clubwomen Discuss Bills" and detailed the open meeting: "The red-light injunction bill, in which women all over the state are taking an active interest, was explained by Mrs. Colby. The club endorsed the measure following Mrs. Colby's discourse.... Plans for a new state board of education ... the minimum wage, mothers' pension bill, equal guardianship, moving picture censorship and other issues were also discussed."[62] The TCC subsequently endorsed all of these measures, popularly termed the "Women's Legislative Agenda" of 1913.

The women also discussed at length the "Ferguson mile-limit bill" (AB 1620), which purported to further restrict the sale of alcohol near churches and schools statewide.[63] Berkeley already had a mile-limit law, an 1876 city ordinance prohibiting the sale of alcohol within one mile of the perimeter of the UC campus. There were recurring efforts in the late nineteenth and early twentieth centuries to revise the law to make the entire town dry, and clubwomen were especially active in these efforts. Berkeley passed a comprehensive temperance ordinance in 1899, rescinded it in 1900, and then reinstated a citywide prohibition in 1906, a measure that lasted until the federal repeal in 1933.[64]

The 1913 Ferguson bill appeared to require university "dry zones" across the state. In reality, Representative Ferguson of Alameda County introduced the bill at the behest of the Claremont Hotel, which wanted a liquor license. Ferguson's bill was carefully crafted to shift the coordinates of the UC campus dry zone to exempt the hotel from Berkeley's prohibition ordinance. The bill was hotly debated across the state, with liquor, hospitality, and commercial interests pitted against women's clubs and the WCTU.

After much debate, the press reported that the clubwomen declared the bill a poorly written "joker" and "decided to use their influence against the passage of the measure."[65] Berkeley remained a WCTU stronghold, with long-standing connections between temperance and women's rights, including the cofounding of the TCC by a WCTU veteran.[66] Oakland business interests nearly succeeded in passing Ferguson's measure in 1913, but the bill failed by a single vote when Berkeley's representative voted against it.[67]

Judging from the TCC's agenda, clubwomen in Berkeley enjoyed an enhanced sense of prominence and prestige in the community in the years between suffrage and World War I. Members of the TCC participated in community boosterism and played a highly visible role in promoting the 1915 PPIE.[68] After 1911, when San Francisco won the bid to host the world's fair celebrating the Panama Canal opening, Bay Area clubwomen promoted the PPIE much as they had campaigned to win it. In 1912 the *Oakland Tribune* reported that the women of Alameda County had sent a quarter of a million postcards across the nation to publicize the PPIE. The article detailed the method employed by Berkeley clubwomen, who had organized card-writers by precinct.[69]

TCC women were well aware of their growing political status. In 1916 they proudly declared, "The Twentieth Century Club is becoming more and more a power in the community."[70] The 1915–1916 Civic Committee report reflects their spectrum of interests from urban to regional to state: "Our first interest was given to civic affairs in the local community—our student population, the youths of the town, and matters of local education," yet "many county interests were discussed as well as state responsibilities concerning proposed legislation."⁷¹ The Civic Committee undertook a "considerable study" of "the girls of the University," who constituted, they thought, "an important element of our population." They found that many female students were struggling financially to put themselves through the University of California. The committee discussed ways of "giving them encouragement in their laudable efforts and of affording them a chance to earn needed expenses," and prompted the TCC to establish a scholarship.⁷² No issue, it seems, was too modest for the club's expansive agenda.

The club's civitas centered on their city, but it protracted into widening spheres of political activism. TCC women embraced international issues from the club's 1904 inception, well before World War I. In December 1908 the TCC held a program entitled "Discussion: The International Peace Movement." Members listened intently as women read papers and discussed such topics as "War, the World's Greatest Blunder," "The History of Arbitration," "The Heroes of Peace," and "What We Can Do for the Peace Movement."⁷³

The club held numerous programs on international issues over the years, finally organizing a formal "Peace Committee" in October 1915, as Americans debated entry into the fighting that already engulfed Europe. The first annual Peace Committee report declared, "This is a crucial time in the world's history. Let us who are far removed from the war zone remember our many blessings, and unite our efforts to make Peace permanent and perpetual."⁷⁴ TCC Peace Committee programs in 1915 included "The Terrible Meek: A Plea For Peace," "The International Mind," and "Wanted—Aggressive Pacifism."⁷⁵ Berkeley clubwomen's interest in pacifism was prescient, since "international peace was, arguably, the major item of concern among organized women in the 1920s," as Nancy Cott has argued.⁷⁶

With the outbreak of fighting in Europe, Berkeley clubwomen shifted from pacifism to relief work. The TCC hosted lectures on war conditions and held relief drives for Armenians, Syrians, Belgians, and French.⁷⁷ TCC officers were guests of honor at the reception in April 1916, when the British suffragist Emmeline Pankhurst visited Berkeley to raise money for Serbian refugees. Two hundred East Bay clubwomen and the leadership of the CFWC attended, the event explicitly blending women's club culture, feminism, and internationalism.⁷⁸ Women's relief work was generally characterized as philanthropy, often by the women themselves, yet for women opposed to militarism, the focus on aiding noncombatant victims of war presented an ideal venue for international activism.

The mobilization of U.S. women during World War I had many far-reaching effects. For TCC members, war work was a unifying, all-encompassing campaign that elevated their political legitimacy. The organizational structure of the women's club movement lent itself perfectly to mobilization activities. The resulting "drives," which the public likely viewed as charity work before the war, now became patriotic and nationalistic; the public viewed the campaigns as essential to national security and international peace.

American entrance into World War I shifted the TCC activities dramatically. The final pre-war program of the club discussed "The Pros and Cons of Single Tax," "Educating Prisoners at Folsom," "The Proposed City and County of Alameda," "The School on Trial," and "Municipal Collection of Garbage."[79] After their summer vacation of 1917 and the country's entrance into the war, the club's attention was almost entirely dominated by war work, and philosophical debates gave way to quotidian projects. The "War Service Work Committee" subsumed club activities, and the TCC adopted the motto "Saving—Service—Sacrifice."[80] The Peace Committee was the war's first casualty, and the new order of business became sewing and knitting for the Red Cross, bandage making, food-conservation forums, and war savings bond drives. The TCC temporarily suspended all regular committees and sections "to concentrate on war service work," and they were supplanted by new ones: Americanization, Service Flag, Sewing Bags for French and Belgians, Tin Foil, Food Conservation, Cancelled Stamps, Old Gloves, Relief Sewing, New Clothes for Relief, the Committee of Thirty Regarding the War Savings Society, and Rennecourt Relief (an aid project "the women of Berkeley" initiated and managed for a small French village near the front that the City of Berkeley had "adopted").[81]

The TCC invited General C. A. Woodruff to speak on "Our Army," and club records duly noted that members had divided into groups of ten "according to government instructions" for selling war bonds.[82] The club's reversal from antiwar lobbying to complete assimilation of militarism and patriotism is hinted at in TCC descriptions of its own mobilization as "Over the Top," a phrase evoking trench warfare.[83]

With the coming of the war, issues of household management became imperative and nationalistic. The women of the TCC had always been concerned with their roles and responsibilities as home managers, expressing that concern in ways that blended private domestic concerns with public policy issues, such as the anti-tuberculosis, pure milk campaign in Berkeley. Conservation of resources (chapter 7 in this volume) had always been a central value for the clubwomen, but now it became a patriotic duty. Club bulletins carried the motto "save lives by saving dollars."[84] The need to conserve food, clothing, and energy fell within the female realm, and so was infused with nationalism. The TCC held demonstrations on "Hoover Luncheons" in September 1917 and "Hoover Breakfasts" in January 1918.[85] (Herbert Hoover headed the federal Food Administration, responsible for national food-conservation efforts.) TCC's Food Conservation Forum held a total of thirty lectures and demonstrations on war cooking, and instructors from the University of California and the U.S. government regularly spoke to members on such topics as "the Housewife's War Time Problem," wheat substitutes, canning without sugar, and cooking with fish, fowl, and game.[86] Attention to these mundane problems was constantly accompanied by political and nationalistic exhortations, as in this notice to members: "The Food Administration has promised 15,000,000 tons of food to the Allies. In addition to the compulsory ration of sugar and wheat flour, we are asked to save voluntarily, in true American spirit, 50% more non-perishable food than last year."[87] For Berkeley clubwomen the concept of the "home front" had merged with civitas.

It was clear by the end of the war that, through their voluntary efforts, local women had elevated their status as citizens. The September 1918 *Oakland Tribune Magazine* addressed some of the changes in gendered citizenship that women's war work had wrought:

> After being classed in the "weaker sex" for some thousands of years, although for the same thousands of years women have been doing most of the really hard work of the world, there must have been a glow of enthusiasm in making clear the foolishness of the classification.... Undoubtedly the war call itself has been a great, perhaps a dominating, incentive.... When help is needed badly in war time ... patriotism has no sex or prejudices.[88]

Women's war mobilization appears to have altered public perceptions and rhetoric regarding their work, at least in the short term. The *Oakland*

Tribune's coverage of local women's activities also suggests this conceptual shift. Before the war, the paper placed women's club activities under its "In Society" section, with a stylized graphic of an aristocratic-looking woman wearing a huge hat with gauze netting over her face. After 1917 the paper moved the same women's clubs to a regular column entitled "Women of Alameda County and Their Work."

Berkeley women continued their mobilization throughout the global influenza pandemic that accompanied the armistice in late 1918, but under even more difficult conditions. The TCC was eager to return to its civic politics as soon as the disruptions of war eased. The club had planned to discuss the state legislative agenda in October (with TCC member and newly elected assemblywoman Anna Saylor as moderator) but the Board of Health banned all public meetings in October and November 1918.[89] TCC members instead volunteered as nurses in Berkeley's makeshift infirmary and, during the second wave of the flu epidemic, at the Municipal Hospital.[90] For organized women, service still trumped politics.

Given the sweeping changes in the world and in women's lives, it was no small question for TCC women to ask what would be "Women's Share in the New Internationalism," as they did in April 1918.[91] Because California women had already won the franchise, their war work did not carry a quid pro quo regarding suffrage. In fact, the reverse was true; as June Underwood argues, "Woman's suffrage was successful in the West not because men recognized the worth of women, but because women needed political power to promote the welfare of others and to extend their roles outside the confines of their home."[92] The long list of Western women's progressive-era accomplishments—child labor laws, minimum-wage and maximum-hour laws, age-of-consent laws, child-care centers, parks and playgrounds, pure food and drug laws, clean city water systems, municipal sewerage and garbage collection systems, and free public libraries—parallels the program agenda of the TCC during the early twentieth century.[93] To this venerable list of achievements, clubwomen could now add their role in the Allied war victory. Women's direct and unprecedented engagement in global movements and struggles during the Great War affected their self-consciousness as citizens in ways that rivaled—or perhaps exceeded—the casting of a ballot. The power that they accumulated is reflected in a 1919 TCC reception for two of its most accomplished members, Mrs. Aaron

Schloss (née Adella Tuttle), the president of the statewide CFWC, and Mrs. Anna Saylor, a member of the state legislature.[94]

TCC women continued their engagement in international issues throughout the interwar years, returning to their public advocacy of the peace movement. The January 1920 *Bulletin* announced: "The Executive Board of the California Federation of Women's Clubs, at a recent meeting DECIDED what a great majority of the women of California would do, i.e., ask for the early ratification of the Peace Treaty and the League of Nations. The Memorial to Congress signature booklets will be at the first Club Meeting, January 6th. Sign then, if not before."[95] The club program for November 1921 included a lecture and discussion of "the Washington conference of the limitation of armaments."[96] In March 1928 the TCC hosted a three-day conference on international relations at its clubhouse. The conference was presented under the auspices of the CFWC, organized by TCC and other local clubwomen, directed by the Alameda District Federation of Women's Clubs, and addressed each day by federation officers. The women had a large view of their conference's significance. Local press coverage indicated that the gathering was intended to be the first in an annual series "to which world leaders will turn for facts leading to a better understanding and amity between nations."[97] Organized in cooperation with the University of California, Stanford University, and Mills College, faculty from several Bay Area colleges participated.[98] Topics included international debt, international labor standards, immigration, trade policies, public opinion, and the promotion of world peace. The proceedings paid special attention to German and Russian economic recoveries and their effects on European stability. Governmental representatives from Germany, Great Britain, and Canada spoke. President of Mills College Dr. Aurelia Reinhardt addressed "Educational Organizations for International Cooperation," and Dean of Women Lucy Ward Stebbins, a professor of social economics at the University of California, presided over a roundtable on the League of Nations, the Peace Treaty of Versailles, and the World Court.[99]

Postwar TCC programs indicate an engaged citizenship that shifted easily between local and global concerns. In March 1919 the club wrote to President Woodrow Wilson "favoring the entrance of the United States into a Society of Nations."[100] In 1929 the TCC debated "Does California

12. Anna L. Saylor, TCC officer and California Assemblywoman (1919–1926), ca. 1922. From Louis S. Lyons and Josephine Wilson, eds., Who's Who among the Women of California (San Francisco: Security, 1922), 120.

Need a New Constitution?" and discussed the just-published antiwar novel *All Quiet on the Western Front*.[101] Berkeley women examined municipal Americanization efforts alongside "The Kellogg-Briand Treaty and the Outlawry of War."[102] The common denominator was "women's influence in politics," a civitas that now transcended the city.[103]

The club's mobilization for World War I enhanced its members' political power and prestige, leading to the 1918 election of one of its leaders, Anna L. Saylor, to the California State Assembly. Observers attributed this unprecedented victory for women to Saylor's leadership in organizing "war work" among Berkeley clubwomen. The *Oakland Tribune* announced Saylor's election victory with the headline "Woman Is Rewarded By Berkeleyans," and enumerated the five war bond drives she had led. The celebratory article carried a picture of Saylor with the caption "she will be the first woman to sit in the legislature of California."[104] (In fact, Saylor was one of four "first women" elected to the California assembly that year.)

Saylor's path through the TCC sheds light on women's political culture in the era. Anna Louise McBride Saylor (1871–1956) began her career as an educator, administrator, and clubwoman in Indiana. In 1901 she successfully lobbied Andrew Carnegie to fund the Elwood (Indiana) Public Library.[105] She was elected president of the Indiana Union of Literary Clubs in 1904, and successfully negotiated a merger with the rival Indiana State Federation of Women's Clubs in 1906, thus creating a more powerful lobby for women.[106] Saylor moved with her family to Berkeley in 1912, soon joined the Twentieth Century Club, and quickly became a leader.[107] She was the original organizer and chair of the Current Events section and was responsible for its activist orientation.[108] Saylor had ascended to the TCC board of directors by 1916.[109] In September 1917 she was elected first vice-president, ensuring her succession to the presidency. By February 1918 she chaired the TCC's War Service Work committee and directed the Berkeley Women Workers of the Liberty Loan bond drive.

In August 1918 Saylor won election to the California State Assembly. The *Oakland Tribune* failed to mention her Republican Party affiliation (or that of any opponent), reporting only that Saylor had been elected by women voters with the campaign slogan "in union there is strength" (which was reminiscent of the CFWC motto, "strength united is stronger"). The *Tribune* declared: "She was the unanimous choice of the women of Berkeley to be their standard bearer for the highest electoral honor accorded a woman in California."[110] Saylor gave credit where it was due, to Berkeley clubwomen: "The success she declares is due entirely to the undivided support of the women of her district, upon whom she lavished unstinted praise. What has been done by the women of Berkeley she declares can be done anywhere, provided there is unity in purpose and strength."[111] Saylor attributed her election to voter "recognition of the wonderful work of service done by the women of Berkeley in carrying out the college city's extensive program of war activities." Saylor's election was the culmination of years of activism by the community of Berkeley clubwomen.

Assemblywoman Saylor led successful campaigns to abolish the death penalty for minors and establish psychiatric clinics in prisons. After serving four terms in the assembly (1919–1926), she declined to run for a fifth in order to accept appointment by Governor C. C. Young to direct the California State Department of Social Welfare. As director from 1927 to 1931, Saylor championed child labor protection, prevention of juvenile crime, mental health assistance, and aid to seniors. Saylor's work brought her national attention, and she was invited by President Herbert Hoover to participate in the 1930 White House Conference on Child Health and Protection. She continued working within the networks she had developed as a Berkeley clubwoman, indicated by her continuing involvement in TCC events throughout the 1920s.

Clubwomen in California generally supported the progressive wing of the Republican Party, yet they formally maintained nonpartisan independence and occasionally opposed Republican candidates who did not conform to their standards. And although clubwomen developed an innovative politics of civitas that was officially nonaligned, they still operated in a male-dominated partisan system, as in the case of Governor Rolph. In his bid for governor in 1930, James "Sunny Jim" Rolph Jr. failed to receive the endorsement of the San Francisco League of Women Voters because they disapproved of his performance as San Francisco mayor. According to Helen Valeska Bary (1888–1973), the deputy director of the California State Department of Social Welfare from 1928 to 1931 (during Saylor's tenure), Rolph "could be a very vindictive person, and he said that he would get even with those women." Bary recalled that in 1931, "with the change of administration, [female] department directors [including Bary and Saylor] were dismissed" by Rolph.[112]

After her retirement from government service, Saylor returned to Berkeley and continued her work in women's clubs. She was a founding member of the Berkeley Women's City Club, established in 1927 and housed in an impressive downtown structure designed by Julia Morgan. Saylor also maintained her membership in the TCC, where she was a popular speaker on social and legislative issues.[113]

The example of the Twentieth Century Club of Berkeley brings a clearer focus to the political culture that developed in California during the progressive era. There was more continuity than change in the goals and methods of the TCC before and after enfranchisement. The club was political from its inception, seven years prior to woman suffrage in the state, and it remained politically active for decades after the vote was won. Berkeley women ran for office and won elections before they could vote, as Elinor Carlisle had done in 1909.[114] The TCC's sustained involvement in urban politics demonstrates the club's emergence in an era of civic activism, as clubwomen forged their own civitas.

Carlisle's election typifies how municipal issues were often interwoven with maternalism. The women of the TCC defied the dichotomy between civic and private. The club's president in 1913 reported that the TCC was engaged with "domestic and public problems" and committed to "the conservation of humanity."[115] In April 1914 the club held a program entitled "Child Welfare Work Through the Parent-Teacher and Mothers' Clubs."[116] TCC women moved within overlapping public and private realms in a way that was consistent with contemporary gender definitions yet, at the same time, their activism challenged dominant social structures. The women's sense of the "conservation of humanity" implies a broad understanding of protecting the common good at multiple levels during the progressive era, as they extended the ideas of "municipal housekeeping" in increasingly sophisticated ways, from pure milk to international arbitration. It is precisely this play of scale that makes the evolution of women's political agency during the progressive era—and the issue of how they viewed their own status as women and citizens—such an intriguing historical question.

Direct linkages between the TCC and the CFWC demonstrate the broad political impact that federated Berkeley clubwomen had on California politics. (CFWC membership was 25,000 in 1911 and 33,500 in 1915.)[117]

Ties between Berkeley and the state federation were strong, evidenced by the constant presence of TCC members as delegates to federation conventions, the frequency of CFWC speakers at TCC meetings, and the number of TCC women who served as CFWC officers. The style of the TCC indicates the substance of the clubwomen's political culture. Issues were addressed in the parliamentary format, which the women viewed as an essential tool and an entering wedge into the political process. To facilitate these meetings, TCC women built their clubhouse, which served as an affirming social and civic space. The women clearly valued their proprietary space for deliberation, excluding the general public in order to promote the full participation of each member, where veterans could get things done, novices might find tutelage, and no one would be shut out of discussions by a few dominant voices. The women of Berkeley's TCC explored the meanings and uses of citizenship in remarkably consistent ways. The TCC's 1904 mission statement emphasized "mutual improvement" and "the good of the community," and their eighty-six-year history indicates that the club successfully integrated social and political concerns in their activism.[118] Winning suffrage was an empowering event for clubwomen, but the vote invigorated, rather than created, their civic focus. They formed a Current Events section in 1905 and added a Civic Section in 1909 to acknowledge what they had long been doing. The club's leadership encouraged increased attention to civic work and social service, but these had been a focus at the club's founding in 1904. TCC women ceaselessly participated in politics, as candidates and legislators, as voters and constituents, forging links between local issues and state initiatives as well as between national and international issues, throughout the progressive era and beyond.

The history of the TCC illustrates more fully the path that early twentieth-century women took to realize full agency as citizens: participation in civic life. The roots of citizenship for California women during the progressive era, both before and after suffrage, were in the city. Twentieth Century Club members understood the relational significance of *civic* as both place and ideology; for TCC women, civitas meant a claimed citizenship derived from their city.

When considering the legacy of progressive-era women's clubs, the question of what constitutes "politics" becomes a defining issue. As Maureen

Flanagan has shown with clubwomen in Chicago, urban planning always takes place in an acutely political context, even when women's club work is defined as "beautification."[119] The fact that progressive women often considered their activism *nonpartisan* has been misconstrued, in both contemporary and subsequent considerations, as an indication that their work was *apolitical*—a grave misunderstanding of the era and of women's political culture.

Assessing the TCC's legacy has been made more difficult because the record of their works and achievements gradually faded from view, but this elision is itself a critical part of the story. A 1941 history of Berkeley compiled by the Works Progress Administration's (WPA) Writer's Project relegates women to a couple of pages, and even these references are oblique. The election of Elinor Carlisle was reduced to a nameless footnote—"the first woman member of the board was elected in July, 1909." Anna Saylor's unprecedented election was similarly truncated to an anonymous notation: "Berkeley sent a woman to the State Legislature in 1919."[120] The WPA history further conveys a sense that women's civic activism was much diminished by the 1940s. In discussing the "civic consciousness" surrounding the planning of the city's "Diamond Jubilee" in 1941, the account mentions thirty-five men, but only four women.[121] This distorted representation of what Berkeley women had done during the early twentieth century makes clear that coverage does not necessarily reflect reality. Of the four women mentioned in 1941, however, it is no surprise that one, Mrs. E. J. Hadden, was a recent TCC president.

The political culture that TCC women developed during the progressive era affected state politics in complex, direct, and far-reaching ways. TCC leaders astutely characterized the club's political philosophy as a blend of progressive and conservative impulses, in keeping with progressive-era women's broad sense of conservation. The 1910 "Women's Issue" of the *Berkeley Daily Gazette* included a "History of the Twentieth Century Club," which declared that founder Annie Little Barry had infused the club with a "wise conservatism." At the same time, members were also likely to boast that the Twentieth Century Club was "the most progressive ... women's club about the bay."[122] This complex mixture of conservative and progressive impulses is key to understanding the work of women's clubs and the political culture that they created in the progressive era.

The history of the Twentieth Century Club of Berkeley is an example of how California women broadened their power as citizens by developing a civitas that used the progressive-era city as an alternative to the ballot, how they expanded the meaning of political culture before and after the fulcra of suffrage and war, and how they accomplished an ambitious agenda with remarkable continuity of purpose across three decades of a radically shifting geography of power.

Notes

1. Paula Baker, "The Domestication of Politics: Women and American Political Society, 1780–1920," *American Historical Review* 89 (1984): 622.

2. *Cassell's Compact Latin Dictionary* (New York: Dell, 1981), s.v. "civitas," and *Webster's Unabridged Dictionary*, 2d ed. (2001), s.v. "civitas."

3. Rosemary Dobbins, "Club History, December 12, 1944," typescript, box 1, folder 35, Twentieth Century Club of Berkeley Records (hereafter "TCC") MSS 90/55 c, Bancroft Library, University of California, Berkeley. All TCC records—mostly unpublished minutes, reports, and scrapbooks—are located at the Bancroft Library, and are hereafter cited as "TCC MSS."

4. Mrs. H. H. Dobbins, "History of the Twentieth Century Club," *Berkeley Daily Gazette*, December 1, 1910, box 1, folder 33; Rosemary Dobbins, "Club History"; California Federation of Women's Clubs (CFWC), *Club Women of California: State Register and Directory, 1916* (San Francisco: CFWC, 1916).

5. Club membership began at 50 in 1904, grew to 129 in 1905, to 150 in 1907, to 272 in 1916, and to 291 by 1917; "Yearbook" (1904–1906), 17, "Yearbook" (1916), 9; "Yearbook" (1917), 7, TCC MSS; CFWC, *California Federation of Women's Clubs Year Book 1906–1907* (San Jose: Murgottens, 1906), 76; CFWC, *Clubwomen of California: Official Register and Directory, 1907* (San Francisco: CFWC, 1907), 98; CFWC, *Clubwomen of California: State Register and Directory, 1916* (San Francisco: CFWC, 1916), 120–21.

6. "Constitution and By-Laws of the Twentieth Century Club of Berkeley," pamphlet, December 1904, "Scrapbook" vol. 1 (1904–1913), TCC MSS.

7. Gayle Gullett, *Becoming Citizens: The Emergence and Development of the California Women's Movement, 1880–1911* (Urbana: University of Illinois Press, 2000), 120.

8. Gullett, *Becoming Citizens*, 123. See also Rebecca J. Mead, *How the Vote Was Won: Woman Suffrage in the Western United States, 1868–1914* (New York: New York University Press, 2004), 121.

9. Gullett, *Becoming Citizens*, 123.

10. Gullett, *Becoming Citizens*, 123, 124.

11. Bureau of the Census, *Thirteenth Census of the United States, vol. 2, Population*, 1910 (Washington DC: GPO, 1913), 180.

12. "Mary Frances Albrier: Determined Advocate for Racial Equality," 1977–78,

oral history interview conducted by Malca Chall, Berkeley Oral Histories of African Americans, Regional Oral History Office, the Bancroft Library, University of California, Berkeley; from part 6: "Clubs and Civic Organizations: Integrating White Women's Groups"; available at: http://content.cdlib.org/view?docId=hb6 96nb3ht&query=&brand=calisphere.

13. "Yearbook" (1908–1909), 11, TCC MSS.

14. Caroline French Benton, *The Complete Club Book for Women* (Boston: Page, 1915), 1–3.

15. "Yearbook" (1908–1909), 13.

16. *Los Angeles Capital*, August 2, 1902, cited in Gullett, *Becoming Citizens*, 120.

17. Eric Foner, *The Story of American Freedom* (New York: Norton, 1998), 161.

18. Mary S. Gibson, *A Record of Twenty-Five Years of the California Federation of Women's Clubs, 1900–1925* (Los Angeles: CFWC, 1927), title page.

19. Bessie Ross Page, "President's Report," "Yearbook" (1910–1911), 12, TCC MSS.

20. December 1905 "Bulletin," October 1909 "Bulletin," April 1911 "Bulletin"; "Scrapbook" vol. 1.

21. January 1916 "Bulletin," "Scrapbook" vol. 2 (1913–1922), TCC MSS.

22. January 1920 "Bulletin," October 1920 "Bulletin," "Scrapbook" vol. 2.

23. "Twentieth Century Club," newspaper clipping (n.d.), box 1, folder 45, TCC MSS.

24. Mrs. A. S. M. to Mrs. W. R. Pond, Pres., letter, January 20, 1914, "Scrapbook" vol. 1.

25. Rosemary Dobbins, "Club History."

26. Julie Roy Jeffrey, *The Great Silent Army of Abolitionism: Ordinary Women in the Antislavery Movement* (Chapel Hill: University of North Carolina Press, 1998), 79.

27. Mary S. Cunningham, *The Woman's Club of El Paso: Its First Thirty Years* (El Paso: Texas Western, 1978), 73.

28. "Yearbook" (1904–1906), 13.

29. Rosemary Dobbins, "President's Report," "Yearbook" (1908–1909), 11.

30. Gibson, *A Record*, 41.

31. "Yearbook" (1904–1906), 12–13.

32. Clipping [n.d., n.p.], "Scrapbook" vol. 1.

33. Mrs. Stephen E. Kieffer, "President's Annual Report," "Yearbook" (1913–1914) [sic] [1912–1913], 14, TCC MSS.

34. Benton, *Complete Club Book*, Chap. 4: "Rules of Order."

35. Gibson, *A Record*, 48.

36. "Scrapbook" vol. 1.

37. "President's Annual Report," "Yearbook" (1912–1913), 13–14, TCC MSS.

38. September 1914 "Bulletin," "Scrapbook" vol. 2.

39. "Interesting Club Meeting," clipping, November 27, 1906, [n.p.], "Scrapbook" vol. 1.

40. April 1909 "Bulletin," "Scrapbook" vol. 1.
41. George Pettitt, *Berkeley: The Town and Gown of It* (Berkeley: Howell-North, 1973), 84–85, 173.
42. Gullett, *Becoming Citizens*, 165–66; WPA Writers' Program, *Berkeley, the First Seventy-Five Years* (Berkeley: Gillick, 1941), 143.
43. Gullett, *Becoming Citizens*, 165–66.
44. April 1909 "Bulletin," "Scrapbook" vol. 1.
45. Rosemary Dobbins, "President's Report," in "Yearbook" (1908–1909), 12, 13.
46. Dobbins, "President's Report," 12, 13.
47. "Women's Edition," *Berkeley Daily Gazette*, December 1, 1910, p. 1 [capitalization in original].
48. Gibson, *A Record*, 61.
49. Bessie Ross Page, "President's Report," "Yearbook" (1910–1911), 12, TCC MSS.
50. Gibson, *A Record*, 62.
51. Pettitt, *Town and Gown*, 142.
52. Sara Bard Field, "Sara Bard Field, Poet and Suffragist," oral history interview by Amelia Fry, June 20, 1961, tape 19: "The Demands of the Suffrage Movement: The Politics of Woman Suffrage," Suffragists Oral History Project, The Bancroft Library, Berkeley, CA, available at: http://content.cdlib.org/view?docId=kt1p30 01n1&brand=calisphere.
53. Nancy F. Cott, *The Grounding of Modern Feminism* (New Haven CT: Yale University Press, 1987), 95.
54. "To Discuss Civic Affairs," clipping, [n.d., n.p.], "Scrapbook" vol. 1.
55. Kieffer, "President's Annual Report," 12–13.
56. Mrs. O. E. Chaney, "Women's Legislative Council of California," in *Who's Who among the Women of California*, ed. Louis S. Lyons and Josephine Wilson (San Francisco: Security, 1922), 116.
57. Chaney, "Women's Legislative Council," 116.
58. Gibson, *A Record*, 190–99.
59. "Clubhouse Plans Ready," clipping [n.p.], February 4, 1913, "Scrapbook" vol. 1.
60. "Pure Food Lore," clipping [n.d., n.p.]; "To Discuss Civic Affairs," clipping [n.p., n.d.], "Scrapbook" vol. 1.
61. Clippings, February 1913; March 1913 "Bulletin," "Scrapbook" vol. 1.
62. "Clubwomen Discuss Bills," clipping [n.d., n.p.], "Scrapbook" vol. 1.
63. "The Need of Young Women in the Temperance Work," January 20, 1900; "Anti-Saloon Mass Meeting," April 9, 1900, both in *Berkeley Daily Gazette*.
64. Charles M. Wollenberg, *Berkeley: A City in History* (Berkeley: University of California Press, 2008), 36.

65. "Clubwomen Discuss Bills."

66. This historic connection remains apparent in the progressive-era Frances Willard Junior High School on Derby Street at Telegraph Avenue near the TCC clubhouse on Derby, another example of Berkeley women's geography of civitas.

67. Franklin Hichborn, "The University 'Dry Zone' Bills," in *Story of the Session of the California Legislature of 1913* (San Francisco: James H. Barry, 1913), 296–309.

68. The December 1914 "Bulletin" noted with pride that TCC member Mrs. J. H. Wood had been elected secretary to the Women's Board of the PPIE.

69. Clipping, *Oakland Tribune*, October 13, 1912, "Scrapbook" vol. 1.

70. "Yearbook" (1915–1916), TCC MSS.

71. "Report of the Civic Committee, Mrs. Richard Boone, Chairman," "Yearbook" (1915–1916).

72. "Report of the Civic Committee, Mrs. Richard Boone," 22.

73. "Discussion: The International Peace Movement," "Program," December 8, 1908; "Twentieth Century Club," clipping, [n.d., n.p.]; all in "Scrapbook" vol. 1.

74. Peace Committee Report, "Yearbook" (1915–1916), 23.

75. October 1915 "Bulletin," "Scrapbook" vol. 2.

76. Cott, *Grounding*, 94.

77. "American Committee for Armenian and Syrian Relief," September 1917 "Bulletin," "Scrapbook" vol. 2.

78. "Berkeley Women Greet Mrs. Pankhurst," clipping [n.p., April 1916]; "Scrapbook" vol. 2.

79. November 1916 "Bulletin," January 1917 "Bulletin," April 1917 "Bulletin," "Scrapbook" vol. 2.

80. February 1918 "Bulletin," "Scrapbook" vol. 2.

81. February 1918 "Bulletin," "Scrapbook" vol. 2. See also "Berkeley's Town is Held By U.S.," *Oakland Tribune*, September 1, 1918, p. 43.

82. March 1918 "Bulletin," "Scrapbook" vol. 2.

83. January 1919 "Bulletin," "Scrapbook" vol. 2.

84. March 1918 "Bulletin."

85. September 1917 "Bulletin," January 1918 "Bulletin," "Scrapbook" vol. 2.

86. September 1917 "Bulletin," February 1919 "Bulletin," "Scrapbook" vol. 2.

87. October 1918 "Bulletin," "Scrapbook" vol. 2.

88. *Oakland Tribune Magazine* (Sunday) September 8, 1918, 1.

89. "Notices," November-December 1918, "Bulletin," "Scrapbook" vol. 2.

90. Mrs. Geo. N. Nash, "World War I," in "Twentieth Century Club of Berkeley," typescript, 1959, 5; box 1, folder 36, TCC MSS.

91. April 1918 "Bulletin," "Scrapbook" vol. 2.

92. June O. Underwood, "Western Women and True Womanhood: Culture and Symbol in History and Literature," *Great Plains Quarterly* 5, no.2 (1985): 101.

93. Underwood, "Western Women and True Womanhood," 101.

94. September 1919 "Bulletin," "Scrapbook" vol. 2. Schloss's obituary described her as a "feminist leader"; see *New York Times*, January 1, 1930, 29. The Berkeley newspaper's front-page eulogy said Schloss was "endowed with all of the qualifications for leadership" and "one of the most prominent and best beloved women in the State in social, club and civic circles." *Berkeley Daily Gazette*, December 31, 1929, p. 1.

95. January 1920 "Bulletin," "Scrapbook" vol. 2.

96. November 1921 "Bulletin," "Scrapbook" vol. 2.

97. "International Relations to be Topic of Institute," clipping [n.d., n.p.], "Scrapbook" vol. 3 (1922–1937), TCC MSS.

98. "International Relations to be Topic of Institute," clipping [n.d., n.p.], "Scrapbook" vol. 3 (1922–1937), TCC MSS.

99. "Institute of International Relations Program," March 6–8, 1928, pamphlet, "Scrapbook" vol. 3.

100. Letter, U.S. Department of State to Mrs. Frederick G. Athearn, President of the TCC, March 18, 1919, "Scrapbook" vol. 2.

101. January 1929 "Bulletin," February 1929 "Bulletin," "Scrapbook" vol. 3.

102. January 1929 "Bulletin," February 1929 "Bulletin," "Scrapbook" vol. 3.

103. September 1928 "Bulletin," "Scrapbook" vol. 3.

104. *Oakland Tribune*, September 1, 1918, p. 48.

105. For Saylor's letter to Carnegie and her efforts to create the library, see http://www.elwood.lib.in.us/historyofourlib3.htm.

106. "Wabash Valley Profiles: Anna McBride Saylor," available at: http://web.indstate.edu/community/vchs/wvp/!saylora.pdf.

107. Membership roster, "Scrapbook" vol. 1; CFWC, *Clubwomen of California: State Register and Directory*, 1916 (Los Angeles: CFWC, 1916), 121.

108. Martha P. Bennett, "Twentieth Century Club Has Notables Among Membership," clipping [n.d., ca. 1929, n.p.], "Scrapbook" vol. 3.

109. September 1916 "Bulletin," "Scrapbook" vol. 2.

110. "Woman Is Rewarded by Berkeleyans," *Oakland Tribune*, September 1, 1918, p. 48.

111. *Oakland Tribune*, September 1, 1918, p. 48.

112. "Helen Velaska Bary: Labor Administration and Social Security: A Woman's Life," 1974, oral history interview conducted by Jacqueline K. Parker, Suffragists Oral History Project, Regional Oral History Office, the Bancroft Library, University of California, Berkeley; from part 8, "California State Department of Social Welfare 1928–1931," available at: http://sunsite.berkeley.edu:2020/dynaweb/teiproj/oh/suffragists/bary/@GenericBookTextView/5129;pt=5192.

113. Information on Saylor's life is thin; see "Wabash Valley Profiles: Anna McBride Saylor," and Laura B. Driemeyer, "The Berkeley Women's City Club: Gender and Architecture" (Master's thesis, San Francisco State University, 1992), 8.

114. Gullett, *Becoming Citizens*, 165–66, 173.
115. Kieffer, "President's Annual Report," 13, 16.
116. April 1914 "Bulletin," "Scrapbook" vol. 2.
117. Gibson, *A Record*, 64, 197.
118. "Constitution and By-Laws."
119. Maureen A. Flanagan, *Seeing with Their Hearts: Chicago Women and the Vision of the Good City, 1871–1933* (Princeton NJ: Princeton University Press, 2002).
120. WPA Writers' Program, *Berkeley: The First Seventy-Five Years* (Berkeley: Gillick, 1941), 143.
121. WPA, *Berkeley*, 146.
122. "Women's Edition," *Berkeley Daily Gazette*, December 1, 1910, p. 1.

9. "WE WANT THE BALLOT FOR VERY DIFFERENT REASONS"

Clubwomen, Union Women, and the Internal Politics of the Suffrage Movement, 1896–1911

SUSAN ENGLANDER

In 1896, California voters defeated a proposition granting women the right to vote. While Southern California and the rural areas supported the measure, San Francisco Bay area voters decisively trounced the proposed amendment to the state constitution. Stunned by the failure, California suffrage organizations limped away from the campaign and effectively went into hibernation for five years. The California Woman Suffrage Association, the statewide coordinating structure, held no state conventions during this period. Only nine local suffrage clubs survived the debacle, most of them in San Francisco, and fewer than a hundred state activists continued to promote suffrage during this period. The state body constructed during the campaign wasted away to a mere skeleton.[1]

California's slump following the 1896 election was not unique. Nationally, the suffrage movement entered a fourteen-year period dubbed "the doldrums," during which no state enfranchised women. This fallow stretch was exacerbated by a leadership crisis in the National American Woman Suffrage Association (NAWSA), which followed the 1896 defeat and Susan B. Anthony's decline as a visible steward of the movement prior to her death in 1906. Anna Howard Shaw, NAWSA president from 1906 to 1915, lacked the dynamism and sense of direction needed to reinvigorate the organization. In the midst of an era of reform and political action, NAWSA seemed, in comparison, becalmed.[2]

The process of revitalizing the suffrage movement began at the state and local level, as the leadership of suffrage groups restructured the clubs and devised new strategies. Concurrently, working-class women rose as a new source of membership and of tactics. In particular, female unionists verbalized an interest in woman suffrage and attempted to join forces with the reform-minded middle-class women who had been the backbone of the movement since its inception. In San Francisco, union women sought an alliance with reform suffragists of the San Francisco Equal Suffrage League in 1907 to advance the suffrage cause. An examination of their tense, fugue-like relationship reveals a series of ideological differences that hindered their ability to work in the same organization and eventually dictated the need for a separate organization for the union women. These differences originated with the nature of the leadership of the 1896 California woman suffrage campaign and carried through the first years of the twentieth-century movement in the Golden State.[3]

Daniel W. Rodes noted in his history of California woman suffrage that temperance adherents comprised most of the leadership of the 1896 campaign.[4] Suffragist Mary McHenry Keith also reported that the Woman's Christian Temperance Union (WCTU) proved to be "a powerful ally" in the 1896 effort and was largely responsible for the "well-organized army of workers" that campaigned for woman suffrage that year. The liquor interests played a large role in the amendment's defeat.[5]

Carrie Chapman Catt, the president of NAWSA and Susan B. Anthony's immediate successor, visited California in 1901 in an attempt to raise the morale of her troops there. The effort succeeded. State leaders recommitted themselves to the cause and began the process of rebuilding the organization. The NAWSA also dispatched the organizer Gail Laughlin to California to give its western sisters a hand.[6] By 1905 the California Woman Suffrage Association boasted fifty-two new clubs in addition to the revival of twenty clubs from the 1896 effort. The federation also renamed itself the California Equal Suffrage Association (CESA) in an attempt to appeal to sympathetic men.[7]

The bulk of leaders after 1900 were drawn from the membership of California's women's club movement. Many of these clubs were a direct outgrowth of the 1896 campaign and mainly involved themselves in civic improvement and humane services. While temperance continued to be a concern for some of these women, it lost its predominance and became one of a number of reform interests. A prime example of this type of activism was the California Club of San Francisco. Formed in 1898 by members of the Forty-First District Suffrage Club, the club hoped to promote the notion of women as responsible and vital citizens through participation in San Francisco's public affairs.[8]

During the first year of its existence, the California Club organized one of the first public playgrounds on the Pacific coast, located at Bush and Hyde streets in San Francisco, and financed its operation for three years. It lobbied for and won the first municipally funded playground in California and took an early lead in the save-the-redwoods movement. After 1900 the Club promoted an anti-racetrack law, conducted a consumer's boycott of stores that did not treat their "shopgirls" fairly or that sold clothing made in sweatshops, and sponsored public art and music presentations through an Outdoor Art League.[9]

The California Club also sought to draw in women not previously identified with the suffrage movement and to educate them about the need for the franchise. Their purpose in this "indirect agitation" was to make woman suffrage more acceptable and desirable to the general public.[10]

More politically inclined members such as Lillian Harris Coffin grew impatient with the club's indirect means. She shifted her attention to the reborn suffrage movement; in 1906 Coffin founded the San Francisco Equal Suffrage League, an amalgamation of several local suffrage clubs. The league elected Mary Gamage, another clubwoman, as its president. Later that year, the California Equal Suffrage Association named Coffin head of its State Central Committee. In addition, fellow California Club members Mary Sperry, Elizabeth Lowe Watson, and Alice Park held office as CESA president, resolutions committee chair, and recording secretary, respectively. Ellen Clark Sargent, a founder of the Century Club, chaired the CESA Literature Committee.[11] Sargent had been part of the California woman suffrage movement since its inception in 1869, and her late husband Aaron had introduced the first bill proposing a woman suffrage amendment to the U.S. Constitution in 1878.[12]

These women probably brought their compatriots in the clubs into contact with the various suffrage organizations at the local and state level. By 1907 Mary McHenry Keith reported that more than five thousand California clubwomen endorsed suffrage. While the figure cannot be documented, it demonstrates that suffragists were anxious to bind clubwomen to the movement.[13]

As Karen Blair has noted in *The Clubwoman as Feminist*, clubwomen at the turn of the century constituted one of many elements of progressive reform.[14] They seem to have shared many characteristics common to progressives, such as the desire for social harmony, the minimization

13. Clubwoman and suffragist Lillian Harris Coffin (left) marches in August 1908 as a College Equal Suffrage League official with Mrs. Theodore Pinther Jr. and Mrs. Theodore Pinther Sr. California Historical Society, FN-19319/CHS2010.222.

of class differences, and abhorrence of conflict, which they perceived as irrational and destructive.[15] This reform consciousness soon clashed with the very different assumptions held by union women active in the suffrage movement.

By 1907, union women were working for the vote alongside other suffragists in the San Francisco Equal Suffrage League. Louise LaRue, the secretary of Waitresses Local 48, claimed that the female unionists joined "with the National Woman's Suffrage League in San Francisco and got along fine with them," asserting, "we endorsed everything they did."[16]

While neither middle-class suffragists nor union sources documented just when the unionists allied themselves with the Equal Suffrage League, the union women probably participated in the effort to secure passage of a woman suffrage resolution in 1907, introduced by Assemblyman Grove L. Johnson of Sacramento. Johnson's bill squeaked through the assembly on the second ballot but failed in the senate by two votes. The bill won the endorsement of San Francisco's Union Labor Party and the California Federation of Labor.[17]

After the turn of the century, liquor continued to be an issue for suffragists. While the temperance and prohibition movement did attract some mainstream feminists, anti-liquor attitudes also seemed to spring from resentment against the political power wielded by the liquor interests. In a 1911 interview in the *San Francisco Examiner*, Mary McHenry Keith fumed, "The 'Saloon in Politics' has for fifteen years been successful in preventing any legislation . . . allowing this question of woman suffrage to get out before the people." Keith also reported that a member of the state senate from San Francisco informed her that if she could convince all the saloon, hotel, and restaurant keepers, liquor dealers, and other purveyors of alcoholic beverages in his district to support woman suffrage, he would vote in kind.[18]

In 1908 California Club leaders backed a proposal to raise license fees for saloons in San Francisco to one thousand dollars. A spokeswoman from the club stated that "all women" supported the measure and that reducing the number of saloons would decrease the chance that young women would come into contact with hard liquor.[19] In July of 1909 the WCTU organized a Congress of Reform in Berkeley. The speakers contained many suffrage leaders, including Mary Sperry, Ellen Clark Sargent, Lillian Coffin, and Mary McHenry Keith of the California Equal Suffrage Association. Elizabeth Gerberding, the future president of the Woman Suffrage Party, was also featured, representing the Citizens' League for Justice.[20]

Though suffragists again feared a close identification with the temperance movement and a resulting backlash from the politically influential liquor industry, historic ties and sympathy persisted between the two movements. Many of those who worked for woman suffrage nationally and locally joined other progressives in decrying the effects of alcohol itself as well as the role of liquor interests in politics.

In contrast, beer, wine, and spirits frequently occupied a central place in many immigrant and working-class communities. Many men and women made their living brewing, fermenting, or distilling alcohol, and bottling, transporting, and vending it. Many German, Irish, and Italian San Franciscans who worked in those industries and consumed their products regarded alcohol both as a means of support and a part of their culture.

The saloon was often a male social and political center. The average San Francisco saloon offered card games, billiards, gambling machines, and other games of chance. In addition, many served free or cheap lunches, lent customers money or extended credit, and afforded a club where men could meet their friends, sometimes carouse, and, on occasion, even sleep. Ward heelers could contact the men of their precinct, build a political following over glasses of beer, and distribute political favors. One historian has reported that in San Francisco in 1915 there was one saloon for every 218 people. In most cities, working-class districts housed the highest proportion of drinking establishments, to the extent that many had one for every fifty adult males.[21]

The labor movement held ambivalent attitudes toward saloons and drinking. Union officials often bemoaned liquor's ability to dull the fighting spirit of local members. On the other hand, most unions were fiercely anti-prohibitionist. San Francisco labor unions resisted the 1908 higher license measure, claiming that the law could put breweries out of business and cost hundreds of men their jobs. In 1909 the *Labor Clarion* announced that the San Francisco Labor Council opposed prohibition and any legislation designed to limit the issuance of liquor licenses. Specifically, it went before the state legislature to condemn the Local Option Bill that would permit each county to place no-license measures on the ballot. While unions did decry excess drinking, working-class and immigrant communities preferred to look to internal institutions to remedy the situation. The *Labor Clarion* of May 28, 1909, reported on labor temperance fellowships in Europe, perhaps in the hope that it would stimulate such organizations in the United States.[22]

Women unionists may also have had mixed feeling about alcohol and saloons. Nationally, women union members resented that some union locals held their membership meetings in saloons, which were widely considered to be unfit places for women. This was not the case in San Francisco, judging from the roster of labor organizations in the *Labor Clarion* from 1907 to 1911. The city's unions either had their own halls, rented halls, or held meetings in the buildings that housed the San Francisco Labor Council and the Building Trades Council; none met in saloons.[23] Some women undoubtedly witnessed the effect of alcoholism on individuals and families. However, such labor agitators as Mary Harris, the United Mine Workers' organizer more commonly known as "Mother Jones," maintained that temperance supporters wanted to ban liquor only in order to squeeze more work out of toilers. She argued that closing saloons deprived workingmen of their own club and denied them one of the few pleasures they had. Because of life's trials, Jones mused, "It's a wonder we are not all drunk all of the time."[24]

In 1906 San Francisco Waitresses Local 48 successfully opposed a local law that would have barred them from working in establishments that served liquor. Temperance activists sponsored a similar bill on the state level in 1911, and Local 48 spoke out again. Louise LaRue warned, "Such a law . . . would have injured the girls all over the state and particularly in this city, as nearly all the restaurants serve liquor." To these women, liquor consumption was less a moral issue than an economic one. They did not wish to be cut out of work in restaurants with bars. This incident also represented one of many efforts by waitresses nationally to preserve or open up jobs in workplaces selling alcoholic beverages and to serve liquor and beer themselves. These working women resented the efforts of moral crusaders to enact these reforms instead of concentrating on economic and social advances.[25]

Liquor was also a source of income for Local 48. The waitresses served liquor at the benefit ball for their sick and death benefit. This fund provided expenses for medical care for Local 48 members and paid for the burial costs of poor members. The bar alone raised six hundred to eight hundred dollars for the fund, money the waitresses could ill afford to turn away. Despite the good works this fund provided, the fact that Local 48 sold alcohol at its affairs "provoked considerable disapproval," according to Lillian Matthews. Similarly, middle-class women rarely approached waitresses with any type of aid because of their association with alcohol and, some imagined, prostitution. Louise Ploeger identified this as a continuing problem between the two classes of women in 1920.[26]

Another point of difference between these two groups of women lay in the reformers' belief in suffrage's potential to transform the lives of working women versus the unionists' equally strong commitment to union organizing for the same reason. Women reformers and suffragists promised that the vote and resultant protective legislation would provide women with the greatest protection and rights on the job. When asked in 1905 how Los Angeles female laundry workers could secure a nine-hour day, Susan B. Anthony replied, "We are heartily in favor of women's trade unions but you will never get full justice until you have the ballot."[27] San Francisco union women dissented. United Garment Workers' Union President Sarah Hale challenged reformers to "expend one-half the energy [you] are now wasting to institute organization" if they truly wished to benefit working women. Matthews similarly observed about women unionists, "To them, the trade union with its power to educate the worker and to make effective the demands of the worker offers the proper medium for the solution of their difficulties." Seven years later, Louise Ploeger concurred on this matter in a study done as a follow-up to Matthews's work. While the vote and legislation were important tools to improve women's work lives, Ploeger described them as incomplete without the power of collective bargaining.[28]

Tension between reform and union suffragists came to a head in the spring of 1907. San Francisco was still in turmoil following the earthquake and fire when, on May 5, more than fifteen hundred members of the Carmen's Union struck the United Railroads, the corporation that owned the franchise for San Francisco's transit system. Patrick Calhoun, the president of the United Railroads, refused to consider granting the streetcar drivers the eight-hour day or raising wages to three dollars per day. The union responded to Calhoun's uncompromising stand with an overwhelming vote by the union membership for a strike.[29]

On the strike's first day, no streetcars rumbled on the rails that connected San Francisco's residential districts with the financial and industrial areas downtown. Residents, out for Sunday church or amusement, either walked or hailed wagons and carriages willing to give them a lift for a fee. That same day, strikebreakers hired by Calhoun quietly entered San Francisco and set up housekeeping in the carbarns, preparing to get the streetcars rolling at any cost.[30]

The following day, the United Railroads erected barbed-wire barriers around the carbarns. Hundreds of strikers, sympathizers, and spectators gathered at the barns in anticipation of an attempt by the company to resume transit service. No cars left the barns, however, and the day passed without incident.[31]

"Bloody Tuesday," as unionists dubbed May 7, dawned as unionists again took their positions outside the carbarns. On this morning, strikebreakers drove six cars out of the barn with private armed guards on board. Enraged, the unionists barraged the cars with rocks and bricks and traded shots with the guards. One elderly female sympathizer reportedly lay down on the tracks to block the cars' way with her body.[32]

In the wake of the melee, two unidentified men were shot to death and at least twenty others sustained injuries in the "street-car war."[33] Chief of Police Jeremiah Dinnan and the labor community placed the blame for the battle on gun-happy strikebreakers, an opinion that the usually pro-labor *San Francisco Examiner* echoed. The *San Francisco Chronicle* compared the day's events to the "lawless days of the 1850s," when the 1856 murder of James King of William, the editor of the *San Francisco Bulletin*, sparked the formation of a Committee of Vigilance. Thus began the most violent strike in pre–World War I San Francisco and probably the bloodiest streetcar strike in the nation's history.[34]

The San Francisco Labor Council had initially hesitated in backing the union's impulse to strike, and instead promoted conciliation. "Bloody Tuesday," however, converted the council to a pro-strike position. Shortly thereafter, the council resolved to boycott the transit lines. "Neither the tens of thousands of loyal union men and women of San Francisco, nor the members of their families, nor sympathizers outside the union ranks, will ride in Calhoun's cars until he has made peace with the Street Carmen's Union," the council proclaimed. The Labor Council also vowed to fine all unionists found riding the streetcars. Many individual unions followed suit. The council additionally pleaded with unionists to refrain from protesting at the carbarns, in the interest of public safety.[35]

At the height of the strike, Father Peter Yorke, labor's priest, responded to those San Franciscans who complained that the strike inconvenienced them or who decried the militance of the Carmen's Union. He bellowed, "We would like to ask those soft-hearted and soft-headed people who snivel over strikes and weep for the miseries inflicted on them by workingmen . . . what consideration have the workingmen ever received from their employers that was not forced?"[36]

While no succeeding day matched the ferocity of that of "Bloody Tuesday," the streetcars continued to be targeted by unionists and their allies for sabotage and skirmishes with the strikebreakers. Hundreds of riders suffered injuries due to this clash of forces and the inexperience of the imported drivers.[37]

Despite the Labor Council's apparent enthusiasm, the boycott failed. Four months into the strike, the Labor Council called off the boycott, tacitly admitting that the Carmen's Union was losing. Sapped of concrete union support, the strike slowly collapsed, ending in March 1908. Soon afterward, the Carmen's Union folded.[38]

Throughout the strike and boycott, the press gave significant attention to the activities of women. The Chronicle was the first to report, on May 9, that women along the route of some streetcars waved and cheered the strikebreakers from their windows. By the next day both the Chronicle and the more labor-oriented Examiner disclosed that female residents of the middle-class Western Addition and Richmond districts, and women along Sutter Street, presented cakes and flowers to the strikebreakers, blew them kisses, and treated them like heroes. According to the Examiner these acts infuriated pro-labor observers, who cursed the women.[39]

When the first women passengers boarded the streetcars on May 11, one paper treated their maiden voyage as a major news event. The Chronicle filled the second page of the next day's edition with pictures of these women, some with children, braving pro-union crowds to defy the boycott. The two cars depicted originated in the Western Addition and traveled to Market Street and the financial district.[40] Women who supported the union were no less vocal and active. In addition to the woman who risked her life by blocking the tracks, female compatriots of the strikers jeered the strikebreakers and joined male unionists in pelting them with debris as streetcar service resumed. The Examiner identified some of these women as "telephone girls," telephone operators who were also on strike at that time for better wages and union recognition.[41]

On May 13, women living at the post-earthquake refugee Richmond Camp on the corner of 13th Avenue (now Funston Avenue) and California Street attacked streetcars with "missiles" and occupied the tracks with babies in their arms. Police arrested one participant during the protest.[42]

Waitress's Union Local 48 joined the unions that fined their members for disregarding the streetcar boycott. Any member found on a streetcar paid a twenty-dollar penalty, a sizable amount for anyone at that time, much less a working woman. In June, Local 48 collected ten cents per week from its members and, in August, each member was assessed an additional twenty-five cents in order to contribute to the nearly three hundred thousand raised by the labor community for strike support. The members of the Steam Laundry Workers Union, most of whom were female, also passed a resolution declaring support for the strike and boycott.[43]

According to Louise LaRue, the unionists in the Equal Suffrage League had earlier sought to bolster ties between the mainstream suffragists and themselves by supporting their actions. When the streetcar strike began, the unionists expected reciprocal aid for the issues they deemed important. That aid was not forthcoming, as middle- and upper-class reform suffragists actively opposed the strike and boycott. LaRue reported that, when pressed to explain why they would not observe the boycott, the reform feminists agreed with critics who argued that "it was not the right time" and charged that the unionists were "wrong" in promoting the strike. LaRue retorted that she saw little "wrong" with "walking back and forth." Remonstrating with her erstwhile allies, she held out the condition, "They would have to stay with us and be friends with us even if we were wrong . . . but if they couldn't stick to us when we were wrong, we didn't want them when we were right."[44]

Because of their commitment to their brothers in the labor movement and to union principles of solidarity, unionists involved in the suffrage movement became enraged when their reformist sisters ignored the plight of the Carmen's Union. Judging from the newspaper reports and from the knowledge that many progressive-era reformers found labor conflict intolerable, some of those women probably hailed the effort to break the strike and quell the upheaval. "So you can just imagine how we felt about it.... We had to pull out," LaRue remarked when she reported the incident.[45]

In reviewing the concerns of the union women and their middle-class counterparts, it appears that other problems along with the dispute over union tactics came into play over the issue of the boycott. LaRue expressed dismay that the more upper-strata women of the city's western tier "objected to walking."[46] Aside from their disinclination as privileged ladies to travel on foot, many of them lived in the Western Addition and Richmond districts. Residents of these neighborhoods depended on mass transit to convey them to their jobs, to the downtown shopping area, and to the theater and other venues for entertainment. Indeed, the two streetcar lines described in the May 12 *Chronicle* article originated in the Western Addition.[47] Working-class San Franciscans, on the other hand, relied less on the trolleys, as sports arenas, dance and music halls, and workplaces honeycombed the Mission and South-of-Market areas. For them, walking was more of a daily reality and less of an onerous chore or stigmatizing act. Indeed, on their wages some residents—including many women—could not afford streetcar fares. Aside from the union issue, then, class influenced residential patterns and streetcar patronage and, therefore, determined support for the boycott.[48]

The San Francisco graft prosecutions of 1906–1910 provided the final nail in the coffin of the relationship between reform and union suffragists. A colorful episode in the city's history, the trials have afforded historians an opportunity to explore such diverse issues as machine politics, progressive-era reform, and the role of class and ethnicity in politics. However, women's involvement in the trials has received only minor mention. A cadre of San Francisco middle-class women made a significant contribution toward promoting the graft trials and disseminating the spirit of reform during this period. These women had gained experience in reform and political organizing through their membership in women's clubs and through their activity in the suffrage movement. Galvanized by their concern that the graft trials were foundering and that the grafters would not be brought to justice, these women turned their attention and their expertise to this pressing issue. In doing so, they won the enmity of union women who opposed or disparaged the graft prosecution.

The background of the trials dated to 1901, when San Franciscans elected

Eugene Schmitz, the Union Labor Party (ULP) candidate, as their mayor. Catalyzed by city police protection of strikebreakers during a violent 1901 waterfront strike, a hodgepodge of politically inexperienced unionists founded the Union Labor Party. Abraham Ruef, who had failed to carve out a following for himself as a reformer in the Republican Party, immediately saw the potential of such a group. Ruef descended upon the ULP with a small body of pro-union men recruited from the Republican Party, a coherent platform, and an attractive mayoral candidate. Handsome, engaging, of Irish and German parentage, and president of the Musicians' Union, Schmitz easily bested his two opponents, with the immigrant, working-class, South-of-Market district providing the bulk of his support. Schmitz and other Union Labor Party candidates again emerged victorious in the municipal elections of 1903 and 1905, reaffirming their solid working-class backing.[49]

In late 1906 a grand jury indicted Schmitz and Ruef for accepting bribes from corporations that had received franchises to operate city railroad lines, a telephone service, and gas and electric service. While most of the members of the San Francisco Board of Supervisors were also implicated, they received immunity in exchange for their testimony, which incriminated Ruef and Schmitz. Following Schmitz's conviction and sentencing, several acting mayors served out the term of the deposed mayor. San Franciscans then elected a progressive Democrat, E. R. Taylor, the dean of Hastings College of Law, as mayor in November 1907. Local suffrage leaders played an active role in Taylor's campaign.[50]

Because the prosecution's long-term goal was to punish those who had proffered bribes and those who had accepted them, indictments against corporate officials from Home Telephone, Pacific State Telephone and Telegraph, the United Railroads, and Pacific Gas and Electric soon followed. The trials were dramatic, righteous spectacles that rated a high level of press coverage.[51]

Initially the novelty and purpose of the trials generated an impressive degree of curiosity and excitement. By 1908, however, public interest was flagging as the trials ground into their second year, Schmitz's conviction was overturned on appeal, juries had acquitted United Railroads Chief Counsel Tirey Ford three times, and Ruef's first trial had resulted in a hung jury. Frustrated by increasing public apathy and hostility, a group of professionals and clergymen were jolted into action when an antiprosecution assailant dynamited a key witness's house. Led by the Reverend C. N. Lathrop, these men organized a citizen's action group that could rally support for the prosecution—the Citizens' League for Justice (CLJ).[52]

The Woman's Branch of the CLJ soon followed. In fact, some women's efforts had preceded those of the CLJ, as Lillian Harris Coffin and Mary H. Gamage had tried to launch a "women's campaign against graft" in March 1908. Pledging to "lend aid" to the district attorney and the graft prosecution, Coffin also made a special plea to union women to join the effort. Apparently the group did not get off the ground because nothing further was mentioned about a women's anti-graft organization until formation of the Woman's Branch of the CLJ. Composed of energetic women who had been active in the women's club and suffrage movement, the Woman's Branch was not about to accept backseat status. Elizabeth Gerberding, the Woman's Branch president and a Century Club member, captained the group and steered its course into the main channel of the CLJ's activity.[53]

Women from the Century and California clubs quickly assumed leadership positions in the Woman's Branch. Ellen C. Sargent, a Century Club founder, became honorary president. After serving as temporary chair, Katherine Hittell became a "District Chairman" [sic]. Hittel belonged to both clubs. Other Century Club members included Mary S. Sperry and Margaret Foster, the club president. The California Club contributed Coffin, Mrs. J. W. Orr, and Alice Park. Park also belonged to the Palo Alto Women's Club. Gamage of the Daughters of California Pioneers Society entertained league meetings in her home. Mrs. J. W. Orr also served as vice-president of the California Federation of Women's Clubs. Gerberding, Sargent, Sperry, Coffin, Gamage, and Park were all major leaders of the California woman suffrage movement.[54] (For more on Park, see chapter 13.)

During the first year of the branch's existence, it took on the responsibility of one of the league's main functions—attendance at the graft trials. Union Labor Party followers were packing the hearings, jeering the prosecution, and attempting to influence the proceedings by verbal intimidation and by their presence. Male members of the league were unwilling or unable to spend time away from their businesses to counter these tactics. Women picked up the torch.[55]

This was no mean feat. Because of the raucous atmosphere, the courtroom was not considered a fit place for women. Elizabeth Gerberding, the Woman's Branch president, noted that the women's initial entrance into court caused "a sensation." They appeared in court day after day, ignoring insults and jeers from the defendants' corner, proudly wearing "the blue button of the League, not aggressively, but fearlessly for the sake of the example it may serve."[56] Gerberding asked women to recruit their friends, fellow church-goers, and club members to the Woman's Branch. She also admonished branch members not to "feed the enemy" or patronize those businesses supporting the trial defendants, but only those "who stood for the right." Gerberding counseled mothers to use the defendants as an object lesson of the consequences of corruption to their children and to teach young ones that all morality was absolute and based on fundamental Christian doctrine. They were to disabuse their children of the notion that one set of morals applied to the home and another applied to the business world and government.[57]

The clubwomen had further incentive to bash the grafters. California Club members still harbored a grudge against Mayor Schmitz for refusing to appoint a woman to the school board in 1902. A delegation from the club had met with Schmitz on the matter, and he reportedly told the women that such an act was not in the interest of the school system. This incident must have riled the women, for Mary McHenry Keith included it as a pertinent event in her history of California suffrage.[58]

While Woman's Branch members witnessed Ruef's conviction and sentencing in December 1908, the jury acquitted another key defendant in the spring of 1909, and public interest in the trials waned again. By the time of the WCTU Women's Reform Congress that July, Elizabeth Gerberding became convinced that the women of the CLJ needed to champion politicians who could renew the momentum needed to propel the trials to their just and moral conclusion. According to Gerberding, "While the League for Justice is nonpolitical, its members must perforce be interested in politics. It is essential that upright honest men be elected to office." When Francis Heney, the chief prosecutor, decided to run for district attorney, the Woman's Branch reorganized into the California Woman's Heney Club and jumped into the campaign with both feet.[59]

While mass meetings attracted attention to the campaign and made the women's work well known, "home meetings and personal contact" were the hallmark of the women's campaign. The Woman's Heney Club gathered at the league headquarters every Thursday afternoon, as the branch had done in the past. In addition, the CLJ's organ, *The Liberator*, announced meetings at the homes of supporters. It reported on September 25, "All of the home meetings have been largely attended. The speakers on all occasions brought home to their hearers the fact that the issue of the campaign for district attorney is primarily a moral issue and that the contest is not between individuals, but is a struggle for a principle."[60]

Heney Club leaders drew in other women's organizations. The club presented its case before the California Equal Suffrage Association in late September. On October 1, Lillian Harris Coffin, the CESA Central Committee chair, enthusiastically endorsed Heney, commenting, "We are for Heney and are organizing in every district of the city." On October 12 the Woman's Christian Temperance Union added its endorsement to the list.[61]

However, Heney's opponent, Charles Fickert, the Union Labor Party's candidate, easily won the race. Fickert's platform included a pledge to end the graft prosecution if he were elected, and Fickert followed through with his promise. Soon afterward, the league disbanded.[62]

San Francisco clubwomen had an additional reason to shift their attention away from the league with the national increase in woman suffrage activity. In 1910 Washington State passed a measure granting woman suffrage. Even earlier, California woman suffrage clubs had regrouped in order to commence the ultimately victorious 1911 campaign. Elizabeth Gerberding became president of the Woman Suffrage Party.[63] Lillian H. Coffin and Mary Sperry returned to the CESA to continue their tenure as vice-president and president. Coffin also founded the Club Woman's Franchise League in 1911. Alice Park headed up the massive literature campaign for the CESA during the 1911 effort. Franchesca Pierce, a Woman's Branch district chair, continued as CESA's corresponding secretary. Mary Gamage, a CESA member became president of the San Francisco Equal Suffrage League and treasurer of the CESA. Presumably, these women also returned to their club work, if they had ever left it.[64]

Woman's Branch activists in the CLJ also applied their acquired political skills during the 1911 California woman suffrage campaign. The Woman

Suffrage Party, led by Gerberding, mobilized feminists on the level of city precincts. Its organizational structure resembled that of the Woman's Branch and its district chairs.[65]

The suffrage movement and women's anti-graft organizations overlapped considerably from 1908 to 1910. The identification of leading suffragists with pro-prosecution forces was clear and unequivocal, and union women came to view it with scorn and contempt.

When news of the graft confessions by members of the Board of Supervisors hit the papers in March 1907, labor's response was immediate. The *Labor Clarion* demanded that the supervisors, most of whom were ULP members, either prove their innocence or resign. The *Clarion* article complained that workingmen had elected the board in 1905 in good faith and that their trust had been violated. The following week, the San Francisco Labor Council announced in the *Labor Clarion* its belief that *all* wrongdoers should be prosecuted and, in the process, disassociated itself from those charged with graft. The *Coast Seamen's Journal* railed against the betrayal of the ULP administration, dubbing it "a crime against union hopes."[66]

Ruef's trial began on May 15, 1907, barely a week after the start of the streetcar strike. While the strike received far more coverage than the graft trials, labor papers still found space to comment on the graft prosecution and its consequences for the labor community. By early summer the *Labor Clarion* ran an article holding the prosecution responsible for the chaotic state of San Francisco's municipal government and blaming it for the non-resolution of the streetcar and telephone strikes. The article implied that the prosecution was more interested in usurping power than guaranteeing capable and honest city government.[67]

During the summer of 1907, three factions vied for power in the ULP. When the smoke had cleared, P. H. McCarthy, the president of the Building Trades Council, touting an anti-prosecution stance, emerged from the party's August primary as its mayoral candidate. In the general-elections campaign, however, McCarthy downplayed this position, sensing rightly that the pro-reform atmosphere would not tolerate criticism of the trials. Louise LaRue reported that members of Waitresses Local 48 supported McCarthy by riding in cars bearing his campaign banners in the Labor Day parade. Labor, however, divided over McCarthy's candidacy, and the ULP ticket went down to defeat. Michael Kazin identified the cause of the rift as "a combination of antagonism towards McCarthy and reluctance to oppose the popular warriors of reform."[68]

By the time of the next municipal election, in 1909, the San Francisco public had grown weary of the seemingly never-ending trials, which had failed to convict anyone except Ruef but which nevertheless continued. Labor united around McCarthy when he again sought the mayoralty. This time, LaRue and Local 48 were backing a winning team. McCarthy won by exploiting growing frustration with the graft prosecution and appealing to workers.[69]

Aside from supporting McCarthy, women unionists supported the anti-prosecution forces in another way during the 1909 campaign. At the same time the Woman's Heney Club began promoting Heney, *The Liberator* produced an article from the *San Francisco Evening Post* reporting that Minna (Mrs. E. H.) O'Donnell, a leader of the Wage Earners' Suffrage League and of the Woman's Auxiliary #18 of the International Typographical Union Local 21 in San Francisco, helped form the Women's Municipal League (WML). The WML sought to end the graft prosecution and propagandized that the money spent on it would be more wisely spent bettering the school system, improving the streets, and acquiring more land for parks and playgrounds. Reformers certainly did not miss the sarcasm of these demands, which snidely parroted measures usually put forth by them.[70]

Despite the deepening wedge between themselves and reform suffragists, the unionists continued to identify themselves as suffragists and to work actively for the women's franchise. In August 1908 LaRue attended the Republican state convention in Oakland as part of a three-person delegation from Local 48. The delegation, along with more than one hundred other suffragists, descended on the convention with signs and banners, demanding that the Republicans include a woman suffrage plank in the party platform. The resolution failed. Undaunted, the Local 48 delegation announced that they planned to travel on to Stockton the next week to lobby for a similar plank in the Democratic Party platform. The Democrats had endorsed votes for women at their previous convention and now reiterated their support. The *Labor Clarion* faithfully recorded each attempt and identified Local 48 as being "active in the suffrage agitation."[71]

In 1909 the San Francisco Labor Council and the San Francisco Building

Trades Council sponsored Louise LaRue as a delegate to the National Woman's Trade Union League Convention in Chicago.[72] At the convention, LaRue reported on the split between the two groups of suffragists. After recalling the blowup between reform and union suffragists, LaRue claimed that the unionists tried to maintain an outward appearance of friendliness toward the Equal Suffrage League to prevent anti-suffrage forces from making hay out of the schism. "We felt that we did not get on together—that the working women and women like that cannot mix, and the only thing to do is to separate and try to be as pleasant as we can and let outsiders think we are harmonious," she explained.[73]

By the time LaRue attended the National Woman's Trade Union League (NWTUL) Convention, she and other union suffragists had taken concrete steps to assure that labor would maintain a presence in the suffrage campaign. They founded the Wage Earners' Suffrage League (WESL) on September 22, 1908. The WESL pledged to advocate and win "better conditions for working women and . . . to promote the suffrage idea." Founding members chose Louise LaRue as their secretary and Mrs. Will French, the wife of the *Labor Clarion*'s editor, as treasurer. Minna O'Donnell became the organization's president. O'Donnell announced the news of the WESL's birth in her column in the *Labor Clarion*'s "Women's Department," which she had initiated one month earlier.[74]

Two weeks after the WESL held its founding meeting, Minna O'Donnell appeared before the San Francisco Equal Suffrage League at their invitation. According to a report in the *San Francisco Call*, the reform suffragists hoped to effect a reunion with their sisters across the class divide. During her speech O'Donnell took the opportunity to remind the reform suffragists of the issues and conditions that differentiated them from the WESL. "It has been suggested that our league join hands with yours," O'Donnell began, "but that is out of the question. . . . We can not join you and we can not send representatives to your gatherings. . . . We want the ballot for very different reasons from the ones you have for wanting it. Our idea is self-protection; you want it to use for some one else."[75] O'Donnell was apparently referring to the reform suffragists' stated intention to pursue the goals of progressivism, such as political reform, slum elimination, and temperance, versus the union suffragists' intent to work for legislation that would directly benefit the women and men of their own class.

Maud Younger, a WESL activist, backed up O'Donnell's point, adding, woman suffrage is "just a question of sex with the women of the league, but with us—and I am a union woman myself—it is a question of the things that affect men and women alike." Younger further noted that unions had remained aloof from the suffrage movement because they suspected that reform suffragists were "using the unions as tools only" and were not interested in labor's aims. Other WESL activists present agreed, charging that the Equal Suffrage League only wanted the strength and influence of the WESL's working-class membership, a point the reform suffragists adamantly denied. The meeting broke up before the reformers made any progress toward reconciliation.[76]

Despite their differences with the reformers and their unyielding position on a separate body, the WESL activists maintained the appearance of solidarity with the Equal Suffrage League. LaRue told the NWTUL convention that she and other unionists traveled to Sacramento in 1909 to speak on behalf of the woman suffrage bill submitted to the state legislature. "We went to the legislature and backed their bill," LaRue said pointedly. John I. Nolan, the legislative agent for the California Federation of Labor, accompanied the hopeful delegation to lobby for woman suffrage. Introduced again by assembly member Grove Johnson, the bill was narrowly defeated in the assembly by a vote of 39–37.[77]

Union suffragists and their reform-minded sisters attempted and failed to merge their energies and resources into a single organization in the effort to win woman suffrage. Unlike feminists in New York, Boston, and Chicago with a brief history of cross-class alliance in organizations such as the Woman's Trade Union League, San Francisco reform suffragists had little experience working with women from a background and culture different from their own. This first effort, apparently initiated by women unionists who were pro-suffrage, proved to be extremely brittle. Preexisting differences between union and reform suffragists on the desirability of union organizing over legislation and on the use of alcohol, compounded by divergent views on the graft trials and Union Labor Party, undermined whatever chance the alliance had for survival. The 1907 streetcar strike seems to have dealt the final blow to their working relationship within the San Francisco Equal Suffrage League.

Class and cultural disparity stood at the heart of this schism. While middle-class suffragists promoted the notion of the commonality of all women and social harmony, other women recognized that merely wishing it would not make it so. Speaking at a 1910 socialist women's conference to discuss working within mainstream suffrage organizations, May Wood Simons warned that suffragists "cannot wipe away class struggle among women and say it is just a beautiful sisterhood." In her role as an organizer for the Industrial Workers of the World, Elizabeth Gurley Flynn echoed this conviction in an article in the *Solidarity*, the journal of the Industrial Workers of the World. Calling the notion of sisterhood "a hollow sham to labor," she caustically disabused her readers of the possibility of an alliance with middle-class feminists. Behind the facade of unity lurked "smug hypocrisy and sickly sentimentality." Flynn maintained that the only gender allies that working-class women had were themselves. Following the split, women such as LaRue probably would have agreed.[78]

While woman suffrage, and indeed gender status, provided an issue these two groups of women could rally around, each group adhered to a separate constellation of values that was often the antithesis of the other's beliefs. These divergences repeatedly polarized them and foiled their attempts to work in concert with one another. As the WESL, union women continued to back the cause for woman suffrage through the movement's victory in 1911 but as a separate group. They sought the support of the labor community and participated in actions directed toward influencing the Democratic and Republican parties and the state legislature. Though disillusioned by the reaction of the Equal Suffrage League to the streetcar boycott, they remained committed to the suffrage cause and to the notion that the vote, in combination with the more powerful force of collective bargaining, was a significant means of improving working conditions for women.

Notes

This chapter is based on Susan Englander, *Class Conflict and Class Coalition in the California Woman Suffrage Movement, 1907–1912* (Lewiston NY: Edwin Mellen, 1992).

1. Donald Waller Rodes, "The California Woman Suffrage Campaign of 1911" (Master's thesis, California State University, Hayward, 1974), 7–10, 23–25; Mary McHenry Keith, "California in 1901–1920," Keith-McHenry-Pond Papers, carton

3, File "Woman Suffrage Campaign in California," Bancroft Library, University of California, Berkeley, California.

2. Eleanor Flexner, *Century of Struggle* (Cambridge MA: Belknap, 1959; New York: Atheneum, 1973), 248–49. Trisha Franzen argues that Shaw is due for a reevaluation; see Franzen, "Singular Leadership: Anna Howard Shaw, Single Women and the U.S. Woman Suffrage Movement," *Women's History Review* 17 (July 2008): 419–34; Franzen, "Convincing Words, Challenging Positions: The Rhetoric and Theory of the Rev. Dr. Anna Howard Shaw," Western Association of Women Historians, Santa Clara, California, May 2, 2009.

3. For solid overall accounts of the California campaign, see *Gayle Gullett, Becoming Citizens: The Emergence and Development of the California Women's Movement, 1880–1911* (Urbana: University of Illinois Press, 2000), and Rebecca J. Mead, *How the Vote Was Won: Woman Suffrage in the Western United States, 1868–1914* (New York: New York University Press, 2004), 73–95, 119–49.

4. Rodes, "The California Woman Suffrage Campaign of 1911," 8; Arthur S. Link and Richard L. McCormick, *Progressivism* (Arlington Heights IL: Harlan Davidson, 1983), 102–3. Prohibitionists relied on a legal tactic called the local option to reduce liquor sales in California. Local option laws permitted each community or county to vote on whether or not liquor would be sold within its borders. See Gilman M. Ostrander, *The Prohibition Movement in California, 1848–1933*, University of California Publications in History, vol. 57 (Berkeley: University of California Press, 1957).

5. Reda Davis, *California Women: A Guide to Their Politics, 1885–1911* (San Francisco: n.p., 1967), 78; Rodes, "The California Woman Suffrage Campaign of 1911," 8; Keith, "California in 1901–1920."

6. Laughlin travelled extensively on behalf of the cause for woman suffrage. She eventually returned to San Francisco in 1914 to set up a law office and became active in state Republican politics. She joined the National Women's Party at the same time as Maud Younger, who figured prominently in the future of the Wage Earners' Suffrage League. Barbara Sicherman et al., *Notable American Women: The Modern Period* (Cambridge MA: Belknap, 1980), 410–11.

7. Keith, "California in 1901–1920."

8. Rodes, "The California Woman Suffrage Campaign of 1911," 27–28; Selina Solomons, *How We Won the Vote in California: A True Story of the Campaign of 1911* (San Francisco: New Woman, n.d.), 4.

9. *San Francisco Chronicle*, August 28, 1949; *San Francisco Bulletin*, January 23, 1909; April 14, 1909; September 1, 1908.

10. Solomons, *How We Won the Vote in California*, 4.

11. Founded in 1888, the Century Club was a bastion of San Francisco high society women such as Phoebe Hearst, the club's first president, and Mrs. Benjamin Ide Wheeler, the wife of the president of the University of California, Berkeley. Like

the California Club, it was affiliated with the General Federation of Women's Clubs. California Federation of Women's Clubs, *Who's Who among the Women of California* (San Francisco: Security Publishing, 1922), 93, 252; Karen J. Blair, *The Clubwoman as Feminist: True Womanhood Redefined, 1868–1914* (New York: Holmes & Meier, 1980), 37, 95; Century Club, *First Report of the Century Club* (San Francisco: Crocker, 1898), 24.

12. Rodes, "The California Woman Suffrage Campaign of 1911," 28–29; Keith, "California in 1901–1920," California Federation of Women's Clubs, *Club Women of California* (San Francisco: California Federation of Women's Clubs, 1907–08), 17–23, 45–47. U.S. Senator Aaron A. Sargent first introduced the "Anthony Amendment" in 1878. Congress eventually passed this same bill in 1919 as the Nineteenth Amendment to the U.S. Constitution, and the states ratified the "Anthony Amendment" in 1920. Flexner, *Century of Struggle*, 173.

13. Keith, "California in 1901–1920." Although the California Federation of Women's Clubs did not endorse woman suffrage until 1911, the California Club did so earlier. Rodes, "The California Woman Suffrage Campaign of 1911," 27–28; Keith, "California in 1901–1920".

14. Karen J. Blair, *The Clubwoman as Feminist*, 93–119.

15. Robert Wiebe, *The Search for Order, 1877–1920* (New York: Hill & Wang, 1967). Link and McCormick, *Progressivism*, 67–104; Sheila M. Rothman, *Woman's Proper Place* (New York: Basic Books, 1978); Blair, *The Clubwoman as Feminist*; and Eleanor Flexner, *Century of Struggle*, 203–215; Robyn Muncy, *Creating a Female Dominion in American Reform, 1890–1935* (New York: Oxford University Press, 1991); Ellen Carol DuBois, *Harriot Stanton Blatch and the Winning of Woman Suffrage* (New Haven CT: Yale University Press, 1997).

16. "Proceedings of 1909 Convention," September 29, p. 24, National Woman's Trade Union League Papers (henceforth NWTUL), Microfilm, Reel 19, Library of Congress, Washington DC.

17. Rodes, "The California Woman Suffrage Campaign of 1911," 36.

18. *San Francisco Examiner*, September 3, 1911.

19. *San Francisco Examiner*, February 28, 1908.

20. *San Francisco Call*, July 22, 1909; *San Francisco Chronicle*, July 22, 1909; *San Francisco Examiner*, July 22, 1909. DuBois, *Harriot Stanton Blatch and the Winning of Woman Suffrage*, 159; Mead, *How the Vote Was Won*, 130).

21. Jon M. Kingsdale, "The 'Poor Man's Club': Social Functions of the Urban Working-Class Saloon," *American Quarterly* 25 (October 1973): 472–89.

22. Kingsdale, "Poor Man's Club," 482; *Call*, February 27, 1908; *Labor Clarion*, March 5, 1909.

23. Alice Kessler-Harris, "Where Are the Organized Women Workers?" *Feminist Studies* 2 (Fall 1975): 92–110; *Labor Clarion*, March 5, 1909, 1907–1911.

24. Mary Jones, *The Autobiography of Mother Jones* (Chicago: Charles Kerr & Co.,

1972), 239; Dale Fetherling, *Mother Jones, The Miner's Angel: A Portrait* (Carbondale: Southern Illinois University Press, 1974), 166.

25. Lucile Eaves, *A History of California Labor Legislation with an Introductory Sketch of the San Francisco Labor Movement*, vol. 2 (Berkeley: University of California Press, 1910), 313; Joan M. Jensen and Gloria R. Lothrup, *California Women: A History* (San Francisco: Boyd & Fraser, 1987), 58; *Mixer and Server* 20 (April 1911): 16; Dorothy Sue Cobble, "'Practical Women': Waitress Unionists and the Controversies over Gender Roles in the Food Service Industry, 1900–1980," *Labor History* 29 (Winter 1988): 15–23; Cobble, *Dishing It Out: Waitresses and Their Unions in the Twentieth Century* (Urbana: University of Illinois Press, 1991), 75–76, 126.

26. Lillian Matthews, *Women in Trade Unions in San Francisco*, University of California Publications in Economics, vol. 3 (Berkeley: University of California, 1913), 81; Louise Ploeger, "Trade Unionism among the Women of San Francisco 1920" (Master's thesis, University of California, Berkeley, 1920), 122.

27. Ida Husted Harper, *Life and Work of Susan B. Anthony*, 3 vols. (New York: Arno, 1969), 1162.

28. *Coast Seaman's Journal*, April 2, 1913; Matthews, *Women in the Trade Unions in San Francisco*, 92; Ploeger, "Trade Unionism among the Women of San Francisco 1920," 130–31.

29. Robert Edward Lee Knight, *Industrial Relations in the San Francisco Bay Area, 1900–1918* (Berkeley: University of California Press, 1960), 186; *San Francisco Chronicle*, May 5, 1907.

30. *San Francisco Chronicle*, May 6, 1907; *San Francisco Examiner*, May 6, 1907.

31. Knight, *Industrial Relations in the San Francisco Bay Area*, 187.

32. *Labor Clarion*, May 10, 1907; Knight, *Industrial Relations in the San Francisco Bay Area*, 187–88; *San Francisco Chronicle*, May 8, 1907; *San Francisco Examiner*, May 8, 1907.

33. *San Francisco Examiner*, May 8, 1907; *San Francisco Chronicle*, May 8, 1907; Knight, *Industrial Relations in the San Francisco Bay Area*, 188.

34. Knight, *Industrial Relations in the San Francisco Bay Area*, 186–88; *San Francisco Examiner*, May 8, 1907; *San Francisco Chronicle*, May 8, 1907. William Issel and Robert W. Cherny, *San Francisco 1865–1932* (Berkeley: University of California Press, 1986), 19–21. For an in-depth examination of the streetcar strike, see Robert Emery Bionaz, "Streetcars and the Politics of Class: Voters, the Union Labor Party, and Municipal Ownership in San Francisco, 1901–1913" (Master's thesis, San Francisco State University, 1997).

35. Knight, *Industrial Relations in the San Francisco Bay Area*, 18; *Labor Clarion*, May 17, 1907; *San Francisco Chronicle*, May 8, 1907.

36. *Labor Clarion*, July 26, 1907.

37. Knight, *Industrial Relations in the San Francisco Bay Area*, 193–97.

38. Knight, *Industrial Relations in the San Francisco Bay Area*, 193–97; *Labor Clarion*, September 13, 1907.

39. *San Francisco Chronicle*, May 9, 1907; *San Francisco Chronicle*, May 10, 1907; *San Francisco Examiner*, May 10, 1907; May 11, 1907.

40. *San Francisco Chronicle*, May 12, 1907; *San Francisco Examiner*, May 12, 1907.

41. *San Francisco Examiner*, May 12, 1907. In early May 1907 approximately five hundred women telephone operators employed by Pacific Telephone and Telegraph Company went on strike to demand union recognition and decent wages, and to protest the firing of union members. Lillian Matthews reported that, at the time of the strike, 10 to 20 percent of operators were members of the fledgling Telephone Operators Union. The San Francisco Labor Council initially solicited funds to support the strike and endorsed a sympathy strike staged by the Electrical Linemen's Union. The telephone operators ended their strike three months later when the Labor Council told the union's leaders that the company agreed to increase wages and rehire the strikers. Despite these reassurances, PT&T refused to reinstate the many Telephone Operators Union members. Drained of its activists, the union eventually dissolved. *Labor Clarion*, May 3, 10, and 31, 1907; Matthews, *Women in the Trade Unions of San Francisco*, 87; Knight, *Industrial Relations in the San Francisco Bay Area*, 186, 191–92; Stephen H. Norwood, *Labor's Flaming Youth: Telephone Operators and Labor Militancy, 1878–1923* (Urbana: University of Illinois Press, 1990), 84–87.

42. *San Francisco Examiner*, May 14, 1907; *San Francisco Chronicle*, May 14, 1907.

43. *Labor Clarion*, May 24, 1907, August 2, 1907; Knight, *Industrial Relations in the San Francisco Bay Area*, 196; *Labor Clarion*, June 14, 1907. The strike fund was a combined effort of the San Francisco Labor Council and the Building Trades Council. *Call*, May 8, 1907; *Labor Clarion*, May 10, 1907.

44. "Proceedings of 1909 Convention," NWTUL, September 29, p. 26.

45. "Proceedings of 1909 Convention," NWTUL, September 29, p. 26. Lack of sympathy for labor struggles was not a given for all women reformers of the period, however. In New York, in a remarkable display of solidarity, middle- and upper-class women joined thousands of women garment workers on picket lines in 1909 to protest miserable wages and working conditions at shirtwaist factories. For a full account of the Great Uprising of the garment workers, see Meredith Tax, *The Rising of the Women* (New York: Monthly Review, 1980), and Barbara M. Wertheimer, *We Were There* (New York: Pantheon, 1977), 293–317. Nancy Schrom Dye described the strike from the Woman's Trade Union League's perspective in *As Equals and As Sisters* (Columbia: University of Missouri Press, 1980), 88–109.

46. "Proceedings of 1909 Convention," NWTUL, September 29, 26.

47. Issel and Cherny, *San Francisco 1865–1932*, 66–68, 78.

48. Issel and Cherny, *San Francisco 1865–1932*, 58–66.

49. Jules Tygiel, "'Where Unionism Holds Undisputed Sway'—A Reappraisal of San Francisco's Union Labor Party," *California History* 62 (Fall 1983): 196–215; Walton Bean, *Boss Ruef's San Francisco* (Berkeley, University of California Press,

1968). Both sources chronicle the emergence and development of the Union Labor Party. Tygiel demonstrated that working-class voters provided the ULP with its primary base of support and that it was entitled to call itself a labor party. Bean's book focuses on the graft trials.

50. Bean, *Boss Ruef's San Francisco*, 188–97; *San Francisco Examiner*, July 12, 1908.

51. Bean, *Boss Ruef's San Francisco*, 188–97.

52. Bean, *Boss Ruef's San Francisco*, 256–267; *The Liberator*, December 12, 1908; *Bulletin*, June 22, 1908.

53. *Call*, March 21, 1908; Minutes, Woman's Branch meeting, September 17, 1908, Citizen's League for Justice Papers (henceforth CLJ), Box 103, Franklin Hichborn Collection, University Research Library, University of California, Los Angeles; *Bulletin*, October 27, 1909. Elizabeth Gerberding, "Women Fight against Graft in San Francisco," *Delineator* 76 (October 1910): 245–246, 322–23, recounts Gerberding's activity in the CLJ.

54. Elizabeth Gerberding to George Boke, September 1, 1909, CLJ, Box 103; "District Chairmen," CLJ, Box 103; Lillian Harris Coffin to the CLJ, June 17, 1909, CLJ, Box 103; *Bulletin*, March 16, 1909; *Liberator*, September 15, 1909; California Federation of Women's Clubs, *Club Women*, 37; *Bulletin*, November 28, 1908; California Federation of Women's Clubs, *Club Women*, 57, 17–23, 45–47; *Bulletin*, April 24, 1909.

55. CLJ recruitment letter, August 28, 1908, CLJ, Box 103; CLJ recruitment letter, September 16, 1908, CLJ, Box 103; Elizabeth Gerberding, "Women Fight Against Graft in San Francisco," *Delineator* 76 (October 1910): 245; CLJ, see Box 103, File "1908–1909 Correspondence"; Gerberding, "Women Fight," 245.

56. *Liberator*, January 16, 1909; Gerberding, "Women Fight," 245.

57. *Liberator*, January 16, 1909; *Bulletin*, March 16, 1909; April 19, 1909; *Liberator*, January 16, 1909.

58. Keith, "California in 1901–1920."

59. *Liberator*, July 24, 1909; *Bulletin*, June 12, August 24, August 31, 1909.

60. Gerberding, "Women Fight," 322; *Liberator*, September 25, 1909, October 9, 1909.

61. *Liberator*, October 2, 1909; *Bulletin*, October 1, October 12, 1909.

62. Bean, *Boss Ruef's San Francisco*, 299; *Liberator*, January 15, January 22, 1910; also CLJ, Box 104.

63. For more on the Woman Suffrage Party, see DuBois, *Harriot Stanton Blatch and the Winning of Woman Suffrage*, 159, and Mead, *How the Vote Was Won*, 130.

64. Solomons, *How We Won the Vote*, 24–25; Schrom Dye, *As Equals and As Sisters*, 130; Mary McHenry Keith, "California in 1901–1920."

65. Schrom Dye, *As Equals and As Sisters*, 130; *Liberator*, December 26, 1908; January 16, 1909.

66. *Labor Clarion*, March 22, March 29, 1907; *Coast Seaman's Journal*, March 27, 1907.

67. *Labor Clarion*, July 12, 1907. Labor did not unanimously oppose the prosecution. Three notable exceptions were Andrew Furuseth, the president of the Sailors' Union of the Pacific; Michael Casey, the Teamster Union's chief; and the Carmen's Union president Richard Cornelius, all of whom backed the prosecution. Furuseth and Casey feared that the scandal would taint the entire labor movement. While Cornelius claimed to have the same motivation, it is clear that he viewed the trials as a way to strike back at Patrick Calhoun, the United Railroad president and a defendant in the graft trials. Michael Kazin, *Barons of Labor: The San Francisco Building Trades and Union Power in the Progressive Era* (Urbana: University of Illinois Press, 1986), 131–32, 137–39.

68. Kazin, *Barons of Labor*, 136–39; "Proceedings of 1909 Convention," NWTUL, September 29, pp. 21–22; Kazin, "Barons of Labor: The San Francisco Building Trades, 1896–1920" (PhD dissertation, Stanford University, 1983), 298.

69. Bean, *Boss Ruef's San Francisco*, 264–267.

70. *Liberator*, September 11, 1909; *San Francisco Evening Post*, September 4, 1909.

71. *Labor Clarion*, May 1, July 10, August 28, 1908; Rodes, "The California Woman Suffrage Campaign of 1911," 38–39; *Labor Clarion*, August 28, 1908.

72. Building Trades Council to San Francisco Labor Council, September 3, 1909, file "Building Trades Council," Box 3, San Francisco Labor Council Papers, Bancroft Library, University of California, Berkeley, California; *Labor Clarion*, August 13, September 3, September 17, 1909.

73. "Proceedings of the 1909 Convention," NWTUL, September 29, p. 26.

74. *Labor Clarion*, September 25, 1908.

75. *Call*, October 4, 1908.

76. *Call*, October 4, 1908.

77. "Proceedings of the 1909 Convention," NWTUL, September 29, p. 27; *Labor Clarion*, January 8, January 22, 1909; Rodes, "The California Woman Suffrage Campaign of 1911," 39. For more on Younger, see Englander, *Class Conflict and Class Coalition*, 110–23, 165–67; Englander, "Maud Younger," in *American National Biography* at http://www.anb.org/articles/15/15-00782.html; *American National Biography Online*, February 2000.

78. Bruce Dancis, "Socialism and Women in the United States, 1900–1917," *Socialist Revolution* 6 (January–March 1976): 119; Tax, *The Rising of the Women*, 12.

10. "AWED BY THE WOMEN'S CLUBS"

Women Voters and Moral Reform, 1913–1914

TERESA HURLEY AND JARROD HARRISON

California women secured the franchise in 1911 when the state's male voters approved a constitutional amendment granting what one woman later called "their right to representation" and "the sovereignty of full citizenship." Some California women immediately set out to make the most of their suffrage. As one later explained, "The newly enfranchised citizens realized that education in public affairs was their first business."[1] Politically active California women now combined strategies of grassroots organization with legislative lobbying in order to bring their influence to bear on an impressive range of public concerns, from environmental degradation to prostitution. Armed with the vote at the high point of progressive-era reform, California's newly enfranchised women came to be perceived by legislators, at least for a time, as a well-oiled, cohesive, and redoubtable voting bloc.

The California Federation of Women's Clubs, the state's largest women's association, took a leading role in these efforts. Clubwomen had formed the Federation in 1900 as the state's affiliate of the national General Federation of Women's Clubs. An umbrella organization for hundreds of clubs around the state, the federation brought many local clubs into a statewide structure with state officers and committees, annual conventions, and regular publications.[2] Many of these women had been leaders or foot soldiers in the suffrage campaign. Now they plunged into politics with enthusiasm and a clear sense of purpose.[3]

In May 1912, six months after securing suffrage, the federation held its annual convention. While some members urged caution in entering the political arena, the keynote was boldly sounded: "Legislation." The federation already had a state legislative committee in addition to several district legislative committees. Marion Swan, chair of the state committee, presented a program based on the understanding that the "franchise for women has given new importance and responsibility to the Legislative Committee." She asserted, "Women, anxious to use their new power in a wise and well-balanced way, cannot depend on intuition in this matter." The goal was to prepare for the next legislative session, seven months away. Swan requested that "clubs appoint legislative chairmen who will be in direct communication with the District and State chairmen." The federation endorsed legislation on topics that had occupied clubwomen for more than a decade: safeguarding the health of women and children, securing community property rights for married women, prohibiting prostitution, preserving the redwoods, and more, including winning universal peace.[4]

Swan planned to coordinate the efforts of as many women's organizations as possible to mount a coherent and unified legislative campaign including a central legislative committee for all the large women's organizations. Invitations soon went out to the Woman's Christian Temperance Union (WCTU), the Young Women's Christian Association (YWCA), the Mother's Congress, the California Civic League, the Women's College Alumnae, and others. Swan then held organizational conferences in Los Angeles, Sacramento, and San Francisco, the last of which produced the Women's Legislative Council of California.[5]

The federation's final legislative platform included seventeen items, most drawn from the list developed at the annual convention that May, including a health certificate for marriage; joint guardianship of children; community property; compensation for mothers; maternity homes; psychopathic parole; a minimum wage for women (the subject of chapter 11); state registration of nurses; a state training school for girls; the raising of the age of majority to twenty-one for women; ethical, vocational, and hygienic training in the public schools; tuberculin tests for dairies; the compelling of fathers to support illegitimate children; conservation; civil service reform; and the Iowa injunction and abatement act.[6]

The federation also endorsed four federal measures: uniform marriage and divorce laws; conservation of womanhood, childhood, and home; an employers' liability and workmen's compensation act; and "Peace Measures." The inclusion of the Iowa injunction and abatement act, also known as the red-light abatement bill, may reflect the influence of the WCTU, which had unsuccessfully supported such a measure in the 1911 legislature.[7]

The California Civic League, with some three thousand members, was an important ally of the federation in its legislative efforts. Based in San Francisco but with centers around the state, the Civic League was dedicated to educating women on political issues. In 1912, in cooperation with the Southern California Civic League, the two organizations began publishing *The Woman's Bulletin*, a monthly magazine devoted to informing women of "civic questions and public affairs ... from the feminine point of view and free from the bias of political partisanship." The magazine became the public medium through which many women discussed political issues and educated themselves on the workings of government.[8] Through the *Woman's Bulletin*, the Civic League publicized the coalition's proposed laws for the upcoming 1913 legislature.

The Women's Legislative Council created a headquarters at the Hotel Sacramento for the duration of the legislative session. Described as a "central gathering place" for the dissemination of daily papers, legislative literature, and the daily proceedings in the senate and assembly, it served as a center for women's lobbying, bringing "together all the women who [were] actively supporting or opposing any legislation, making them acquainted with each other and giving them accurate knowledge of the progress of bills in which women [were] interested." As Swan later recalled, "Our headquarters at the Hotel Sacramento was a great help, bringing us into close and helpful companionship with the experienced women of other organizations—especially the W.C.T.U."[9]

With establishment of the office, women could now keep close watch on legislators and bills. In the process, the headquarters also became an expression of the women's political and social identity, fulfilling Nancy Cott's three-tiered definition of feminism—California women not only saw themselves as a "biological sex" and a "social grouping" but now also now sought to draw upon "the community of action among women to impel change."[10]

On the opening morning of the legislature, every legislator found on his desk a card with the "First Legislative Platform of the Women's Legislative Council of California" and the list of seventeen proposed bills. By the end of the session, a substantial majority of the council's proposed bills had been written into law. The Joint Guardianship Bill was the first of the federation's bills to pass both houses and receive the governor's signature. The bill gave the father and mother of an unmarried minor child joint custody; previously, the father had sole rights. The Health Certificate for Marriage Bill was drafted by an expert from the State Board of Health and, according to the federation, was designed to "do away with reckless marriages" and to save young women from venereal diseases. The bill passed both houses of the legislature but failed to receive the governor's signature because a last-minute amendment required only men to obtain a health certificate for marriage.[11]

As the federation's chair of health, Katherine Philips Edson led the effort to eliminate the threat of tuberculin-infected milk. Edson had begun her campaign in Los Angeles, as the chair of the Committee on Public Health of the Friday Morning Club, the most prominent women's club in that city. She had gained appointment to the Los Angeles City Charter Revision Committee as a way to change the city charter so that the city's health department could regulate milk, and then served on the Los Angeles County Board of Health. She extended her purview from the city to the state; it was at her urging that the federation agreed at its 1912 convention to include a bill for "clean milk from healthy cows" in its list of legislative proposals. Edson had also argued that the work of the organization extended beyond legislation: "Our business," she proclaimed, "is to send men to Sacramento" who will support these bills.[12] The federation's Pure Milk Bill called for rigid inspection of dairies and their regulation by the State Board of Health; it was among the women's bills passed in 1913.

The Psychopathic Parole Law allowed the mentally ill to be released on parole from court-ordered confinement and provided for their care and maintenance throughout their parole and until recovery. The Psychopathic Parole Society of Los Angeles, under the leadership of Mrs. O. P. Clark, had already established Resthaven, which became a model for such parole houses. The Regulation of Nurses Act provided for certification of nurses by an appointed state board and for criminal action against any nurse practicing without registration. Similar proposals had been before the legislature several times before but had failed to pass. Senate Bill 46 appropriated funds for a state training school for girls. The Mother's Pension Act provided an annual fund to benefit orphans and half-orphans. Another long-standing goal of the federation was realized with the passage of a measure that established a State Civil Service Commission.[13]

Central to the concerns of the women's coalition was eradication of the "social evil"—prostitution. Assemblyman George W. Wyllie (R-Tulare and Inyo counties) had carried a red-light abatement bill for the WCTU in 1911, but it died in committee. Following a nationwide trend to eradicate prostitution by attacking those who profited from it, the 1911 red-light abatement bill was patterned after Iowa's law of 1909, which targeted the owners of buildings used as brothels. Any citizen could charge the owner of such property with maintaining a public nuisance and, if the charge were proven, the property could be sold. After the failure of the red-light abatement bill in 1911, the state WCTU embarked upon an educational campaign in support of such a law. The WCTU had long been committed to a broad legislative program that centered on temperance but also included woman suffrage and other reforms. WCTU members condemned the notion that prostitution was necessary, declaring: "Segregation and regulation [are] wrong in principle and utterly inadequate to lessen the evil. . . . [T]hey provide for its perpetuation, not its extermination."[14]

The WCTU recruited Franklin Hichborn's assistance. A leading journalist, Hichborn had attended every session of the California legislature since 1891; he was widely viewed as an authority on California politics in general and reform issues in particular. The WCTU asked him to write a leaflet on the red-light abatement bill's merits and its history in the legislature, and "whatever else [he] might think well to add [that] would be very effective." The California Civic League also enlisted Hichborn to lecture at its twenty-three centers. The league's education chair, Dr. Mary Roberts Coolidge, a professor of social economics at Stanford University, reported that members were studying Hichborn's *Story of the Session of the California Legislature of 1911* and "preparing themselves to coerce their local representatives in the right direction." Coolidge also prepared and distributed her own leaflets on the "social evil."[15]

Well before the opening of the legislative session, Hichborn had been lobbying for a new red-light abatement bill. In a letter to Assemblyman Lewis D. Bohnett (R-Santa Clara County), Hichborn suggested that it "would be a mighty good thing" for the Republican Party to include a plank in the platform endorsing red-light abatement at the state convention because "it is right," and "it is good politics." Hichborn informed Bohnett that the women of California were almost unanimously behind the bill and that it would soon be "one of the most popular measures before the people." He added that subsequently "it would pay politically to get behind the measure." Bohnett replied that the Republicans opposed including the bill in the platform but would support it in the legislature and that it had a good chance of passing. The WCTU also asked Bohnett to introduce the red-light abatement bill in the assembly, giving him a copy of the Iowa law, which he asked the deputy district attorney of San Jose to revise to meet California conditions.[16]

On January 16, 1913, shortly after the fortieth legislative session convened in Sacramento, Senator Edwin E. Grant (D-San Francisco) and Assemblyman Bohnett introduced red-light abatement bills in their respective houses. Both houses referred the Grant-Bohnett bill to their Committees on Public Morals. Meanwhile, voters, particularly women, petitioned the legislature to enact the bill. A few days before the first half of the legislative session ended, the senate and assembly Public Morals committees held a joint meeting to discuss the measure. The senate chambers were "packed to the doors" as clergymen, women's groups, and members of law enforcement spoke on behalf of the bill. Tim J. Crowley, a San Francisco attorney representing realtors, opposed the bill, contending that it was unnecessary as there were already statutes addressing prostitution. He also argued that apartments and office buildings in San Francisco would be vulnerable if citizens had the power to attack property rights.[17]

During the legislative recess, women's organizations publicized the measure throughout the state. The WCTU deployed speakers to twenty-three counties. In an article in the *Woman's Bulletin*, the California Civic League explained the red-light abatement bill and listed those who endorsed it, including David Starr Jordan, president of Stanford University, and Jane Addams of Hull House. In all, more than fifty thousand women endorsed the bill, and many of them went beyond a simple endorsement to engage in some effort to persuade the legislature to approve the bill.[18] By coordinating their legislative work under the umbrella provided by the State Federation of Women's Clubs, women's groups formed an effective, influential interest group.

Due to the women's organizations' blitz during the thirty-four-day recess, senators and assemblymen received an avalanche of letters and telegrams from their constituents urging them to vote for the red-light abatement bill. Many legislators now perceived women as a voting bloc and feared that, if they did not support women's issues, their political futures might be in question. Assemblyman H. C. Nelson (R & Prog-Humboldt County), the chair of the Assembly Public Morals Committee, claimed that he had received about fifty letters a day on the issue, or approximately eighteen hundred letters during the recess. The *San Francisco Examiner* quoted an unnamed senator as stating, "I'd hate to go home and face my constituents after I had voted against [the bill.] Women vote now and they are making a tremendous fight." Senator John Curtin (D-Tuolomne County), who also served as the district attorney, claimed to have received more letters on the abatement bill than on any other piece of legislation.[19] Curtin later voted for the bill, explaining that he did so against his "better judgment" because he doubted that the measure would accomplish its purpose but that he felt pressured by his constituents to vote for it.[20]

As a result of the women's publicity campaign, the red-light abatement bill received extensive attention when the legislature reconvened in March 1913. Senator Grant, a member of the Senate Public Morals Committee, announced that when the legislative session resumed he planned to introduce "a concurrent resolution to provide for a legislative commission to make thorough investigation of the contributory and resultant causes of the white slave traffic." However, when the senate assembled on March 10, Senator Dominick Beban (R-San Francisco), whose district included the notorious Barbary Coast vice district, introduced a similar resolution calling for a five-member senate committee to investigate the relationship between inadequate wages for women and the "social evil, or white slave traffic." Since there was pending legislation relating both to the abatement of houses of prostitution and to a minimum wage for women, Beban argued that an investigation should be made before any action was taken in the legislature. Beban also claimed that the Grant-Bohnett bill was "too drastic and would work too much havoc in [his] district." He added, "I don't believe in trying to stamp these places out." By long-standing practice, Beban's resolution, if adopted, assured him a position on the investigation committee. The Committee on Rules corrected defects in the resolution, provided a thousand-dollar investigation fund, and recommended its adoption.[21]

The formation of an investigation committee as proposed by Beban linked the red-light abatement bill to the pending minimum-wage bill. Katherine Philips Edson, now the deputy inspector in the Bureau of Labor Statistics, had drafted the minimum-wage bill at Governor Johnson's request. The bill called for the establishment of a five-member commission to investigate wages, hours, and working conditions among women and children. The commission had the authority to determine the cost of living, hours to be worked in a day, and a minimum wage. Sponsored by the National Consumers League and supported by the California Civic League, the bill faced opposition from employers and labor alike. The bill nonetheless passed and was signed by Governor Johnson on May 26 (see chapter 11).

Meanwhile, Grant introduced his resolution for a joint legislative investigation, composed of five senators and five assemblymen, which was referred to the Senate Committee on Public Morals. Senators Grant, John Anderson (R-Riverside), Edwin Butler (Prog-LA), and Lee C. Gates (R-LA) sought to refer Beban's resolution to the Committee on Public Morals in order to examine it alongside Grant's resolution. Beban objected, charging that the Public Morals Committee would stall his resolution. San Francisco Senators Beban, Edward Bryant (R), George Cassidy (R), Thomas Finn (R), and Daniel Regan (R), along with Senators Albert Boynton (R-Butte), George Hans (R-Alameda), Louis Juilliard (R-Sonoma), and Leroy Wright (R-San Diego), voted against sending the resolution to the Public Morals Committee, and, in the end, all nine of these senators voted against the red-light abatement bill. Beban's resolution drew enough votes to bypass the Public Morals Committee, and on March 11, at Senator Boynton's urging, the senate approved it by a vote of 21 to 10. Hichborn saw this "as a defeat for those who were advocating the passage of the Abatement act."[22]

Throughout the debate on the Beban and Grant resolutions, senators continually referred to the red-light abatement bill. According to the *San Francisco Bulletin*, Boynton, president pro tempore of the senate and a leader of the progressive faction, led the opposition to the abatement bill. Boynton encouraged other senators "who before had been awed by the campaign of women's clubs" to vote in favor of Beban's resolution, although he acknowledged that a group of ministers had told him that if he voted against the red-light abatement bill, it would be "political suicide." Boynton was resigned to the fact that he was likely to retire from politics after his term expired, but contended that many legislators who opposed the bill were afraid to vote against it.[23]

The following day Lieutenant-Governor Albert Wallace—whose wife and sister had visited the Women's Legislative Council's headquarters in the Hotel Sacramento—selected the committee of five senators to investigate the relationship between low wages and prostitution as outlined by Beban's resolution. Though the senator who introduced such a resolution was traditionally named committee chair, Wallace instead named Lee C. Gates (R-LA). Gates, chair of the Senate Judiciary Committee, had voted for Beban's resolution. In addition to Gates and Beban, the other committee members were Senators Grant, Butler, and William Kehoe (R-Humboldt)—all of whom had voted against Beban's resolution. The committee quickly objected to Beban's proposal for an immediate inquiry into those involved in the "underworld," on the ground that a thorough investigation into the "social evil" would be impossible to complete during the legislative session. The committee concluded that, since both the appropriation and the time were inadequate, there should be a special committee for the work, composed of members of both houses, or else a commission with the powers of a legislative committee. Given this, the red-light abatement and minimum-wage bills were no longer linked, and it was once again possible for the women's groups to focus their full attention on securing passage of the red-light abatement bill.[24]

Though the bill moved slowly through the senate, it passed much more smoothly in the assembly. On March 14, 1913, the Assembly Public Morals Committee referred the bill back to the full assembly, with the recommendation to pass as amended. One amendment called for protections for property owners unjustly accused of housing prostitutes, providing that complainants would pay all costs if owners were found innocent, thus mitigating the possibility of blackmail.[25]

On March 20 the assembly debated a motion by Milton Schmitt (R-San Francisco) to conduct the discussion of the measure in closed chambers "to protect the sensibilities of the ladies." Bohnett opposed Schmitt's motion, and Wyllie argued that "the women who have forced this matter to an issue should be allowed to hear it." The assembly defeated Schmitt's motion. A five-hour public debate now unfolded. According to the San Francisco and Sacramento newspapers, the San Francisco delegation adamantly opposed the bill. Assemblyman James Ryan (R-San Francisco), who was also a deputy sheriff, presciently argued that prostitutes would scatter throughout San Francisco, which "would be detrimental to the morals of the community." When one assemblyman questioned the legality of the measure, Bohnett replied that every legal principle in the bill had already been upheld by the courts.[26] In the end, the assembly passed the bill by a vote of sixty-two to seventeen. Only one of the thirteen San Francisco assemblymen voted for the bill. Democrats, a hapless minority at 31 percent, were more likely to oppose than were Republicans, but a majority of both Democrats and Republicans voted for the bill. [27]

After the bill passed the assembly, the senate continued its discussion. On March 28 Grant opened a seven-hour debate by stating that one of the purposes of the bill was to give citizens the power to close down houses of prostitution, which was nominally the responsibility of district attorneys, some of whom were failing to act. He introduced the bill, he said, to fulfill an election promise that he would fight to abolish the white slave traffic.[28] Opponents of the bill argued that the white slave traffic was likely to increase under the act and that the bill threatened property rights. San Francisco Senator Thomas Finn (R) defended his city's "moral soundness" by praising segregation and medical inspection of prostitutes as effective methods for regulating the "social evil."[29]

According to Hichborn and the press, Californians displayed more interest in Boynton's speech against the bill than they did the words of any other speaker. Boynton reported he'd received a letter from a Mrs. M. E. Skinner of Cupertino urging him to vote for the bill and threatening him with "political annihilation" if he did not. Others tried to bribe him "by letter and telegram," stating that they represented "so many voters" who would stand by him if he supported them. Some voters even threatened to recall Boynton from office. In debate, Boynton insisted that he condemned and abhorred prostitution but that the bill would abolish neither prostitution nor the white slave traffic; instead, it would scatter the "social evil" and lead to the spread of venereal diseases. Fearing for the safety of decent women when the streets were filled with prostitutes, Boynton claimed that his main concern was the bill's consequences for all women, rather than with property interests.[30]

The senate approved the bill 29–11. "Scores of women who packed the lobbies and gallery" of the senate "rushed forward to congratulate Senator Grant when the result was announced." As in the assembly, partisanship was not an issue, since a majority of Democrats and Republicans voted for the bill, which had been sponsored by Grant, a Democrat, and Bohnett, a Republican. Democrats voted two to one in favor of the bill, while Republicans, Republican-Progressives, and Progressives voted three to one in favor. Only two of the seven San Francisco senators voted for the bill.[31]

The legislative debate provides ample evidence for the influence that women had exerted to gain votes for the red-light abatement bill. Several assemblymen had questioned whether the bill would produce the desired effects, but said that they endorsed it because of pressure from their female constituents. William Sutherland (R-Fresno) opposed the bill, believing that the "social evil" was inevitable, but, by voting against it, he said, he knew that he was signing his "political death warrant." Sutherland explained that "the good women who overwhelmed the members of the assembly with requests to support the bill, did so with the best of motives, but absolutely without knowledge either of the bill itself or of the subject of which it treats."[32] Women's organizations had especially targeted legislators who held key leadership positions, including Boynton, president pro tempore of the senate, and H. C. Nelson (R & Prog-Humboldt County), chair of the Assembly Public Morals Committee. Some women lobbyists bombarded their representatives with letters urging them to support the bill, while others went so far as to threaten the legislators' political careers.

On April 7, 1913, Governor Hiram Johnson held a public hearing on the red-light abatement bill at the request of Charles B. Callahan, a real estate dealer in San Francisco. Although Callahan opposed the bill, he was unable to attend the hearing. When Callahan and other opponents of the bill failed to attend the hearing, Johnson signed it. He symbolically presented the pen he'd used to Sara J. Dorr, the president of the WCTU. Mary Roberts Coolidge of the California Civic League and Katherine Philips Edson of the State Labor Bureau later agreed that the WCTU had earned chief credit for passage of the bill. The bill's passage signified the effectiveness of women's groups in lobbying legislators. Conducted through a publicity campaign and legislative networking, the women's war on prostitution proved successful. Coolidge contended that the measure "would not have passed but for the steady, intelligent, co-operative pressure of the women voters upon their representatives." Having successfully pressured legislators to support measures of concern to the welfare of women and children, women had carved out a space for themselves in the political spectrum. Edson claimed that the outcome confirmed women's central role in state politics. Now that "women in California stand absolutely equal with men, politically and legally," she said, it would be the woman's job "to keep alive the ideals and not to forget them."[33]

California's Red Light Abatement Act was to take effect on August 10, 1913. However, a San Francisco organization, the Property Owners' Protective Association, circulated petitions to place the measure on the ballot in a referendum. Despite claims of fraudulent signatures on the petitions, the measure was approved for the next general election on November 3, 1914.[34] This development put organized women into a second phase of political campaigning. To contest the referendum, the WCTU president, Sara J. Dorr, and Dr. D. M. Gandier of the Anti-Saloon League requested Hichborn to manage a statewide campaign. According to Hichborn, the WCTU wanted a single, statewide organization that it would dominate. Hichborn and others, however, wanted two separate campaigns, one in the north and one in the south.[35]

In November 1913 Bohnett and J. E. White, a San Francisco attorney and former Progressive candidate for the Twenty-seventh Assembly District, sought to mobilize clergymen, writing to inform them of a new organization supporting the red-light abatement act. This organization became the Northern California Campaign Committee for the Red-Light Abatement Bill with headquarters in San Francisco. Progressives in southern California organized a similar campaign committee for the same purpose. Bohnett and White asked the clergy to act on November 9, designated as "Purity Sunday," to inform their congregations about the red-light abatement act and the referendum. They also urged clergymen to encourage their parishioners to vote in favor of the act in the election the following Tuesday. They enclosed a leaflet written by Bohnett describing the purposes of the measure and a leaflet by Hichborn "showing the real source of the opposition to such legislation." Finally, they asked the clergy to distribute cards seeking endorsements and volunteers to their congregations on Purity Sunday.[36]

On December 1, 1913, the Northern California Campaign Committee for the Red-Light Abatement Bill opened its headquarters in San Francisco and drafted a budget. The committee included legislators, members from women's groups, clergymen, and journalists. Bohnett and Grant, co-authors of the Red Light Abatement Act, were chairman and vice-chairman, respectively, and Charlotte Anita Whitney, a member of the California Civic League and the president of the Women's College Suffrage Clubs, was Oakland vice-chairman.[37] Other officers included J. E. White as secretary, Hichborn as corresponding secretary, and Reverend Charles Lathrop as treasurer. The committee placed Hichborn in charge of the San Francisco headquarters and the publicity campaign. Among the group's members were assembly speaker (later governor) C. C. Young; Sara J. Dorr; Mrs. James W. Orr, the president of the Federation of Women's Clubs; Reverend Terence Caraher, the pastor of St. Francis Catholic Church and an early advocate of abolishing prostitution in North Beach (see chapter 12); Bishop Edwin Holt Hughes of San Francisco's Methodist Episcopal Church; Chester H. Rowell, the editor of the *Fresno Republican*; Irving Martin, the editor of the *Stockton Record*; and Francis J. Heney, the crusading prosecutor in the San Francisco graft cases.

The Northern California Campaign Committee embarked on a vigorous campaign to publicize the fabricated signatures on the referendum petitions and to garner support for the act in the November election. Hichborn estimated that, in the end, total expenditures for the campaign amounted to six thousand dollars (a significant sum for the times—equivalent to nearly $130,000 in 2010).[38] The committee planned a letter to each person who endorsed the red-light abatement act on the cards distributed on Purity Sunday.[39] The committee also petitioned Governor Johnson to order California Attorney General Ulysses S. Webb to become involved in the forgery scandal, since the San Francisco district attorney had failed to prosecute members of the Property Owners' Protective Association. Subsequently, on February 20, 1914, the grand jury charged one person with perjury, but members of the committee remained frustrated that a larger criminal conspiracy had not been exposed.[40] Hichborn claimed that if all the forged names were eliminated, there would not have been enough valid signatures to secure the referendum.[41] He used this argument to discredit the opponents of the act, and assured Chester Rowell that he intended to keep the issue of forgery at the forefront of the campaign because he believed the forgery issue reinforced the larger issues:

> If the public can be aroused to the fact that we have opposed to this Red-Light Abatement act exploiters of prostitution who have literally millions at stake, who have political and financial connections in all parts of the country, who have already resorted to forgery and perjury to hold the bill up in California, and who will stop at no misrepresentation to defeat the measure, there is no question in my mind but that the bill will be overwhelmingly ratified at the polls.[42]

Thus, Hichborn did not merely defend California's Red Light Abatement Act but also attacked its opponents, namely the Property Owners' Protective Association.[43]

Meanwhile, voters in San Francisco had signed petitions to recall Senator Grant, the coauthor of the Red Light Abatement Act. Grant blamed the recall on the "dive keepers and white slavers" who opposed his fight for the bill. The former senator, Edward Wolfe, campaigned to be Grant's replacement. Wolfe, allegedly a "machine" politician, had voted against the woman's suffrage and recall amendments in the 1911 legislative session. In the 1912 election Wolfe had lost to Grant by only ninety-five votes. At the October 8 election, however, Grant was recalled by 53 percent of the votes cast and Wolfe was elected. Grant lost by more than three to one in the city's vice and financial districts. The affluent and middle-class residential parts of the district also voted for recall, but by narrower margins. Grant contested the legality of the recall election, charging that the registrar of voters had not given him the full twenty days required by law before certifying the signatures on the petition. Grant conducted his own investigation and discovered that there were more than six hundred fraudulent signatures on the petition. Hichborn again stepped in on Grant's behalf and sent a letter to every legislator alerting them of the controversy regarding the recall. Grant sought relief in the courts but was unsuccessful.[44]

Grant's recall sparked further interest in the red-light abatement referendum. The California Civic League, which had supported Grant in his recall battle and assisted in his investigation, also joined in the referendum campaign. It circulated a leaflet which, in addition to providing the exact text of the measure, publicized the legislative vote and defined the object of the act as "to check commercialized vice by placing the penalty on the owner of property used for prostitution." The leaflet also explained the bill's method and its advantages. Another league leaflet dealt with existing laws on prostitution and the effectiveness of the abatement law in other cities and states. Dr. Coolidge also continued her efforts to educate women about prostitution, by writing articles and giving lectures.

The league also gave the Red Light Abatement Act a great deal of attention in *The Woman's Bulletin*. From August 1913 to November 1914, the magazine consistently carried articles on the league's educational campaign, publicizing the 1913 legislators' stance on moral reform and women's issues, explaining and promoting the measure, and recommending further readings on the subject, including the leaflets circulated by the WCTU. After Grant's defeat in San Francisco, the league claimed he had been "punished for his services to decency." Alarmed that the Red Light Abatement Act was in danger, the league urged "every decent citizen of the south to go to the polls" and vote in favor of the act. While both men and women were encouraged to vote for the Red Light Abatement Act, women were reminded that it was their duty as mothers to clean up the vice interests in the state by endorsing moral legislation. Thus, as justification for their new political role as voters, women had a higher responsibility to reform society.[45]

While the California Civic League conducted its own educational campaign for the Red Light Abatement Act, Hichborn managed and controlled the northern California committee's publicity campaign. Not only did he disseminate information through lectures, newspapers, and numerous pamphlets, but he also directed the committee's campaign strategy. Hichborn, along with other committee members, made every effort to keep the red-light abatement campaign separate from the Dry State campaign, a prohibition measure that was on the same ballot. Hichborn had little sympathy for "liquor interests" but realized that statewide prohibition would injure the wine industry and, therefore, that a "sense of business justice" would deter thousands of people from voting for it. Members of the committee were therefore unwilling to join forces with the Dry State campaign, which they saw as doomed, and risk losing support for the red-light measure. Hichborn feared that thousands might vote against the Red Light Abatement Act "in protest against what they will term too much reform legislation."[46]

In all, the committee expended $6,798.08 on its eleven-month campaign; more than $1,200 was spent during the month before the election. The money went for weekly letters to the press, cards, pamphlets, and other ways of answering the claims of the act's opponents. It paid for speakers' expenses and for distribution of a total of 1,255,750 pieces of literature.[47]

Throughout the eleven-month campaign, committee members reiterated the same arguments for the ratification of the Red Light Abatement Act that legislators had used to secure its passage. The committee publicized the fact that an enormous amount of profit was generated by commercialized prostitution. It disputed claims that the act was experimental or an innovation by citing similar laws already in effect in other states. The committee argued that property owners were safeguarded from blackmail by the false-claim provision. It also claimed that "scatteration" had not occurred in other states with abatement laws and that, similarly, crimes against women in those areas had not increased. Red-light abatement advocates often presented their arguments in terms of virtuous people versus corrupt interests.[48]

Despite the efforts by property ownership groups to defeat the Red Light Abatement Act, the measure was upheld by a vote of 402,629 to 352,821, with 53.2 percent of California voters giving approval. Opposition was centered in the north: all but two of the twenty-five counties where a majority voted against the act were from the northern part of the state. San Franciscans voted against the measure 38,556 to 68,114, with 63.9 percent opposing the measure, and it failed in every San Francisco assembly district.[49] Although the Northern California Campaign Committee for the Red-Light Abatement Bill had publicized the issue, sending speakers throughout the state to mobilize and educate voters, a majority of the northern counties voted to void the measure.

Many reformers believed the measure's success was due to Hichborn, who had campaigned fifteen to sixteen hours a day, seven days a week. Hichborn himself felt that the concurrent prohibition campaign had been a "heavy handicap," and claimed that the Red Light Abatement Act would have passed by 150,000 votes (instead of the narrower 50,000-vote margin by which it passed) had it not been for the prohibition amendment. Splitting regionally over the issue, Californians responded to arguments as presented by proponents and opponents alike. Many felt that property rights could come under attack, with insufficient recourse afforded the owners. Others wanted prostitution to remain where it was, in segregated areas such as the Barbary Coast district and adjacent Chinatown, rather than scattered throughout the city or in residential areas. Nonetheless, advocates for red-light abatement—Hichborn and his group, the California Civic League, and the WCTU—proved that a highly organized publicity and educational campaign could carry the day.

In December 1914, soon after the Red Light Abatement Act came into effect, a number of San Franciscans organized the Law Enforcement League to compel its use. Under the supervision of Bascom Johnson, the director of the American Social Hygiene Association's department of law enforcement and investigations, the Law Enforcement League brought several actions against property owners. Johnson, along with members of the American Social Hygiene Association and the Anti-Saloon League, investigated dance halls (see chapter 12) and saloons in the Barbary Coast in an attempt to permanently abolish prostitution and the sale of alcohol. Despite reformers' efforts, many of the resorts operated unchecked during the Panama–Pacific International Exposition in 1915.[50]

Shortly thereafter, the Reverend Paul Smith, pastor of the Central Methodist Church in San Francisco, launched his own vice crusade. In response to Smith's pressure on the police commission to enforce the act, on January 15, 1917, Mayor James Rolph promised to close every brothel in San Francisco. Ten days later, three hundred to four hundred prostitutes organized by the newspaper editor Fremont Older and Maude Spencer, a brothel operator, assembled in Smith's church to voice their complaints. Smith proved unable to solve the prostitutes' dilemma—that is, what they should do and where they should go when the city deprived them of their occupation. With the meeting at an impasse, the prostitutes left the church. On January 30, Assistant District Attorney James Brennan announced that he was preparing to file actions under the Red Light Abatement Act against every brothel in the city. In February the police systematically raided and closed the Barbary Coast brothels. Prostitutes dispersed throughout the city, producing the "scatteration" predicted by the act's opponents.[51]

14. The Barbary Coast (Pacific Street between Kearny and Montgomery), ca. 1910. The Hippodrome, in the center, was one of the gaudiest and best known of the Barbary Coast pleasure palaces. Curiously, the Thalia, seen here to the left of the Hippodrome, was actually to its right. California Historical Society, FN-01708/CHS2010,223.

The state appellate court upheld the constitutionality of the Red Light Abatement Act twice in 1917. Now assured of judicial support, Reverend Smith organized the State Law Enforcement and Protective League to assist police in enforcing the act. The act's longtime advocates Edwin E. Grant, J. E. White, and Sara J. Dorr joined the league's executive committee. Hichborn was the director of publicity, which coincided with his campaign for a prohibition amendment. The league's effectiveness was reinforced by a 1917 wartime measure that prohibited prostitution within five miles of a military encampment. By 1920 the league reported that it had closed brothels in twenty-two counties.[52]

Passage of the Red Light Injunction and Abatement Act by the state legislature and the ensuing referendum campaign and vote reveal important patterns in California progressivism. Some historians have contended that women gained little political power as a result of winning the vote, but the legislative session of 1913 in general, and the campaign to abolish prostitution in particular, demonstrates how significantly woman suffrage changed California politics.[53] Women perceived themselves differently, and politicians, in turn, felt obliged to respond to the demands of their new constituents. Women seized the opportunities that came with political empowerment, organizing and mobilizing in novel ways. Once armed with the right to vote, women wielded a powerful tool to garner support for particular measures of interest. For California women's groups, the formation of a lobby group with headquarters in Sacramento during the 1913 legislative session was unprecedented. Working in concert, various women's groups entered the political arena and effectively pressured state legislators to vote for reform measures. When the WCTU first attempted to gain support for red-light abatement in 1911, it failed. But when women secured the vote and the WCTU joined with other women's groups, the red-light abatement bill at last received serious consideration. Given strong opposition to the measure, California women inundated their legislators with letters to vote in its favor. Countering their opponents' claims that the measure would hurt women, advocates emphasized that the abatement bill struck at the profiteers of vice, the brothel owners. Intent on curing society's moral ills, more than fifty thousand women mobilized in support of obliterating prostitution and, in the process, proved that they could make a difference in politics. In the abatement act's second phase, the referendum campaign, women again demonstrated their new sense of civic responsibility. Their efforts showed that California women viewed the elimination of prostitution as equal in importance to the minimum wage, joint custody of minor children, and other measures designed to improve the status of women and protect children. In the end, the redlight abatement bill passed due to the women's efforts.

Considerations of class reveal an unexpected coalition. The Red Light Abatement Act lost in all of the assembly districts in San Francisco but fared better in working-class districts than it did in middle- and upper-class neighborhoods. Thus, moral reformers—most of whom were middle- or upper-class—enjoyed greater support from the city's working-class than from their own, same-class counterparts. This has significant ramifications on the historiography of prostitution and the reformers who sought to abolish it. Historians have contended that middle- and upper-class men and women, or "social progressives," sought to eradicate the "social evil" in order to improve the overall status of women. Contemporary rhetoric reflected this class stratification in many of the anti-prostitution campaigns, including California's red-light abatement campaign. However, this comparison of election returns against moral-reform rhetoric demonstrates that more research is needed to explain why the electorate responded as it did to the issues the social progressives raised.

Analyzing registration rates and election returns also helps us determine how the electorate responded to reform measures. While many women sought to prove their political worth by exercising their new right to vote, it is evident that others did not. Based on an estimate derived from 1910 and 1920 census records, approximately two-thirds of all eligible men actually registered to vote in San Francisco, while probably no more than one-third of all eligible women did. However, women rapidly improved their rate of registration. From fiscal year 1912–1913 to fiscal year 1914–1915, the registration figure increased for women by 20.5 percent. For this same period, the registration rate for men increased by only 4.2 percent.[54] Clearly, women were responding to suffrage.

Aided by sweeping legal measures, and making effective use of the print media, moral reformers abolished segregated vice districts, such as the Barbary Coast. Prostitutes, afforded no recourse as they continued to ply their trade, scattered throughout the city to avoid arrest. They were deprived of their support networks and forced to solicit customers off the streets. In the end, the moral reformers succeeded by demonstrating the political clout of aroused, organized, and enfranchised women. They failed, however, to "rescue" the prostitutes and to eradicate prostitution; instead, they merely obliterated its more glaring forms by driving prostitution underground.

Notes

This chapter is the result of combining Jarrod Harrison's paper on women's activities in the 1913 legislative session with Teresa Hurley's shortened version of her master's thesis, "California's Moral Reformers: The Redlight Injunction and Abatement Act, 1913–1914" (San Francisco State University, 1995). The two were combined and edited by Robert Cherny.

1. Mary Gibson, *A Record of Twenty-Five Years of the California Federation of Women's Clubs 1900–1925* (California Federation of Women's Clubs, 1927), 68, 181.

2. For the early years of the federation, see Gibson, *Record of Twenty-Five Years*.

3. Mrs. Seward Adams Simons, for the Committee of Political Science, *A Survey of the Results of Woman Suffrage in California* (n.p.: California Federation of Women's Clubs, 1917), Bancroft Library, University of California, Berkeley. The report also details numbers of registered women voters in San Francisco and Los Angeles.

4. Simons, *Survey of the Results*, 182–83.

5. Simons, *Survey of the Results*, 188n1; 184–87.

6. Simons, *Survey of the Results*, 186.

7. Franklin Hichborn, *Story of the California Legislature of 1913* (San Francisco: James H. Barry Company, 1913), 322–323. For more information on this measure, see the next chapter.

8. *The Woman's Bulletin* 1 (June 1912): 5.

9. "Items of California's Legislative Session, 1912–13," *The Woman's Bulletin* 1 (March 1913): 12–13. In December 1912 Marion Swan wrote to Hichborn informing him that a legislative council composed of women's groups was going to establish headquarters in Sacramento during the 1913 legislative session. She asked him for suggestions "to get ready for the fray." Marion Hawley Swan to Franklin Hichborn, December 18,1912, Hichborn Papers, box 126, folder Correspondence: 1912 M-Z, 6.

10. Nancy F. Cott, *The Grounding of Modern Feminism* (New Haven CT: Yale University Press, 1987), 4–5.

11. Gibson, *Record of Twenty-Five Years*, 187, 188, 190–91, 201; California State Legislature, *Sessions of California State Legislature Bill Sets*, 1913 session (Micro Photo Division, Bell & Howell), hereafter "*Sessions*". The dates of introduction,

amendment, and passage are all taken from the Sessions Bill Sets. Unless otherwise noted, the numbers and contents of the bills are taken from Hichborn's *Legislature of 1913*.

12. Jacqueline Braitman, "Katherine Philips Edson: A Progressive Feminist in California's Era of Reform" (PhD Dissertation, University of California at Los Angeles, 1988), 81; *Woman Citizen* 3, no. 5 (December 1912): 12.

13. Gibson, *Record of Twenty-Five Years*, 191, 194–95; Emily Karns, "New California Civil Service Law," *Woman Citizen* 3, no. 6 (September 1913): 20–21.

14. "California Women and the Vice Situation," *The Survey* 30 (May 3, 1913): 162; Franklin Hichborn, *Story of the Session of the California Legislature of 1911* (San Francisco: James H. Barry, 1911), 177–78; Hichborn, *Story of the Session of the California Legislature of 1913*, 322; *San Francisco Call*, October 22, 1912.

15. Anna E. Chase, Corresponding Secretary of WCTU to Franklin Hichborn, February 14, 1912, Franklin Hichborn Papers, Special Collections, University Research Library, University of California, Los Angeles, box 126, folder Correspondence: 1912 A-H, 4; Mary Roberts Coolidge, "Educational Work of California Civic League," *The Woman's Bulletin* 2 (August 1913): 13–15.

16. Franklin Hichborn to Hon. L. Bohnett, September 21, 1912, Hichborn Papers, box 126, folder Correspondence: 1912 A-H, 2; L. D. Bohnett to Franklin Hichborn, October 1, 1912, Hichborn Papers, box 126, folder Correspondence: 1912 A-H, 2.

17. *Journal of the Assembly during the Fortieth Session of the Legislature of the State of California, 1913* (Sacramento: Friend W. Richardson, Superintendent of State Printing, 1913), 66–67, 135, 453, 507; *Journal of the Senate during the Fortieth Session of the Legislature of the State of California, 1913* (Sacramento: Friend W. Richardson, Superintendent of State Printing, 1913), 470; Hichborn, *Story of the Session of the California Legislature of 1913*, 324–326.

18. Hichborn, *Story of the Session of the California Legislature of 1913*, 327; Mary Roberts Coolidge to Franklin Hichborn, November 6, 1913, Hichborn Papers, box 127, folder Correspondence 1913: A-C.

19. *Sacramento Bee*, March 10, 1913; *San Francisco Examiner*, March 11, 1913.

20. *Sacramento Bee*, March 28, 1913; Hichborn, *Story of the Session of the California Legislature of 1913*, 341n350; *Journal of the Senate*, 849–850.

21. Hichborn, *Story of the Session of the California Legislature of 1913*, 329; *Journal of the Senate*, 555; *San Francisco Chronicle*, March 11, 1913; *Bulletin*, March 11, 1913.

22. Hichborn, *Story of the Session of the California Legislature of 1913*, 330–333. Hichborn's account also appears in the *Sacramento Bee*, March 12, 1913.

23. *Bulletin*, March 12, 1913; *San Francisco Examiner*, March 11, 1913. Boynton did retire, and spent several years in the 1920s as head of the aggressively anti-union Industrial Association of San Francisco.

24. *Bulletin*, March 12, 1913; Hichborn, *Story of the Session of the California Legislature*

of 1913, 335; Sacramento Bee, March 12, 1913; San Francisco Examiner and San Francisco Call, March 13, 1913.

25. Sacramento Bee, March 14, 1913; Journal of the Assembly, 617–618.

26. Sacramento Bee, March 20, 1913; Bulletin, March 20, 1913; Journal of the Assembly, 813–814; San Francisco Chronicle and San Francisco Examiner, March 21, 1913; Sacramento Bee, March 21, 1913.

27. William Issel and Robert W. Cherny, San Francisco, 1865–1932: Politics, Power, and Urban Development (Berkeley: University of California Press, 1986), 192; Journal of the Assembly, 815; Bulletin and San Francisco Chronicle, March 21, 1913; Hichborn, Story of the Session of the California Legislature of 1913, 340n348.

28. Sacramento Bee, March 28, 1913; Hichborn, Story of the Session of the California Legislature of 1913, 341n350; Journal of the Senate, 849–850.

29. Sacramento Bee, March 28, 1913; Hichborn, Story of the Session of the California Legislature of 1913, 341; Bulletin, March 29, 1913. For San Francisco's experiment with legalized prostitution, see Mary Ann Irwin, "Making Sex Safe for the Married Man: Prostitution and the San Francisco Municipal Clinic, 1911–1913," paper, National Coalition of Independent Scholars, October 24–26, 2008, Berkeley, California; Hiroyuki Matsubara, "The Anti-Prostitution Movement and the Contest of the Middle-Class Reformers over Cultural Authority: San Francisco, 1910–1913," Japanese Journal of American Studies, 12 (2001): 83–104; Neil Larry Shumsky, "The Municipal Clinic of San Francisco: A Study of Medical Structure," Bulletin of the History of Medicine 52 (1978): 542–559; Neil Larry Shumsky, "Vice Responds to Reform: San Francisco, 1910–1914," Journal of Urban History 7 (1980): 31–48.

30. Senator A. E. Boynton to Mrs. M. E. Skinner, March 24, 1913, Hichborn Papers, box 120, folder Red-light Abatement Correspondence: 1913. Also reprinted in the Sacramento Bee, March 25, 1913; Sacramento Bee and Bulletin, March 29, 1913.

31. Bulletin and San Francisco Examiner, March 29, 1913; Hichborn, Story of the Session of the California Legislature of 1913, 342n351.

32. Hichborn, Story of the Session of the California Legislature of 1913, 339; Sacramento Bee, San Francisco Chronicle, and San Francisco Examiner, March 21, 1913; Sutherland was not a candidate for the 1915 legislature; State of California, Secretary of State, California Blue Book: 1913–1915, 400; Journal of the Assembly, 815.

33. Sacramento Bee, April 7, 1913; Hichborn, Story of the Session of the California Legislature of 1913, 343–344; Mary Roberts Coolidge to Franklin Hichborn, November 6, 1913; Katherine Farwell Edson, "Woman's Influence on State Legislation," California Outlook 14 (June 14, 1913): 7, 19; Coolidge, "Educational Work of California Civic League," 15.

34. Leaflet No. 1 entitled "Abatement and Injunction Law," by the California Civic League, n.d., Hichborn Papers, box 118, folder Red-light Abatement-Miscellaneous. Bulletin, December 9, 1913.

35. Franklin Hichborn, California Politics: 1891–1939 (Los Angeles: Haynes Foundation, 1950), 1311–16.

36. L. D. Bohnett and J. E. White to Dear Sir, ca. November 1913, Hichborn Papers, box 120, folder Red-light Abatement Correspondence A-J 1914, 3.

37. Whitney later served as a leader and frequent candidate of the California Communist Party, and was the subject of *Whitney v. California*, (274 U.S. 357), the 1927 court challenge to California's Criminal Syndicalism Act. See Lisa Rubens, "The Patrician Radical: Charlotte Anita Whitney," *California History* 65 (1986): 158–71.

38. S. Morgan Friedman, "The Inflation Calculator," http://www.westegg.com/inflation, accessed August 22, 2010.

39. Statement to Finance Committee, December 29, 1913, Hichborn Papers, box 120, folder Redlight Abatement Financial Reports.

40. C. M. Fickert to J. E. White, February 21, 1914, Hichborn Papers, box 119, folder Redlight Abatement Articles, 2; C. M. Fickert to Hiram Johnson, February 21, 1914, Hichborn Papers, box 120, folder Redlight Abatement Correspondence A-J 1914, 1.

41. Leaflet, Franklin Hichborn to the Editor, n.d., Hichborn Papers, box 120, folder Forged Referendum Petitions; Franklin Hichborn to Dear Friend, June 27, 1914, Hichborn Papers, box 120, folder Redlight Abatement Correspondence A-J 1914, 1.

42. Franklin Hichborn to Chester Rowell, April 17, 1914, Chester H. Rowell Papers, Bancroft Library, University of California, Berkeley, box 16, folder Franklin Hichborn.

43. Franklin Hichborn to Hiram W. Johnson, February 7, 1914, Hichborn Papers, box 120, folder Redlight Abatement Correspondence A-J1914, 1.

44. Edwin E. Grant to Franklin Hichborn, June 3, 1913, Hichborn Papers, box 127, folder Correspondence 1913: G-H; Edwin Grant, "Sample Ballot," Hichborn Papers, box 4, folder Grant Recall; Hichborn, *Story of the Session of the California Legislature of 1911*, xlv–xlvi; sample letter from Franklin Hichborn, December 29, 1914, Hichborn Papers, box 4, folder Grant Recall; *San Francisco Call*, October 31, 1914; Franklin Hichborn, "The Recall of Senator Grant," Hichborn Papers, box 4, folder Grant Recall.

45. Coolidge, "Educational Work of California Civic League," 31; "What the California Civic League Is Doing for the Red-light Abatement and Injunction Bill," *Women's Bulletin* 2 (February 1914): 13; *Women's Bulletin* 2 (April 1914): 23; "Recall of Senator Grant," *Women's Bulletin* 3 (September-October 1914): 7.

46. Franklin Hichborn to L. B. Mallory, February 19, 1914, Hichborn Papers, box 120, folder Redlight Abatement Correspondence K-Z 1914, 1; Franklin Hichborn to L. D. Bohnett, February 19, 1914, Hichborn Papers, box 120, folder Redlight Abatement Correspondence A-J 1914, 3; Franklin Hichborn to Dr. William F. Snow, April 10, 1914, Hichborn Papers, box 120, folder Redlight Abatement Correspondence K-Z 1914, 1.

47. Financial Statement for October 31, 1914, Hichborn Papers.

48. Edwin E. Grant, "Argument in Favor of Chapter 17 of the California Statutes of 1913, Known as the Redlight Abatement Bill," Hichborn Papers, box 120, folder Redlight Abatement Articles; Franklin Hichborn, *Arguments Which Are Used against the California Redlight Abatement Act*, (San Francisco: James H. Barry, n.d.); Pauline Jacobson, "The Red Light on the Ballot: A Summary of the Arguments for and against Abatement," *Bulletin*, October 31, 1914.

49. State of California, Secretary of State, *Statement of Vote at General Election held on November 3, 1914 in the State of California*, 6, 41–42. The referendum campaign is covered in more detail in Hurley's thesis, where she outlines the dissension among several health organizations regarding the endorsement of the measure and the opponents' arguments to the measure. See Hurley, "California's Moral Reformers," 80–89.

50. Bascom Johnson, "Moral Conditions in San Francisco and at the Panama–Pacific Exposition," *Social Hygiene* 1 (1914–1915): 589–609.

51. Liston F. Sabraw, "Mayor James Rolph, Jr. and the End of the Barbary Coast" (Master's thesis, San Francisco State University, 1960), 187–93; Neil Larry Shumsky and Larry M. Springer, "San Francisco's Zone of Prostitution, 1880–1934," *Journal of Historical Geography* 7 (1981): 85; Herbert Asbury, *The Barbary Coast: An Informal History of the San Francisco Underworld* (Garden City: Garden City Publishing, 1933), 307–314.

52. Franklin Hichborn, "A Gratifying Record of Good Work Done," Publicity Slip of State Law Enforcement League, Hichborn Papers, box 115, folder Paul Smith Correspondence; Franklin Hichborn, "The Anti-Vice Movement in California," *Social Hygiene* 6 (April 1920): 213–326.

53. Paula Baker, "The Domestication of Politics: Women and American Political Society, 1780–1920," *American Historical Review* 89 (1984): 645; Eleanor Flexner, *Century of Struggle: The Woman's Rights Movement in the United States* (Cambridge MA: Belknap, 1975), viii.

54. In order to estimate the number of eligible male voters for 1914, Hurley used the total number of men of voting age for 1910 and 1920 and multiplied the difference between the two totals by 40 percent. She added that figure to the 1910 total in order to derive the 1914 estimate for eligible male voters. The 1920 census had a total for women of voting age, but the 1910 census did not. She calculated the percentage decrease for men from 1920 to 1910. She used that percent (approximately 18.7 percent) and multiplied it by the 1920 figure in order to derive the 1910 estimate of women twenty-one and over. She then multiplied the difference between the two figures by 40 percent. Although she was able to create only very rough estimates for 1914, she considers the ratio between men and women who actually registered versus the total eligible population to be generally accurate. See *Municipal Reports for the Fiscal Year 1913–14, Ended June 30, 1914* (San Francisco: Neal Publishing, 1916), 274; *Municipal Reports for the Fiscal Year 1914–15, Ended June 30, 1915* (San Francisco: Neal Publishing, 1917), 522.

11. "WE ARE NOT KEEN ABOUT THE MINIMUM WAGE"

Union Women, Clubwomen, and the Legislated Minimum Wage, 1913–1931

REBECCA J. MEAD

California women's struggle for the suffrage coincided with a number of efforts to pass protective legislation in addition to efforts at moral reform. As indicated in chapter 10, the campaign for red-light abatement was linked at crucial points with efforts to define a minimum-wage law for women. When middle-class clubwomen became involved in campaigns for protective legislation, however, they quickly encountered working-class women who often had their own ideas about the appropriateness of such legislation. Working women sometimes challenged unrealistic middle-class prescriptions for morality, maternity, and domesticity that undervalued their identities as workers. In California, women trade unionists developed a critique of minimum-wage legislation that emphasized self-sufficiency through organization and disputed popular characterizations of female workers as physically or morally weak, defenseless, and thus in need of "protection."

California had a long tradition of political activism by a vigorous labor movement centered in San Francisco. Powerful if unstable progressive-labor coalitions installed a reformist state legislature and elected Hiram Johnson governor in 1910, reelected him in 1914 (with the active support of newly enfranchised working-class women), and passed several important pieces of labor legislation during his administration.[1] Male labor leaders had long since offered qualified support to women workers, resulting in a higher than average rate of unionization among San Francisco women that facilitated their politicization. In 1911 the state labor federation endorsed eight-hour-workday legislation for women, but in 1913 women unionists convinced the labor establishment to oppose a legislatively mandated minimum wage.[2] Subsequently, working women played key roles in the implementation of the minimum-wage law by the Industrial Welfare Commission (IWC) under the leadership of Katherine Philips Edson (for more on Edson, see chapter 13).[3]

Such California progressives and feminists as Edson quite consciously referred to themselves as "pioneers," noting that the state's growing importance as an industrial center made it "an ideal laboratory for industrial experiments."[4] Indeed, such progressive-era bureaucracies as the IWC provided the programmatic prototypes and administrative professionals for the emergent federal welfare state of the New Deal. Nevertheless, another important aspect of this history must emphasize the political and organizational sophistication of the labor movement and the feminism of trade-union women. Wary of the ideological feminism they associated with middle-class women, they developed their own pragmatic version by selectively combining labor's collective orientation and self-protection rhetoric with the political demands of the women's movement. An official of the laundry workers' union, Carrie Parmer, asserted, "If the working women want to become really emancipated they should organize and secure conditions that will make their lot a less unenviable one.... When that is done... women may then be called emancipated with some degree of truth."[5]

Women trade unionists argued that, while protective legislation offered material benefits, it also reinforced pernicious notions about women as inferior and undesirable workers who deviated from the domestic ideal, notions that circumscribed their employment opportunities and placed them at the mercy of government largesse. Alliances with working-class men were burdened by male ambivalence toward women wage earners; to curb female competition, male labor leaders sometimes advocated labor legislation for women that they rejected for themselves. For example, the American Federation of Labor (AFL) position on legislated standards remained equivocal and applied differentially to men and women. In a 1913 letter to the San Francisco Labor Council (SFLC), AFL president Samuel Gompers vehemently rejected the concept of a minimum-wage law for men and stated that "statutory enactment [of] wages... will only be another step to force workingmen to work at the behest of their employers, or at the behest of the State, which will be equivalent to and will be slavery." When it came to women, however, he qualified this position: "I hope you will have none of it, that is, not for men. It may be justifiable and defensible for women, but if so then only on the theory that they are in a sense the 'wards of the State.'"[6] Sarah Hagan, the leader of San Francisco United Garment Workers' Local #131 (UGW) and an SFLC official, responded with bitter irony: "Men are very kind to women wage-earners all of a sudden. ... If this minimum wage is so good for women, why isn't it good for men wage-earners? Why make a difference? The men say, try it on the women first. We're tired of being tried on."[7]

The political involvement of working-class women was a logical extension of their increasing organizational sophistication. Before the early 1920s, San Francisco was widely characterized as the quintessential labor town, dominated by powerful locals, central councils, and sympathetic political parties.[8] In the early 1900s the city's labor establishment began to encourage unionization among women, and by 1910, 7.6 percent of the wage-earning women of San Francisco were members of trade unions, often in predominantly female locals, while the national average was only 1.5 percent.[9] The men responded to the enthusiasm and determination of the women—and broadened their base of female support—by endorsing issues such as woman suffrage. In fact, contrary to accepted wisdom that stresses working-class opposition to woman suffrage, the labor vote was probably instrumental in winning passage of the California state suffrage amendment in 1911.[10]

Winning the vote was a crucial step in the ambitious reform agendas of both middle- and working-class women (see chapter 9). For several years wage-earning women had advocated an eight-hour law for women workers as an extension of labor's long-term efforts to achieve this goal through organization. Women's involvement in reducing their working hours arose internally within the affiliated women's organizations of the labor movement, particularly the Women's Union Label League (WULL), and won the support of numerous middle-class women's clubs and organizations as well. Delegations of San Francisco working women testified twice before the state legislature, where their assertive presentations about harsh working conditions won them significant public support, especially when contrasted to the hardhearted stance of the opposition (primarily employers of women). Louise LaRue of the waitresses' union pointed out that "the average waitress walks ten miles a day, and the Government will not allow an army mule to walk more than thirteen miles in the same time." Workers could also be scientific in collecting data: the waitresses had used pedometers to gather this information. The women took advantage of the hearings to proudly emphasize cases in which they had reduced their hours and improved their working conditions and wages through their own unions.[11]

In contrast to the 1911 eight-hour law for women, the minimum-wage measure passed in 1913 over the strident objections of the powerful California labor establishment and was thus perceived by labor as imposed by progressive reformers. From labor's perspective, there were important differences between hours and wage legislation. The former established fixed standards and vested enforcement responsibility in the state labor commissioner, who was usually responsive to labor interests. The latter created a novel form of government agency, the independent commission, with the power to determine the wage standards, which it then administered. Minimum-wage legislation for women roused the opposition of many of the state's male trade unionists, who feared that it would encourage excessive government intrusion into the collective bargaining process and weaken all labor organizations. In California, organized labor originally had four major points of objection to the minimum-wage law for women: that it would create maximum-wage ceilings, increase unemployment by speeding up production and eliminating less productive workers, obviate the need for organization among women, and, most significantly, place women at the mercy of unsympathetic future administrations and excessively powerful appointed officials who were not accountable to the electorate. In theory, commissions were neutral, objective bodies. In reality, their appointments often reflected the difficulty of trying to balance labor, management, and public interests. In this context, it is not so surprising that the measure elicited a spirited reaction from working-class women, who already had their own activist traditions and who rejected their characterization as marginal workers, victims, and subjects for social experimentation.[12]

Hagen and the other trade-union women who anticipated potentially detrimental effects from minimum-wage legislation insisted that organization was the ultimate source of strength and self-protection, and they never referred to themselves as victims or dependents. Instead, they concentrated on their complex identities as workers, labor activists, and newly enfranchised voters as well as women, wives, and mothers. Their infrequent use of maternalist rhetoric was often sarcastic. For example, while campaigning for Governor Johnson in 1914, Adelaide Walden, a San

Francisco laundry union official, referred to the persistent complaints of laundresses and waitresses about legal hour limitations when she told the San Francisco Daily News, "Sometimes we workers have to be saved from ourselves.... They didn't realize then, as they do now, that they were hurting not only themselves, but their future children."[13] During this period many middle-class women did indeed use the ideological power of motherhood as the basis of their own authority and as a legal justification for programs designed to aid children and women (usually defined as actual or potential mothers).[14] Union women understood how easily condescending prescriptions for motherhood ignored the economic exigencies affecting working-class practices.

Many progressive policy initiatives, including protective legislation, were experimental and could be evaluated only in the course of implementation. This contingent quality helps explain how the same female unionists who supported eight-hour-day legislation for women in 1911 could oppose minimum-wage legislation in 1913 and, in the 1920s and 1930s, argue for better enforcement, maintenance of standards, and budgetary support for the Industrial Welfare Commission (IWC) even as they continued to criticize the basic premise of the law. Regional differences were important in this regard, as the northern Californians controlled a labor movement that wielded significant economic and political clout until the 1920s. Labor influence in southern California was generally much weaker, but there was a greater socialist presence in the south, especially among women reformers. This orientation probably reinforced their tendency to seek statist solutions that seemed naive to the cynical labor veterans of the north.[15]

Among middle-class reformers, the prevailing rationale for minimum-wage legislation was the perceived connection between low wages and the chastity of working-class women, and was, as noted in chapter 10, only one of many moral-reform initiatives championed by middle-class women.[16] Morality issues titillated and shocked the general public in ways that the poverty, racial-ethnic, or immigrant status of working women in general did not.[17] The assumption that poverty led almost inevitably to prostitution infuriated working women, who objected to the sensationalist politicization of their economic exploitation and to the slander on their moral standards. Trade-union women vigorously challenged these condescending and voyeuristic judgments along with their inherent assumptions about superior middle-class virtue. They maintained that they had just as much control over the use of their bodies as did other self-respecting women, and they preferred to emphasize issues of personal dignity, self-protection, and economic justice. Sarah Hagan insisted, "This talk about white slavery and low wages is all stuff and nonsense.... The working women haven't time to go wrong." The labor press echoed this indignation, asserting, "Our working women have character enough to stand firm against temptation, and they do not take the 'easiest' way.... The minimum wage advocates ... must cease their slanders of working women."[18]

Middle-class reformers who saw the minimum wage as an important step toward the goal of greater economic equity for women were thus bewildered, but not deterred, when the intended recipients felt offended and patronized by the proposed legislation. With faith in scientific investigation and their own capacities for impartial administration, middle-class reformers generally discounted labor's focus on latent class-based power conflicts by dismissing the desire to perpetuate trade-union influence and industrial control as potentially, if not inherently, corrupt. This position was personified by Katherine Philips Edson, the Los Angeles clubwoman, suffragist, and prominent progressive activist who was instrumental in gaining passage of the minimum-wage law and who subsequently served as the chief executive officer of the IWC for many years. Initially, Edson held relatively neutral attitudes toward labor. In 1914 she proposed that working-class women's organizations be admitted as affiliates of the California Federation of Women's Clubs, a group not noted for its sympathy to working-class concerns. She told federal investigators that since unskilled women in female trades were unlikely to unionize, the legislation actually might help stimulate organization. As a result of Edson's subsequent confrontations with the labor movement, however, her position hardened.[19]

In reward for her political support, Governor Johnson appointed Edson as deputy inspector of the Bureau of Labor Statistics in 1912, where her review of an earlier investigation into the wages of women workers showed that approximately 40 percent of the women of California received less than nine dollars per week. At the governor's request, Edson then drafted a minimum-wage measure, one of a number of similar proposals introduced in the legislature early in 1913. She subsequently worked with other progressives, including Florence Kelley of the National Consumers League (NCL), and key California legislators to develop an effective and judicially defensible bill.

At first, both union officials and employers were distracted by the introduction of several other important labor bills, including workmen's compensation, and by the entanglement of the minimum-wage issue with the controversial "Red Light Abatement" act. In support of the red-light bill, Edson joined Elizabeth Gerberding and Helen Todd, fellow middle-class reformers, in presenting testimony on the condition of wage-earning women. After that law passed, over the clamorous objections of most of the San Francisco delegation, these women continued to press for a separate minimum-wage bill. Far from being grateful for their efforts on behalf of working women, the labor press castigated female reformers such as Edson and her colleagues as typical examples of "the woman politician who has invaded the field in recent years either to further her own interests or the interest of a political party with which she is affiliated." Significantly, this tirade foreshadowed the problems Edson would experience later when she refused to accept labor claims to authority over the welfare of working women.[20]

Evidently, the mobilization of their own female activists was more acceptable to male trade unionists, as labor women passed resolutions against the minimum-wage measure, distributed flyers, debated male colleagues, and spoke to middle-class women's clubs. Sarah Hagan was instrumental in this effort, leading the members of the San Francisco UGW local in opposing minimum-wage legislation as early as the 1912 California Federation of Labor (CFL) convention and convincing the SFLC to go on record against the proposal soon thereafter. By focusing on the potential for government arrogation of trade-union authority as a threat to their organizational autonomy, the women convinced the CFL to support their opposition to the measure over the objections of several powerful labor officials aligned with the progressive administration of Governor Johnson. They also appeared before the state legislature on several occasions, indignantly refuting the putative connection between morality and low wages. During one session in March, Hagan stated that working women "know something about the causes which lead women to the red-light district," adding, "Holier-than-thou women and men who prate about a minimum wage being the remedy do not know." She alluded to persistent class tensions when she suggested that "if these people are serious and really are bent upon doing something that will be beneficial to the working women, rather than advertise themselves, let them expend about one-half the energy they are now wasting in an endeavor to institute organizations among them."[21]

In spite of these efforts, the minimum-wage measure passed by wide margins in both houses of the legislature, and Governor Johnson signed it in May 1913. The law authorized the five-member Industrial Welfare Commission to conduct investigations, hearings, and conferences to determine the cost of living, hours of work per day, wages, and conditions of labor necessary to provide an adequate standard of living for women workers, and to issue orders establishing basic minimum-wage rates in each industry. Its major innovation was in its enforcement power. Failure to comply was a misdemeanor punishable by fines or imprisonment. Section 1 required only that one of the five commissioners be a woman; the composition of the board was otherwise left up to the governor. At labor's insistence, Section 17 of the law prohibited the commission's involvement in strike arbitration. As protection against judicial challenge, the legislature also passed a corollary constitutional amendment. California voters confirmed this measure in the fall of 1914 in spite of the renewed oppositional efforts of labor activists—many of whom simultaneously supported Governor Johnson and worked for his reelection.[22] According to the *Daily News*, Hagan apparently managed to convince at least some San Francisco clubwomen to reject the amendment with the argument: "The women wage-earners are opposed to it and they are the only ones to be considered," but the measure won easily based on widespread support elsewhere in the state.

The following year, Hagan's counterpart in Los Angeles, Daisy Houck, told a local group of clubwomen, "We of the union are not keen about the proposed establishment of a minimum wage." Nevertheless, the well-meaning middle-class ladies in her audience reiterated their commitment to state protection for "the women, who, unorganized, would otherwise be unable to help themselves."[23]

Anticipating deleterious long-term effects, the labor press noted suspiciously that certain employers otherwise known for long-standing antagonism to labor also had endorsed the legislation. The majority opposed the law because they worried that they would be placed at a competitive disadvantage relative to unregulated states, shared labor's objections to the commission form of government, or insisted more generally that the government should not meddle in business affairs. Some employers, including proprietors of smaller companies heavily dependent upon local market conditions, did support the measure. Others, particularly large department store owners, appreciated the potential capacity of government regulation to stabilize wages, increase efficiency, and deter unionization. One of these, A. B. C. Dohrmann, the president of the Emporium department store, was a powerful early member of the commission. His store was the target of several labor boycotts in the 1910s, while its manager, B. F. Schlesinger, opposed the eight-hour law for women and was accused by the SFLC of profiteering during World War I; he was also a confidant of Katherine Edson. In 1913, describing the attitudes of his fellow commissioners toward the new minimum-wage law, Walter Mathewson, a San Jose trade unionist, wrote to Edson that Chairman Dohrmann "was, if anything, against the measure."[24] One of Edson's subordinates at the commission, Helen Bary, subsequently criticized her boss as being too dependent upon Dohrmann, who she reported as saying frankly that he had "accepted the appointment to keep the commission from doing anything wild." Edson probably relied heavily on Dohrmann for help because he was one of the few people who actively supported the work of the commission—for whatever reason—and he became her loyal ally.[25]

Partly as a result of the women workers' lack of cooperation, much of the early cost-of-living documentation derived from material provided by the YWCA and Mrs. M. V. Greene, the Emporium's welfare director. The store's program was an early example of the corporate welfare strategy that became popular in the 1920s. By offering a variety of miscellaneous benefits and amenities, employers hoped to enhance employee well-being, circumvent unionization, and rationalize business operation.[26]

Under these difficult circumstances, the IWC remained a focus of controversy as Edson began the thankless task of trying to balance these competing interests and establish an effective agency. She opened an office in San Francisco in January 1914 and immediately alarmed the state's businessmen by her announced intention of using San Francisco's high wage rates as the norm, noting that "the board could not well fix a lower standard wage than $9 a week, what the organized workers of San Francisco have fixed for themselves." Edson was not unsympathetic to employers, but she articulated the progressive vision of a harmonious relationship between labor and capital, asserting that while "industry is the life blood of the nation," nevertheless "anything that affects the industrial life of the nation is the business of the whole people."[27]

The IWC initiated two difficult tasks in the face of multilateral opposition. The first project, a general survey of wages, occupations, apprenticeships, and working conditions, revealed that almost half of the female workers of the state received less than ten dollars per week. In the garment industry, the hostility of members of Sarah Hagan's San Francisco UGW local impeded IWC investigative attempts. Mathewson tried to mediate, but he also expressed frustration with IWC bureaucratic insensitivity. Mathewson criticized a draft report for its elitist attitudes and indifference to the displacement of older workers, and he noted that the organized women wished "the commission to leave . . . [them] well alone."[28]

The commission's second major undertaking was an intensive investigation of the canning industry, the state's largest employer of women. Due to concentrated industry lobbying efforts, the 1911 eight-hour law had explicitly exempted canneries, in spite of their notoriously low wages and primitive working conditions. Early in 1916 the IWC issued its first order that set wages, established sanitary standards, and limited hours to ten per day (sixty per week), with provision for overtime. Developed in close cooperation with those canners interested in standardization and quality control, the regulations were designed to ensure compliance by basically reflecting the employers' concerns, especially in retaining piece rates. The women workers ostensibly enjoyed higher wages, limitations on hours of work, improved conditions, and the protection of the state. Yet enforcement was erratic, the interpretation of regulations often favored the employers, and the commission allowed many modifications and exclusions, especially in the 1920s.[29]

Furthermore, spontaneous strikes by cannery workers continued to disrupt the industry. The largest of these, in July 1917, began in San Jose and soon spread to San Francisco and Oakland. Because the fledgling union did not include the women who formed 80 percent of the cannery workforce, government mediators, concerned about production during World War I, separated the women's issues and asked Edson to mediate their disputes. When Bary objected that the law prohibited IWC involvement in arbitration during a strike or lockout, Edson replied that because of the war, "things were different." Edson was reluctant to address the women's needs by altering the standards so recently set by her own commission after great effort. The final settlement granted the men a 20 percent wage increase (without union recognition) but did little for the women.[30] Also in July 1917 the IWC finally began to extend the minimum wage of ten dollars per week for women to other industries, seventeen months after setting the cannery standards. Part of the delay resulted from anxiety over a pending challenge in the United States Supreme Court, but the court's decision in April was inconclusive. After another cost-of-living study in response to post–World War I inflation pressures, the weekly minimum wage for women was raised to $13.50 in 1919 and increased again to $16 per week in 1920.[31]

World War I marked a major watershed for women workers, who eagerly filled the better paying jobs in previously male-dominated industries now vacated by soldiers. Although distracted by her campaign to mobilize citizen participation in the war effort, Edson was concerned that the exigencies of wartime might endanger established protective legislation measures. In fact, however, federal regulation of war-production industries advanced the developing rationale for government intervention in productive processes. To some extent, industry-wide application of rules promulgated for women workers also benefited men, but the regulations only affected government contractors and noncompliance was common, especially in the matter of wage rates. After the war, observers noted that the combination of government protection, labor organization, and market demand for workers had produced more skilled and confident female wage earners—who now faced displacement by returning veterans and because of the demilitarization of the economy. In 1919 the *Labor Clarion* reported that the U.S. Employment Service had found, "Jobs for women are plentiful at low wages [but] the women are refusing to work for less than they have been receiving." The partial preemption of the

IWC's regulatory responsibilities by the federal government combined with the growing confidence of women workers (reflected in another surge in female organization) to bolster labor's charge that the IWC was dilatory, self-serving, and already obsolete.[32]

As government agencies became increasingly involved in the collective-bargaining process, some of labor's concerns proved to be unfounded, but other anticipated consequences were realized. At least in the case of hours limitations, subsequent research has indicated that the material effects were generally beneficial for most women, a major exception being those who were prohibited from earning additional overtime income. Minimum-wage legislation resulted in unmistakable wage improvements for women in three California industries. For example, in 1920, after the rate was raised from $13.50 to $16 per week, the percentage of women making less than $16 dropped to 14 percent from 72 percent the year before. The effect within a single industry varied greatly by city, however, indicating that the workers in the more highly unionized areas probably enjoyed consistently higher earnings, undoubtedly as a result of unrelenting labor pressure. For example, when the ten-dollar weekly standard was established for the laundry industry in 1917, improvements were most dramatic in San Francisco. They were also impressive in Oakland, which shared the generalized strength of labor throughout the Bay Area. In the staunchly anti-union city of Los Angeles, however, 21.3 percent of working women continued to earn substandard wages, often through the manipulation of apprenticeship regulations, even after the ten-dollar minimum wage went into effect. Significantly, it was frequently the vigilance of labor activists that guaranteed reliable government enforcement of the laws, because evasion and retribution against unorganized workers who filed complaints were common practices. Organized labor continued to emphasize this point long after it had grudgingly accepted the reality of government intervention.[33]

The California Industrial Welfare Commission and the Women's Bureau issued careful reports documenting these positive effects, although the small size of their samples is one indication that this was not an easy task. The primitive scientism of progressive reformers often cloaked their own vested interests and class orientation, whether this effect was intended or not. On the other hand, both federal and state agencies asserted that female unemployment did not increase significantly in spite of large numbers of women receiving higher pay. In California there were threats and isolated dismissals, but women workers were still preferred for a number of reasons. As John Millar, the general manager of the California Cotton Mills and a perennial foe of labor, reported to a Women's Bureau interviewer, even at minimum wage "they [women] are still cheaper than men for most jobs." Millar was apparently unconcerned about admitting that "he was theoretically disregarding minimum wage," but he also acknowledged that he "found it hard to get women for less than $16.00 as [the] minimum wage idea has educated [women] to expect it and most women refuse to work for less." As Adelaide Walden had noted earlier, a common complaint of the working women themselves was the elimination of opportunities for overtime by hours limitations, a serious blow to subsistence-wage earners, and they frequently colluded in infractions to augment their earnings.[34]

Compared to similar (but weaker) statutes in Massachusetts and New York, 93.7 percent of the California women surveyed by the Women's Bureau reported that their hours had decreased, while 6.3 percent stated that legislation had had no effect, compared to figures of 55.2 and 38.5 percent, respectively, in the other states. Although the majority of California workers surveyed did not indicate whether hour reductions had affected their wages, of those who did (N=13), five reported pay increases while seven reported that there had been no effect. More than half of the small California sample responded that their employment opportunities had improved, while the rest indicated that the legislation had had no effect. Significantly, they were not asked if these chances had deteriorated. These figures indicate the comparative success of regulation in California, but this data precludes differential analysis of the importance of private union pressure compared to the effects of public enforcement.[35]

Although protective legislation immediately improved working conditions, hours, and pay rates for large numbers of working women, the San Francisco trade union women who had already earned this power through their own organizational efforts still worried that trade union autonomy could be subverted by a hostile IWC. By the early 1920s a shifting political climate had installed an arch-conservative governor, Friend W. Richardson, who disapproved of social and regulatory programs. In addition, the commission was increasingly sympathetic to the interests of employers, some of whom shared labor's opinion that the law was undermining organizational incentives among women. Privately, Ben Schlesinger confided to Fred Boegle of the California Manufacturers Association that "a minimum wage law, properly administered, is the best kind of a barrier to closed shop conditions." At a meeting of fellow employers in 1921, Schlesinger remarked that the minimum wage was "a bulwark against Labor Unions and radicalism, because if the State causes a fair minimum wage to be paid, it takes a great deal of argument to say to the average woman that she could do better through other means." Schlesinger clearly believed that the IWC was the less odious alternative, and he advised his colleagues to make the best of the situation, assuring his audience that if they could "show good reason for changing the present minimum wage" due to a decline in the high cost of living, "you will find the Minimum Wage Commission just as ready to lower it as it has been to increase it." "There is no doubt about it," he stated. As if on cue, during a recession in the fall of 1921 the IWC began a series of public hearings to review a request by the California Manufacturers' Association (CMA) for a wage-rate reduction from $16 to $12.50 per week.[36]

When Edson advised a one-dollar reduction in the basic weekly wage, infuriated labor activists developed a tripartite strategy of legal challenges, revised cost-of-living studies, and a vituperative personal attack on Katherine Edson. Articles in the labor press charged her with political opportunism, compared her moral insensitivity to "that Austrian woman who became queen of France," accused her of misappropriation of state funds based on irregularities in her financial arrangements, and petitioned the governor for her dismissal. Aggrieved working women communicated with her personally and publicly, suggesting that she try living on fifteen dollars per week before recommending it for others. In a response that recalls Bary's criticism of their professional relationship, IWC Chairman Dohrmann attempted to deflect some of the criticism by issuing an "apology" for Edson that did more harm than good by undercutting her authority. The labor establishment sarcastically suggested that "the apparent remedy . . . is for the women victims go before the next session of the Legislature and insist upon having a majority of women on the commission . . . so that if women are to be whipped they may at least enjoy the satisfaction of having it done by their sisters instead of by tyrant man."[37] Although Edson insisted that the only reason she supported the wage reduction was that she feared the effects of unemployment, she admitted privately that she did not believe that "a decrease of $1 a week is going to make a tremendous difference in the actual cost of production." Edson appeared more concerned that the IWC was "rapidly losing the confidence of the employers" who accused the commission of "being a political board." She added, "I am sure that the life of this Commission has been lengthened by this concession." Thus, the regulators regarded the continued existence of their agency to be at least as important as the legislative mandate to provide the working women of California with an adequate wage.[38]

Sarah Hagan, a SFLC official, had served earlier as a workers' representative on the IWC's needle-trades wage board. Considering her long-standing animosity, she had probably justified her participation as an evil necessary to counter powerful employer interests. Now Hagan renewed her attack on the principle of regulation, helped compile the SFLC's cost-of-living estimates, and insisted that the current minimum of sixteen dollars per week was already inadequate: "Working girls cannot live on this schedule, I do not care how hard they try. . . . If it is reduced I do not know what is going to happen."[39] None of the budget estimates included accommodations for dependents, nor were they very generous in addressing the individual needs of single women, such as savings or entertainment expenses. Employers' estimates and those of the women unionists varied considerably. In both northern and southern California, working women complained vociferously in letters to the local newspapers and in testimony during IWC hearings, which they criticized as biased and perfunctory. Hagan told the *San Francisco Bulletin* of the humiliating treatment she experienced at one of those meetings. In that incident, the employers held a fashion show to demonstrate the types of garments a woman could afford on their meager cost-of-living allowance, but the items were so cheap and flimsy that the women were offended and objected vehemently. Most emphasized their constant frugality, but a few insisted that they had as much right to nice things as any woman.[40]

In their protests, the labor women appealed directly to the community, and some middle-class women's organizations responded by passing

15. "How to Dress on $12.50" (clipping of newspaper cartoon in the San Francisco Labor Council Collection). Courtesy Curator of Pictorial Collections, the Bancroft Library, University of California, Berkeley CA.

resolutions in support of their position. In speaking to women's clubs, both Sarah Hagan and Frances Noel, a Los Angeles trade unionist and socialist, exchanged heated words in debate with Katherine Edson. Of very different social and political backgrounds, Edson and Noel had a complex relationship. They had collaborated on suffrage, but by the time they confronted each other in San Diego, Noel had publicly denounced Edson as a "catspaw of capital," apparently a reference to her support of

Charles Evans Hughes in the 1916 presidential election. In San Francisco the *Labor Clarion* republished a story from the *Los Angeles Citizen* on the San Diego incident, which observed that "Mrs. Noel refrained from mentioning the fact that Mrs. Edson receives about six times the amount of pay deemed sufficient for other women." Apparently, "Mrs. Edson's aristocratic face became as red as a California sunset when Mrs. Noel declared: 'Fear of losing our own bread and butter makes cowards of us all, including newspaper editors and public officeholders.'"[41] Writing to Mrs. Raymond Robins of the Women's Trade Union League, Edson sniffed that Noel was "one of those people whose early environment" seemed "impossible to overcome." In her elitist opinion, Noel had "no sense of things that to us seem almost as essential as good morals," especially "good taste."

Edson was deeply hurt and disillusioned by the virulence of the personal criticism, never realizing how her condescending elitism compromised her good intentions, affected her relations with labor, and vitiated her best efforts. Yet she realized that the California law set an important precedent and defended it energetically in spite of her vexation. She was very gratified, therefore, to receive help from an unexpected source when the Los Angeles United Garment Workers Local #125 issued public statements protesting the proposed cut but defending Edson's character. The courageous Los Angeles women defied the powerful state and San Francisco labor groups that repudiated their position, complained to the international union, and attempted to harass them into compliance.[42] While condemning the defiant insubordination of female trade unionists, the men saved some vitriol for apathetic women wage earners as well: "Had the women indicated intelligence enough to organize years ago there never would have been such a State Commission. . . . It is to be hoped that the recent decision . . . will serve to convince them that organization is their only salvation." The underlying misogyny of male labor leaders is clearly revealed by this episode, but the situation is complicated by the fact that the men had also learned to appreciate the strength of their sister unionists. The labor press noted that no reductions had been made in the laundry and restaurant industries, ostensibly because no request had been made by the employers, but in reality because "the women workers in these particular lines happen to be organized and capable of taking care of their own wage matters." Basically, "the unions would not permit [reductions]."[43] Nevertheless, the fact that so many working-class women joined in criticizing Edson underscores their sensitivity to unresolved class tensions that subverted any residual notions of common sisterhood.

Upon receiving notice of the wage reduction, members of the San Francisco UGW Local #131 immediately filed a brief in San Francisco Superior Court alleging that the reduced fifteen-dollar weekly minimum was inadequate to maintain the health and welfare of workers as explicitly required by the law. The garment workers further maintained that the IWC had held "secret meetings" instead of the required conferences and public hearings. A writ of review blocked implementation of the new rate two days before it was to become effective. The reduction controversy was never really resolved. While preparing the state's defense, the attorney general found irregularities in the order, which technically invalidated it and potentially all previous orders as well. The IWC was severely embarrassed publicly, but privately Edson was not sorry to be relieved of responsibility for the wage reduction. By the time the IWC initiated a new series of hearings in the fall of 1922, the economic situation had improved and the reduction was no longer considered necessary.[44]

Confused in vision and weakened by judicial challenge, the IWC was further handicapped by two events the following year. In April 1923 the U.S. Supreme Court ruled that minimum-wage legislation in the District of Columbia interfered with freedom of contract (*Adkins v. Children's Hospital*), casting similar state statutes into legal limbo. Labor leaders reacted to the decision by expressing concern for the unorganized women of the state, but they also emphasized how this action confirmed the fundamental importance of self-determination through organization. Sarah Hagan confidently asserted that "women who are organized are not affected one way or the other." Frances Noel stated, "The Supreme Court decision against the minimum wage illustrates clearly that even at best a minimum wage for women requires an artificial or state-made union of workers, which, therefore, depends on the mercy and fluctuating power of politics." She continued, "The wage-earning women's true salvation depends on the strength of their own trade unions and on their own political representatives in government." If labor felt vindicated in their objections, middle-class reformers were seriously disturbed by this threat to one of their most significant achievements. Some employers volunteered to continue paying the established minimum, but others vowed to challenge the California law immediately. The progressive momentum had largely dissipated during World War I, and Edson had difficulty raising the interest of women's clubs, her traditional power base. Nevertheless, considerable reformist sentiment had been institutionalized in government agencies by the 1920s, although this situation did not prevent conservative officials from attempting to undermine existing policies.[45]

In response to the Supreme Court decision, Governor Richardson announced that he "would not be a party to any plan that might discredit the supreme court of the United States," but progressive members of the California state senate introduced a resolution memorializing the U.S. Congress to amend the Constitution if necessary to protect such laws. This possibility was also under consideration by a number of reform organizations and, perhaps surprisingly, by some employers as well. Edson wrote frankly to Margaret Robins of the National Women's Trade Union League that she knew that many employers believed the law to be a disincentive to organization. Thus, she was worried about accepting financial support from Dohrmann, Schlesinger, and others to go to Washington DC, to work for the contemplated constitutional amendment. Robins replied that since Edson was "not, speaking technically, a working woman," or part of the labor movement, she could accept this offer from a "group of finer manufacturers." Edson's friends were probably also motivated by personal concern, for Edson's position with the IWC was a casualty of Richardson's drastic reduction of the agency's budget appropriation in the spring of 1923. Echoing labor's earlier contention that her *per diem* reimbursement arrangement was illegal, Richardson cut Edson's salary and forced her into a reduced role on the commission (she had been serving as executive commissioner in order to have a vote, rather than as executive secretary with a secure salary but less power). Edson, a stalwart and respectable clubwoman, was further enraged when Richardson called her "an anarchist," because she "dared to criticize the opinion of the United States Supreme Court in reference to the minimum wage decision."[46] Ironically, Edson's bitter antagonists of the previous year, Hagan and the trade union women of San Francisco, joined her in protesting the proposed cuts, and they achieved a partial but inadequate restoration of funding. On July 1, 1923, the IWC staff was reduced by half and Edson lost her influence. In

1927, with the progressive C. C. Young in the governor's office, the IWC was nonetheless further weakened by the loss of its enforcement power when it was subsumed under the Division of Industrial Welfare. Although she felt pressured to resign, Edson remained with the commission until 1931, when ill health and the partisan hostility of Governor James Rolph finally forced her to retire.[47]

In summary, the material condition of most women workers improved as a result of protective legislation, but at the risk of debilitating effects on union organization and the potential, later realized, for unsympathetic government action. Whether the measure actually weakened women's unions is probably impossible to determine because of the general decline in the influence of labor in the 1920s. Both trade unionists and employers believed that the effectiveness of union activity among women had been compromised, yet trade unionism remained an important factor in determining women's wages, especially in San Francisco, where pay rates continued to be higher than in the other major cities of California. Some male labor leaders were probably willing to be relieved of the responsibility of addressing the specific difficulties of organizing women, but trade-union women—who had struggled against such indifference for years to encourage a sense of collective responsibility among marginalized female workers—were very upset. At the time of the reduction controversy, an angry Sarah Hagan said, "Let the women alone. . . . I don't approve of this minimum wage law for 'women and minors'! Let the women get their wages as men do by collective bargaining and organization. Like children they lean too much on the minimum wage and the eight-hour day, which makes them feel protected without organization, and then the employers have it their own way." Labor women worried that government protection was illusory and that the new relationship between the individual and the state promised direct intervention in specific cases but often failed to fulfill this obligation. Although they could not deny the improvements enjoyed by many unorganized workers, and sometimes acknowledged that labor-government cooperation seemed to work best to ensure enforcement, disillusioned unionists never lost an opportunity to stress situations where women had benefited more from organization than from regulation.[48]

More invidiously, such laws perpetuated the concept of women as a separate group of secondary wage earners requiring special treatment. Trade-union women in California actively resisted this characterization by drawing upon labor solidarity and discipline, supplemented by contemporary feminist rhetoric, to defend their hard-won economic and political autonomy. They shared the labor movement's concern about who would have the power to define the elusive concept of the "common good," identify target populations, design and implement programs, and evaluate the results. Over the years, they addressed the issue of extending protection to larger groups of oppressed women, rejected middle-class moral determinism, which cast them in passive and victimized roles, and tried to understand the long-term consequences of the establishment of a modern social welfare bureaucracy during a formative period. Through their involvement, labor women impressed their claims for self-definition and self-determination into the processes of state building and policy implementation. Although they failed to block the initial legislation, and eventually grudgingly acceded to government protection for the unorganized majority of women workers, they consistently stressed the need for strong independent organizations to monitor the enforcement of problematic policies. Unfortunately, the realization of several of labor's anticipated concerns in the 1920s and 1930s confirmed their suspicions about administrative bias and made it clear that implementation under such circumstances relied more than ever upon constant vigilance by dedicated unionists.

Notes

This chapter derives from Rebecca J. Mead, "'Let the Women Get Their Wages as Men Do': Trade Union Women and the Legislated Minimum Wage in California," *Pacific Historical Review* 67 (1998): 317–47.

1. Spencer C. Olin Jr., *California's Prodigal Sons: Hiram Johnson and the Progressives, 1911–1917* (Berkeley: University of California Press, 1968); Mary Ann Mason, "Neither Friends nor Foes: Organized Labor and the California Progressives," in *California Progressivism Revisited*, ed. William Deverell and Tom Sitton (Berkeley: University of California Press, 1994), 57–71.

2. For some previous work on early "labor" or "industrial" feminism, see Ardis Cameron, *Radicals of the Worst Sort: Laboring Women in Lawrence, Massachusetts, 1860–1912* (Urbana: University of Illinois Press, 1993); Mary Jo Buhle, *Women and American Socialism, 1870–1920* (Urbana: University of Illinois Press, 1981); Sarah

Eisenstein, *Give Us Bread but Give Us Roses: Working Women's Consciousness in the United States, 1890 to the First World War* (London: Routledge, 1983); Annelise Orleck, *Common Sense and a Little Fire: Women and Working-Class Politics in the United States, 1900–1965* (Chapel Hill: University of North Carolina Press, 1995); and Maurine Weiner Greenwald, "Working-Class Feminism and the Family Wage Ideal: The Seattle Debate on Married Women's Right to Work, 1914–1920," *Journal of American History* 76 (1989): 118–49.

3. Jaclyn Greenberg, "The Limits of Legislation: Katherine Philips Edson, Practical Politics, and the Minimum-Wage Law in California, 1913–1922," *Journal of Policy History* 5 (1993): 207–30. Other previous studies include Earl C. Crockett, "History of California Labor Legislation, 1910–1930" (PhD dissertation, University of California, Berkeley, 1931), 64–94; Jacqueline Braitman, "Katherine Philips Edson: A Progressive Feminist in California's Era of Reform," (PhD dissertation, University of California, Los Angeles, 1988), and Jacqueline Braitman, "A California Stateswoman: The Public Career of Katherine Philips Edson," *California History*, 65 (1986): 82–95, 151–52fn; Norris C. Hundley Jr., "Katherine Philips Edson and the Fight for the California Minimum Wage, 1912–1913," *Pacific Historical Review* 30 (1960): 271–85; Sherry Katz, "Dual Commitments: Feminism, Socialism, and Women's Political Activism in California, 1890–1920," (PhD dissertation, University of California, Los Angeles, 1991), 566–637; and Susan Diane Casement, "Katherine Philips Edson and California's Industrial Welfare Commission, 1913–1931," (Master's thesis, Kansas State University, 1987). See also Lucile Eaves, *A History of California Labor Legislation* (Berkeley: University of California Press, 1910), 311–17.

4. California Industrial Welfare Commission (IWC), *Second Biennial Report, 1915–1916* (Sacramento, 1917), 13–14.

5. *Daily News*, September 27, 1910.

6. *Labor Clarion*, February 21, 1913; Alice Kessler-Harris, *Out to Work: A History of Wage-Earning Women in the United States* (New York: Oxford University Press, 1982), 35–36, 180–214; Vivien Hart, *Bound by Our Constitution: Women, Workers, and the Minimum Wage* (Princeton: Princeton University Press, 1994); Susan Lehrer, *Origins of Protective Labor Legislation for Women, 1905–1925* (Albany: State University of New York Press, 1987); Judith A. Baer, *The Chains of Protection: The Judicial Response to Women's Labor Legislation* (Westport CT: Greenwood, 1978); Nancy Erickson, "Muller v. Oregon Reconsidered: The Origins of a Sex-Based Doctrine of Liberty of Contract," *Labor History* 30 (1989): 228–50; Alice Kessler-Harris, *A Woman's Wage: Historical Meanings and Social Consequences* (Lexington: University Press of Kentucky, 1990), 33–56; and Ann Corinne Hill, "Protection of Women Workers and the Courts: A Legal Case History," *Feminist Studies* 5 (1979): 247–73.

7. *Garment Worker*, January 3, 1913.

8. William Issel and Robert Cherny, *San Francisco, 1865–1932: Politics, Power, and Urban Development* (Berkeley: University of California Press, 1986); Michael Kazin,

Barons of Labor: The San Francisco Building Trades and Union Power in the Progressive Era (Urbana: University of Illinois Press, 1987); Robert Knight, Industrial Relations in the San Francisco Bay Area, 1900–1918 (Berkeley: University of California Press, 1960); Walton Bean, Boss Ruef's San Francisco: The Story of the Union Labor Party, Big Business, and the Graft Prosecution (Berkeley: University of California Press, 1952); Jules Tygiel, "'. . . Where Unionism Holds Undisputed Sway': A Reappraisal of San Francisco's Union Labor Party," California History 62 (1983): 197–215; and Philip J. Ethington, The Public City: The Political Construction of Urban Life in San Francisco, 1850–1900 (Berkeley: University of California Press, 2001).

9. Kessler-Harris, Out to Work, 152; Lillian Ruth Matthews, Women in Trade Unions in San Francisco, University of California Publications in Economics, Vol. 3 (Berkeley: University of California Press, 1913); Jessica B. Peixotto, "Women of California as Trade Unionists," Publications of the Association of Collegiate Alumnae 3 (1908): 40–49; Louise M. Ploeger, "Trade Unionism among the Women of San Francisco, 1920," (Master's thesis, University of California, Berkeley, 1920); U.S. Department of Commerce and Labor, Report on Condition of Women and Child Wage-Earners in the United States, Vol. 10: John Andrews and W. D. P. Bliss, History of Women in Trade Unions (Washington DC, 1911), 136–139, 149.

10. Susan Englander, Class Coalition and Class Conflict in the California Woman Suffrage Movement, 1907–1912: The San Francisco Wage Earners' Suffrage League (Lewiston NY: Mellen University Press, 1992).

11. Labor Clarion, September 23, 1910, February 24, April 7, 1911; Daily News, February 15, March 11, May 1, 1911; San Francisco Examiner, February 17, 1911; California Federation of Labor, Proceedings of the Tenth Annual Convention (1909), 33; Earl C. Crockett, "History of California Labor Legislation, 1910–1930" (PhD dissertation, University of California, Berkeley, 1931), 5–21; Franklin Hichborn, Story of the Session of the California Legislature of 1911 (San Francisco, 1911), 246–60.

12. Labor Clarion, January 24, March 28, April 4, 1913, October 2, 30, 1914; Coast Seamen's Journal, January 22, March 5, 12, 19, April 2, 1913.

13. Daily News, September 16, 1914.

14. Linda Gordon, Pitied but Not Entitled: Single Mothers and the History of Welfare, 1890–1935 (New York: Harvard University Press, 1998); Theda Skocpol, Protecting Soldiers and Mothers: The Political Origins of Social Policy in the United States (Cambridge MA: Belknap, 1992); Robyn Muncy, Creating a Female Dominion in American Reform, 1890–1935 (New York: Oxford University Press, 1991); Seth Koven and Sonya Michel, Mothers of a New World: Maternalist Politics and the Origins of Welfare States (London: Routledge, 1993); Barbara J. Nelson, "The Gender, Race, and Class Origins of Early Welfare Policy and the Welfare State: A Comparison of Workmen's Compensation and Mother's Aid," in Women, Politics, and Change, ed. Louise A. Tilly and Patricia Gurin (New York: Russell Sage Foundation, 1992), 413–35; Lynn Y. Weiner et al., "Maternalism as Paradigm," Journal of Women's History 5 (1993): 96–131.

15. Katz, "Dual Commitments," 581–99.

16. Gayle Gullett, "City Mothers, City Daughters, and the Dance Hall Girls: The Limits of Female Political Power in San Francisco, 1913," in *Women and the Structure of Society*, ed. Barbara J. Harris and JoAnn K. McNamara (Durham NC: Duke University Press, 1984), 149–59, 281–85.

17. Joanne J. Meyerowitz, *Women Adrift: Independent Wage Earners in Chicago, 1880–1930* (Chicago: University Of Chicago Press, 1988); Ruth Rosen, *The Lost Sisterhood: Prostitution in America, 1900–1918* (Baltimore: Johns Hopkins University Press, 1982).

18. *San Francisco Examiner*, March 26, 1913; *Labor Clarion*, October 17, 1913.

19. Braitman, "Katherine Philips Edson," 72–168, 387–88; Katz, "Dual Commitments," 569.

20. *Daily News*, March 17, April 1, 1913; *Labor Clarion*, April 4, 1913; Hundley, "Katherine Philips Edson," 271–76; Crockett, "History of California Labor Legislation," 64–83; Franklin Hichborn, *Story of the Session of the California Legislature of 1913* (San Francisco: James H. Barry, 1913), 320–44, 350–52; Florence Kelley to Edson, November 22, 1912, Katherine Philips Edson Papers, Department of Special Collections, University Research Library, University of California, Los Angeles, California.

21. *Daily News*, September 26, 1914; *San Francisco Bulletin*, March 24, 1913; *Labor Clarion*, March 21, 28, 1913, Oct. 2, 1914; *Coast Seamen's Journal*, April 2, 1913; *San Francisco Examiner*, March 26, 1913; California Federation of Labor (CFL), *Proceedings of the Thirteenth Annual Convention* (1912), 34–35, and *Proceedings of the Fifteenth Annual Convention* (1914), 22–23.

22. California IWC, First Biennial Report, 1913–1914 (Sacramento, 1915), 101–6.

23. *San Francisco Daily News*, October 29, 1914; *Los Angeles Examiner*, December 12, 1915.

24. *Labor Clarion*, March 21, April 4, 1913; Walter Mathewson to Edson, November 28, 1913, Edson Papers; Greenberg, "The Limits of Legislation," 214–15.

25. Helen Valeska Bary, "Labor Administration and Social Security: A Woman's Life," Suffragist Oral History Project, Bancroft Library, University of California, Berkeley (1974), 49–53; Casement, "Katherine Philips Edson," 123–124; Braitman, "Katherine Philips Edson," 228–29.

26. Pamphlet, "What the Emporium is Doing," n.d., Edson Papers; Greenberg, "The Limits of Legislation," 218–19.

27. *San Francisco Daily News*, January 8, February 24, 1914.

28. California IWC, First Biennial Report, Second Biennial Report, 1915–1916 (Sacramento, 1916), 13–57, 77–168; Mathewson to Edson, September 30, 1914, Edson Papers.

29. California IWC, Second Biennial Report, 231–75; Jaclyn Greenberg, "Industry in the Garden: A Social History of the Canning Industry and Canning Workers in

the Santa Clara Valley, California, 1870–1920," (PhD dissertation, UCLA, 1985), 147–191; Bary, "Labor Administration and Social Security," 62–71.

30. Greenberg, "Industry in the Garden," 192–233; Bary, "Labor Administration and Social Security," 67–68, 70–71; Edson to Bertha von der Nienburg, August 9, 1917, Edson to Margaret Dreier Robins, August 27, 1917, Edson Papers.

31. California IWC, Fourth Biennial Report, 13–26.

32. Labor Clarion, July 19, August 30, September 20, 1918, January 31, 1919; Knight, Industrial Relations in the San Francisco Bay Area, 299–368; Braitman, "Katherine Philips Edson," 243–56.

33. California IWC, Third Biennial Report, 49–93, and What California Has Done to Protect Its Women Workers (Sacramento, 1923), 10; Ploeger, "Trade Unionism," 19–22.

34. Nancy Breen, "Shedding Light on Women's Work and Wages: Consequences of Protective Legislation," (PhD dissertation, New School for Social Research, 1989). See also the California IWC biennial reports and its pamphlet series entitled What California Has Done to Protect Its Women Workers (Sacramento, 1921, 1923, 1927); and the U.S. Department of Labor, Women's Bureau, History of Labor Legislation, The Effects of Labor Legislation on the Employment Opportunities of Women, Bulletin 65, (Washington DC, 1928); and The Development of Minimum-Wage Laws in the United States, 1912–1927, Bulletin 61, (Washington DC, 1928); interviews with Mr. Unger, Louis Kurtzman, and John Millar, Long Hour Day Schedules, California (interviews for Bulletin 65), Record Group 86, Women's Bureau Collection, National Archives, Washington DC. For examples of working women evading the law, see Minutes of Bindery Women's Local #125, February 14, July 10, December 11, 1912, August 20, 1915, March 17, 1916, Bookbinders and Bindery Women's Union, Local 31–125 Collection, Labor Archives, San Francisco State University, San Francisco, California.

35. Women's Bureau, Effects of Labor Legislation, 134–144.

36. B. F. Schlesinger to Edson, October 7, 1914; Report of speech by Schlesinger, February 16, 1921; Fred Boegle to Schlesinger, June 14, 1921, and Schlesinger to Boegle, June 16, 1921, Edson Papers; Labor Clarion, February 25, May 24, 1918.

37. A. B. C. Dohrmann, Letter to the editor, San Francisco Bulletin, November 30, 1922; Labor Clarion, January 13, April 14, 21, May 5, 12, 19, 1922; Coast Seamen's Journal, May, June, 1922; San Francisco Examiner, April 17, 1922; Jane Sullivan to Edson, December 19, 1922, Edson Papers.

38. Edson to Mary Anderson, May 10, 1922; Anderson to Edson, April 28, May 19, 1922, Edson Papers.

39. Labor Clarion, December 16, 1921; UGW Local #131, "Report on the Cost of Living for a Single Girl in California," n.d. [late 1921?] (and related material), SFLC Collection.

40. Labor Clarion, January 6, 1922; Call-Bulletin, February 6, December 15, 1922; Daily News, November 30, 1922; San Francisco Examiner, December 15, 1922.

41. *Labor Clarion*, January 13, June 9, 1922; *Oakland Post*, October 29, 1921; Edson to Robins, November 29, 1916, and Edson to Florence Kelley, November 22, 1922, Edson Papers.

42. *Labor Clarion* June 9, 1922; *San Francisco Call-Bulletin*, May 8, 1922; UGW Local #125 to Los Angeles Central Labor Council, April 29, 1922, and UGW #125 to Edson, April 29, 1922, Henry W. Louis to Edson, May 15, 1922, Report to Local #125 by Daisy Houck, May 10, 1922, Edson to Houck, May 3, 1922, Edson to Mabel Still, May 3, June 8, 1922, Edson to Louis, May 12, 1922, and Edson to Dewson, August 17, 1923, Edson Papers; Correspondence between UGW #125 and the SFLC, May 11–June 28, 1922, SFLC Collection.

43. *Labor Clarion*, April 14, April 28, 1922.

44. Brief and related documents, SFLC Collection; *Labor Clarion*, June 2, July 14, October 6, December 22, 1922; Edson to Louis, May 12, 1922, Edson Papers.

45. *Labor Clarion*, April 13, 20, 1923; *Call-Bulletin*, April 12, 1923; *Los Angeles Record*, April 13, 1923; California IWC, *What California Has Done* (1927), 8; Jackson K. Putnam, "The Persistence of Progressivism in the 1920's: The Case of California," *Pacific Historical Review* 35 (1966): 395–411.

46. *Daily News*, April 12, 1923; *Sacramento Union*, April 13, 1923; Edson to Robins, April 24, 1923, Robins to Edson, May 4, 1923, Edson Papers; Braitman, "Katherine Philips Edson," 394–401, 408–12.

47. IWC circular, February 21, 1923, Edson Papers; Edson to Mary Dewson, August 17, 1923, Edson Papers; Braitman, "Katherine Philips Edson," 389–91, 415–19.

48. Ploeger, "Trade Unionism," 43, 60–63, 129; Report [by Frances Noel?], n.d. [ca. 1923], Frances N. Noel Papers, Department of Special Collections, University Research Library, University of California, Los Angeles, California; Braitman, "Katherine Philips Edson," 386–88; Anne Martin, "The Woman's Wage Controversy in California," ca. 1922, Anne Martin Collection, Bancroft Library, University of California, Berkeley.

12. "NO UNDUE FAMILIARITY"

Gender, Vice, and the Campaign to Regulate Dance Halls, 1911–1921

MARK HOPKINS

As California clubwomen mobilized statewide to push the Red Light Abatement Act through the legislature, defend it in a statewide referendum, and close down the Barbary Coast brothels (chapter 10), some San Francisco women were joining with a wide variety of other groups in opposition to other Barbary Coast establishments: commercial dance halls. However, such businesses varied significantly in character, and the reformers concluded that the best solution was to close some but reshape others through regulation. Working with the Board of Police Commissioners, reformers succeeded in closing some halls and regulating the rest, and clubwomen themselves took on major responsibilities for supervising the surviving commercial dance halls.

In a 1924 report, Maria Lambin, the chief supervisor of the Public Dance Hall Committee of the San Francisco Center, remarked, "San Francisco has long recognized that it had a dance hall problem." She traced the origins of the perceived problem to the dance halls and saloons of the city's Barbary Coast district, which, since its inception during the Gold Rush, had been a center for commercialized vice and crime.[1] Its dance halls enjoyed a worldwide reputation for sensual dancing, prostitution, and liquor and were also known as haunts for outlaws.

Herbert Asbury's *Barbary Coast* (1933)—a popular history closely based on primary sources—recounts the evolution of the city's commercial dance halls. Before 1906, says Asbury, virtually every resort that featured dancing or entertainment also employed prostitutes. Called "pretty waiter girls," these women solicited liquor sales on commission, stripped, or otherwise plied their trade; dancing with customers was incidental. As the Barbary Coast rebuilt following the earthquake and fire of 1906, a nationwide dance craze produced a proliferation of commercial dance halls, and Barbary Coast dance hall owners began to cater more to dancers and tourists.[2]

By 1910 or so, San Francisco dance halls could be divided into two basic types. Non-commercial dance halls were establishments where social, ethnic, fraternal, and occupational organizations hosted dances for their members, families, and friends. Typically, such dances were not for profit, though they may have raised funds for the sponsoring organization. San Francisco's Recreation League, for example, sponsored nonprofit dances for the general public as a means of promoting a sense of community, and as a wholesome form of recreation.[3] Commercial or public dance halls, on the other hand, aimed to earn a profit by charging an entrance fee; they catered to a broad, heterogeneous, and generally youthful clientele drawn from the public at large, and typically sold alcohol. A variation of the public hall was the "closed" hall (later known as "taxi-dance" halls), a business that was closed to women as patrons. Instead, proprietors employed young women "instructors" to dance with the male customers.[4] Although these commercial halls varied in character, many San Franciscans associated all commercial establishments with viciousness and sought to abolish them entirely.[5]

The San Francisco Center was the most prominent of the women's organizations that mobilized against the commercial dance halls. A chapter of the California Civic League (discussed in chapter 10), the Center was founded to push for woman suffrage. After 1911 the organization shifted its focus to education and reform, and supported many of the campaigns California women undertook in the 1913 legislative session. Local women attended the Center's open forum, where they heard intellectuals and statesmen discuss the nation's civic and social life. The group's political work centered on social welfare work, especially services to women and children. Leaders worked to secure the appointment of women to key governmental positions at the state and local level, and lobbied the state legislature for various reforms, including sanitary milk laws, the Mother's Pension Bill, and the Red Light Abatement Act.[6] When clubwomen and clergymen set their sights on the Barbary Coast, the Center was quick to enter the fray.

The campaign against the commercial dance halls coincided with efforts to close the brothels, and included many of the same groups and individuals. Clubwomen were often in the lead, but typically as part of a broad coalition of neighborhood improvement associations, men's civic organizations, and religious groups. At times, women's organizations were recruited by other organizations; at other times, it was the women who cultivated these broader coalitions. In the end, the reformers worked closely with the police commission to close some local dance halls and, in the others, to implement a system of supervision by clubwomen.

The campaign against the dance halls began in earnest after the 1911 municipal election, when voters turned out the incumbent mayor, P. H. McCarthy. His opponents had blamed McCarthy for promoting a "wide-open town" through his policies on vice, and had charged his administration, particularly his police commissioners, with patronage and graft. The new mayor was James Rolph Jr., a businessman devoted to the "Good Government" principles of non-partisanship, honesty, efficiency, and expertise. In 1911, San Franciscans had just learned that they'd won the competition to host the Panama–Pacific International Exposition (PPIE), scheduled to begin in 1915, and Rolph was firmly committed to making a success of it. That same year the State of California gave women the right to vote. Before woman suffrage, while Rolph was still campaigning for mayor, San Francisco clubwomen had given him their support. With Rolph's success, and encouraged by his campaign promises, clubwomen felt the time had come for a moral reform crusade.[7]

The women were not alone: Rolph's election had also mobilized members of the city's clergy, notably Father Terence Caraher, of St. Francis of Assisi parish, a largely Italian congregation only a few blocks from the heart of the Barbary Coast. Together, clubwomen and clergymen renewed their efforts to shut down local vice districts.[8]

Though Rolph was committed to reforming city government and cleaning up the city's image for the PPIE, he wavered on issues of moral reform. Personally, he did not believe that vice could be suppressed, and he favored policies regulating rather than abolishing it.[9] For example, he supported a system of regulated prostitution, in which prostitutes plied their trade in segregated districts and were licensed and regularly tested for venereal diseases.[10] Though their views differed from his own, Rolph understood that religious and women's groups constituted a significant voting bloc and that he would have to find some way to overcome their opposition.[11]

Rolph's solution was to shift responsibility for managing the city's segregated vice districts to the Board of Police Commissioners. Rolph's choice of police commissioners reflected his views on good government. Within a year of assuming office, he had filled the board's four seats with a former chief of police, a businessman, and two attorneys. Theodore Roche, one of the attorneys, was a close political ally of Rolph. As president of the commission, Roche often sought to shield Rolph from political fallout caused by efforts to curb vice in the Barbary Coast.[12]

Two weeks after Rolph took office, the North Beach Promotion Association (NBPA) launched a campaign to clean up the Barbary Coast, which occupied several city blocks just south of the largely Italian neighborhood of North Beach. Like other neighborhood improvement clubs, the NBPA often petitioned the city for improvements such as street lights, paving, and better police protection, but the NBPA was also concerned about the neighboring Barbary Coast, which exposed the women and children of North Beach to lewd behavior as they passed through that district on their way to and from downtown. Father Caraher led the NBPA in its struggle to clean up the "dens of vice and degradation." The police board heard arguments from both the NBPA and defenders of the Barbary Coast in January 1912. Two weeks later, the board placed some restrictions on Barbary Coast dance halls and saloons.[13]

When it became apparent that these regulations were inadequate, the NBPA lodged new protests with the police commissioners. When their complaints proved unproductive, Caraher, on behalf of the NBPA, appealed for support from the Juvenile Protective Association. Three months later, Caraher led a delegation in a meeting with the police commission and was joined by the president of the NBPA, Attilio Musante, and several women's organizations, including the California Club, the Vittoria Colonna Club (the city's only Italian women's club, centered in North Beach), and the Juvenile Protective Association.[14] (The Juvenile Protective Association, formed by clubwomen the previous year, had a religiously diverse leadership and met at Temple Emanu-El, the city's leading Jewish congregation.)[15]

Caraher demanded that liquor sales be separated from dancing on the Barbary Coast.[16] The commissioners met the reformers halfway, barring female patrons and visitors from establishments where liquor was sold and prohibiting saloon and dance hall proprietors from paying female employees commissions on liquor sales. If enforced, the regulations would have negative consequences for women, putting some out of work and denying others the right to enjoy the local pleasure resorts that served alcohol. Still, the NBPA and women's groups were not satisfied; they continued to demand the complete separation of liquor and dancing.[17]

On September 12, 1913, the *San Francisco Examiner*, the flagship newspaper of the Hearst press, embarked on a campaign to abolish the city's vice districts. In a full-page editorial the *Examiner* argued that a "widespread change in public opinion and public manners" had overtaken the "civilized world." This "new order" embodied higher moral standards, a better conscience, and a concern for the common welfare and prosperity. San Franciscans, by tolerating vice districts, were losing ground to the great cities of the East, which had passed stringent legislation to end public displays of immorality. From an economic standpoint, the editors argued, if San Franciscans wanted to attract a higher class of tourists and residents, they had to trade "vulgar vice for decent entertainment." With opening ceremonies of the PPIE just a few months away, public officials and private citizens needed to unite in ridding the city of "open dens of debauchery and crime."[18]

Within a day, the *Examiner*'s call was answered by hearty endorsements from leaders of women's clubs and churches. Dr. Mariana Bertola, the founder and president of the Vittoria Colonna Club, concurred with the *Examiner* that recent years had seen a change in the "spirit of the public." Mrs. A. E. Graupner, the director of the San Francisco Center and the chairwoman of the Dance Hall Section of the Recreation League (an organization created in March 1912 by representatives of neighborhood improvement clubs, women's clubs, and athletic organizations, and, like the Juvenile Protective Association, led by a cross-section of the city's elite, including Catholics, Protestants, and Jews[19]), commented that the *Examiner*'s plan would be beneficial to "all men and women who want healthy, happy, safe recreation [to] surround our boys and girls, as well as our men and women." Father Caraher proclaimed, "It is time evil is driven out. The argument that it is a 'necessary' evil will not stand. What is necessary cannot be evil, and what is evil cannot be necessary."[20]

The *Examiner* carried on its campaign over the next ten days, publishing letters, articles, and sermons by a great diversity of women, along with male religious, civic, educational, and business leaders from around the Bay Area. The San Francisco Center took the lead in working with the

Recreation League and the Commonwealth Club (a leading men's civic organization) to form a coalition on the issue. On September 22, 1913, representatives of reform from women's and men's clubs, including the San Francisco Center, the Recreation League, the Woman's Political League, the Civic League of Improvement Clubs, and the Commonwealth Club, joined saloon-keepers and dance-hall men in packing the hearing room of the Board of Police Commissioners. The board voted to ban dancing in Barbary Coast establishments where liquor was sold, and prohibited the hiring of female employees in district saloons. Barbary Coast dance-hall owners now faced a simple choice: they could operate dance halls that employed women and give up selling liquor, or they could operate straight saloons with no dancing and no women. The editors of the *Examiner* appeared satisfied with the new regulations and declared their mission "fulfilled" in September 1913.[21]

Commissioner Roche's prepared statement focused on the city's clubwomen. Pointing out that the new regulations were likely to put "500 or more" dance-hall women out of work, Roche suggested that "the clubwomen and others who insisted on the wiping out of the dance halls" should find "legitimate" jobs for the women. His singling out of the clubwomen is instructive: although the women were part of a broad reform coalition, including Father Caraher, the NBPA, the Commonwealth Club, and the Recreation League, Roche specifically mentioned only the clubwomen when assigning responsibility to aid the displaced Barbary Coast workers.[22]

There matters rested until 1917. During World War I the San Francisco Center became directly involved in the regulatory process by supervising several of the city's public dance halls. This new role began with a request from the United States Commission on War Training Camp Activities (CWTCA), a body charged with maintaining the morale of sailors and soldiers and providing them with wholesome recreational opportunities.[23] Of special concern was preventing the spread of venereal disease, especially by young women who were not prostitutes but who were drawn to the men in uniform.[24] Since the United States military had naval and army bases in San Francisco, the CWTCA mobilized the San Francisco Center and other local civic and recreational organizations to help maintain the morale, morals, and good health of the fighting man.[25] In addition to its other war-related services, the San Francisco Center agreed to assist the CWTCA by supervising the closed halls. One leader recognized that war work gave the Center a number of "unparalleled opportunities," including the means to reshape local dance hall culture.[26] Ensuring that leaders would have both political support and the authority their work would demand, the San Francisco Center gained promises of cooperation from the police department and the board of police commissioners.[27]

In November 1917, leaders of the San Francisco Center created the Girls' Advisory Council to protect the virtue of San Francisco women in wartime. Soon after its inception, the Girls' Advisory Council was also selected as a CWTCA affiliate. Initially, the council focused on preventive work, such as instituting army patrols around the military base at the Presidio to protect both the soldiers and the local women. The San Francisco police department cooperated in the program, designating a policewoman as a field worker and council liaison. The council soon realized that successful preventive work hinged on proper supervision of the dance halls. Leaders appointed Lucile Wollenberg to the task. After conducting a three-month survey, Wollenberg concluded that the halls ranged from "conservative and acceptable" to "low-grade dance halls that were mostly assignation places." The council took Wollenberg's study to the police, who then ordered dance hall operators to hire supervisors.[28]

In 1918 the San Francisco Center organized its Public Dance Hall Committee, which assumed supervision of seven of the "low-grade" dance halls. These were actually closed halls that had sprung up in the districts adjacent to the Barbary Coast in 1913. The Public Dance Hall Committee's Maria Lambin described these establishments as "feeders to prostitution, dope selling [and] drunkenness" and as "centers for gang fights, crime planning, etc." Lambin declared that the committee's chief concern was the welfare of the young women dancers who worked in the halls. But she admitted that the committee also intended to keep minors out of the halls and to "prevent exploitation of the clientele by avaricious and unscrupulous interests, such as dope sellers [and] panderers."[29]

Lambin further explained that, although conditions in these halls were deplorable, the Public Dance Hall Committee was not demanding their abolition, because it "recognized at the outset that the halls were furnishing amusement of a sort to a considerable proportion of the population."[30] In other words, in 1918, committee members decided that they would tolerate the low-grade halls for the sake of the war effort, since they provided supervised recreation for men from the city's naval and army bases.[31]

As an affiliate of the CWTCA, the Center's Public Dance Hall Committee became a quasi-governmental body, able to select its own women supervisors and to assign them to various dance halls. Supervision was shared by the police commission, which had the power to regulate the halls; the committee's women supervisors, who were vested with "police powers"; and the chief supervisor, who served as the women supervisors' liaison to the police commission. Although the supervisors were paid by the dance-hall proprietors, they worked at the will of the chief supervisor, who was always a prominent clubwoman.[32]

According to Lambin, the supervisors were case workers experienced in handling the "problems of modern life," such as poverty, ignorance of U.S. manners and customs, lack of sex education, and unmarried motherhood. Lambin reported that the supervisors did more than raise the standards of decorum in the halls. They also improved the social lives of the dancers and clientele, expelled recognized prostitutes, broke up fights and removed the combatants, and secured the prosecution of dope sellers and panderers.[33] The Center's Emma Moffat McLaughlin agreed that the Public Dance Hall Committee had a very long reach due to the support the women received from the police commission.[34] (Mrs. McLaughlin herself had a very long reach as a member of the prestigious Century Club, a nonpolitical women's club that included members of the city's Catholic, Jewish, and Protestant elite; she was active in a wide range of social reform groups, serving as president of the San Francisco Center during the transition of the Civic League to the California League of Women Voters in 1921.[35])

That relationship was put to the test in May 1920, when San Francisco City Supervisor Charles Nelson proposed an ordinance that would divest the police commissioners of the responsibility for issuing dance hall permits and dance hall supervision and place it in the hands of a committee under the Board of Supervisors. John Tait, a dance hall owner, denounced the proposal: "Every Supervisor who had a friend who wanted a permit would get one." Consequently, it would be bad for business because dance halls would spring up "all over" and "loose control inevitably would result."

In an editorial, the *Examiner* argued that putting matters in the hands of the Board of Supervisors would increase the "opportunities for 'political' maneuvering" and that, for the most part, the Police Commission had administered its regulations in an "equitable manner."[36]

Representatives of the San Francisco Center feared that, if the ordinance were passed, the Board of Supervisors would undercut the Center's work in the dance halls, particularly by interfering with their selection of women supervisors. As testimony to the good work accomplished by the women supervisors, Mrs. Ansley K. Salz stated that these supervisors had established such a fine rapport with "girls of every kind" at the dance halls that the girls, almost invariably, called them "mother." Salz believed that this bond was important to the Center's social work in the city, in that the women supervisors provided a variety of services to the girls, directing them to "hospitals, employment offices, and clubs."[37]

Emma Moffat McLaughlin went to the City Federation of Women's Clubs for help in protecting the Center's civic role. The federation passed a resolution protesting the ordinance and promised to have a large number of women on hand when the measure came to a vote before the Board of Supervisors.[38] Although the federation delivered on its promise, the supervisors decided, 11–4, in favor of the ordinance. However, Acting Mayor Ralph McLeran vetoed it two days later.[39] Even though unsuccessful in winning a majority of supervisors, the women were able to express their support for the Center's long-time allies in the police commission—strengthening a relationship that would prove valuable in the near future.

Tough new regulations for commercial dance halls emerged several months later, when an episode in a dance hall spiraled into violence that held the front page for weeks. According to the *Chronicle* (the less sensationalist of the city's major papers), it began on the evening of Thanksgiving, November 24, 1920, when a number of men "lured" two young women—newcomers to San Francisco who worked as telephone operators—from the Winter Garden Dance Hall. The women were taken to a "shack" on Howard Street, forced to drink "cheap liquor," and "tortured and attacked by nine men." One woman escaped; she returned with the police, who rescued the other woman and arrested two men. Two other men were soon in custody. The press began describing the men as "the Howard Street gang," and drawing connections to local prizefighting.

Most of those arrested bore Irish (and the occasional Italian or Slavic) surnames. Two other young women then came forward with similar accounts involving the Howard Street shack, and police eventually accused the gang of twenty attacks on women. On December 6, 1920, fifty miles north of San Francisco in Santa Rosa, two San Francisco police detectives and the Sonoma County sheriff were shot and killed while attempting to apprehend three of the accused. Four nights later, a mob stormed the Sonoma County jail and lynched the suspects.[40]

As was true in other U.S. cities at the time, San Francisco was caught up in a wave of postwar hysteria brought on by the Red Scare, a rash of strikes and, in 1920–21, widespread unemployment. Thus, when the Howard Street assaults were made known, many San Franciscans were prepared to believe that their city was in the midst of a crime wave. Many joined the clamor for law and order.[41] In an effort to deprive local gangs of a perceived source of income, the police commission cancelled all permits for boxing and prizefighting. In the meantime, San Francisco attorneys refused to defend members of the Howard Street Gang. Chief of Police Daniel O'Brien directed his police captains to make a "clean-up" of "objectionable characters," including "all persons, male or female, who have no legitimate occupation." Police quickly picked up 161 "vagrants, loungers, former convicts," and jobless individuals. For their part, groups of private citizens—women's clubs, civic organizations, parent–teacher associations, improvement clubs, and former servicemen's groups—passed resolutions "against permitting San Francisco to be the gathering place for thugs, gangsters, and degenerates who have been driven out of other cities." Many of these groups also blamed police judges for treating accused criminals too leniently. Claiming that the police courts had been entirely too soft on criminals, the Civic League of Improvement Clubs formed a committee to investigate the courts and passed a resolution to sponsor a recall of two police court judges.[42]

Against this backdrop, representatives from nearly all of the city's women's clubs met to discuss vice in San Francisco. According to the *Chronicle*, after a thorough discussion the women unanimously decided that the time was ripe to "take prompt and energetic action to curb the criminals and clean up their haunts." The women enlisted the cooperation of a number of male-led business and professional organizations, including the city bar association, and formed a committee to pressure the municipal government to control vice in the city. In a later meeting, clubwomen clarified that cleaning up their "haunts" meant closing poolrooms and extending supervision to all of the city's dance halls. With wartime recreation no longer a concern, and with an anxious public clamoring for better law enforcement, San Francisco clubwomen saw that the moment was ripe to take on the closed dance halls. Leaders demanded a new regulatory policy and, with it, the authority to supervise all local dance halls. A cross-section of civic leaders organized themselves as the Woman's Vigilant Committee, drawing representatives from all of the member organizations, to lobby for the committee's demands. The participants included almost every imaginable group, from the California Club to the Salvation Army, the Colored Women's Federation, the Booker T. Washington Community Center, the Council of Jewish Women, the Vittoria Colonna Club, the Catholic Professional Women's Club, and the San Francisco Center and the Juvenile Protective Association. Among the officers of the Woman's Vigilant Committee were Dr. Mariana Bertola and Emma Moffat McLaughlin.[43]

Within a week of the formation of the Woman's Vigilant Committee, the United States government entered the campaign to clean up San Francisco's dance halls. Florence Calderwood, a field agent for the United States Interdepartmental Social Hygiene Board (created by Congress in 1918 to address the social hygiene of U.S. troops, especially the spread of venereal disease), drew on investigations conducted by federal agents to prepare a report for police commissioners.[44] Her report criticized the general character of San Francisco's public dance halls. Calderwood singled out the closed halls, noting that male patrons had "no difficulty in 'making dates' with female instructors" and observing that the women supervisors were "frequently negligent in their duty of 'supervising.'" In condemning San Francisco's plan of regulation and supervision, Calderwood made the federal government's position clear. While "we are not in favor of closing all dance halls," she said, "the 'closed' places must go."[45]

The following day the Board of Police Commissioners met to hash out these accumulated grievances against the dance halls. Those present included Calderwood, women's civic organizations, and local labor groups. Emma Moffat McLaughlin and Alicia Mosgrove of the San Francisco Center spoke, as did Calderwood. The federal spokeswoman demanded abolition of San Francisco's closed halls, characterizing them as "breeding places of vice." She argued that the "closed" halls had taken the place of San Francisco's former vice districts in attracting "women of the underworld" who had been ejected from other cities. Mrs. L. M. Culver of the Federated Women's Clubs agreed that the closed dance halls should be abolished, and she advocated supervision of all dancing resorts by various women's organizations.[46]

Two men representing organized labor protested the abolition of the closed dance halls and argued against supervision of the remaining halls by women's organizations. John A. O'Connell, the secretary of the San Francisco Labor Council, explained his position: "You cannot make people good by legislation. . . . Young people must have places of recreation and they can be regulated without the aid of so-called reformers." Both O'Connell and P. H. McCarthy, the former mayor and the head of the Building Trades Council, argued that if the closed halls were wiped out, many people would be thrown out of work. While both men were "heartily" opposed to vice, they advocated that the police commissioners delay before making any changes in the dance halls. Despite the men's protests, the following day the commissioners ordered the closing of San Francisco's closed dance halls, to become effective at the end of the year.[47]

Faced with the prospect of losing their jobs, some seventy-five women dance-hall workers, claiming to represent more than five hundred others, put their case before an open meeting of the Women's Vigilant Committee. Bessie Voigt, representing a Market Street dance hall, the Pacific, succinctly appraised their situation:

> Of our sixty instructors there are twenty-eight who have children to support—one to three little ones each. Work as domestics is too hard for us and it takes us away from our children altogether. Department stores do not pay enough to feed them and it is difficult to get work any other place since you have accused us publicly. All the stores tell us they are turning girls away instead of taking them on at this season of the year. I have two children to support. I can not do it on small wages, and at the dance halls I am able to take good care of them.

16. This photograph of discouraged dance-hall workers was taken outside the law offices of police commission president Theodore Roche. The young women turned to Roche after appearing the previous day at an open meeting of the Women's Vigilant Committee to plead (unsuccessfully) to be allowed to keep their jobs.
San Francisco Bulletin, December 31, 1920.

Other representatives spoke similarly, portraying themselves as respectable and responsible workers facing a hardship that affected their loved ones. After the dancers had finished speaking, an apparently unmoved Dr. Bertola suggested that the girls consider careers as educators or businesswomen.[48]

On January 3, 1921, the police commissioners' assembly room at the Hall of Justice was packed with representatives of organizations with some stake in San Francisco's dancing establishments. Speaking first, the young women of the closed dance halls claimed hardship and begged the commissioners to give them their jobs back. Commissioner Roche declined, declaring that the commissioners could not countenance "the occupation of a woman commercializing herself to dance with any stranger [which] places her in an environment that is not good for herself."[49]

Next, the young women and their lawyer explained the difficulties they faced in trying to find other lines of work. Mrs. Eleanor Fisher, of the State Board of Health, supported the young women on this point, saying that businesses in the city were cutting back. The only jobs available to unskilled young women were in domestic service, and it was doubtful that these young women could be placed as domestic servants since, as Fisher observed, they had been unjustly classed along with prostitutes. Commissioner Roche then offered to give the young women money out of his own pocket. Alicia Mosgrove of the San Francisco Center announced that arrangements had already been made for "those in need." But the young women cried: "We don't want charity!"[50]

The police commissioners ended the discussion by adopting stringent regulation for all commercial dance halls. The San Francisco Center, the Woman's Vigilant Committee, and their allies scored another victory when the commissioners adopted fourteen of the regulations proposed by the Center's Public Dance Hall Committee. In effect, these regulations gave the commissioners much wider control over the city's commercial dance halls and, most importantly to local clubwomen, placed supervisors in all the halls. Proprietors and managers of commercial halls would be required to demonstrate good character in their person and in their halls and would have to provide bright lights at all times, close their halls at 12:30 a.m., and adhere to more stringent rules on licensing. One rule governed the conduct of the patrons on the dance floor: "There must be no undue familiarity, exaggerated, suggestive or freak dancing between partners."[51]

The adoption of these new regulations spoke not only of a happy marriage between the police commission and the Public Dance Hall Committee but also of a new relationship between the municipal government and the public. Within ten years San Francisco's dance halls had been domesticated—at least on paper—and the supervision by clubwomen lasted well into the 1930s.

Thus, between 1911 and 1921, clubwomen, especially those of the San Francisco Center, had taken a large measure of control over the city's commercial dance halls by skillfully using the regulatory process. Often the Center's success was due to members' willingness to work in coalitions with a wide array of other civic, business, and religious bodies. Their accomplishment owed much, as well, to the willingness of the Board of Police Commissioners to reform the city's dance halls. In the initial stages of reform, women's organizations did not take the lead but proved consequential in the *Examiner*'s early campaign, which resulted in taming the Barbary Coast's pleasure resorts. With the advent of World War I, the San Francisco Center seized the opportunity to introduce women supervisors with police powers into the city's closed halls. In 1921, capitalizing on several dramatic and highly publicized crimes, the city's clubwomen struck again by ramming through a host of new police regulations that effectively gave them management and supervision over the public dance halls.

White, middle-class notions about class and gender were codified in the new police regulations. Although women reformers saw the dance halls as breeding grounds for promiscuous contact between the sexes, the regulations they helped shape consistently discriminated against women. The police rules of 1912 and 1913 not only defined the working conditions for female employees but also barred women patrons from dance halls where liquor was sold.

The creation of closed halls, where women were paid to dance with male patrons, was an unintended consequence of these regulations. Reformers despised these halls because, they believed, such dance halls encouraged promiscuous behavior that resembled prostitution. The Center's women consistently justified their work in the dance halls by likening their women supervisors to "mothers" who were protecting their "girls." This self-ascribed role was viewed as legitimate not only by the city's reformers but also by the *Examiner* and the police commissioners. Nevertheless, in 1920–21 a group of dance hall "girls" challenged the moral authority of the clubwomen in tones reminiscent of those used in the conflict between clubwomen and working-class women in the campaign for suffrage and in the contest over a legislated minimum wage (as discussed in chapters 9 and 11).

Notes

1. Maria Lambin, *Report of the Public Dance Hall Committee of the San Francisco Center of the California Civic League of Women Voters* (San Francisco: San Francisco Center of the California Civic League of Women Voters, 1924), 14.

2. Herbert Asbury, *The Barbary Coast: An Informal History of the San Francisco Underworld* (New York: Alfred Knopf, 1933), 107–8, 280, 284–93.

3. "Municipal Dance Hall Will Open," *San Francisco Chronicle*, September 11, 1912.

4. Paul Goalby Cressey, *The Taxi-Dance Hall: A Sociological Study in Commercialized Recreation and City Life* (Chicago: University of Chicago Press, 1932), 17–27.

5. Lambin, *Report of the Public Dance Hall Committee*, 3.

6. Emma Moffat McLaughlin, "Emma Moffat McLaughlin: A Life of Community Service," interview by Helene Maxwell Brewer and Willa Baum, Outstanding Women of California Oral History Collection, University of California, Berkeley, 116–17; California Civic League, San Francisco Center (SFC), *Report 1913–1918/San Francisco Center of the California Civic League* (San Francisco: The Center, 1918), 1–3.

7. Liston Sabraw, "Mayor James Rolph Jr. and the End of the Barbary Coast"

(Master's thesis, San Francisco State College, 1960), 43–44, 48–49, 55–56, 67–69, 81–82, 102.

8. Sabraw, "Mayor James Rolph" 81–82, 102–3.

9. Sabraw, "Mayor James Rolph," 150–55.

10. For San Francisco's brief experiment with legalized prostitution, see Mary Ann Irwin, "Making Sex Safe for the Married Man: Prostitution and the San Francisco Municipal Clinic, 1911–1913," National Coalition of Independent Scholars, October 24–26, 2008, Berkeley, California; Hiroyuki Matsubara, "The Anti-Prostitution Movement and the Contest of the Middle-Class Reformers over Cultural Authority: San Francisco, 1910–1913," *The Japanese Journal of American Studies* 12 (2001): 83–104; Neil Shumsky, "The Municipal Clinic of San Francisco: A Study of Medical Structure," *Bulletin of the History of Medicine* 52 (Winter 1978); Neil Larry Shumsky, "Vice Responds to Reform: San Francisco, 1910–1914," *Journal of Urban History* 7, no. 1 (November 1980).

11. Sabraw, "Mayor James Rolph," 169–71.

12. Sabraw, "Mayor James Rolph," 110–11, 150–55, 169–71.

13. "North Beach Association Will Elect Its Officers," *San Francisco Chronicle*, March 22, 1911; "Numerous Improvements Wanted for North Beach," *San Francisco Chronicle*, May 27, 1911; "Dr. Giannini to Address Citizens of North Beach," *San Francisco Chronicle*, January 14, 1912; "Lights May Go Out on Coast," *San Francisco Chronicle*, January 24, 1912; "Dead Line Drawn for Dance Halls," *San Francisco Call*, February 7, 1912.

14. "Protest Fails to Bar Dance Hall," *San Francisco Chronicle*, April 19, 1912; "Protests Fail to Bar Dance Hall," *San Francisco Chronicle*, September 6, 1912; "Clergy Denounce Morals of City," *San Francisco Chronicle*, October 9, 1912; "Demand Reforms for North Beach," *San Francisco Chronicle*, January 18, 1913.

15. "New Plans for the Juvenile Auxiliary Changes," *San Francisco Chronicle*, April 4, 1912; "Federation Specials Are Arriving," *San Francisco Chronicle*, June 23, 1912.

16. Caraher's demand that the Barbary Coast be regulated by separating liquor from dancing was not novel. According to Elisabeth Perry, dance hall reformers generally "opposed only the serving of alcohol to minors in dance halls." The idea that liquor be separated from dancing came from a belief that "alcohol weakened a girl's ability to resist sexual temptation." See Elisabeth I. Perry, "'The General Motherhood of the Commonwealth': Dance Hall Reform in the Progressive Era," *American Quarterly* 37, no. 5 (Winter, 1985): 719–33, 720.

17. "More Regulations Given the Coast," *San Francisco Chronicle*, February 18, 1913; "Condemn Partial Closing of 'Lid,'" *San Francisco Chronicle*, February 20, 1913; "Political Defi Is Hurled at Board," *San Francisco Chronicle*, July 15, 1913. For the efforts of 1913, see also Gayle Gullett, "City Mothers, City Daughters, and the Dance Hall Girls: The Limits of Female Political Power in San Francisco, 1913," in *Women and the Structure of Society*, ed. Barbara J. Harris and JoAnn K. McNamara, 149–59 (Durham NC: Duke University Press, 1984).

18. "Make San Francisco Clean City for Clean People," *San Francisco Examiner*, September 12, 1913.

19. "Recreation League Comes into Being," *San Francisco Chronicle*, March 11, 1912; "Recreation League to Hold Luncheon," *San Francisco Chronicle*, April 20, 1912.

20. "Women Back Examiner Fight," *San Francisco Examiner*, September 13, 1913; "By Fr. Terence Caraher," *San Francisco Examiner*, September 13, 1913.

21. "Co-operation May Yet Prevail in Women's Clubs, *San Francisco Chronicle*, September 14, 1913; "Brief Work Is Made of Evil Zone," *San Francisco Examiner*, September 23, 1913.

22. Theodore Roche, "Roche Writes of Board Action: Women Are Problem," *San Francisco Examiner*, September 23, 1913.

23. Jesse W. Lilienthal, "A Message from the President of the League," *Recreation League Bulletin*, May 1918, p. 1.

24. See Allan M. Brandt, *No Magic Bullet: A Social History of Venereal Disease in the United States since 1880* (New York: Oxford University Press, 1985), esp. chap. 2.

25. Lilienthal, "A Message," 1; McLaughlin, "Emma Moffat McLaughlin," 135, 136; SFC, *Report 1913–1918*, 8–9.

26. SFC, *Report 1913–1918*, 1–3.

27. SFC, *Report 1913–1918*, 8–9.

28. SFC, *Report 1913–1918*, 8–9.

29. Lambin, *Report of the Public Dance Hall Committee*, 14–15.

30. Lambin, *Report of the Public Dance Hall Committee*, 14.

31. McLaughlin, "Emma Moffat McLaughlin," 135, 136; SFC, *Report 1913–1918*, 8–9.

32. Lambin, *Report of the Public Dance Hall Committee*, 14–15.

33. Lambin, *Report of the Public Dance Hall Committee*, 14–16.

34. McLaughlin, "Emma Moffat McLaughlin," 142–43.

35. McLaughlin, "Emma Moffat McLaughlin," 142–43.

36. "Women Score New Rule on Dance Halls, *San Francisco Examiner*, May 7, 1920; "Revival of Dance Hall Days Fought," *San Francisco Examiner*, May 8, 1920; "Keep Control of Dance Halls in Hands of the Police Department," *San Francisco Examiner*, May 10, 1920.

37. "Women Score New Rule on Dance Halls," *San Francisco Examiner*, May 7, 1920; "Revival of Dance Hall Days Fought," *San Francisco Examiner*, May 8, 1920; "Dance Hall 'Mother' Plan Lauded," *San Francisco Examiner*, May 8, 1920.

38. "Vote on Dance Hall Control Set for Today," *San Francisco Examiner*, May 11, 1920.

39. "Board Assumes Control over Dance Halls," *San Francisco Chronicle*, May 18, 1920; "McLeran Vetoes Dance Hall Law; End of Case Seen," *San Francisco Chronicle*, May 20, 1920.

40. "Two Young Women Tortured and Attacked by Gang of Nine Men in Howard-

Street Shack," *San Francisco Chronicle*, November 26, 1920; "Fourth in Gang That Attacked Girls Arrested," *San Francisco Chronicle*, November 28, 1920; "2 Suspects in Gang Assault Case Captured," *San Francisco Chronicle*, November 29, 1920; "Suspects Face Ten Counts in Assault Case," *San Francisco Chronicle*, December 2, 1920; "Girl Victims of Assaults Incommunicado," *San Francisco Chronicle*, December 3, 1920; "Confession of Assault on 2 Girls Expected," *San Francisco Chronicle*, December 4, 1920; "Girls Report New Outrages by Gangsters," *San Francisco Chronicle*, December 5, 1920; "Santa Rosa Mob Storms Jail Seeking S.F. Brutes Who Killed 3 Officers," *San Francisco Chronicle*, December 6, 1920; "Howard-St. Gangsters Lynched at Santa Rosa by Infuriated Citizens," *San Francisco Chronicle*, December 10, 1920; "Girl, 17, Tells of Assault by 'Spud' Murphy," *San Francisco Chronicle*, December 11, 1920.

41. Frederick Lewis Allen characterized the period 1919–1920 as "an era of lawlessness and disorderly defense of law and order, of unconstitutional defense of the Constitution, of suspicion and civil conflict—in a very literal sense, a reign of terror." Frederick Lewis Allen, *Only Yesterday: An Informal History of the 1920s* (New York: Perennial Classics, 2000), 39–40. For a contemporary account linking the aftermath of World War I to San Francisco's crime conditions, see William Randolph Hearst, "Free San Francisco of Criminal Elements, Is Plea of Mr. Hearst," *San Francisco Examiner*, December 19, 1920; for further reading on the turbulence that followed World War I, see Lynn Dumenil, *The Modern Temper: American Culture and Society in the 1920s* (New York: Hill & Wang, 1995), 201–49; Robert H. Zieger, *America's Great War: World War I and the American Experience* (Oxford UK: Rowman & Littlefield, 2000), 187–215.

42. "Confession of Assault on 2 Girls Expected," *San Francisco Chronicle*, December 4, 1920; "Police Ban Prize Fighting," *San Francisco Chronicle*, December 7, 1920; "Police Guard Gangsters as They Plead," *San Francisco Chronicle*, December 7, 1920; "O'Brien Tells Men S.F. Must Protect Women," *San Francisco Chronicle*, December 7, 1920; "Chief O'Brien Demands Sift: Will Fix Blame," *San Francisco Chronicle*, December 8, 1920; "Recall of Sullivan, Oppenheim Launched by Civic League," *San Francisco Chronicle*, December 8, 1920; "S.F. Phone Girl Assaulted: 4 Arrests Made," *San Francisco Chronicle*, December 9, 1920; "Gangsters Held under $400,000 in Girls' Case," *San Francisco Chronicle*, December 9, 1920; "San Francisco Civic Leagues Unite in Movement to Drive 'Lawless Element from City,'" *San Francisco Chronicle*, December 11, 1920.

43. "Women's Clubs to Investigate Crime Wave, *San Francisco Chronicle*, December 11, 1920; "Women's Clubs Launch League to Fight Vice," *San Francisco Chronicle*, December 14, 1920; "Abolish Vice, S.F. Women's Clubs Demand," *San Francisco Examiner*, December 15, 1920.

44. T. A. Storey, "The Work of the Interdepartmental Social Hygiene Board," *Social Hygiene* 5 (1919): 443.

45. "Police in Pay of Dance Hall, U.S. Charges," *San Francisco Examiner*, December 17, 1920.

46. "'Closed' Dance Halls Breeding Places for Vice, Aver Opponents," *San Francisco Chronicle*, December 18, 1920; "U.S. Charges against City Dances Aired," *San Francisco Examiner*, December 18, 1920.

47. "'Closed' Dance Halls to Be Shut Dec. 30," *San Francisco Examiner*, December 19, 1920.

48. "Girl Employees of S.F. Dance Halls Plead for Jobs," *San Francisco Chronicle*, December 31, 1920; "'Instructors' Invade Parley of Vigilants," *San Francisco Examiner*, December 31, 1920.

49. "Dance Halls Must Close Sunday P.M.," *San Francisco Examiner*, January 4, 1921.

50. "Jury Dissents with Police on Dance Halls," *San Francisco Chronicle*, January 4, 1921.

51. "Dance Halls Must Close Sunday P.M.," *San Francisco Examiner*, January 4, 1921.

13. "HEARTS BRIMMING WITH PATRIOTISM"

Katherine Edson, Alice Park, and the Politics of War and Peace, 1914–1921

EUNICE EICHELBERGER

Sometime after World War I, Katherine Philips Edson wrote that women had "entered politics at one of the most critical times in our History" and had "helped to win a world war." However, she lamented, the "sacrifice of blood and treasure, poured out with hearts brimming with patriotism" had been taken advantage of by "heartless profiteers who have grown swollen and fat off the peoples' sorrow and sacrifice."[1] Besides reflecting widespread disillusionment in the aftermath of World War I, Edson's statement pointed to the connection between the growing political activism of women, particularly in the area of woman suffrage, and their activism during the period of World War I.

California women displayed their patriotism in varying ways during World War I. Barbara Steinson has written that war-related activities and the continuing campaign for woman suffrage at the national level "drew unprecedented numbers of women into the public sector," but many California women, including Katherine Edson and Alice Park, both of whom engaged in wide-ranging reform efforts and held important roles in the campaign for woman suffrage, had been activists well before the war.[2]

Edson and Park provide prominent examples of the differing forms that women's patriotism took in the context of wartime. Edson apparently displayed little interest in the issues of war and peace during the years before the United States entered the war, but she then devoted her considerable energy to helping the war effort from her position as the most influential member of the California Industrial Welfare Commission and as a member of various government wartime agencies. Alice Park expressed her patriotism before American intervention by helping organize a local branch of the Woman's Peace Party to oppose U.S. entry into the war and by participating in the Ford Peace Ship Expedition. After U.S. intervention, Park fought to uphold civil liberties in the face of government repression. At war's end, a disillusioned Edson worked to prevent the coming of another war by serving on the Advisory Commission to the American delegation at the Washington Limitation of Armaments Conference. Park continued her work for peace, civil liberties, and women's rights for the rest of her long life. The lives of these two women illustrate the links between prewar engagement in politics by women and women's wartime activism, and suggest that, as women became more politically active, they also became more interested and involved in issues of international affairs. The stories of Edson and Park also permit a consideration of the relationship of gender to their views and activism.

War broke out in Europe in August 1914, following more than a decade of reform in the United States. Though the spirit of reform had come to California later than in other states, it proved to be particularly strong and productive once it appeared. Under the administration of Governor Hiram Johnson, the state enacted far-reaching reform legislation.[3] The progressives' faith in progress and in the betterment of humanity undoubtedly added to the shock that many of them felt over the coming of war.

In May 1915 the sinking of the English passenger liner the *Lusitania* by a German U-boat, with the loss of 162 American lives, aroused anti-German sentiment but had little effect on the determination of the United States to stay out of the war. However, in early 1917 the resumption by the Germans of unrestricted submarine warfare, the sinking of U.S. ships, and the publication of a telegram from Arthur Zimmermann, the German secretary for foreign affairs, to the German ambassador to Mexico, proposing an alliance between Germany and Mexico if the United States and Germany were to go to war, caused a sharp change in sentiment. The telegram angered Californians because the Germans offered to return to Mexico the territory in the southwest United States that Mexico had lost to the United States in the Mexican–American War and further suggested an alliance between Mexico and Japan, a country many Californians feared and against whose immigrants to California they discriminated.[4] On April 6, 1917, the United States declared war on Germany and, as many progressives had feared, the coming of war brought a halt to most reform efforts and also brought the abridgment of civil liberties.

Katherine Philips Edson was the most prominent woman in California progressivism. She worked toward key progressive goals related to women and children, both in the workplace and in the home, and served as a key link between California women and the state progressives.[5] (Some of

17. This portrait of Katherine Philips Edson is from 1929, toward the end of her service in state government. San Francisco History Center, San Francisco Public Library.

Edson's activities are explored in chapters 10 and 11.) Jacqueline Braitman, her biographer, notes that she was a "close personal friend" to many of California's leading progressives, including Chester H. Rowell, the intellectual leader of the movement and one of the founders of the Lincoln–Roosevelt League, the group that led the state's progressives, and was "probably as close as any woman could become" to Hiram Johnson, the governor and later U.S. senator, the most important progressive in California.[6] Rowell referred to Edson's ability to get along with Governor Johnson: "It is not easy for him to take a serious woman seriously, especially in politics, and so far as I know you are the only women whom he does so take."[7]

She was also a good friend of Meyer Lissner, the chief organizer of the progressives within the state Republican Party and Johnson's closest adviser in southern California. To Jane Addams, Lissner described Edson as the "Jane Addams of California."[8] To Theodore Roosevelt, the former president, Lissner wrote, "She is just about the leading progressive woman in California, and you can talk to her as you would to a man."[9]

Edson was a member of the Progressive Party's state central committee from 1912 to 1916. When she returned to the Republican Party in 1916, she joined the executive committee of the Republican state central committee and served for the next four years. In 1920 she was a delegate to the Republican National Convention and for the next four years served as a member of the executive committee of the Republican National Committee.[10]

Katherine Philips Edson was born in Ohio in 1870. Her father, Dr. William Philips, served as a surgeon in the Civil War and was involved in a number of reform movements, including woman suffrage. At least a part of Edson's devotion to reform can be attributed to her father's influence. After receiving her primary and secondary education, she attended a music conservatory in Chicago, where she met her future husband, Charles Edson. In 1891 they settled with Charles's parents in Antelope Valley, California, where Katherine lived the hard life of ranch wife and mother. When Katherine and Charles moved to Los Angeles in 1899, she joined the Friday Morning Club, the most prominent women's club in Los Angeles.[11] Edson played a large role in what her biographer describes as the "evolution" of that organization from one "devoted to cultural and philanthropic affairs to one advocating reform of municipal and state agencies, political rights, conservation, public health, labor legislation, consumer consciousness, and a host of other issues."[12] As chairman of the club's Committee on Public Health, Edson embarked on a campaign for pure milk that led to her appointment to the Los Angeles City Charter Revision Committee and then to efforts to secure a state law mandating tuberculin tests for cows.

According to Walton Bean, Edson was credited with persuading the Lincoln–Roosevelt League, at its first meeting in May 1907, to endorse woman suffrage, although there is no record of Edson, or of any woman, attending the meeting.[13] The Lincoln–Roosevelt League's program became Hiram Johnson's platform in his campaign for governor in 1910, and much of that platform was adopted after Johnson's successful election. Edson was active in the campaign to elect Johnson as governor in 1910. During the 1911 suffrage campaign, Edson was a cochairman of the Southern California Political Equality League, the most important woman suffrage group in southern California. Edson traveled hundreds of miles by car, speaking on behalf of the constitutional amendment.

In 1912 Governor Johnson appointed her as a deputy inspector in the State Bureau of Labor Statistics—making her one of the first women in California to receive such a major political appointment.[14] Her investigations of the working conditions of women and children revealed the unhealthful conditions under which they worked, the long hours they endured, and the meager pay they received. Within a month of her appointment to the bureau, Edson announced that she would work for the protection of the state's women and children.[15] During her career she worked tirelessly for that purpose. As explained in chapter 11, she carefully studied the Massachusetts minimum-wage bill, the first in the nation, then enlisted the support of Governor Johnson. A minimum-wage bill became one of the "Ten Commandments" to be enacted by the 1913 state legislature. The final act set up an Industrial Welfare Commission (IWC) of five members, with broad powers to investigate the working conditions of women and children and to set minimum wages, maximum hours of work, and working-condition standards.[16]

Johnson appointed Edson as a member of the IWC, which was to include at least one woman among the five members. She served on the IWC for eighteen years under five governors, and was its chief executive officer from 1927 to 1931. During her first three years on the IWC, Edson commuted by train to its office in San Francisco, but in 1916 she took an apartment in San Francisco. A prominent merchant from Santa Cruz praised Edson's administration of the IWC, pointing out that the compulsory minimum-wage law "was a really beneficent force over quite a number of years" and that in no other state where such law was in effect "had results been secured at all comparable to what was accomplished by Mrs. Edson in California." He concluded that Mrs. Edson "played a proud part in the political regeneration of California" and was "a pioneer in dedicating our government to human needs; more than any one person, she brought hope to unorganized toiling women, and into the lives of those who had had little, she brought a bit of God's sunlight."[17]

In 1916 Edson, like many other California progressives, rejoined the Republican fold and supported Charles Evans Hughes, the Republican candidate for president. In answering the question of an eastern friend as to how Hughes had lost California's electoral votes to Woodrow Wilson, the incumbent, Edson discounted the peace issue as being important and suggested, "The understanding of our foreign relations has not pressed so deeply upon the imagination of the West as it has upon the East, where you are more closely connected with European matters."[18]

Edson's discounting of the peace issue reflected her own limited interest in "European matters" and set her apart from Alice Park and from many other California women who were deeply concerned that the United States not be involved in the war in Europe. George Mowry noted that "the Democratic slogan, 'He kept us out of war' was particularly effective among California women."[19] Spencer Olin has also cited the importance of the peace issue in California, particularly among women voters.[20] In *The Presidential Election of 1916*, S. D. Lovell quotes Gilson Gardner in concluding that, in California, "labor and women are Wilson's strongest hold," adding, "The women are for peace."[21]

Edson's limited interest in foreign affairs may have been due to lack of time to study the issues because of her duties with the IWC and her devotion to other reform efforts. Without strong pacifist convictions and aware that her fellow progressives' admiration for her was partially based on a perception that, as Meyer Lissner said, "Her brain works like a man's, she thinks like a man and talks a language that a man can understand," Edson may have adopted their views on intervention in the war in order to preserve this perception.[22] Their opinions on the question of intervention changed from firm opposition in the early days of the war to a more interventionist stance in late 1916 and early 1917.

Once the United States entered the war, Edson focused her energies on helping the war effort while attempting to keep the reform spirit alive in the face of the state and national governments' obsession with winning the war. Like her fellow California progressives, she feared that war would halt reform or even destroy the reforms that had been achieved by California progressives, such as the eight-hour day for women and the state commissions created under the Johnson administration. The day before the war resolution passed Congress, in a letter to Governor William D. Stephens, who had succeeded to the governorship when Johnson entered the Senate, Edson objected to an amendment to the eight-hour law for women, which had been proposed by the executive of a large insurance company. Noting that there had been "a very determined effort" in the East to "utterly destroy" certain protective labor laws that had been "slowly and painstakingly built up," Edson argued that there was still an "adequate supply of labor for all the factories in California that had government contracts or were likely to get them, so that they would be able to maintain the eight-hour day, if necessary on two shifts." She warned that "to amend the eight-hour day law would be an entering wedge for the destruction of all our protective legislation."[23]

Writing to Chester Rowell, Edson mentioned a labor situation in the glove industry that the IWC was to investigate. She suggested that such investigations by state commissions could prevent any curtailment of their activities. Edson urged that progressives publicize the ability of the Industrial Accident Commission and the Immigration and Housing Commission, headed by two prominent progressives, Meyer Lissner and Simon Lubin, as well as the ability of the IWC, to provide expert information and thus help the state in wartime. She reasoned that, instead of thinking of them as "peace commissions, they should be considered as very important adjuncts in wartime."[24]

During the course of the war, both the state and the national governments called on Edson to serve on various wartime commissions and committees. In response to demands for preparedness, the federal government had created the Council of National Defense and its Civilian

Advisory Commission in August 1916. The Advisory Commission, was to represent labor, among other groups.[25] Samuel Gompers, the chairman of the council's Committee on Labor, appointed Edson as chairman of the Committee on Women in Industry for California on August 21, 1917.[26]

Not until after Edson's appointment to the National Council of Defense did Governor Stephens appoint her to the State Council of Defense. The California legislature had enacted a special war emergency bill authorizing the governor to create the council "for the immediate preservation of the public peace and safety." The state council both carried out directives from the Council of National Defense and initiated its own programs.[27] Edson had written to Governor Stephens shortly before the war declaration, suggesting that women and labor be represented on the state council. However, when Stephens announced his appointments to the state council on April 5, 1917, there were just three women among the thirty-three members.[28]

At the first meeting of the members of the State Council of Defense, there was no labor committee among the fourteen subcommittees appointed.[29] When the executive committee of the council suggested a committee on labor, Edson seconded this suggestion in a letter to the governor's private secretary in October 1917, declaring that it was "essential that such a committee be appointed." She made the further suggestions that it would be more "workable if the committee were made seven, rather than six, and that Chester Rowell be made chairman of the committee."[30] Governor Stephens accepted Edson's suggestions, naming a labor subcommittee to the state council and making Rowell its head, and also appointed Edson as a member of the state council.

Edson received another appointment to a wartime agency when she was made bureau chairman of California for the Bureau of Information and Registration of the National League for Woman's Service. The league was charged with organizing volunteer workers for emergency service; the bureau was engaged in mobilizing and caring for wage-earning women whose services were needed on war orders. In the early period of U.S. involvement in the war, the majority of war contracts were concentrated in the East, so the focus of the league's early efforts was to get the War and Navy departments to distribute more contracts to the West, rather than send workers east.[31]

Edson, who liked clarity and efficiency and prided herself on being able to accomplish a task promptly and well, occasionally complained about the confusion, lack of clear authority, and duplication of agency functions. In a letter to Bertha von der Nienburg at the bureau, she confided that, because she had "tried to simplify the organization of the women in the state," she had angered an official of the National League for Women's Service on the latter's visit to California when she attempted to discourage the official from organizing the league "by taking in other women's organizations which properly came under the women members of our State Council of Defense." Edson declared, "We are over-organized to death here as I suppose they are every place else in the United States."[32]

Edson accepted still another job with the federal government when Secretary of War Newton Baker appointed her as Industrial Mediator for California to listen to disputes arising in connection with government contracts. A newspaper article noted that this was the "first time a woman has been appointed to such a position."[33]

Felix Frankfurter, the assistant to the United States secretary of labor and head of the War Labor Policies Board, invited Edson to attend a conference of state officers in the industrial field to consider women's work and the proper control of contracts let by the federal government in the states.[34] When Frankfurter later proposed that Edson head a program in the Labor Department concerning the introduction of women into industry, she was unable to accept the position immediately; by the time she was able to accept, the war was ending and the department had dropped the program.[35]

In early 1918 the federal food commissioner for California appointed Edson as head of the Women's Land Army of California, which recruited and organized women to work on California farms.[36] She made a number of speeches urging women to work to aid the war effort. At a convention of the Women's Federation in Stockton, she asked that the audience help "save California from an influx of Mexicans and Orientals for our children and our children's children" by opposing the importation of laborers from Mexico and East Asia to work in California's fields.[37] Edson feared that the growing number of migrant workers would make it difficult for American-born workers to maintain a living wage. In a letter to the United States Department of Labor about the presence of several thousand laborers from Mexico in the Imperial Valley, she pointed out that this resulted from the department's representative taking the word of employers, who "were looking for cheap labor" and had claimed that they needed three thousand laborers, whereas an investigation by the state Immigration and Housing Commission revealed that "they did not need five hundred."[38]

While the war continued, Edson worked on behalf of the United States' war effort, but after the war ended, she expressed her anger at the war's outcome. She stated that women had helped win the war, but that war profiteers had taken advantage of their sacrifice. She decried the chilling of hopes for world peace "by such an exhibition of imperialism as we never dreamed we would witness after 'crushing the Kaiser.'" She condemned censorship and repression and pointed out, "[Any person] who dares to challenge the existing order is branded 'Bolshevik-red-radical.'" Those who desired ignorance, she continued, were "trying to control our schools by threatening the teachers who teach progressive and liberal ideals to the youth" and trying as well to control the churches and the press, and advising businessmen to watch what their wives "were being taught in their organizations."[39]

Edson eventually switched from support for membership of the United States' in the League of Nations after reading John Maynard Keynes's *Economic Consequences of the Peace*, and agreed with Hiram Johnson's opposition to league membership and his stand against "sending our boys all over the civilized and uncivilized world." However, unlike Johnson, Edson's disillusionment with the war did not turn her toward a policy of isolation.[40] She was attracted instead to efforts for international cooperation in the limitation of armaments. When President Warren Harding nominated her as one of four women to serve with twenty-one men on the American Advisory Committee to the Limitations of Armaments Conference at Washington DC she promptly accepted.[41] After attending the Republican National Convention in 1920 as a delegate for Johnson, where she and six other women gave nominating speeches, she had campaigned for Harding's election when the convention selected him instead of Johnson.

Harding chose Edson for the advisory board in recognition of her efforts in his campaign, her membership on the Republican National Committee, and her position with the National League of Women Voters, whose first vice-president wrote to Edson, "[It was] marvelous for the League of Women Voters to have you there, an honor to Republican women, and a fine guarantee for women all over the United States." She pointed out that Edson was "just about the finest type of 'political woman'" in the United States at the time, and one who made "the most of political connections to give intelligent public service." The League of Women Voters' official also wrote of her sense of encouragement about the "whole reduction of armament proposition" and said that it meant "a lot to have women in on it and it means still more to have you there." Edson's appointment also constituted an acknowledgment of her political influence among California's women and among many prominent women throughout the country, and her excellent work as a member of the IWC in California and her work for state and national agencies and committees during the war.[42]

The newly enfranchised women of the United States claimed significant responsibility for the calling of the Limitation of Armaments Conference. The Women's Committee for World Disarmament was an early advocate of a disarmament conference, and the National League of Women Voters was the first major national organization to join the cause. Other women's organizations also promoted the notion of a disarmament conference.[43]

In a letter, Edson explained that the women on the advisory committee were "not appointed as a separate women's committee but were on the committee just as any other citizen" and that they did "not organize themselves in any sense as a woman's committee but took part in all discussions just as American citizens." She pointed out that eastern women's organizations had insisted that President Harding appoint women as delegates to the conference and that the president was "exceedingly anxious that such representation as the women had would be real." When he discussed the matter with the women leaders of the Republican Party, they insisted that the "functions" of the women delegates be "real and not just honorary." The president asked them to submit names and, among those submitted, four were chosen: Mrs. Charles Sumner Bird, the chairman of the State Republican Club of Massachusetts and an "active member of the National League of Women Voters"; Mrs. Thomas G. Winter, the president of the General Federation of Women's Clubs and a "great orator"; Mrs. Eleanor Franklin Egan, a "brilliant magazine writer" who "had large experience in the Far East"; and Katherine Philips Edson, the only woman on the committee from "west of the Mississippi River."[44] Among the twenty-one men were General John J. Pershing, chief of staff of the United States Army; Samuel Gompers of the American Federation of Labor; Secretary of Commerce Herbert Hoover; and Congressman Stephen G. Porter, chairman of the House Committee on Foreign Affairs.[45]

Meyer Lissner congratulated Edson: "You certainly are 'highly honored' in appointment on the American Advisory Committee."[46] It was an honor for her and an honor for California women. On taking office as a member of the advisory committee, Edson wired a colleague on the IWC, "Yesterday was the greatest day in my life."[47]

On November 26, 1921, Edson and the other women members of the advisory committee made public a letter they were sending to Lady Astor, a member of the British House of Commons, stating that public opinion had "found its way to power" and was "affecting the course of statesmen who once could settle everything behind closed doors." Pointing to the recent world war as demonstrating the need for peace, the four women declared that, if people wanted "our type of civilization and culture to endure and to progress, then this fierce race for armament must cease." They warned that another world war would be "more swift, aggressive, more destructive" and might be the "beginning of the degeneration of our race," and stressed the need to remove "suspicions, hatreds, and fears."[48]

Edson's interaction with Stephen G. Porter, the head of the House Committee on Foreign Affairs, who served with Edson on the Committee on Far Eastern Questions and Pacific Questions, helps support her claim that women on the advisory committee served on an equal basis with the men. Porter wrote to Edson after her return to California, requesting the name and address of the representative of a far eastern republic, where he hoped to travel.[49] In another letter he asked her to try to influence Hiram Johnson to approve the confirmation of the conference treaties. He wrote of the "fascinating" work of their committee and said that it was "with deep regret that I realize our duties are over" and hoped that "when you again visit Washington I may have the pleasure of your congenial companionship."[50]

Throughout her career, Edson's continued focus was on the well-being of workers, particularly women who worked out of economic necessity.

Even when her work for federal wartime agencies expanded her focus from state affairs to national affairs and when nomination to the Limitation of Armaments Conference expanded her focus to international affairs, she maintained her allegiance to the cause of the welfare of workers. Before leaving for the conference, Edson, speaking in San Francisco, declared, "A life-sustaining wage is more vital to world peace than battleships," and if every worker could "keep body and soul together, there would be no need for navies and armies."[51]

Alice Park was a leader of the California suffrage movement and a strong advocate for peace. Among her other reform efforts was her work for the passage of the Equal Guardianship Law in California, which provided that mothers and fathers were equal guardians of minor children, in place of a law that had given fathers sole guardianship; her crusade to abolish child labor; and her work to improve jail conditions, and to promote humane education, vegetarianism, simplified spelling, and sex education. She authored the California Bird and Arbor Day Law, which went into effect in 1909 (see chapter 6). She was a strong opponent of the death penalty, writing one of the first pamphlets against it in California and speaking and demonstrating against it. Park summed up her philosophy and the motivation for her reform efforts in a response to a question about her religion. "My religion," she wrote, "is humanity—humanitarianism—confident that the present time is all that we are sure of and our duty, our progress and our usefulness are all here and now—If we think earnestly of the present and try to do all we can right here and now—we are at least sure of immediate results. My religion is boundless—Nothing human is alien to me."[52]

Alice Park was born in Boston, the daughter of John G. Locke, a lawyer, who died in 1869 when she was only eight and her three siblings were even younger. Her mother, Harriet Brown Pinkham of Nantucket, Rhode Island, died just five years later, as Park wrote, of "hard work and worry."[53] Park and her youngest sibling, a boy, went to live with an aunt and uncle in Providence, Rhode Island. She graduated from the Rhode Island State Normal School at eighteen and began teaching in Rhode Island and Massachusetts. Suffrage leaders in Massachusetts recommended her for a scholarship to Smith College, but, unable to afford the costs of room and board, she could not accept. Her desire to attend college never

18. Alice Park, shown here in approximately 1915, was involved in the California suffrage campaign beginning when she first arrived in California in 1902. After the successful California campaign, she participated in suffrage campaigns in other states. She was known for her use and occasional design of "personal advertising," such as the sash shown here, identifying her as a voter. From the Special Collections Department, Mariam Coffin Canaday Library, Bryn Mawr College, Bryn Mawr PA.

left her, and years later when her two children began college at Stanford University, she considered joining them but could not do so because there was no money saved for the children's tuition.[54]

In 1884 she married Dean W. Park. The couple lived in various remote regions of the United States and Mexico while he followed his career as a mining engineer. When his work took him to Peru in 1902, his family moved to San Francisco so the two children could attend the Lick School of Mechanical and Industrial Arts. After the San Francisco earthquake and fire in 1906, they moved to Palo Alto, where the children entered Stanford University. Dean Park died in 1909.

Alice Park became active in woman suffrage movements when she moved to California. She was the recording secretary for the California Equal Suffrage Association, headed the state publicity committee in the successful 1911 campaign for woman suffrage, and authored a pamphlet "Women under the Laws of California." She also began what she termed "personal advertising" in conjunction with the campaign for woman suffrage—the use of badges, pins, stickers for baggage and stationary, pennants, and posters with "Votes for Women" on them.[55] Her use of "personal advertising" carried over to her peace activities. She displayed a peace flag on her home throughout World War I, published leaflets about peace flags, and displayed one at many of her lectures.[56]

Park's activities on behalf of woman suffrage in California led to her appointment as a delegate to woman suffrage conventions in Portland, Oregon, in 1905 and in Seattle in 1909. Park had worked with Mary McHenry Keith as officers of suffrage groups in California, and Keith suggested that Governor Johnson appoint Park as one of the six California delegates to the International Women's Suffrage Alliance Congress that was to meet in Budapest in June 1913. Keith also provided the funds for Park's trip. At the Congress, Park read a paper that described what women had accomplished in California after attaining the vote, including passage of the Red Light Abatement Bill, forcing the recall of a judge who had abused two young girls, raising the age of consent from sixteen to eighteen years, increasing the penalty for rape, gaining recognition that women and girls were not paid a living wage for what was called "honest labor," and securing the subsequent enactment of minimum-wage legislation.[57] After the suffrage conference, Park traveled to the Hague to attend a peace conference in August and then to England, where she picketed Holloway Jail to protest the jailing of Emmeline Pankhurst, a leading English suffrage worker.[58]

After California women won the right to vote, Park continued her suffrage work elsewhere, participating in suffrage parades throughout the country and spending weeks in both Arizona and Iowa during their suffrage campaigns. Park delayed joining the Woman's Christian Temperance Union until after the suffrage amendment was passed in California because she knew that some men would not vote for the amendment for fear that enfranchised women would seek to restrict alcohol.[59]

Among all the causes undertaken by Alice Park, the cause of peace was probably closest to her heart. In her typewritten autobiography in the Hoover Institution Archives, Park explained that she could not remember when she became a pacifist. She speculated that "abhorrence of war was a family tradition" and recalled being strongly impressed by paintings exhibited in St. Louis in 1889 and by reading a magazine article by E. L. Godkin on the "Absurdity of War."[60] She joined a peace society when the United States declared war on Spain and distributed pacifist literature by mail.

After the outbreak of war in Europe in August of 1914, American women assumed a much more important role in the U.S. peace movement. They organized an antiwar parade in New York in late August, in which approximately fifteen hundred women clad in black participated; helped initiate the Ford Peace Ship; were among the leaders of the American Union against Militarism; and were the "moving spirits" behind the American Neutral Conference Committee, the Emergency Peace Federation, and the People's Council.[61]

Alice Park did not attend the meeting of women concerned with peace, called by Jane Addams in January 1915, which produced the Woman's Peace Party (WPP). Although Joan Jensen has reported that Park was a member of the California delegation to the International Congress of Women at the Hague in 1915, there is no record of her attending.[62] The only delegate from California to the Hague Congress of Women in 1915, according to three sources, was Rose Morgan French of San Francisco, who represented the National Federal Suffrage Association, the California Suffrage Association, and, unofficially, the Women Voters of California.[63]

Park did attend the 20th Universal Peace Congress at the Hague, which met from August 18 to August 24, 1913, the same summer that she attended the woman suffrage convention in Budapest.[64] A calling card in Park's papers in the Hoover Institution Archives describes her as "Mrs. Alice Park, Delegate to Hague Peace Congress, 1913 Representative of *Woman's Journal*, Boston," a journal to which Park contributed articles.[65]

The WPP of Northern California had its headquarters in San Francisco. Park was one of the chief organizers of the Palo Alto branch of the WPP, formed in March 1915. Many of its members were connected with Stanford University. Its president was Ellen Coit Elliot, whose husband was the first registrar of the university. Jesse Knight Jordan, the wife of Chancellor David Starr Jordan, was the chairman of the Northern California Branch of the WPP's advisory council, and Evelyn Wight Allan, the dean of woman, was its corresponding secretary. Frances (Mrs. C. E.) Cumberson, the president of the Northern California Branch of the WPP, lived in Palo Alto. [66]

In July 1915 the Palo Alto branch of the WPP helped sponsor the International Conference of Women Workers to Promote Permanent Peace, held in San Francisco in conjunction with the Panama Pacific International Exposition, which opened in January of that year. Alice Park was an advisor. At a meeting on June 4, Park spoke about "the Peace Movement in Hawaii," from where she had recently returned.[67] In November of the same year, the Northern California branch of the WPP protested a proposal to introduce military training in high schools. Park sent a request to a meeting of the American Federation of Labor, being held in San Francisco, that they pass a resolution in opposition to military training in high schools. She wrote, "Educators, as a class, ... opposed ... military drill," but continued that the question now was "How many of them have the courage of their convictions and how many of us?"[68] Park was a delegate from California to the meeting of the WPP in Washington DC in December 1916.[69]

Park was also a member of the Ford Peace Expedition that left New York for Europe aboard the ship *Oscar II* on December 4, 1915. Her invitation came at the suggestion of Rosika Schwimmer, whom Park had met at the International Woman Suffrage Congress in Budapest in June 1913, which Schwimmer had organized; Park had seen Schwimmer two months later when both women were delegates to the Universal Peace Congress at the Hague.[70] In November 1915 Schwimmer enlisted Henry Ford's financial support for a Peace Expedition to neutral European nations in an endeavor to set up a conference for continuous mediation.[71] On November 25 Ford announced the Ford Peace Mission, which was to sail on a Norwegian vessel to neutral nations to "create machinery where those who so desire[d] [could] turn to inquire what [could] be done to establish peace and begin relations with those who also desire[d] peace."[72] In an address to the WPP, Ford's rash slogan, "Out of the trenches by Christmas, never to go back," created a sensation and, in the minds of many who heard it, a skepticism about the Peace Mission that was magnified by many in the press, which subjected the venture to criticism and often derision. The hasty planning and selection of delegates further undermined its possibility of success. Lisa Secor, a young journalist, whose participation in the Peace Expedition converted her to lifelong peace activism, attributed the dissension that developed among delegates to the fact that some of the delegates joined the expedition for "the opportunity of a luxurious trip abroad at Mr. Ford's expense" and had very little interest in its peace aims.[73] Barbara Kraft cast a major share of the blame on Schwimmer's authoritarian leadership of the expedition and her overbearing and often unpleasant manner.[74]

Park defended the expedition in an interview in 1950 on the thirty-fifth anniversary of the sailing of the Ford Peace Ship, claiming "of the reports sent back by the fifty-four newspapermen who went along on the trip—their expenses were also paid by Mr. Ford—only the inaccurate dispatches achieved much prominence." She declared, "Our object was to arrange continuous mediation without an armistice."[75] She was perhaps attempting to counteract Ford's statement about ending the fighting "by Christmas" in pointing out that the Peace Mission had a more realistic and long-term goal than immediately ending the war. Park expressed her admiration of Henry Ford in a letter to her children written from the Peace Ship in December 1915: "Mr. Ford is so absolutely sincere and so simple and so altogether admirable" and has "the right strength and splendid confidence that a great man or woman has."[76] In her typewritten autobiography, written in 1946, she declared that the Ford Peace Expedition "did more than people knew in 1916 and came nearer the Big Peace than people know." She wrote that the British minister to Sweden had stated that the Ford Neutral Conference was one of the principal influences that kept Sweden out of the war.[77] Park was one of the few U.S. delegates who remained in Holland, for a month after the other expedition members sailed for home, to cooperate with Scandinavian delegates. Stockholm was made the head office for "continuous mediation without armistice." After her return to the United States in March 1916, Park gave many lectures about the Ford Peace Expedition, and the Lecture Bureau of the WPP of Northern California listed her for the 1916–1917 season as a lecturer on the Ford Expedition and world peace.[78]

As the United States moved closer to intervention in the European war in early 1917, Park continued her crusade for peace. In February, Carrie Chapman Catt, the president of the National American Woman Suffrage Association (NAWSA), in an effort to advance the cause of woman suffrage, decided to reject the association's stand for peace and instead called for a meeting of the members of its executive board in Washington DC to offer the association's services to the government if it declared war. Park protested vehemently. In a letter written on behalf of Mrs. Keith, the president of the California Suffrage Association, Park argued that just because war would disrupt suffrage work was "no reason ... we should turn aside from our chosen work and take up other work." She complained that the short notice given for the meeting and the long distance involved made "it almost certain" that the conference would be one for eastern women, and she insisted that the "voice of the west, could it be heard, would be a voice for Peace." Park indicated that the desire for peace was evidenced in the 1916 presidential election when California voted for President Woodrow Wilson, whose slogan was "he kept us out of war." She noted that California's fear of Japan, "trotted out from time to time, and the demand upon Congress for increased fortifications on this coast [had] not made the west into a people planning for war."[79]

On April 1, 1917, when U.S. entry into the war was imminent, Park attempted to cheer up a Mrs. Spencer (probably Anna Garland Spencer, an officer of the WPP) by emphasizing the contrast between the eastern and western views on the European war in Europe, saying that the "West was for peace." Park wrote, "The great body of the common people—especially the young men of military age—is for peace." She urged her friend not to "feel so down in the minority." She explained, "We are right. We must stand and be counted—however few. And standing and being counted in the west you would not feel so lonesome." Park mentioned a protest about the war she had written, not knowing that "anyone else would stand up with me." "But I had to make it," she said. When the protest was "printed in full in the San Francisco paper, it was understood and approved at once—cut out by friends and sent east."[80]

After the United States entered the war, Park courageously continued her peace activities despite the strongly pro-war attitude quickly assumed by most Americans. When the Palo Alto chapter of the WPP disbanded,

Park continued to attend meetings of the other WPP organizations in the area. She became involved with the American Union against Militarism and held monthly meetings of the organization at her Palo Alto home, beginning on April 16, 1917, shortly after war was declared, when the members met to discuss plans for immediate actions and actions to be taken during the war.[81]

Park's activities sometimes subjected her to the threat of arrest. When she placed a newspaper ad giving her address as a place where conscientious objectors could enroll their names by mail with the Palo Alto branch of the American Union against Militarism, a federal agent appeared at her door, bearing a telegram from Washington stating that such ads must stop and that the person responsible for them should be investigated.[82]

Throughout the war Park remained active in, and attempted to assist, the American Union against Militarism, which printed leaflets about conscientious objectors.[83] Park also followed the cases of women convicted under the Espionage Act and often aided them, according to Kathleen Kennedy in *Disloyal Mothers and Scurrilous Citizens*.[84]

Park attended the first meeting held in San Francisco of the People's Council on July 7, 1917, with approximately eighty persons in attendance. The People's Council was an organization of opponents of war, formed by Louis Lochner, a pacifist and a leader of the Ford Peace Expedition. One of its original leaders was John D. Works, a former U.S. senator from California. The council's principal aims were a public statement of peace aims and a negotiated peace. Its slogan was "Peace by Negotiation—Now."[85] At a meeting of the council in San Francisco in August 1917, Park was presiding when police proceeded to the speakers' platform, where along with Park were sitting David Starr Jordan and Works, and "plucked" Daniel O'Connell off the platform. O'Connell was the leader of the American Patriots Association, which had issued a document entitled "Legal Opinion and Advice on the Conscription Law to American Patriots." When O'Connell read aloud the complaint under which he was charged for violating the Espionage Act by helping young men avoid the draft, the audience applauded him for three minutes.[86]

Two days later Park left on a long journey that took her to twenty states and kept her away from home for eight months. During those eight months, she attended meetings, lectured, and otherwise devoted herself to her many reform efforts in various cities. In Seattle she spoke at a conference on conscientious objectors. She attended the national convention of the People's Council, which had been forbidden to meet in Minneapolis by the governor, who stated that its meeting would give "aid and comfort to the enemies of the United States," and was then discouraged from meeting in Fargo, North Dakota, by officials there. When it finally met in Chicago, it was broken up by police on the first day, and by troops sent by the governor of Illinois on the second day. In its brief meeting time it adopted a platform calling for progressive disarmament by all nations, repeal of the draft law, a concrete statement of war aims by the administration, and peace without conquest or indemnities.[87] On the third day the delegates from California met in Park's Chicago hotel room. When in New York, Park spoke at a People's Council meeting.[88]

Park attended the national convention of the Woman's Peace Party in Philadelphia in December. There the WPP adopted resolutions to initiate a campaign for an Inter-Allied Conference to formulate and announce the political and economic aims of the Allied governments, to oppose congressional action for universal compulsory military service, and to support an agreement that a League of Nations be made the basis for the war settlement.[89]

On her way back west in January 1918, Park spent more than two months in southern California, where she attended meetings of the American Alliance for Labor and Democracy, the Fellowship of Reconciliation, the People's Council, and other organizations, and gave speeches on the Ford Peace Expedition, Holland and the press, internationalism, and "some examples of press fiction." The latter speech caused agents from the Department of Justice to call to inquire about her at the office of a friend.[90]

She was warned in February not to return home, but to stay in southern California. She supposed that the threats were of mob violence, and she confessed, "It was one of the first times in my life that I have been afraid." If she had known it was actually military authorities that made the threats of personal violence, she said, she "should not have been afraid." She added, "It took courage to come home."[91]

She also visited in Santa Barbara with a group called the Christian Pacifists, headed by Reverend Floyd Hardin and Reverend George Greenfield. After Park returned to Palo Alto, federal officers went to her home with a search warrant and obtained correspondence from Hardin and Greenfield, who were on trial in Los Angeles for sedition.[92]

In the fall of 1918, while Park was in Portland, Oregon, two officers from the Portland district attorney's office searched her hotel room without a warrant. They took with them a "large armful of miscellaneous papers" and one book, Men in War. After the officers had examined the papers, an officer and the district attorney questioned her and told her four or five times that she was "flirting with jail" and must change her views. They finally released her due to her "previously clean life" and her age. Park believed that the basis of the incident was her reading at a Woman's Christian Temperance Union (WCTU) meeting from her article reviewing two books, Children of Fate and Men in War.[93]

After the war Park continued to work for conscientious objectors. In 1919 she published a pamphlet entitled, "Dungeons in America." She planned a meeting at the Palo Alto Community House to promote the release of all political prisoners, featuring as speaker Philip Grosser of Boston, the first conscientious objector arrested and the last released. Park noted in her autobiography that "even at that late date, the general public was unfriendly and the meeting broke up in disorder."[94]

Although Edson and Park took differing paths in expressing their patriotism during World War I, the two women shared much in common. They were both activists before the war; the war increased their activism; and their activism, particularly in the field of woman suffrage, led both of them to activism on the international scene.

Gender influenced both Edson's and Park's activism and often their rhetoric. Edson's fight for woman suffrage continued throughout her career, as did her fight to improve working conditions for women. Her concern for peace after the war was one often identified as a woman's issue.[95] Park's activism focused on two main causes: woman suffrage and peace. Her authorship of and work toward the Equal Guardianship Law and her membership in the WCTU were also gender related.

Edson, unlike many other women progressive activists, held government positions. Her appointments to these positions were made mostly by men, and she worked often with men. Meyer Lissner attributed Edson's ability to get along with her male progressive colleagues to her being able to "think like a man." An article in *Collier's* magazine stated that it was doubtful that there was any woman in California who could "appeal more convincingly to the masculine mind" than Edson. Edson's remark in the same article, "I am not a lady," and her husband's "she's a good fellow" indicate that Edson herself wanted to reinforce that impression.[96]

Nonetheless, Edson often expressed herself in terms related to gender. When talking about the need for woman suffrage, she pointed out that women needed the vote because men would not look after their concerns: "They never have and they never will!"[97]

Barbara Steinson has written that during World War I women used the rhetoric of "nurturant motherhood" to "justify and promote their efforts."[98] When Edson wrote of the wartime repression of civil liberties, she used such rhetoric in questioning whether "we women, the mothers of free men and women, [were] going to be their soft dupes to carry out these programs of reaction, intolerance and enslavement."[99]

Park expressed herself on the subject of woman suffrage in a feisty manner. When a commencement speaker at Stanford University spoke about the "consent of the governed" when he really meant the consent of men and "of universal suffrage" when he meant suffrage for men only, Park asked: "Are not women people? Isn't it about time that these men speakers were instructed that half the human race are women?" When another speaker spoke in the same manner, Park sent him a letter, pointing out that women, who had been patient and humble in the past, would no longer tolerate being ignored.[100]

Park's rhetoric about peace emphasized a feminist viewpoint regarding the connection between war and women's subjugation when she wrote in her letter to Carrie Chapman Catt protesting her plan to offer NAWSA's services to the government if it declared war. Park stated that she longed "for suffragists who will recognize the close connection between militarism and the subjection of women, and who will refuse to hold out their necks so the yoke may be more firmly riveted upon them." She also pointed out the propensity for men to wage war when she noted that, if war came, it would come through the "action of a man-made government" because "men know of no better way to settle questions." She suggested a "cooling off period and a conference where men and women together confer and pledge themselves to peace." She emphasized that the crisis they faced was "a golden opportunity for women to stand for women's rights and to refuse to help the men murder each other."[101]

Before the United States intervened in the war, Edson and Park had each written to women colleagues in the East that the views of the West differed from those of the East on the war. Despite any alleged difference in views between East and West about foreign relations before intervention, Edson's and Park's activities, although channeled in different directions, demonstrated that women in the West were as much involved in wartime activism as were women in the East, and, in Edson's and Park's individual cases, because of their unlimited energy, courage, and deep devotion to their causes, probably much more so.

Notes

This chapter is based in part on Eunice A. Eichelberger, "California Progressives and World War I" (Master's thesis, San Francisco State University, 2004).

1. Katherine Edson, "Paper on World War I and the Conservation of American Freedom," undated, Edson Papers, Special Collections, Young Research Library, University of California at Los Angeles (hereafter "Edson Papers"), Box 4, Folder 1.

2. Barbara Steinson, *American Woman's Activism in World War I* (New York: Garland, 1999), i.

3. Among these reforms were the initiative, referendum, and recall; state civil service; empowerment of railroad commission to set fair rates; Weights and Measures Law; Pure Food Act; Water and Power Conservation Act; Employers' Liability Act; minimum-wage law for women; eight-hour law for women workers; reform of state tax system; free textbooks for school children; laws against child labor; woman suffrage; direct primary law; popular election of United States senators; nonpartisan election of judges; and old-age pensions. J. Gregg Layne, "The Lincoln–Roosevelt League: Its Origin and Accomplishments," reprinted from the *Quarterly of the Historical Society of Southern California* (September 1943): 23.

4. See, e.g., Roger Daniels, *The Politics of Prejudice: The Anti-Japanese Movement in California and the Struggle for Japanese Exclusion* (New York: Atheneum, 1974).

5. Jacqueline Braitman, "Katherine Philips Edson: A Progressive Feminist in California's Era of Reform" (PhD dissertation, University of California at Los Angeles, 1988), 119.

6. Braitman, "Katherine Philips Edson," 151.

7. Chester Rowell to Katherine Edson, August 29, 1913, Edson Papers, Box 2, folder 3.

8. Meyer Lissner to Jane Addams, January 13, 1915, Meyer Lissner Papers,

Special Collections, Green Library, Stanford University, Box 6 (hereafter "Lissner Papers").

9. Meyer Lissner to Theodore Roosevelt, January 13, 1915, Lissner Papers, Box 6.

10. "Civic Affairs' Leader Passes," *Los Angeles Times*, November 6, 1933.

11. Caroline Severance founded the first women's club in Los Angeles in 1878, which in 1890 became the Friday Morning Club, one of the most successful women's clubs in the state. See Judith Rafferty, "Los Angeles Clubwomen and Progressive Reform," in *California Progressivism Revisited*, ed. William Deverell and Tom Sitton, 144–74 (Berkeley: University of California Press, 1994).

12. Braitman, "Katherine Philips Edson," 81.

13. Walton Bean, *California: An Interpretive History*, 3rd ed. (New York: McGraw-Hill, 1978), 282.

14. Norris C. Hundley Jr., "Katherine Philips Edson and the Fight for the California Minimum Wage, 1912–1923," *Pacific Historical Review* 29 (1960): 272.

15. Hundley, "Katherine Philips Edson," 272.

16. Hundley, "Katherine Philips Edson," 274.

17. Samuel Leask, as quoted in a letter from Will J. Smith to Philips J. Edson, MD, October 26, 1937, or October 18, 1935, Edson Papers, Box 4, Folder 3.

18. Katherine Edson to Mrs. Lyndsay Van Rensslaer, December 16, 1916, Edson Papers, Box 1, Folder 4.

19. George Mowry, *The California Progressives* (Berkeley: University of California Press, 1951), 272.

20. Spencer C. Olin Jr., *California's Prodigal Sons: Hiram Johnson and the Progressives 1911–1917* (Berkeley: University of California Press, 1968), 160.

21. S. D. Lovell, *The Presidential Election of 1916* (Carbondale: Southern Illinois University Press, 1980), 72.

22. Meyer Lissner to Theodore Roosevelt, January 13, 1913, Lissner Papers, Box 6.

23. Katherine Edson to Hon. William D. Stephens, April 5, 1917, Edson Papers, Box 1, Folder 5.

24. Katherine Edson to Chester Rowell, April 6, 1917, Edson Papers, Box 1, Folder 5.

25. David M. Kennedy, *Over Here: The First World War and American Society* (New York: Oxford University Press, 1980).

26. Samuel Gompers to Katherine Edson, August 17, 1917, Edson Papers, Box 2, Folder 12.

27. Diane North, "The State and the People: California during the First World War" (PhD dissertation, University of California at Davis, 2001).

28. "State Council of Defense is Named," *San Francisco Chronicle*, April 5, 1917.

29. "State Council of Defense Is Ready for War," *San Francisco Chronicle*, April 7, 1917.

30. Edson to Martin C. Madsen, October 4, 1917, Edson Papers, Box 1, Folder 5.

31. Bertha von der Nienburg to Katherine Edson, July 10, 1917, Edson Papers, Box 2, Folder 12.

32. Katherine Edson to Bertha von der Nienburg, August 9, 1917, Edson Papers, Box 1, Folder 5.

33. "The Quiet Revolution in Women 'Firsts'; How 'First to Be Chosen' Is Making New Chapter in the History of Women's Rise," *Oakland Tribune*, March 10, 1918.

34. Katherine Edson to Governor William Stephens, August 31, 1918, Edson Papers, Box 1, Folder 6.

35. George Bell telegram to Katherine Edson, October 29, 1918, Edson Papers, Box 2, Folder 13.

36. Charlotte P. Ebbets to Katherine Edson, March 1918 (no day given), Edson Papers, Box 2, Folder 13.

37. *Stockton Record*, February 14, 1918.

38. Katherine Edson to Marie Obenauer, November 27, 1917, Edson Papers, Box 1, Folder 5.

39. Edson Papers, Box 4, Folder 1.

40. Katherine Edson to Mrs. Shelley Tolhurst, April 17, 1920, Edson Papers, Box 1, Folder 8.

41. Charles Evans Hughes telegram to Katherine Edson, November 3, 1921, Edson Papers, Box 3, Folder 2; Katherine Edson telegram to Charles Evans Hughes, November 4, 1921, Edson Papers, Box 1, Folder 10.

42. Marie Stuart Edwards to Katherine Edson, November 14, 1921, Edson Papers, Box 3, Folder 2.

43. C. Leonard Hoag, *Preface to Preparedness: The Washington Disarmament Conference and Public Opinion* (Washington DC: American Council of Public Affairs, 1941), 89.

44. Katherine Edson to Mrs. Josephine Wilson, February 1, 1922, Edson Papers, Box 1, Folder 10.

45. "Committee Named to Advise Parley," *New York Times*, November 2, 1921.

46. Meyer Lissner to Katherine Edson, November 2, 1921, Edson Papers, Box 3, Folder 2.

47. Katherine Edson telegram to Marian Mel, November 13, 1921, Edson Papers, Box 1, Folder 10.

48. *Los Angeles Times*, November 27, 1921.

49. Stephen G. Porter to Katherine Philips Edson, January 9, 1922, Edson Papers, Box 3, Folder 3.

50. Stephen G. Porter to Katherine Philips Edson, February 1922 (no day given), Edson Papers, Box 3, Folder 3.

51. "Kill Avarice in Men's Souls, Outranks Junking of Navies: Peace Views of Mrs. Edson," *Stockton Record*, November 4, 1921.

52. Alice Park to Mr. Lara, October 26, 1919; Alice Park, "Autobiography," Park Papers, Box 29.

53. Park, "Autobiography."

54. Park, "Autobiography."

55. Park, "Autobiography"; Rebecca J. Mead, *How the Vote Was Won: Woman Suffrage in the Western United States, 1868–1914* (New York: New York University Press, 2004), 136.

56. The Huntington Library has a collection of badges, buttons, posters, and flags that were collected, and some designed, by Park in support of her main causes, women's suffrage and peace.

57. "Team Work of California Women Voters," Leaflet, Park Papers, Box 29.

58. Park, "Autobiography."

59. Park, "Autobiography."

60. Park, "Autobiography."

61. Steinson, *American Women's Activism*, 1.

62. Joan Jensen, "When Women Worked: Helen Marston and the California Peace Movement, 1915–1945," *California History* 67 (1988): 122.

63. Wendy E. Chmielewski, Curator, Swarthmore College Peace Collection, Swarthmore College; Jane Addams, Emily Balch, and Alice Hamilton, *Women at The Hague: The International Congress of Women and Its Results* (reprint, New York: Garland, 1972); *San Francisco Chronicle*, April 14, 1915.

64. International Peace Bureau, Bulletin officiel du XXeme Congrès universel de la paix, tenu à La Haye du août 1913 (Berne: Bureau international de la paix, 1914).

65. Calling card, Park Papers, Box 29.

66. Park Papers, Box 23.

67. May Wright Sewall, *Women, World War and Permanent Peace* (San Francisco: John J. Newbegin, 1915), xxii.

68. Protest Against Military Drill," *Palo Alto Times*," November 19, 1915, Park Papers, Box 23.

69. Record of Women's Peace Party, Series A, Box 4, Swarthmore Peace Collection.

70. Schwimmer was a Hungarian journalist, suffragist, and pacifist. After war broke out in Europe, Schwimmer, who was now an enemy alien in Britain, moved to the United States and promoted a plan to offer mediation by the United States and other neutral nations. In 1915 she helped organize the Women's Peace Party and served on one committee of the Hague Congress of Women in the interest of the plan for continuous mediation.

71. Marie Louise Degen, *The History of the Woman's Peace Party* (New York: Burt Franklin Reprints, 1974), 131.

72. Degen, History of the Woman's Peace Party, 134.

73. Lilia Secor Florence, "The Ford Peace Ship and After," reprinted in Degen, Woman's Peace Party, 282.

74. Barbara S. Kraft, The Peace Ship: Henry Ford's Pacifist Adventure in the First World War (New York: Macmillan, 1978).

75. Palo Alto Times, December 5, 1950, Park Papers, Box 6.

76. Alice Park to "Children," December, 1915; Park, "Autobiography."

77. Park, "Autobiography."

78. Lecture Bureau of the Woman's Peace Party, Park Papers, Box 6.

79. Alice Park to Carrie Chapman Catt, February 17, 1917; Park, "Autobiography."

80. Alice Park to Mrs. Spencer, April 1, 1917, Park Papers, Box 6.

81. Alice Park, Diary, 1917, Park Papers, Box 24.

82. Alice Park, Diary, 1917, Park Papers, Box 24.

83. The American Union against Militarism changed its name to the American Civil Liberties Bureau and later to the America Civil Liberties Union. Park's son was a conscientious objector and worked in New York under its director Roger Baldwin.

84. Kathleen Kennedy, Disloyal Mothers and Scurrilous Citizens: Women and Subversion During World War I (Bloomington: Indiana University Press, 1999), 79.

85. H. C. Peterson and Gilbert C. Fite, Opponents of War, 1917–1918 (Madison: University of Wisconsin Press, 1957), 74–75.

86. "U.S. Orders Men and Women Draft Foes Arrested," San Francisco Chronicle, August 9, 1917.

87. Peterson and Fite, Opponents of War, 76–77.

88. Alice Park, Diaries, 1917, 1918, Park Papers, Box 24.

89. Degen, History of the Woman's Peace Party, 207–8. In early 1919 the WPP held an international convention in Zurich, where it reorganized and renamed itself the Women's International League for Peace and Freedom (WILPF). Although Park did not attend the Zurich convention, she was a delegate to the WILPF International Convention in Dublin in 1926 and to one in Duisburg, Germany, in 1927. Park remained active in the WILPF, attending local meetings and conventions. In her later years she was named honorary president of its Palo Alto chapter.

90. Alice Park, Diaries, 1917, 1918, Park Papers, Box 24.

91. Alice Park, Diaries, 1917, 1918, Park Papers, Box 24.

92. Park, Diary, 1918, Park Papers, Box 24.

93. Park, Diary, 1918, Park Papers, Box 24.

94. Park, "Autobiography."

95. See Harriet Hyman Alonso, Peace as a Woman's Issue: A History of the U.S Movement for World Peace and Women's Rights (Syracuse NY: Syracuse University Press, 1993).

96. Peter Clark MacFarlane, "A California Stateslady: An Everyday American of To-Morrow," *Colliers: The National Weekly* 52 (November 1, 1913): 29, 5.

97. Katherine Philips Edson to Mrs. Bryan Thomas, January 23, 1914. Edson Papers, Box 1, Folder 2.

98. Barbara J. Steinson, "'The Mother Half of Humanity': American Women in the Peace and Preparedness Movements in World War I," in *Women, War and Revolution*, ed. Carol R. Berkin and Clara M. Lovett (New York: Holmes & Meir Publishers, 1980), 259.

99. Katherine Philips Edson, paper on World War I, Edson Papers, Box 4, Folder 1.

100. Quoted in Ronald Schaffer, "The Problem of Consciousness in the Woman Suffrage Movement: A California Perspective," *Pacific Historical Review* 45 (November 1976): 478–79.

101. Alice Park to Carrie Chapman Catt, February 17, 1917; Park, "Autobiography."

14. HISTORIANS, POLITICS, AND CALIFORNIA WOMEN

MARY ANN IRWIN

Recent studies of women's politics in California from the mid-nineteenth through the early twentieth century make clear that voting was only one form of political activity in which women engaged, and a fairly narrow one at that. If we take a broad view of what counts as "politics," we can see California women behaving politically long before 1911, when they actually gained the ballot. Like Paula Baker, we define politics as "any action, formal or informal, taken to affect the course or behavior of government or the community."[1] With this broad definition in mind, this essay surveys recent scholarship on women's politics in California in the years between the Gold Rush and the Great Depression.

If we begin at the beginning, with indigenous women and those of Spanish/Mexican descent, the value of a roomy conception of politics is immediately apparent. Although they constituted the majority of the state's female population at the time of conquest, women of color were excluded from public decision-making. Indeed, from 1850 to 1929 and well beyond, formal politics in California was mostly a white affair.[2] Linda Heidenreich (chapter 1 in this volume) illuminates the difficulties historians face when they attempt to reveal California Native women as political actors. Because they left few written records of their own, historians are often left to find Indian women in the narratives of others. Unfortunately, Spanish and European observers—missionaries, soldiers, settlers, and the like—placed little value on indigenous women. As a result, these narratives typically reveal little about Native women's lives, much less their political activities. As Virginia Bouvier explains, "If female experience was not valued enough to be documented, reconstructing that history becomes problematic."[3]

Like Heidenreich, Bouvier sees political action in Native women's efforts to resist colonization. In the Spanish era, Native women engaged in the politics of resistance when they ran away from missions and presidios, when they retained their traditional roles as healers and religious leaders, and when they refused to alter their sexual practices, attend church, wear clothes, or speak Spanish.[4]

Albert Hurtado describes how the influx of white, Anglo-European gold-seekers further limited the agency of Native women.[5] Maria Raquel Casas provides a fascinating case in point in her sketch of Victoria Reid, a Gabrieleño woman whose birth, marriages, and multiple widowhoods moved her back and forth across Native, Spanish, and Anglo-European identities.[6] And yet, despite the overwhelming nature of the American conquest, Indian women found ways to protect their lives and cultures. Greg Sarris studies resistance among the Pomo of north-central California.[7] In the winter of 1871–1872, the revivalist Bole Maru (Dream Dance) cult spread through Pomo and Miwok territory. Pomo dreamers like Annie Jarvis, head dreamer for the Kashaya Pomo from 1912 to 1943, stressed the Bole Maru doctrines of Indian nationalism and isolationism. Jarvis outlawed intermarriage with non-Indians, forbade gambling and drinking, and halted attempts by government officials to take Indian children to boarding schools.[8]

As was true for indigenous women, the American influx to California was often disastrous for Latinas.[9] Spanish and Mexican women had begun immigrating to California as early as the Anza expedition of 1773. Doyce B. Nunis Jr., Susanna Bryant Dakin, and others have demonstrated that Latina immigrants such as Maria Feliciana Arballo could exercise considerable independence. Antonia Castañeda suggests that Arballo's numerous gestures of defiance—from arguing with Anza to singing bawdy songs in public—were essentially political acts.[10]

Scholarship on Latina politics in this era is limited in terms of the electoral process, but a growing body of scholarship on Latinas' civil rights and labor activism is available for the 1930s, 1940s, and beyond.[11] Antonia Castañeda's "Gender, Race, and Culture: Spanish Mexican Women in the Historiography of Frontier California" provides the essential starting point for understanding Latina politics in California.[12] Newer studies explore the ways that women of Spanish, Mexican, and mestizo ancestry struggled to survive, maintain their independence, and protect their cultural identities following the discovery of gold.[13] Anne E. Goldman gives thoughtful consideration to Helen Hunt Jackson's *Ramona* and to Maria Ampara Ruiz de Burton's *The Squatter and the Don*, which Goldman describes as "two significant exceptions to the willful amnesia" that naturalized the American conquest of California.[14] Nicole M. Guidotti-Hernandez explores one of the better-known episodes of race-based violence against women, the 1851 lynching of a Latina, Josefa, by an outraged mob of miners, most of whom were American. Guidotti-Hernandez examines how competing accounts of Josefa's death have been interpreted and manipulated in ways that justify and confirm "male domination, cultural superiority, and imperialistic practices in the American southwest."[15]

The numbers of white women in California grew slowly during the Gold Rush era, from 1850 to roughly the end of the 1860s. As newcomers living on an isolated frontier, some were quick to adopt the time-honored benevolent association as a means of shaping public policy. As Mary Ann Irwin argues in chapter 2, women's charities could be quite influential. In San Francisco, California's most populous city, the wives of civic leaders used their class connections to press for social welfare services for women and children. By soliciting funds and political support for woman-led hospitals, orphanages, and other programs, charity leaders became key players in San Francisco's political economy. Although deprived a formal political voice, middle-class white women nonetheless commanded a good deal of authority and power in California from the 1850s to the 1880s and well beyond.

Nationally, Anne Firor Scott, Lori Ginzberg, and others have looked at benevolence work as one of the most potent kinds of political power available to women in the nineteenth century. Charity work allowed American women to engage in politics without jeopardizing their class standing or femininity.[16] Theda Skocpol labels this kind of women's activism "maternalism," a feminine version of politics that placed women outside the patronage-driven model of public service more typical of male political involvement in the late nineteenth century.[17]

The Gold Rush brought with it a growing population of Europeans and Americans from other parts of the country, which added to the region's ethnic and religious complexity. Although the newcomers attempted to limit the options available to indigenous peoples, mestizos, mulattos, and others who arrived before the American conquest, those groups continued to assert their rights to life and liberty. Historians in recent decades have acknowledged that the West was a truly multiracial environment; this shifting conceptualization from a binary "white people versus minority group" model allows us to study the interactions between and among Native, Latino, and Asian settlers.[18] Examining the Gold Rush era, Leigh Dana Johnsen considers the interaction of African Americans with San Francisco's Chinese.[19] In the progressive era, Linda Pitelka looks at relations between Italian immigrants and their Native American neighbors in rural northern California. Pitelka argues that Italians, often treated as non-white when they arrived, allied themselves with neighboring Indians, working, socializing, and even praying together at *rancheria* churches. The Italians' later efforts at assimilation sometimes meant distancing themselves from their Indian friends.[20]

For women of color, forays into the political sphere usually involved self-preservation. Latina, African American, and Asian women often made use of the legal system to defend their rights and property. Maria Ampara Ruiz de Burton, mentioned above, spent years in court, attempting to hold onto land that she and her husband had purchased, in addition to lands in Mexico that were granted to her grandfather by the Mexican government.[21]

African American women also turned to the courts, despite their disadvantages under California law, especially its ban on blacks testifying against whites.[22] In 1856 a Missourian named Brown attempted to have Lucy, a free black female living in Auburn, arrested as a fugitive slave. Local opinion in Auburn held that Brown was well aware that his father had freed Lucy before she immigrated to California but had hoped to profit from the testimony ban. Lucy called for her (white) lawyer, with whom she had prudently deposited her freedom papers. With proof plus influential friends, Lucy used the legal system to successfully defend her freedom.[23]

That same year, Bridget "Biddy" Mason used the courts to escape slavery. Owned by Robert Smith, a Mississippi Mormon, Mason accompanied Smith from Utah to California in 1851. Some urged Mason to contest her slavery under California's new "free soil" constitution, but Mason waited to petition for her freedom until 1855, when Smith was preparing to relocate to Texas. A sympathetic judge took Mason's testimony in chambers, thus thwarting the testimony ban. In a landmark decision, the court freed Mason, her three children, and eleven others. Mason later amassed a sizable fortune in southern California real estate and became well known for her public and private philanthropy. Biddy Mason still awaits a full biography.[24]

In 1850 the federal census counted only 962 blacks living in California, most of them male, but even these small numbers faced Jim Crow restrictions beyond the ban on court testimony.[25] African American women turned to the courts to attack these forms of discrimination. Barbara Welke and Lyn Hudson explore the efforts of black women to desegregate public transportation in nineteenth-century San Francisco.[26] When Mary Ellen Pleasant, a successful entrepreneur, was ejected from a city trolley, she sued the streetcar company. As Welke observes, Pleasant wanted more than transportation—through her suit, she was making "a very personal claim about her right to be accorded the respect a lady deserved in public."[27] In what later proved to be a landmark decision, Pleasant won her suit but lost her case when the company appealed. Black women's legal challenges did not end segregation, but lawsuits like Pleasant's ultimately undermined the legal foundations on which segregation in California rested.[28]

Asian women in California—another group with little formal political power—also resorted to law to achieve their objectives. Erika Lee finds that in the 1880s Chinese immigrant women actively resisted exclusion, in one of the few forms of political action then available to them.[29] Chinese women hired "the very best attorneys" and sometimes succeeded in gaining entry into the country. With unequal positions in the United States and in their own communities as well, Chinese women, Lee finds, were nonetheless resilient public actors.[30] George Anthony Peffer agrees; by filing affidavits and presenting testimony in judicial proceedings against them, Chinese women fought immigration officials' efforts to label them as prostitutes and thus justify their deportation.[31] Of course, only elite Chinese women had the resources to resist exclusion by these means.

Like their black counterparts, Chinese women used California courts to battle segregation in public facilities. Judy Yung and Mae M. Ngai detail the lawsuit filed by Mary and Joseph Tape, a middle-class Chinese couple who sued San Francisco over its refusal to allow their daughter to attend an all-white public school. They succeeded in their 1884 lawsuit, but it was a hollow victory. The city escaped integration by establishing a separate school for Chinese children.[32] Like other minorities, Asian women were often frustrated in their attempts to shape public policy.

Elite white women, on the other hand, often found great success in the public sphere. As discussed above, charity organizers relied on class and gender ideals to smooth their entry into the public sphere. The maternalist politics described by Theda Skocpol flowered in California's progressive era, as a new generation of women leaders built upon the private-welfare model founded in San Francisco in the 1850s and 1860s. Mildred Nichols Hamilton (chapter 4) notes that such women as Phoebe Apperson Hearst made a career of philanthropy. Hearst's public service grew out of a larger reform tradition common among wealthy women in late nineteenth-century America. According to Kathleen D. McCarthy, such female philanthropists as Mary Rozet Smith and Louise deKoven Bowen in Chicago found legitimacy for their public roles by focusing on service to women and children. In the process, they carved out space for women as public policy-makers. "Unlike men, who enjoyed a host of political, commercial, and social options in their pursuit of meaningful careers," McCarthy points out, "women most often turned to nonprofit institutions and reform associations as their primary points of access to public roles." She notes, "[They] forged power structures that ran parallel to those used by men, and created new social, educational, and professional opportunities for their sisters and themselves." In the process, such philanthropists as Hearst shaped the direction of reform in progressive-era America.[33]

The differences between the philanthropic activities of elite and middle-class white women and those activities undertaken by African American, Chinese, Japanese, and Korean women in this era warrant close consideration. Members of California's minority groups used fundraising methods that were well known to leaders of white women's charities. Women of color organized community entertainments, crafts fairs, teas, and luncheons to raise money to aid the needy. Like their white contemporaries, minority women dispensed funds to the destitute, used them to buy food, fuel, and medicines for the poor, or to provide social services, such as burial or instruction in the English language.

Recent studies by Willi Coleman, Barbara Y. Welke, Delores Nason McBroome, Lyn Hudson, and others offer new insights into the politics that lay behind black charitable work in California. According to Coleman, by the early 1860s San Francisco's small African American community had organized at least two woman-led charities, the Ladies' Benevolent Society and the Ladies Pacific Accumulating and Benevolent Society. Both provided the community with medicines, nursing care, burial, and other services.[34]

Despite their similarities, there were profound differences between white women's charities and those founded by women of color. Black women also used their charitable associations to raise funds for explicitly political ends—pressing for civil rights for their community.[35] The significance of this work has been neglected until recently. Earlier works on black politics in California stressed the role of the male-led California Colored Conventions, which fought tirelessly for black (male) suffrage. But Susan Bragg, Willi Coleman, Barbara Welke, and others complain that the emphasis on suffrage obscures the important civil rights work undertaken by the state's black women.[36] Bragg, for example, finds African American women at the forefront of the battle to integrate California's public schools. Welke agrees, asserting that the most striking aspect of the nineteenth-century California civil rights movement was the extent to which black women led it.[37]

Alternatively, Elsa Barkley Brown argues that the state's black civil rights movement was more race- than gender-conscious. Brown holds that African American women saw suffrage, testimony, and the other rights of citizenship as crucial to both women and men.[38] Thus black women engaged the public sphere—writing letters to the editor, attending public meetings, penning editorials—much as black men did.[39] The careers of women like Oakland's Delilah Leontium Beasley—a pioneer newspaperwoman and essayist, and the author of the first history of black California—support Brown's view, showing black women participating in California politics on equal terms with black men.[40]

Where women of color in this era focused their political energies on racial discrimination, white women working alone and in groups focused their energies on various reforms. Because they deployed a broader range of political tools than could women of color, elite white women pursued a broader array of political changes than their minority-group counterparts, and they were often successful. Temperance, or the campaign to limit the consumption of alcohol, inspired many to political action, but some combined their zeal for temperance with a variety of moral causes.

Ruth Bordin and others agree that, nationally, the temperance movement gave tens of thousands of middle-class American women the tools to work for profound changes in American manners and mores.[41] Usually, these were endeavors that seemed to extend logically from the domestic sphere—examples include efforts to regulate dairies, as a way of protecting children from contaminated milk, and campaigns designed to protect working girls from sexual and economic exploitation. Members of elite white women's social clubs, such as Berkeley's Twentieth Century Club or San Francisco's California Club, took on a variety of explicitly political campaigns, such as woman suffrage and the Red-Light Abatement Act. As informal activist groups, women's associations were endlessly flexible in this regard, able to turn easily from member education to charity to temperance to woman suffrage.

But, as Joshua Paddison reflects in chapter 3, even such single-issue organizations as California's Woman's Christian Temperance Union (WCTU) often pursued multiple agendas. Paddison finds that California women's campaign to ban the sale of alcohol was, in reality, a broad assault on the political structure itself. As they tried to reform society, WCTU members were attempting to stamp their own values onto the political sphere.[42] Leaders of California's WCTU promoted members' vision of social purity—personal, sexual, political, and racial. In California, the WCTU often collaborated with other reform-minded groups, especially elite women's clubs, to curb prostitution; end child labor; censor "impure" books, theater, and film; and, most of all, curb the use of alcohol.[43] Teresa Hurley and Jarrod Harrison (chapter 10) illustrate the flexibility with which woman-led organizations came together in 1913 to produce the First Legislative Platform of the Women's Legislative Council of California. Reformist energies sometimes collided in unexpected ways, as Mark Hopkins (chapter 12) shows in his study of the unlikely groups that joined forces to regulate commercial dance halls in San Francisco.

Some of the reforms undertaken by white clubwomen in this era were prescient. One example is the campaign to save California redwoods, a project undertaken by the California Federation of Women's Clubs (CFWC). In chapter 7, Cameron Binkley explains the symbiotic relationship that developed between the CFWC and various organizations launched to save California's ancient trees. By banding together for nature preservation, women in different groups learned a great deal about political mobilization. Working through the CFWC, Save the Redwoods, and the California Club, they also learned to form alliances with like-minded men in order to achieve common goals. Today, we would view such efforts as environmental activism. The same is true of the efforts California women undertook to protect songbirds. Michelle Kleehammer (chapter 6) makes clear that those efforts involved not only lobbying for protective legislation but also educating consumers as a long-term approach to transforming public opinion.

In *The Clubwoman as Feminist: True Womanhood Redefined, 1868–1914*, Karen Blair argues that clubwomen were all "feminists under the skin." For them the ideology of voluntarism often cloaked their strategic feminism, the underlying goal of which was female autonomy.[44] Sandra L. Henderson's study of the Twentieth Century Club of Berkeley (chapter 8) takes Blair's work as its starting point. Henderson finds that, among other things, Berkeley women used their collective might to shape the "Women's Legislative Agenda" at the 1913 California state legislature (the first legislative session after California women gained suffrage). The club campaigned for peace and internationalism in the second and third decades of the twentieth century, lobbied for the Panama–Pacific International Exposition of 1915, and even managed to get their own Anna Saylor sent to Sacramento as one of the first four women to serve in the California State Assembly (1919–1926). From this vantage point, Saylor was able to promote new child labor legislation; spearhead successful campaigns to reduce juvenile crime; provide mental health assistance; abolish the death penalty for minors; establish psychiatric clinics in prisons; and provide aid to the elderly. Thus, individually and in groups, these women leaders moved the issues that mattered to them onto the formal legislative agenda. In the end, California women's clubs helped transform the relationship between citizens and their government, a move that most historians agree was at the heart of progressive reform.

The clubs founded by women of color were no less flexible. Willi Coleman finds that, like their white counterparts, black women's social clubs served multiple purposes. In Oakland the Fanny Jackson Coppin Club offered members social and educational events, but it also built and operated that city's Home for Aged and Infirm Colored People.[45] More subtly, though, black women's clubs and charities asserted black women's claims to the gentility and respectability that middle-class white women could take for granted.[46] Douglas Flamming's work on southern California reveals African American clubwomen using their clubs in precisely this way. Flamming writes that in 1902 the all-white National Federation of Women's Clubs was scheduled to hold its biennial convention in Los Angeles. The National Association of Colored Women's Clubs spent all of 1901 urging white leaders to permit black organizations to attend. A very public controversy played out in the local newspapers, exposing "large deposits of race hatred in California, much of it expressed by 'southern' women who sounded like crusaders for the Jim Crow ideal." The spurned clubwomen organized the California Association of Colored Women's Clubs shortly thereafter, and the association devoted itself to publishing spirited defenses of the morals and manners of its members.[47]

However, as Mark Hopkins observes in this volume, moments of interracial cooperation were possible. In 1920, when the San Francisco Women's Vigilant Committee was organized, it included two black-led organizations: the Colored Women's Federation and the Booker T. Washington Community Center. The alliance suggests that black women's clubs and charities had gained at least some measure of credibility with white-led civic groups.

The clubs organized by Asian women and girls, like their African American counterparts, also served multiple functions. Japanese American girls' clubs in Los Angeles, for example, used charitable activities to deliver a layered message about their place in mainstream society. According to Valerie Matsumoto, in 1928 a girls' club called the Blue Triangles gave a large Thanksgiving basket to a widowed mother and her five children. It was the girls' first venture into what would become a regular club activity. In banding together for charity work, these daughters of Japanese immigrants not only helped needy women and children in their own community but also confirmed their identities as all-American girls.[48]

California's women of color shared with their white, middle-class counterparts a reliance on separate, woman-led organizations to accomplish multiple goals, from distributing goods and services to pressing for social and legal reforms. Like black women's clubs and charities, Chinese, Korean, and Japanese women's organizations also served multiple purposes, some of them unique. Sucheng Chan discusses Korean women's mutual assistance associations, including the Hankuk Puin-boe (Korean Women's Association) and the Taeban Puin Kuje-boe (Korean Women's Relief Society), both organized in San Francisco in the early twentieth century. The groups raised funds and provided badly needed social welfare services. The groups also had nationalist aims. Excluded from participation in U.S. politics, leaders raised funds for Korean independence at home. The Taeban Yoja Aikuk-dan (Korean Women's Patriotic Society) had branches in every California town with a sizable Korean population. Bong-Youn Choy calculates that, for decades, virtually every Korean in the United States annually gave the equivalent of one month's wages to end the Japanese occupation of Korea.[49]

Chinese immigrant women and their daughters likewise founded multifunctional women's groups, some of which blended Chinese nationalism with U.S. political forms. Judy Yung describes San Francisco's Square and Circle Club, founded by young, middle-class Chinese American women. In 1924, when the young women read of flooding and famine in China, they immediately organized a club and began planning a jazz dance to raise funds for victims.[50] Liu Yilan relates the political activism of San Francisco's Chinese Women's Jeleab (Self-Reliance) Association, founded in the wake of China's 1911 revolution. Taking their model from white women's clubs, Jeleab leaders explained that they had organized for the purposes of "social intercourse, benevolent work, educational advantages, and mutual assistance and benefit."[51] Like members of Korean women's organizations, these Jeleab members committed most of their charitable efforts to their ancestral homeland, raising funds for Dr. Sun Yat-sen's revolutionary cause and for victims of war and famine. Yilan holds that the Jeleab represented the awakening of a new social consciousness among California's Chinese women. Leaders linked women's education to their political advancement, encouraging members to take advantage of their opportunities in the United States to improve the status of Chinese American women and that of their sisters in China.[52]

Japanese American leaders met community needs through voluntary associations as well. Modeling themselves after white Protestant societies, Japanese immigrants founded the country's first Japanese voluntary association in San Francisco in 1877, the male-led Gospel Society Fukuin

Kai.⁵³ Japanese wives and daughters founded their own separate, subsidiary associations, *fujinkai*. These woman-led groups offered English classes, youth activities, Japanese language schools, and social events.⁵⁴ Buddhist Japanese women also founded *fujinkai*. In *Growing Up Nisei*, David Yoo finds that Buddhist women used their associations to expand their roles in public life. In Sacramento in 1900, for example, the Buddhist Women's Association raised funds and provided social welfare services for the immigrant community.⁵⁵ More work is needed to discover if, like other minority women's charities, these *fujinkai* also served more explicitly political functions.

Recent studies of Asian women in California reveal that they, too, used their social and recreational clubs as political pressure groups. Judy Yung, Judy Tzu-Chun Wu, and other students of Chinese California observe that the twentieth century brought new political sway for immigrant women and their daughters.⁵⁶ Yung reports that, after their initial fundraising efforts for flood victims in China, members of San Francisco's Square and Circle Club turned their gaze homeward. Clubwomen wrote letters to federal officials demanding more favorable immigration legislation for the Chinese. They registered voters among American-born Chinese and protested racist legislation such as the Dickstein Nationality Bill and the Texas Alien Land Bill. Yung notes that Square and Circle members lobbied state and municipal leaders for "public housing, longer hours and better lighting in Chinatown parks and playgrounds, a dental and health clinic, and retention of Chinatown's only Chinese-speaking public health nurse." When the United States entered World War I, members of San Francisco's Chinatown Young Women's Christian Association—like the clubwomen described by Sandra Henderson and Eunice Eichelberger—solicited donations, wrapped bandages, and knitted socks for soldiers. Eichelberger (chapter 13) also notes that World War I provoked a pacifist response, as when other local Chinese women organized a Peace Society.⁵⁷ As was true for other minorities, Asian women found mixed results in their efforts to shape public policy.

New research suggests that American-born Chinese women enjoyed greater opportunities than did their immigrant mothers. By 1910 more than 64 percent of Chinese American women in California were native born. With citizenship, education, and growing economic clout, some

Chinese American women were able to achieve individual success, as Judy Tzu-Chun Wu demonstrates in her study of Margaret Jessie Chung. In 1916 Chung graduated from the University of Southern California's College of Physicians and Surgeons, becoming the first known American-born Chinese woman physician. Wu argues that Chung's strategies to succeed in a white, male-dominated profession give us insight into the ways that Asian American women negotiated gender, sexual, racial, and class boundaries, both in mainstream U.S. society and within their own communities.[58]

Japanese women also used their social clubs for political ends. For 1920s and 1930s Los Angeles, Valerie J. Matsumoto finds that members of Japanese American girls' clubs saw themselves as "cultural ambassadors." In 1926, for example, members of the Japanese Young Women's Christian Association performed in a local "Festival of Nations" to raise funds for the Council on International Relations. They had all been born in the United States and would probably have been more comfortable dressed in the flapper style, but the local press reported that the girls donned kimonos and performed a "pretty dance" for the sake of building a "cultural bridge" of understanding between the United States and Japan.[59]

More work is needed on Japanese women's organizations in this era. In San Francisco, Los Angeles, and elsewhere, Japanese community leaders founded such political organizations as the Japan Society of Northern California, formed in 1905 to represent the Japanese community in the United States as a whole. Wives and daughters sometimes established subsidiaries to these male-led organizations. These separate entities suggest another potentially profitable avenue of research.[60]

Promising work on the South Asian experience in California is now underway. A handful of studies of Filipino and South Asian immigrant experiences in California are available, although none to date focus on the political activities of Filipinas or South Asian women in this time period. Arleen de Vera "imagines community" among Filipino migrants in California during the early to mid-twentieth century. She explores the tensions and conflicts that emerged as nationalist elites clashed with women, laborers, and others who rejected traditional hierarchies of gender and class in favor of the "popular" ideals of gender, power, and community.[61] Karen Isaksen Leonard studies the meaning of exclusion for South Asian immigrants, and the flexibility of ethnic identity. In the early twentieth century, men from India's Punjab province came to California to work on the land. They found very few marriageable South Asian women, and miscegenation laws and racial prejudice limited their marriage options. Discovering an unexpected compatibility, Punjabis married women of Mexican descent. These alliances inspired others, as the men introduced their bachelor friends to the sisters and friends of their wives. Leonard finds that these bi-ethnic families developed workable identities not only as "Hindus" but also as Americans.[62]

Dawn Bohulano Mabalon shows that, despite their small numbers, immigrant and second-generation Filipinas in California before and during World War II were critical in building cohesive and vibrant Filipina/o American communities. This was particularly so in the San Joaquin Delta region and in the city of Stockton, where Filipino leaders sometimes exploited the extreme gender imbalance in their community. Organizers used Filipinas as a draw for fundraising events, such as beauty queen contests and dances called "social boxes," in which single Filipinos bid to dance with young Filipinas. Beauty queen contests organized by Filipino American community groups similarly exploited men's desire for social and romantic proximity to their countrywomen. Social boxes and beauty queen contests had the potential to raise thousands of dollars for various charitable purposes, including the campaigns Filipino American community organizations led for Philippine independence from the United States. Contests also enabled young Filipinas to earn pocket money for college. During World War II, Filipinas were again the centerpiece of community campaigns, this time to sell war bonds. With the Philippines then at war with Japan as well—and with still so few Filipinas in the United States—these young beauty queens became symbols of the Philippine nation. Mabalon notes that these contests were often fraught with tension for young Filipina American women, some of whom rejected the traditional gender ideals they were expected to uphold. By the 1930s and 1940s, Filipina immigrant women and second-generation Filipina Americans were organizing their own separate, gender-specific women's clubs and charitable community groups.[63]

Turning from the state's agricultural regions to the bustling South-of-Market district of San Francisco, we find yet another means by which some women exercised public influence. Ann Marie Wilson's study of Lucile Eaves and the San Francisco Settlement Association (chapter 5) reveals how Eaves used the settlement's woman-centered institutional space to secure changes in the state's child-labor law and, at the same time, to further her own career. Drawing upon the work of Estelle Freedman, Kathryn Kish Sklar, Suzanne Lebsock, and Linda Kerber, Wilson recognizes that the South Park Settlement served as an incubator for activist and professional networks and helped launch individual women into public life.[64] More importantly, its story provides a useful addition to the historiography of the settlement movement, which has focused primarily on New York, Boston, and Chicago.[65]

Ruth Hutchinson Crocker, Elizabeth Lasch-Quinn, and other historians have criticized eastern settlements, highlighting the repressive aspects of reformers' programs and goals.[66] However, as Wilson points out, under Eaves's leadership, South Park consciously built bridges between workers and the local elite. The presence of the Chinese also made the San Francisco settlement experience unique. Like the unionists with whom she worked, Eaves believed that competition with Chinese workers reduced wages for white craftsmen. But in 1910 Eaves acknowledged the debt California labor owed the despised race. Their presence as a "common enemy" had "contributed more than any other factor to the strength of the California labor movement."[67]

Race always mattered in the world of California women's politics, but class also created insurmountable divides, as Susan Englander finds in her study of cross-class alliances in San Francisco (chapter 9). There, women labor leaders had hoped to work with the San Francisco Equal Suffrage League toward the common goal of woman suffrage. That alliance broke down after 1900, when elite white women's clubs claimed leadership of the California suffrage movement. Englander's study reveals that ideological differences thwarted the women's genuine desire to work across class lines. Eventually, union women were moved to organize their own, separate suffrage organization. In chapter 11 Rebecca Mead likewise found union women and clubwomen at loggerheads over the legislated minimum wage for women.

Although the significance of race cannot be denied, historians disagree about the relative importance of gender ideals versus class connections.

Michael McGerr finds gender the more useful tool in explaining U.S. women's public activism. According to McGerr, "Women's politics in the nineteenth century developed in counterpoint to male politics," which was characterized by intense partisanship, rituals, rallies, parades, and massive public displays. These forms of political participation excluded middle-class white women. As a consequence, such women developed a new, educational style of politics that favored persuasive argument: pamphlets, petitions, and conventions. Although the twentieth-century suffrage campaign divided along class lines nationally, McGerr concludes that it also fostered a radical new political style among women, one with the vitality needed to move women "well beyond the confines of voluntarism."[68]

Maureen Flanagan develops these themes further in "The City Profitable, the City Livable: Environmental Policy, Gender, and Power in Chicago in the 1910s." Flanagan decries historiographical references to women's urban activism as a domestication of politics, and rejects the endless debates over women's transit between public and private spheres. She argues that these tactics tend to perpetuate false gender distinctions. "While historians generally understand and sympathize with the idea of efficiency," writes Flanagan, "they have usually seen housekeeping as meaning little more than public tidying up." Flanagan suggests instead that "municipal housekeeping" is best understood as a challenge to the "pervasive progressive-era metaphor of government as a business," suggesting that clubwomen imagined a more profound restructuring of city government and urban welfare than did their male counterparts.[69]

The essays in *California Women and Politics* support Flanagan's view. They also demonstrate what California's women of color shared with their white, middle-class counterparts: a reliance on separate, woman-led associations formed to accomplish multiple goals, including social, political, and economic reforms. With wealth and political connections, white women's associations were far more likely than minority-led associations to achieve their objectives.

Another way that race divided California women's organizations was in the kinds of reforms that participants sought. Where women of color rallied for civil rights and an end to discrimination in public facilities, white women seldom demonstrated an interest in reforms of this kind. And yet, despite the chasms of race, class, and nativity that divided women's efforts, California women of all colors were harbingers of a new style of political participation dominated by special interests. As Samuel P. Hays and others have suggested, the emergence of special interest groups such as these was a key phenomenon of the progressive era. The rise of interest group politics accompanied the erosion of traditional partisan politics. As once all-powerful political parties were increasingly regulated and deprived of many of their former functions, the number of special interest groups—corporations, labor unions, trade associations, suffragists, charities, conservationists, and numerous men and women's civic organizations—multiplied.[70] In this era, white clubwomen were at the forefront of this surge of interest group politics, a surge that helped reshape formal political participation in California. Such elite women's groups sought influence by lobbying elected leaders to support their various goals, and often succeeded. Women of color had less success at the time in shaping the sphere of formal party politics. All the same, standing upon foundations erected by individuals such as Mary Ellen Pleasant, and such organizations as the Square and Circle Club, the California Association of Colored Women's Clubs, and untold others, later generations were to dismantle the barriers that once made equality a dim hope.

Notes

1. Paula Baker, "The Domestication of Politics: Women and American Political Society, 1780–1920," *American Historical Review* 89 (1984): 622.

2. William Issel and Robert W. Cherny, *San Francisco, 1865–1932: Power, Politics, and Urban Development* (Berkeley: University of California, 1987); Philip J. Ethington, *The Public City: The Political Construction of Urban Life in San Francisco, 1850–1900* (New York: Cambridge University Press, 1994); Michael Kazin, *Barons of Labor: The San Francisco Building Trades and Union Power in the Progressive Era* (Urbana: University of Illinois Press, 1989); Neil Larry Shumsky, *The Evolution of Political Protest and the Workingmen's Party of California* (Columbus: Ohio State University Press, 1991).

3. Virginia M. Bouvier, *Women and the Conquest of California, 1542–1840: Codes of Silence* (Tucson: University of Arizona Press, 2001). See also Victoria Brady, Sarah Crowe, and Lyn Reese, "Resist! Survival Tactics of Indian Women," *California History* 63, no. 2 (Spring 1984): 140–51. New information about California Indian life before Spanish conquest is slowly emerging. Ramón Gutiérrez and Richard J. Orsi provide a comprehensive study in *Contested Eden: California Before the Gold Rush*, ed. Ramón Gutiérrez and Richard J. Orsi, California History Sesquicentennial

Series, no. 1 (Berkeley: University of California Press, 1998). New studies also shed light on indigenous life during the Spanish colonial era, although information about individual Native women remains scarce. See James A. Sandos, *Converting California: Indians and Franciscans in the Missions* (New Haven CT: Yale University Press, 2008); Robert F. Heizer and Albert L. Hurtado, *The Destruction of the California Indians* (New Haven CT: Yale University Press, 1988). Edward D. Castillo discusses the effect of mission life on Native women in Edward D. Castillo, "Gender Status and Decline, Resistance, and Accommodation among Female Neophytes in the Missions of California: A San Gabriel Case Study," *American Indian Culture and Research Journal* 18, no. 1 (1994): 67–94.

4. Californianas would later resist Americanization in the same way, as when Rosalía Vallejo de Leese refused to learn to speak English. See Linda Heidenreich, *This Land Was Mexican Once: Histories of Resistance from Northern California* (Austin: University of Texas Press, 2007); James A. Sandos takes the same theme in "'Because He Is a Liar and a Thief': Conquering the Residents of 'Old' California, 1850–1880," in *Rooted in Barbarous Soil: People, Culture, and Community in Gold Rush California*, ed. Kevin Starr and Richard J. Orsi (Berkeley: University of California Press, 2000), 86–112; see also Lisbeth Haas, *Conquests and Historical Identities in California, 1769–1936* (Berkeley: University of California Press, 1995). For the period before the Gold Rush, see Miroslava Chavez, "*Pongo mi demanda*: Challenging Patriarchy in Mexican Los Angeles, 1830–1850," in *Over the Edge: Remapping the American West*, ed. Valerie J. Matsumoto and Blake Allmendinger (Berkeley: University of California, 1999), 272–92. On the need to extend the racial boundaries of western women's history, see Susan H. Armitage, "Revisiting 'The Gentle Tamers Revisited': The Problems and Possibilities of Western Women's History—An Introduction," *Pacific Historical Review* 61 (1992): 459–99.

5. Albert L. Hurtado, *Indian Survival on the California Frontier* (New Haven CT: Yale University Press, 1990); see also Albert L. Hurtado, *Intimate Frontiers: Sex, Gender, and Culture in Old California* (Albuquerque: University of New Mexico Press, 1999). On California women in the gold rush, generally, see Nancy J. Taniguchi, "Weaving a Different World: Women and the California Gold Rush," in Starr and Orsi, *Rooted in Barbarous Soil*, 142; Elisabeth Margo, *Taming the Forty-Niner* (New York: Rinehart, 1955); Jo Ann Levy, *They Saw the Elephant: Women in the California Gold Rush* (Hamden CT: Archon Books, 1990); Christiane Fischer, *Let Them Speak for Themselves: Women in the American West, 1849–1900* (Hamden CT: Archon Books, 1977).

6. Reid was born to a prominent Gabrieleño family (actually a Tongva-speaking group called Gabrieleños by Spanish settlers) and educated at Mission San Gabriel. Dona Eulalia Peréz took Victoria under her wing, training her in the Spanish language and customs, and taking her on visits to Los Angeles. There Victoria met Hugo Reid, a Scottish merchant who settled in the tiny pueblo in 1834. When her Indian husband died, Victoria married Hugo; he converted to Roman Catholicism

and adopted Victoria's children; the family lived in her small adobe. In 1838 Mexico acknowledged Victoria's service to the church with a 128-acre parcel of land. This was one of the few Mexican land grants to an Indian. Hugo Reid was not listed on the title; he was not a Mexican citizen until he was naturalized in 1839. Maria Raquel Casas, "Victoria Reid and the Politics of Identity," in *Latina Legacies: Identity, Biography, and Community*, ed. Vicki L. Ruiz and Virginia Sanchez Korrol (New York: Oxford University Press, 2005), 19–38; John R. Kielbasa, "Hugo Reid Adobe," Historic Adobes of Los Angeles County, at http://www.laokay.com/halac/HugoReidAdobe.htm, accessed June 8, 2008.

7. Greg Sarris, *Keeping Slug Woman Alive: A Holistic Approach to American Indian Texts* (Berkeley: University of California Press, 1993), 8–10.

8. Essie Parrish, the last Kashaya Pomo dreamer, held sway from 1943 until her death in 1979. Sarris, *Keeping Slug Woman Alive*, 8–10.

9. Vicki L. Ruiz and Virginia Sánchez Korrol use *Latina* as an umbrella term referring to all women of Latin American birth or heritage, including women from North, Central, and South America, and from the Spanish-speaking Caribbean. *Californianas* are Mexican women born in California prior to conquest; *Mexicana* refers to women born in Mexico, and *Mexican American* indicates birth in the United States. *Chicana* and *Chicano* reflect a political consciousness that emerged out of the Chicano student movement, often a generational marker for those who came of age during the 1960s and 1970s. Ruiz and Korrol, *Latina Legacies*, 5.

10. Antonia Castañeda and Doyce Nunis discuss Apolinaria Lorenzana, another Latina who defied class and gender expectations. See Doyce B. Nunis Jr., ed., *Women in the Life of Southern California* (Los Angeles: Historical Society of Southern California, 1996), xii; Antonia I. Castañeda, "Engendering the History of Alta California, 1769–1848," in Gutiérrez and Orsi, *Contested Eden*. See also Susanna Bryant Dakin, *Rose, or Rose Thorn? Three Women of Spanish California* (Berkeley: Friends of the Bancroft Library, 1963), 1–11; Vicki L. Ruiz and Virginia Sánchez Korrol, *Latinas in the United States: A Historical Encyclopedia* (3 vols.; Bloomington: Indiana University Press, 2006), 55–56; Ruiz, *Latina Legacies*, 8; Zaragosa Vargas, *Major Problems in Mexican American History* (Boston: Houghton Mifflin, 1999); Steven Mintz, *Mexican American Voices* (St. James NY: Brandywine, 2000); Carlos Híjar, E. Pérez, A. Escobar, and T. Savage, *Three Memoirs of Mexican California* (Berkeley: University of California Press, 1988).

11. These works are beyond the time frame of this essay, of course, but for interested readers, Antonia Castañeda recommends Vicki Ruiz, *Out of the Shadows: Mexican Women in Twentieth-Century America*, an invaluable overview of Chicana sociopolitical activism; Antonia I. Casteñeda to Mary Ann Irwin, personal communication, November 5, 2007. Recent reference works are also helpful: Ruiz and Korrol, eds., *Latinas in the United States*, includes general entries (politics, electoral politics), brief biographies of political activists, and entries for specific

organizations. Similarly, Sussane Oboler and Deena J. Gonzalez, eds., *The Oxford Encyclopedia of Latinos and Latinas in the United States*, 4 vols. (New York: Oxford University Press, 2005), has general entries on women in politics, biographies of political activists, and entries for organizations. See also Vicki L. Ruiz, "Feminism," in *Latinas in the United States*, 253–55; Diane-Michele Prindeville, "Identity and the Politics of American Indian and Hispanic Women Leaders," *Gender & Society* 17, no. 4 (2003): 591–608; Yolanda Flores Niemann, Susan Armitage, Patricia Hart, and Karen Weathermon, eds., *Chicana Leadership: The Frontiers Reader* (Lincoln: University of Nebraska Press, 2002).

12. Antonia Castañeda, "Gender, Race, and Culture: Spanish Mexican Women in the Historiography of Frontier California," in *Unequal Sisters: A Multicultural Reader in U.S. Women's History*, ed. Vicki L. Ruiz and Ellen Carol DuBois (New York: Routledge, 2000), 58–79; Castañeda, "Engendering History," 230–59; Antonia I. Castañeda, "The Political Economy of Nineteenth-Century Stereotypes of Californianas," in *Between Borders: Essays on Mexicana/Chicana History*, ed. Adelaida R. Del Castillo (Encino CA: Floricanto, 1990), 213–36.

13. Much of the scholarship on Latino/a history focuses on southern California. See, e.g., Gloria E. Miranda, "Racial and Cultural Dimensions of *Gente de Razon* Status in Spanish and Mexican California," *Southern California Quarterly* 70 (Fall 1988): 265–78; Douglas Monroy, *Thrown among Strangers: The Making of Mexican Culture in Frontier California* (Berkeley: University of California Press, 1990); George J. Sánchez, *Becoming Mexican American: Ethnicity, Culture, and Identity in Chicano Los Angeles, 1900–1945* (New York: Oxford University Press, 1993). Juan Gómez-Quiñones, *Roots of Chicano Politics, 1600–1940* (Albuquerque: University of New Mexico Press, 1994) offers little on women. Students who have sought Spanish-language sources for northern California in the late nineteenth and early twentieth centuries have reported finding only scattered issues of newspapers and few other sources.

14. Anne E. Goldman, "'I Think Our Romance Is Spoiled'; or, Crossing Genres: California History in Helen Hunt Jackson's *Ramona* and Maria Ampara Ruiz de Burton's *The Squatter and the Don*," in Matsumoto and Allmendinger, *Over the Edge*, 65–84.

15. Nicole M. Guidotti-Hernandez, "Reading Violence, Making Chicana Subjectivities," in *Technofuturos: Critical Interventions in Latino/a Studies*, ed. Nancy Raquel Mirabal and Agustin Lao-Montes (Lanham MD: Lexington Books, 2007), 10.

16. The literature on American women's benevolence work is extensive, especially for areas east of the Mississippi River. See Barbara Welter, "The Cult of True Womanhood, 1820–1860," *American Quarterly* 18 (1966): 151–74; Anne Firor Scott, *Natural Allies: Women's Associations in American History* (Urbana: University of Illinois Press, 1993); Lori D. Ginzberg, *Women and the Work of Benevolence: Morality, Politics, and Class in the 19th-Century United States* (New Haven CT: Yale University

Press, 1990); Nathan Irvin Huggins, *Protestants against Poverty: Boston's Charities, 1870–1900* (Westport CT: Greenwood, 1971); Wendy Kaminer, *Women Volunteering: The Pleasure, Pain, and Politics of Unpaid Work from 1830 to the Present* (Garden City NY: Anchor, 1984); Kathleen McCarthy, ed., *Lady Bountiful Revisited: Women, Philanthropy, and Power* (Chicago: University of Chicago Press, 1990); Anne M. Boylan, *The Origins of Women's Activism: New York and Boston, 1797–1840* (Chapel Hill: University of North Carolina Press, 2002). Peggy Pascoe looks at a woman-led San Francisco benevolent–reform organization in Peggy Pascoe, *Relations of Rescue: The Search for Female Moral Authority in the American West, 1874–1939* (New York: Oxford University Press, 1990). Philip J. Ethington briefly mentions San Francisco woman-led charities in Philip J. Ethington, *The Public City: The Political Construction of Urban Life in San Francisco, 1850–1900* (Cambridge UK, 1994), 331–32. Bruce Dorsey discusses the intersections of nineteenth-century notions of masculinity and benevolence in Bruce Dorsey, *Reforming Men and Women: Gender in the Antebellum City* (Ithaca NY: Cornell University Press, 2002). For a transnational perspective, see Carmen Nielson Varty, "'A Career in Christian Charity': Women's Benevolence and the Public Sphere in a Mid-Nineteenth-Century Canadian City," *Women's History Review* 14 (2005): 243–64.

17. Theda Skocpol, *Protecting Soldiers and Mothers: The Political Origins of Social Policy in the United States* (Cambridge MA: Belknap, 1992); see also Seth Koven and Sonya Michel, *Mothers of a New World: Maternalist Politics and the Origins of Welfare States* (New York: Routledge, 1993). Karen Anderson considers the racial implications of maternalist politics in Karen Anderson, "Changing Woman: Maternalist Politics and 'Racial Rehabilitation,'" in Matsumoto and Allmendinger, *Over the Edge*, 148–59.

18. Suggested readings in this paragraph are drawn from Quintard Taylor, "Bibliographic Essay on the African American West," *Montana: The Magazine of Western History* 46 (1996): 18–21.

19. Leigh Dana Johnsen, "Equal Rights and the 'Heathen Chinee': Black Activism in San Francisco, 1865–1875," *Western Historical Quarterly* 11 (1980): 57–68.

20. Linda Pacini Pitelka, "Indians and Italians: The Boundaries of Race and Ethnicity in Rural Northern California, 1890–1920," in *Italian Immigrants Go West: The Impact of Locale on Ethnicity*, ed. Janet E. Worrall, Carol Bonomo Albright, and Elvira G. Di Fabio (Chicago Heights IL: American Italian Historical Association, 2003). Quintard Taylor examines black–Asian relations in Seattle from the progressive era through the 1930s in Quintard Taylor, "Blacks and Asians in a White City: Japanese Americans and African Americans in Seattle, 1890–1940," *Western Historical Quarterly* 22 (1991): 401–29; James Smallwood takes up black–Tejano cooperation in nineteenth-century Texas in James Smallwood, "Blacks in Antebellum Texas: A Reappraisal," *Red River Valley Historical Review* 2 (Winter 1975): 459–60; while Arnold Shankman looks at twentieth-century rivalries between

blacks and Latinos in Arnold Shankman, "The Image of Mexico and the Mexican American in the Black Press, 1890–1930," *Journal of Ethnic Studies* 3 (1975): 43–56. In 1993 Sumi K. Cho took a long view at conflict among Latinos, Koreans, and African Americans following the Rodney King verdict, in Sumi K. Cho, "Korean Americans vs. African Americans: Conflict and Construction," in *Reading Rodney King/Reading Urban Uprising*, ed. Robert Gooding-Williams, 196–211 (New York: Routledge, 1993).

21. Rosaura Sanchez and Beatrice Pita, "Maria Amparo Ruiz de Burton and the Power of Her Pen," in Ruiz, *Latina Legacies*, 81–82; Jesse Alemán, "Novelizing National Discourses: History, Romance, and the Law in *The Squatter and the Don*," Mario Herrera-Sobek and Virginia Sánchez Korrel, eds. *Recovering the U.S. Hispanic Literary Heritage*, vol. 3 (Houston: Arte Público, 2000), 38–49, and John M. González, "Romancing Hegemony: Constructing Racialized Citizenship in María Amparo Ruiz de Buron's *The Squatter and the Don*," in *Recovering the U.S. Hispanic Literary Heritage*, ed. Ramon A. Gutierrez, Virginia Sánchez Korrol, Maria Herrera-Sobek, and Genaro M. Padilla (6 vols.; Houston: Arte Público, 2000), vol. 2, 23–39; José F. Aranda Jr., "Contradictory Impulses: María Amparo Ruiz de Burton, Resistance Theory, and the Politics of Chicano/a Studies," *American Literature* 70 (1998): 551–79; Kathleen Crawford, "María Amparo Ruiz de Burton: The General's Wife," *Journal of San Diego History* 30 (1984): 198–211; Amelia María de la Luz Montes, "María Amparo Ruiz de Burton Negotiates American Literary Politics and Culture," in *Challenging Boundaries: Gender and Periodization*, ed. Joyce W. Warren and Margaret Dickie (Athens: University of Georgia Press, 2000), 202–25; Frederick Bryant Oden, "The Maid of Monterey: The Life of María Amaparo Ruiz de Burton, 1832–1895" (MA thesis, University of California, San Diego, 1992).

22. In April 1850 the legislature decreed that anyone with "one-eighth part or more of Negro blood . . . and every person who shall have one-half Indian blood" could not testify in cases involving whites. That same year, a black woman undertook one of the earliest attempts to overcome the ban when Sarah Carrol of Sacramento filed a charge of grand larceny against her white common-law husband. Her case was dismissed when the defendant pointed out that there was "none but Colored testimony against him"; see Willi Coleman, "African American Women and Community Development in California, 1848–1900," in *Seeking El Dorado: African Americans in California*, ed. Lawrence B. De Graaf, Kevin Mulroy, and Quintard Taylor (Seattle: University of Washington Press, 2001), 104. For African Americans in the West, generally, see Quintard Taylor, *In Search of the Racial Frontier: African Americans in the American West, 1528–1990* (New York: W. W. Norton, 1998); see also Albert S. Broussard, *Black San Francisco: The Struggle for Black Equality in the West, 1900–1924* (Lawrence: University Press of Kansas, 1993).

23. Rudolph M. Lapp, *Blacks in Gold Rush California* (New Haven CT: Yale University Press, 1977), 140.

24. California's testimony ban stood until 1870, when it was overturned by the federal Civil Rights Act, passed to enforce the post–Civil War amendments to the U.S. Constitution. Shirley Ann Wilson Moore, "'We Feel the Want of Protection': The Politics of Law and Race in California, 1848–1878," in *Taming the Elephant: Politics, Government, and Law in Pioneer California*, California History Sesquicentennial Series, ed. John F. Burns and Richard J. Orsi (Berkeley: University of California Press, 2003), 115; Barbara Y. Welke, "Rights of Passage: Gendered-Rights Consciousness and the Quest for Freedom, San Franciso, California, 1850–1870," in *African American Women Confront the West, 1600–2000*, ed. Quintard Taylor and Shirley Ann Wilson Moore (Norman: University of Oklahoma Press, 2003), 75. For one of the few scholarly essays available on Biddy Mason, see Dolores Hayden, "Biddy Mason's Los Angeles, 1856–1891," *California History* 68 (1989): 86–99; see also Women in History, "Biddy Mason," at http://www.lkwdpl.org/wihohio/maso-bid.htm, accessed June 9, 2008.

25. Susan Bragg, "'Anxious Foot Soldiers': Sacramento's Black Women and Education in Nineteenth-Century California," in Taylor and Wilson, *African American Women*, 98.

26. Charlotte Brown, another black San Franciscan, had filed a similar suit three years earlier. Brown's suit resulted in a jury award of five cents, the cost of her streetcar fare. Moore, "We Feel the Want," 118. Douglas Henry Daniels considers the African American experience in San Francisco in Douglas Henry Daniels, *Pioneer Urbanites: A Social and Cultural History of Black San Francisco* (Philadelphia: Temple University Press, 1980).

27. Welke, "Rights of Passage," 80.

28. The streetcar company appealed and the California Supreme Court reversed Pleasant's victory in 1868. Lynn M. Hudson, *The Making of "Mammy Pleasant": A Black Entrepreneur in Nineteenth-Century San Francisco* (Urbana: University of Illinois Press, 2003). Pleasant's lower-court victory set a legal precedent that was used in future black civil rights efforts, such as an 1893 case over segregated housing; see Jason B. Johnson, "A Day for 'Mother of Civil Rights': Entrepreneur Sued to Desegregate Streetcars in 1860s," *San Francisco Chronicle*, February 10, 2005; Moore, "We Feel the Want," 118. California legal scholars revisited Pleasant's case in 1958, when a law review article used the Pleasant case to illustrate the difficulties plaintiffs faced in proving that discriminatory treatment caused real damages. Lynn M. Hudson, "Mining a Mythic Past: The History of Mary Ellen Pleasant," in Taylor and Moore, *African American Women*, 68n18.

29. Congressman Horace F. Page (R-California) proposed the Page Act (1875), which prohibited the entry of "undesirable" immigrants, including Chinese immigrants bound for America as contract laborers, in addition to any Asian woman likely to engage in prostitution. In effect the Page Law precluded the immigration of most Asian women. The Chinese Exclusion Act (1882)—also passed at

the behest of Californians—suspended most Chinese immigration, particularly "skilled and unskilled laborers and Chinese employed in mining." Later provisions allowed the entry of wives and minor children to join certain classes of Chinese, especially merchants and diplomats, already residing in the United States. The ban remained in effect until 1942. This exception encouraged many Chinese women to claim exempt status and attempt entry. Immigration officials expected merchant families to possess fine clothing, a respectable manner, and, especially, bound feet, so Chinese women highlighted these traits. An early example involved Jow Ah Yeong and Chun Ah Ngon, a merchant's wife and daughter who arrived in San Francisco in 1885. The applications of mother and daughter emphasized that both applicants had "compressed feet," which was "a mark of respectability." In 1901 Gee See, a Los Angeles merchant's wife, submitted her full-length portrait, revealing luxurious silk robes and tiny, bound feet. She even included an X-ray of her tiny feet. Erika Lee, "Exclusion Acts: Chinese Women during the Chinese Exclusion Era, 1882–1943," in Shirley Hune and Gail M. Nomura, *Asian/Pacific Islander American Women: An Historical Anthology* (New York: NYU Press, 2003): 78–82.

30. Lee, "Exclusion Acts," 81–82. Sucheng Chan explores the experiences of Chinese in California agriculture in Sucheng Chan, *This Bittersweet Soil: The Chinese in California Agriculture, 1860–1910* (Berkeley: University of California Press, 1989). Transnational studies of the Chinese American experience are increasingly popular; see Yong Chen, *Chinese San Francisco, 1850–1943: A Trans-Pacific Community* (Stanford: Stanford University Press, 2000); Madeline Y. Hsu, *Dreaming of Gold, Dreaming of Home: Transnationalism and Migration between the United States and South China, 1882–1943* (Stanford: Stanford University Press, 2000).

31. George Anthony Peffer, "Forbidden Families: Emigration Experiences of Chinese Women under the Page Law, 1875–1882," *Journal of American Ethnic History* 6 (1986): 28–46. See also Lisa Lowe, *Immigrant Acts: On Asian American Cultural Politics* (Durham NC: Duke University Press, 1996).

32. Judy Yung, *Unbound Feet: A Social History of Chinese Women in San Francisco* (Berkeley: University of California Press, 1995), 101–5; Mae M. Ngai, "History as Law and Life: *Tape v. Hurley* and the Origins of the Chinese American Middle Class," in *Chinese Americans and the Politics of Race and Culture*, ed. Sucheng Chan and Madeline Y. Hsu, (Philadelphia: Temple University Press, 2008). See also Victor Low, *The Unimpressible Race: A Century of Educational Struggle by the Chinese of San Francisco* (San Francisco: East/West, 1982), esp. chap. 4. At this writing, Mae M. Ngai is completing a book-length treatment of the Tape lawsuit in Mae M. Ngai, *The Tape Family and the Origins of the Chinese American Middle Class* (Boston: Houghton Mifflin Harcourt, forthcoming); see http://www.columbia.edu/cu/history/fac-bios/Ngai/faculty.html, accessed February 24, 2010.

33. McCarthy, *Lady Bountiful Revisited*, 1; Kathryn Kish Sklar, *Florence Kelley and*

the Nation's Work: The Rise of Women's Political Culture, 1830–1900 (New Haven CT: Yale University Press, 1997); Robyn Muncy, Creating a Female Dominion in American Reform, 1890–1935 (New York: Oxford University Press, 1994).

34. Coleman, "African American Women"; Welke, "Rights of Passage"; Hudson, The Making of "Mammy Pleasant"; Delores Nason McBroome, Parallel Communities: African Americans in California's East Bay, 1850–1963 (Berkeley: University of California Press, 1994). Earlier works that consider black women in California include Glenda Riley, "American Daughters: Black Women in the West," Montana 38 (1988): 14–27; Lapp, Blacks in Gold Rush California; James A. Fisher, "A History of the Political and Social Development of the Black Community in California, 1850–1950" (PhD dissertation, State University of New York at Stony Brook, 1971); Philip M. Montesano, "Some Aspects of the Free Negro Question in San Francisco, 1849–1870" (MA thesis, University of San Francisco, 1967); Quintard Taylor, "The Emergence of Black Communities in the Pacific Northwest, 1850–1920," Journal of Negro History 64 (1979) 346–51.

35. Several works deal specifically with charity associations in San Francisco, including Ruth Shackelford, "To Shield Them from Temptation: 'Child-Saving' Institutions and the Children of the Underclass in San Francisco 1850–1910" (PhD dissertation, Harvard University, 1991); Bradford F. Luckingham, "Associational Life on the Urban Frontier: San Francisco, 1848–1856" (PhD dissertation, University of California, Davis, 1968).

36. Coleman, "African American Women." In this vein, see also Evelyn Brooks Higginbotham, "African-American Women's History and the Metalanguage of Race," Signs 17 (1992): 251–76; Higginbotham, "Beyond the Sound of Silence: Afro-American Women in History," Gender & History 1 (1989): 50–67; and Paula Giddings, When and Where I Enter: The Impact of Black Women on Race and Sex in America (New York: William Morrow, 1984).

37. Bragg, "Anxious Foot Soldiers," 107–8; Welke, "Rights of Passage," 73.

38. Elsa Barkley Brown, "Negotiating and Transforming the Public Sphere: African American Political Life in the Transition from Slavery to Freedom," Public Culture 7 (1994): 107–46; Welke, "Rights of Passage," 88n10.

39. Bragg, "Anxious Foot Soldiers," 107–8.

40. Works by Beasley include Delilah Leontium Beasley, The Negro Trail Blazers (Whitefish MT: Kessinger, 2005), and Delilah L. Beasley, "California Colored Women Trail Blazers," in Hallie Q. Brown, ed., Homespun Heroines and Other Women of Distinction (Xenia OH: Adline, 1926). For a biography of Beasley, see Lorraine Jacobs Crouchett, Delilah Leontium Beasley: Oakland's Crusading Journalist (El Cerrito CA: Downey Place, 1990).

41. Ruth Bordin, Woman and Temperance: The Quest for Power and Liberty, 1873–1900 (Philadelphia: Temple University Press, 1981), 3; Estelle B. Freedman, "Separatism as Strategy: Female Institution Building and American Feminism, 1870–1930," Feminist Studies 5 (1979): 512–29.

42. Histories of the California temperance movement include Mrs. Dorcas James Spencer, *A History of the Woman's Christian Temperance Union of Northern and Central California* (Oakland CA: West Coast, 1911), 17; Gilman M. Ostrander, *The Prohibition Movement in California, 1848–1933* (Berkeley: University of California Press, 1957), 58.

43. On the social purity movement, see David J. Pivar, *Purity Crusade: Sexual Morality and Social Control, 1868–1900* (Westport CT: Greenwood, 1973); Alison M. Parker, *Purifying America: Women, Cultural Reform, and Pro-Censorship Activism, 1873–1933* (Urbana: University of Illinois Press, 1997); Alison M. Parker, "'Hearts Uplifted and Minds Refreshed': The Woman's Christian Temperance Union and the Production of Pure Culture in the United States, 1880–1930," *Journal of Women's History* 11 (1999): 135–58.

44. Karen J. Blair, *The Clubwoman as Feminist: True Womanhood Redefined, 1868–1914* (New York: Holmes & Meier, 1980), 1. More recent treatments of clubwomen include Michael McGerr, "Political Style and Women's Power, 1830–1930," *Journal of American History* 77 (December 1990): 864–85.

45. Coleman, "African American Women," 111. A. W. Hunton provides an early twentieth-century discussion of black social clubs in A. W. Hunton, "The Club Movement in California," *Crisis* 5 (December 1912).

46. Coleman, "African American Women," 111. On the pioneer educator Fanny Jackson Coppin, see Linda M. Perkins, "Fanny Jackson Coppin and the Institute for Colored Youth: A Model of Nineteenth-Century Black Female Educational and Community Leadership, 1837–1902" (PhD dissertation, University of Illinois, 1978); Linda M. Perkins, "'Heed Life's Demands': The Educational Philosophy of Fanny Jackson Coppin," *Journal of Negro Education* 51, no. 3 (Summer 1982): 181–90.

47. Douglas Flamming, *Bound for Freedom: Black Los Angeles in Jim Crow America* (Berkeley: University of California Press, 2006), 135–42.

48. Valerie J. Matsumoto, "Japanese American Girls' Clubs in Los Angeles during the 1920s and 1930s," in Hune and Nomura, *Asian/Pacific Islander Women*, 181.

49. Mary Paik Lee, *Quiet Odyssey: A Pioneer Korean Woman in America* (Seattle: University of Washington Press, 1990).

50. Yung, *Unbound Feet*, 48, 69, 153–55, 160. Sue Fawn Chung explores the battles waged by the Chinese American Citizens Alliance in Sue Fawn Chung, "Fighting for Their American Rights: A History of the Chinese American Citizens Alliance," in *Claiming America: Constructing Chinese American Identities during the Exclusion Era*, ed. K. Scott Wong and Sucheng Chan, 95–126 (Philadelphia: Temple University Press, 1998). See also Sucheng Chan, *Asian Californians* (San Francisco: MTL/Boyd & Fraser, 1991; Sucheng Chan, *Asian Americans: An Interpretative History* (Boston: Twayne, 1991).

51. Elizabeth Young, "The Most Unique Club in America: A Club of Chinese Women," *San Francisco Chronicle*, February 8, 1914, quoted in Liu Yilan, "The Purpose

of the Chinese Women's JELEAB Association," in Judy Yung, *Unbound Voices: A Documentary History of Chinese Women in San Francisco* (Berkeley: University of California Press, 1999), 242.

52. Young, "Most Unique Club."

53. California Department of Parks and Recreation, Office of Historic Preservation, "Five Views: An Ethnic Historic Site Survey for California," at http://www.nps.gov/history/history/online_books/5views/5views4.htm, accessed June 13, 2008.

54. California Department of Parks and Recreation, "Five Views."

55. David Yoo, *Growing Up Nisei: Race, Generation, and Culture among Japanese Americans of California, 1924–1949* (Urbana: University of Illinois Press, 1999), 43–46. See also David Yoo, "Enlightened Identities: Buddhism and Japanese Americans of California, 1924–1941," *Western Historical Quarterly* 27 (1996): 281–301.

56. Wilma Mankiller, "Asian Pacific Women," in *The Reader's Companion to U.S. Women's History*, ed. Gwendolyn Mink, Marysa Navarro, Wilma Mankiller, Barbara Smith, and Gloria Steinem (New York: Mariner Books, 1999), 47–48.

57. Yung, *Unbound Feet*, 48, 69, 153–55, 160.

58. Mankiller, "Asian Pacific Women," 47–48; Judy Tzu-Chun Wu, "'The Ministering Angel of Chinatown': Missionary Uplift, Modern Medicine, and Asian American Women's Strategies of Liminality," in Hune and Nomura, *Asian/Pacific Islander Women*, 155.

59. Valerie J. Matsumoto, "Japanese American Girls' Clubs in Los Angeles during the 1920s and 1930s," in Hune and Nomura, *Asian/Pacific Islander Women*, 182–83.

60. California Department of Parks and Recreation, "Five Views." Valerie Matsumoto studies Japanese American women in the Great Depression era in Valerie J. Matsumoto, "Japanese American Women and the Creation of Urban Nisei Culture in the 1930s," in Matsumoto and Allmendinger, *Over the Edge*, 291–306.

61. Arleen de Vera, "The Tapia-Saiki Incident: Interethnic Conflict and Filipino Responses to the Anti-Filipino Exclusion Movement," in Matsumoto and Allmendinger, *Over the Edge*, 201–14. Although it deals primarily with men, see also Sucheta Mazumdar, "Punjabi Agricultural Workers in California," in *Labor Immigration Under Capitalism: Asian Workers in the United States before World War II*, ed. Lucie Cheng and Edna Bonacich (Berkeley: University of California Press, 1984).

62. Karen Isaksen Leonard, *Making Ethnic Choices: California's Punjabi Mexican Americans* (Philadelphia: Temple University Press, 1994).

63. Dawn Bohulano Mabalon, "Beauty Queens, Bomber Pilots and Basketball Players: Second Generation Filipina Americans in Stockton, California, 1930s–1950s," in *Pinay Power: Peminist Critical Theory*, ed. Melinda L. de Jesus (New York: Routledge, 2005), 117–33. See also Dawn Bohulano Mabalon, "Life in Little Manila: Filipinas/os in Stockton, 1917–1927" (PhD dissertation, Stanford

University, 2003). Although much of it lies beyond our time period, see also Dawn Bohulano Mabulon, "Losing Little Manila: Race and Redevelopment in Filipina/o Stockton, California," in *Positively No Filipinos Allowed: Building Communities and Discourse*, ed. Antonio Tiongson, Ricardo Gutierrez, and Edgardo Gutierrez, 57–89 (Philadelphia: Temple University Press, 2006).

64. Freedman, "Separatism as Strategy"; Kathryn Kish Sklar, "Hull House in the 1890s: A Community of Women Reformers," *Signs* 10, no. 4 (1985): 658–777; Linda Kerber, "Separate Spheres, Female Worlds, Woman's Place: The Rhetoric of Women's History," *Journal of American History* 75 (1988–1989): 9–39; Allen F. Davis, *Spearheads for Reform: The Social Settlements and the Progressive Movement, 1890–1914* (New Brunswick NJ: Rutgers University Press, 1994); John P. Rousmanier, "Cultural Hybrid in the Slums: The College Woman and the Settlement House, 1889–1894," *American Quarterly* 22, no. 1 (1970): 45–66; Mina Carson, *Settlement Folk: Social Thought and the American Settlement Movement, 1885–1930* (Chicago: University of Chicago Press, 1990); Mary Jo Deegan, *Jane Addams and the Men of the Chicago School, 1892–1918* (New Brunswick NJ: Transaction Books, 1988).

65. The Russell Sage Foundation's 1911 *Handbook of Settlements* lists sixty-one active settlements west of the Mississippi, including twenty-one in California. Robert A. Woods and Albert J. Kennedy, eds., *Handbook of Settlements* (New York: Arno, 1970). For an architectural exploration of the West Oakland Settlement, see Marta Gutman, "Inside the Institution: The Art and Craft of Settlement Work at the Oakland New Century Club, 1895–1923," in *People, Power, Places: Perspectives in Vernacular Architecture*, ed. Sally McMurry and Annmarie Adams, 248–79 (Knoxville: University of Tennessee Press, 2000). See also Carol Roland, "The California Kindergarten Movement: A Study in Class and Social Feminism" (PhD dissertation, University of California Riverside, 1980).

66. Ruth Hutchinson Crocker, *Social Work and Social Order: The Settlement Movement in Two Industrial Cities, 1889–1930* (Urbana: University of Illinois Press, 1992); Rivka Shpak Lissak, *Pluralism and Progressivism: Hull House and the New Immigrants, 1890–1919* (Chicago: University of Chicago Press, 1989); Judith Ann Troylander, *Professionalism and Social Change: From the Settlement House Movement to Neighborhood Centers, 1886 to the Present* (New York: Columbia University Press, 1984); Elizabeth Lasch-Quinn, *Black Neighbors: Race and the Limits of Reform in the American Settlement House Movement, 1896–1945* (Chapel Hill: University of North Carolina Press, 1993); Howard Jacob Karger, *The Sentinels of Order: A Study of Social Control and the Minneapolis Settlement House Movement, 1915–1950* (New York: University Press of America, 1987).

67. Lucile Eaves, *A History of California Labor Legislation* (Berkeley: University of California Publications in Economics, 1910), 5–6. Both Alexander Saxton and Michael Kazin cite Eaves in their work. Alexander Saxton, *The Indispensable Enemy: Labor and the Anti-Chinese Movement in California* (Berkeley: University of California

Press, 1971); Michael Kazin, "The Great Exception Revisited: Organized Labor and Politics in San Francisco and Los Angeles, 1870–1940," *Pacific Historical Review* 55 (August 1986): 371–402.

68. McGerr, "Political Style and Women's Power," 880.

69. Maureen A. Flanagan, "The City Profitable, the City Livable: Environmental Policy, Gender, and Power in Chicago in the 1910s," *Journal of Urban History* 22 (January 1996), 165; see also Maureen A. Flanagan, "Gender and Urban Reform: The City Club and the Woman's City Club of Chicago in the Progressive Era," *American Historical Review* 95 (October 1990): 1032–50.

70. One of the earliest statements linking the emergence of organized interest groups to the decline of party politics is Samuel P. Hays, "Political Parties and the Community–Society Continuum," in *The American Party Systems: Stages of Political Development*, ed. William Nisbet Chambers, 152–81 (New York: Oxford University Press, 1975). See also Joel H. Silbey, *The American Political Nation, 1838–1893* (Stanford: Stanford University Press, 1991), for a more detailed discussion of nineteenth-century political partisanship.

THE CONTRIBUTORS

Cameron Binkley is the deputy command historian at the Defense Language Institute and Presidio of Monterey, Monterey, California. He was previously a historian with the National Park Service. He received his bachelor's degree from the University of Denver in 1984, a master's degree from the Monterey Institute of International Studies in 1990, and a master's degree in history from San Francisco State University in 2000. He is the author of five books published by the National Park Service and of several articles in scholarly journals.

Robert W. Cherny is a professor of history at San Francisco State University. He received his bachelor's degree from the University of Nebraska in 1965, and his master's degree and PhD from Columbia University in 1967 and 1972. He is the author of several books, chapters in anthologies, and articles in scholarly journals, most dealing with politics in the American West, especially California. He has been an NEH fellow, a Distinguished Fulbright Lecturer at Moscow State University, a Senior Fulbright Scholar at the University of Heidelberg, and a Visiting Research Scholar at the University of Melbourne, and has served as treasurer of the Organization of American Historians and on the council of the American Historical Association, Pacific Coast Branch.

Eunice Eichelberger is retired. She received her bachelor's degree from Stanford University, a law degree from the University of Oregon in 1974, and a master's degree in history from San Francisco State in 2004. She is a member of the California State Bar and the author of many annotations in *American Law Reports*.

Susan Englander is an adjunct in history at City College of San Francisco. She received her master's degree from San Francisco State in 1989, and a PhD in history from UCLA in 1999. She is the author of *Class Coalition and Class Conflict in the California Woman Suffrage Movement, 1907–1912* (1992), the lead editor for *Volume VI: Advocate of the Social Gospel, September 1948-March 1963* of *The Papers of Martin Luther King, Jr.* (2007), a coeditor of the *Martin Luther King, Jr., Encyclopedia* (2008), and the author of articles in scholarly journals.

CONTRIBUTORS

Mildred Nichols Hamilton received her bachelor's degree in journalism from the University of Oklahoma in 1943. Her career included thirty years with the *San Francisco Examiner* as a top feature writer. Always a feminist, she took pride in "liberating" the press box at the University of Oklahoma stadium when she took the seat reserved for the editor of the student newspaper. She later covered national and international conferences on women's rights. In 1955 she received a fellowship for a year in Europe to study the effect of the United Nations; her series on women was nominated for a Pulitzer Prize. After retiring, she earned a master's degree in history from San Francisco State University in 1996. She died a few days after reviewing the page proofs for her chapter here. She was eighty-eight.

Jarrod Harrison is the social studies department chair at Carlmont High School, Belmont, California. He received the California League of High Schools Educator of the Year award for his region in 2009. His bachelor's degree is from California State University, Stanislaus, in 1994, and his master's degree is in history, from San Francisco State University in 1997.

Linda Heidenreich is an associate professor and the chair of women's studies and a member of the graduate faculty in American studies at Washington State University. Her bachelor's degree is from San Francisco State University in 1987 and her PhD is from the University of California, San Diego, in 2000. She is the author of *"This Land Was Mexican Once": Histories of Resistance from Northern California* (2007). Her articles have appeared in the *Journal of Chicana/Latina Studies*, the *Journal of American Ethnic History*, and other scholarly journals.

Sandra L. Henderson is a doctoral candidate in history at the University of Illinois, Urbana–Champaign, where she has been the managing editor of the *Journal of Women's History*. She received her bachelor's degree in 1999 and her master's degree in 2002, both in history, from San Francisco State.

Mark Hopkins received his bachelor's degree from San Francisco State University and is currently a graduate student there.

Teresa Hurley is a senior paralegal at Morrison and Foerster, in San Francisco. She received her bachelor's degree in history from the University of California, Berkeley, in 1988, and her master's degree in history from San Francisco State University in 1995.

CONTRIBUTORS

Mary Ann Irwin teaches in the California community college system, serves on the steering committee of the Coalition for Western Women's History, and is a member of the editorial board of the *Pacific Historical Review*. She received her bachelor's degree from the University of California, Berkeley, in 1980 and her master's degree in history from San Francisco State University in 1995. She has published a number of articles in scholarly journals, is a coeditor of *Women and Gender in the American West* (2004), and a coauthor of *Elusive Eden: A New History of California* (4th ed.). In 2003 she won one of six fellowships presented by the Jewish Women's Archives. She is the recipient of the 1999 Joan Jensen-Darlis Miller Prize from the Coalition for Western Women's History for the best journal article in western women's history for the article on which her chapter in this collection is based.

Michelle Kleehammer is a doctoral candidate and instructor in history at the University of Illinois, Urbana–Champaign. She received her bachelor's degree from SUNY College at Geneseo in 1998 and her master's degree from San Francisco State in 2002. She is the recipient of a Science, Technology, and Society grant from the National Science Foundation.

Rebecca J. Mead is an associate professor of history at Northern Michigan University. She received her BS in psychology from the University of New Mexico in 1978, her master's degree in history from San Francisco State in 1991, and her PhD from UCLA in 1999. She is the author of *How the Vote Was Won: Woman Suffrage in the Western United States, 1868–1914* (2004). Her articles have appeared in the *Pacific Historical Review* and other journals and anthologies.

Joshua Paddison is an American Council of Learned Societies new faculty fellow at Indiana University, where he teaches courses on comparative race and ethnicity, religion, and the American West. He received his bachelor's degree in journalism from the University of Oregon in 1996, his master's degree in history from San Francisco State University in 2001, and his PhD in history from UCLA in 2008. He is the editor of *A World Transformed: Firsthand Accounts of California before the Gold Rush* (1999). He also received the Western History Association's 2010 Arrington-Prucha Prize for the best article on the history of religion in the American West.

Ann Marie Wilson is a college fellow and lecturer on history at Harvard University, where she teaches courses on nineteenth-century U.S. history, transnational social movements, and women's and gender history. She received her bachelor's degree in interdisciplinary social science from the University of Michigan in 1994, her master's degree in history from San Francisco State University in 2003, and her PhD in history from Harvard in 2010. She is the recipient of Phi Alpha Theta's George P. Hammond Prize for the paper on which her article in this collection is based. She is also the recipient of the 2010 Fischel-Calhoun Prize of the Society for Historians of the Gilded Age and Progressive Era.

INDEX

Page numbers in italic indicate illustrations

activism. *See* bird-protection movement; conservation; consumer activism; environmental movement; municipal activism; political activism
Addams, Jane, 99, 101, 107, 178, 242, 312, 324. *See also* Hull House
Adkins v. Children's Hospital, 280
African Americans: charity work of, 344–45; civil rights efforts of, 343, 361n28; kindergartens for, 83; political interests of, 342–45, 347–48; population in California, xv, 75n38, 342–43; and segregation of women's clubs, 178–79; teacher-training for, 83; use of legal system, 342–43
age-of-consent laws, 195, 238, 323
Alameda CA, 183
Alameda County, 177, 181, 187, 188, 191–95
Alameda District Federation of Women's Clubs (ADFWC), 181, 190, 196
Albee, Edith S., 162
Albee, George B., 161–62
Albrier, Mary Frances, 178–79
alcohol: Bole Maru doctrines on, 340; comparative cost of, 67; immigrant and working-class attitudes toward, 214–16, 228; Isidora Filomena Solano on, 11; sales at dance halls, 289, 290, 292–95, 303, 304n16; sales in Barbary Coast, 253; sales in California, 190–91, 210, 214–16, 230n4; Twentieth Century Club on prohibition of, 176. *See also* business interests; prohibition; saloons; temperance; Woman's Christian Temperance Union (WCTU)
Allan, Evelyn Wight, 325
Allen, Joel A., 126
All Quiet on the Western Front (Remarque), 198
Alms House, 28, 41, 42, 45–49, 47
American Alliance for Labor and Democracy, 329
American Civil Liberties Bureau, 336n83. *See also* American Union against Militarism
American Civil Liberties Union (ACLU), 336n83. *See also* American Union against Militarism
American Federation of Labor (AFL), 264, 320, 325
American Museum of Natural History, 163
American Neutral Conference Committee, 324
American Ornithologists' Union, 128, 137
American Patriots Association, 328
American Social Hygiene Association, 253
American Union against Militarism, 324, 328, 336n83
American University, 84
Anderson, John, 244
Angell, Frank, 100
Antelope Valley CA, 312
"Anthony Amendment" (1878), 211, 231n12
Anthony, Susan B., 91, 209, 210, 216
Anthracite Coal Strike of 1902, 108
Anti-Saloon League, 248, 253
Apperson, Drucilla Whitemire, 78, 79
Apperson, Elbert, 78
Apperson, Randolph Walker, 78, 79
apprenticeships, 272, 274
Arballo, Maria Feliciana, 340
Arbor Day, 130, 132, 137, 141, 321
Arizona, 323
Armenians, 192
Armer, Elizabeth, 41
Armitage, Kevin C., 127
arms limitation, 309–10, 318–21, 329. *See also* peace
articles. *See* literature
Asbury, Herbert, 289
Ashe, Elizabeth, 115
Asians, xv, 64, 65, 317, 342–44, 348–49, 351–52. *See also* Chinese; Japanese; Koreans; South Asians
Associated Charities of San Francisco, 100, 102

INDEX

Association of Collegiate Alumnae, 88–89, 100, 110, 113
Astor, Lady, 320
Auburn CA, 342
Audubon, John James, 128
Audubon Magazine, 146n27
"Audu-bonnet," 139
Audubon societies: Catherine Hittell in, 132; formation in California, 134, 143; gender of organizers, 135; literature about birds, 126; membership of, 146n27; motives for bird-protection, 125; role in protective legislation, 123–24; spread through United States, 133, 143; teachers in, 134. *See also* Berkeley Audubon Society; California Audubon Society (CAS); Junior Audubon Society; Los Angeles Audubon Society; Santa Cruz Audubon Society
The Auk, 133
"Australian" ballots, 70

Bacon Library, 87
Baker, Newton, 317
Baker, Paula, xi, 175, 339
Baldwin Bird Law, 137–38
Baldwin, Roger, 336n83
ballots, 69–70, 72, 179, 185. *See also* electoral politics
Bancroft, Hubert H., 1, 4, 16–18, 24n80. *See also* Cerruti, Henry
Barbary Coast (Asbury), 289
Barbary Coast (San Francisco), 254; alcohol sales restrictions in, 292, 294, 304n16; campaign to clean up, 302; campaign to close dance halls in, 290, 291; kindergarten in, 81; and red-light abatement bill, 243, 253, 289. *See also* business interests; dance halls; San Francisco CA
Barrow, Mark V., Jr., 126
Barry, Annie Little, 181–83, 185, 202
Bary, Helen Valeska, 52n17, 199, 271, 273
Bean, Walton, 313
Bear Flag Revolt, 1–2, 5–6, 14–15, 17–18
Beasley, Delilah Leontium, 345
Beban, Dominick, 243–44
Becoming Citizens (Gullett), xiii–xiv
Beebe, Rose Marie, 2
Belgians, 192, 193

benevolent societies. *See* charitable organizations
Berkeley Audubon Society, 132
Berkeley Board of Education, 187
Berkeley Board of Health, 195
Berkeley CA: alcohol sales restrictions in, 190–91; A. L. Saylor in, 198–200; Audubon societies in, 132, 134, 141; charter (1909), 186–87; civic art commission in, 187; "Diamond Jubilee," 202; dressmaker trade in, 87; election of Socialist mayor, 188; Hearst Hall in, 87; history of, 202; Jane Addams's visit to, 99; racial composition of, 178–79; rejection of partisanship in, 188–89; unity of clubwomen in, 183; wartime work in, 192–94, 198; WCTU Congress of Reform in, 213. *See also* Twentieth Century Club of Berkeley (TCC)
Berkeley Daily Gazette, 187, 202
Berkeley Municipal Hospital, 195
Berkeley Political Equality Society, 131
Berkeley Women's City Club, 131, 200
Berkeley Women Workers of the Liberty Loan, 198
Berlin, 81
Berryessa, Remijio, 10
Bertola, Mariana, 293, 299
Bicknell, Carrie Elizabeth Fargo (Mrs. F. T.), 140, 141
Big Basin, 158–61, 159, 166
Billings, Frederick, 27, 35
Binkley, Cameron, 346
Bird, Mrs. Charles Sumner, 319
Bird Day, 127, 130, 132, 137, 141, 321
Bird-Lore, 125, 133, 134, 137
bird-protection movement: anthropomorphization of birds in, 127–28, 131; Audubon societies' role in, 127–43; clubwomen in, 123–24, 128–30, 138, 142–43; for community, 132; comparison to women's issues, 127–28, 131; grassroots efforts in, 123, 124, 138, 142–44; literature on, 126–28; motives for, 125; for non-game birds, 136; in political sphere, 131, 135; public interest in, 137–42; women's approach to, 347; during World War I, 140. *See also* conservation; environmental movement

The Bird's Convention (Myers), 127–28
birds of paradise, 125, 137
Birney, Alice, 85
blackbirds, 125, 136
Blair, Karen, 82, 211, 347
Bliss, Rev. W. D. P., 103
"Bloody Tuesday," 217
Blue Triangles, 348
boardinghouses, 37, 59, 62, 68. *See also* housing
Board of Police Commissioners: and dance hall closures, 289, 299–301, 303; dance hall permits issued by, 296–98; on dance hall regulations, 302; hearing on cleanup of San Francisco vice districts, 294; reshaping of dance hall culture, 295; responsibility for vice districts, 291–92; and supervision of dance halls, 296–97
Board of Supervisors, 296–97
Boegle, Fred, 276
Bohemian Club, 100
Bohnett, Lewis D., 241–42, 245–49. *See also* Grant-Bohnett bill
Bole Maru (Dream Dance) cult, 340
Booker T. Washington Community Center, 299, 348
books. *See* literature
Bordin, Ruth, 346
Boring, Jesse, 31, 53n25
Boston Herald, 92–93
Boston MA, 99, 100, 115, 128, 228, 353
Bouchard, Hippolyte de, 13
Bouvier, Virginia, 339
Bowen, Louise deKoven, 77, 344
boxing, 297, 298
Boynton, Albert, 244–47, 258n23
Bragg, Susan, 345
Braitman, Jacqueline, 312
Breckinridge, Sophonisba, 105
Brennan, James, 253
Brooks, Adele, 79
brothels, xiii, xvii, 241, 246, 253–57, 289, 290. *See also* prostitution; red-light injunction and abatement act
Brothers of the Order of St. Dominic, 41
Brown, Charlotte, 361n26
Brown, Elsa Barkley, 345
Browne, Mary Frank (Mrs. P. D.), 62–64, 66, 70

Brown (Missourian), 342
Bryant, Edward, 244
Budapest, 323, 324, 325
Buddhist Japanese women, 350
Buddhist Women's Association (Sacramento), 350
Budd, James H., 77, 88
Buford Kitchengarten, 100, 117n14
Building Trades Council (San Francisco), 215, 225–27, 233n43, 300
Bull Creek Flat, 165, 167
Burchard, George, 161–62
Burdette, Clara Bradley, 151–52, 154, 167, 168
Bureau of the Biological Survey, 136
business interests: and alcohol sales restrictions, 191, 214–16; and bird-protection movement, 123, 139, 347; and cleanup of San Francisco vice districts, 293, 298–99; clubwomen's disinterest in, 153–54; and conservation, 151, 153, 155, 156, 158, 166; and labor legislation, 110, 112, 114; and minimum-wage law, 271–72, 276, 277, 281, 282; on San Francisco waterfront, 37–40; as special interest groups, 355; WCTU's influence on, 72. *See also* alcohol; Barbary Coast (San Francisco); canning companies; dance halls; economy; millinery trade; prostitution; wine industry
"business unionism," 107. *See also* unionists
Butler, Edwin, 244, 245
Butterfield, Ada, 84

Cahn, Frances, 52n17
Calaveras "Big Trees," 155–58, 160, 166
Calderwood, Florence, 299–300
Calhoun, Patrick, 216–17, 235n67
California: defined as "American," 4–5; demography of, xiv–xv; effect of women's activism in, 143–44; historical understanding of politics in, 3; mining in, 79; north-south division of, xv, xvi, 267, 277, 358n13; as subject of study, xi–xii, xiv; women's participation in public policy in, xiii, xvii, 341; women's representation in, 237
California Association of Colored Women's Clubs, 348, 355

California Audubon Society (CAS): *Annual Report* (1907), 134–36; California Club as liaison of, 131; H. W. Myers as president of, 127; legislative victories of, 134–40; M. M. Keith's affiliation with, 131; mobilization of public, 138–42; school secretary position in, 141; structure of, 129–30; success of, 133–34. *See also* Audubon societies
California Bureau of Information and Registration of the National League for Woman's Service, 316
California Bureau of Labor Statistics, 110–11, 244, 268, 313
California Civic League, 167, 238–39, 241, 242, 244, 247, 249–51, 253
California Club: affiliation with GFWC, 231n11; and bird-protection movement, 123, 130–32, 136, 138; on child labor, 113; cleanup of North Beach, 292; and dance hall closures, 299; foundation and leadership of, 152; and graft prosecutions, 222, 223; political focus and influence of, xiii, 110, 346; promotion of arts and literature, 211; and redwoods campaign, 155–58, 160, 166, 168, 347; on saloon license fees, 213; and South Park Settlement, 104, 105; suffrage activities of, 210–11, 231n13. *See also* San Francisco CA; San Francisco Center
California Colored Conventions, 345
California Communist Party, 260n37
California Cotton Mills, 275
California Division of Industrial Welfare, 282
California Equal Suffrage Amendment, 187–88. *See also* suffrage
California Equal Suffrage Association (CESA), 131, 132, 210, 211, 213, 224, 323. *See also* California Woman Suffrage Association
California Federation of Women's Clubs (CFWC): and bird-protection movement, 130, 132, 135, 140, 141; creation and leadership of, 151–52; Eleventh Annual Convention of, 162; endorsement of suffrage, 231n13; and graft prosecutions, 222; legislative agenda of, 237–40; motto of, 181, 198; parliamentary procedures in, 185; political power through, 152; and redwoods campaign, 157, 167–69, 346–47; segregation in, 178; at Serbian relief drive, 192; and South Park Settlement, 105; and Twentieth Century Club, 181, 196, 200–201; widespread involvement of, xiii; and Women's Legislative Council, 189–90; and working-class women, 268
California Immigration and Housing Commission, 315, 318
California League of Women Voters, 296
California legislature: authorization of State Council of Defense, 316; and bird-protection movement, 132, 135–38, 143; charitable appropriations of, 32; on child labor legislation, 112; Chinese women's lobbying of, 350; Committees on Public Morals, 242, 243; Ladies' Seaman's Friend Society appeal to, 38 39; on minimum wage, 269, 270, 281; and organized labor, 110, 263; on P. A. Hearst's death, 92; and red-light abatement bill, 241–57; and redwood protection, 156, 157, 160–61, 166, 167; on saloon license fees, 214; San Francisco Center's lobbying of, 290; suffrage bill before, 213; on temperance instruction law, 68; on testimony ban, 342, 360n22; on University of California, 88; WCTU's petitioning of, 69, 71; women's legislative agenda before, 189–90, 255, 347; Women's Legislative Council's following of, 239; working-class women before, 228, 229, 265–66. *See also* California State Assembly; California State Senate; legislation; Sacramento CA
California Manufacturers Association (CMA), 276
Californianas/os: definition of, xiv–xv, 357n9; education of, 16; engendered space of, 15; European Americans' description of, 6, 17, 18; Isidora Filomena Solano on history and culture of, 10–12; lifeways of, 13–14; passage of histories to children, 17; preservation of culture, 5; resistance strategies of, 7, 18–19; scholarship on, 3, 339–42;

testimonios of, 2, 4–5; theft from, 1, 9–10, 17–18. *See also* Chicanas; Latinas/os; Mexicans; Spaniards
California Police Gazette, 42
California State Federation of Labor (CFL), 97, 119n49, 213, 228, 269
California Society for the Prevention of Cruelty to Children (CSPCC), 41–42
California State Assembly: A. L. Saylor in, 179–80, 196, 198–99, 347; passage of suffrage amendment, 188; Public Morals Committee of, 242, 243, 245, 247; Twentieth Century Club's appeals to, 182. *See also* California legislature
California State Board of Health, 240
California State Department of Social Welfare, 199
California State Law Enforcement and Protective League, 255
California State Marine Hospital, 49, 51n6
California State Normal School, 134
California State Reform School at Whittier, 56n76
California State Senate, 240, 242–45. *See also* California legislature
California State Senate Bill no. 46, 240
California State Senate Committee on Rules, 243
California State Senate Judiciary Committee, 245
California State Senate Public Morals Committee, 242–44
California Suffrage Association, 324, 327
California Supreme Court, 112, 361n28
California v. Whitney, 249, 260n37
California Woman Suffrage Association, 131, 209, 210. *See also* California Equal Suffrage Association (CESA)
California Women's Heney Club, 223–24, 226
Callahan, Charles B., 247
Canada, 136, 196
canning companies, 110, 112, 272–73. *See also* business interests
Cannon, "Uncle" Joe, 156
Caraher, Reverend Terence, 249, 291–93, 304n16
Carlisle, Elinor, 187, 200, 202
Carmen's Union, 216–20, 235n67

Carnegie, Andrew, 198
Carnegie Foundation, 115
Carquin people, 8
Carrol, Sarah, 360n22
Casas, Maria Raquel, 340
Casey, Michael, 235n67
Cassidy, George, 244
Castañeda, Antonia, 3, 18, 340
Castro, Don Angel, 15
Cathedral Hill, 35
Catholic Laborers Union Association, 31
Catholic Professional Women's Club, 299
Catholics: in Century Club, 296; charitable donations from, 31, 32; and cleanup of San Francisco vice districts, 293; Indians as, 8, 9; and management of San Francisco City Hospital, 44; prejudice against immigrants, 64; social welfare organizations and institutions of, 41–47. *See also* religion; Roman Catholic Sisters of Mercy
Catt, Carrie Chapman, 210, 327, 331
censorship, 63, 176, 190, 318, 346
Central Methodist Church (San Francisco), 253
Century Club, 90, 211, 230n11, 296
Cerruti, Henry, 1–2, 4, 7, 13–14. *See also* Bancroft, Hubert H.
CFWC. *See* California Federation of Women's Clubs (CFWC)
Chamberlain, J. P., 112
Chan, Sucheng, 349
Chapin, Mrs. Lou V., 155
Chapman, Frank, 125–26, 129, 130
charitable organizations: for African Americans, 344–45, 347–48; for Asians, 348–49; and Berkeley City Charter, 187; of Buddhist Japanese women, 350; for Chinese, 349; comparison to women, 27; efficiency of woman-run, 46–49; for Filipinas/os, 352; in Gold Rush San Francisco, 29, 52n15, 341; near South Park Settlement, 102; political economy of, 27–28, 341; private in San Francisco, 28–30, 41–50, 344; scholarship on, 100, 341, 358n16; significance in women's political action, xiii; South Park Settlement's cooperation with, 101; support for women's, xvii, 27, 30–31, 34, 40–41;

377

charitable organizations (cont.) women's entry into public sphere through, 341, 344. See also club movement; philanthropy; social welfare services; voluntarism
Chávez-Garciá, Miroslava, 3
Chicago Herald, 82
Chicago IL: clubwomen in, 202; K. P. Edson in, 312; Lucile Eaves in, 105; National Women's Trade Union League Convention in, 227; nineteenth ward in, 99, 102; People's Council meeting in, 329; settlement movement in, 99, 353; suffragists in, 228; women's philanthropy in, 344
Chicanas, 3, 4, 18, 357n9. See also Californianas/os; Latinas/os
Chico CA, 134
child-care centers, 41, 195
child labor: Alice Park on, 321; legislation on, 98–99, 110–14, 332n3, 347; Lucile Eaves on, 353; relationship with social scientists and settlement movement, xiii; Twentieth Century Club on, 180, 186, 199; WCTU on, 59, 69, 346; Western women on, 195. See also children
children: Alice Park's concern for, 321; and bird-protection movement, 123, 130, 140–43; of Bole Maru, 340; as clubwomen's concern, 151, 346; and conservation, 138, 154; and graft prosecutions, 223; K. P. Edson's concern for, 310, 313; legislation to benefit, 238–40, 248, 267; Lucile Eaves's reports on, 121n81; P. A. Hearst's interest in, 78, 80–81, 91–92; as philanthropic interest, 344; protection from vice of dance halls, 292, 295; San Francisco Center's focus on, 290; San Francisco Settlement's focus on, 115; social welfare services for, 27, 29–30, 32–33, 35–36, 41–43, 45–46, 49–50, 341; at South Park Settlement, 103; Twentieth Century Club's concern for, 200; wages and hours of, 244; WCTU on, 62, 63, 68, 72; on women's legislative agenda, 189, 238, 240. See also child labor; joint guardianship; juveniles; kindergartens; orphans and orphanages; public schools

Children of Fate (Rutledge), 330
Children's Hospital, 84
Children's Hospital, Adkins v., 280
Children's Hospital and Training School for Nurses, 42
China, 349, 350
Chinatown, 102, 104, 253, 350. See also Chinese
Chinese: in Berkeley, 178; competition for work, 353; Edward Ross on, 106; and labor movement, 109–13; merchant families, 362n29; political focus of, 348, 349; population in California, xv, 342; population in United States, 350–51; resistance to exclusion, 343, 361n29; WCTU on treatment of, 64. See also Asians; Chinatown
Chinese Exclusion Act (1882), 361n29
Chinese Women's Jeleab (Self-Reliance) Association, 349
Chiructos, 8, 10
cholera epidemic of 1850, 29, 30, 44
Choy, Bong-Youn, 349
Christian charity, 49
Christian doctrine, 223
Christian Pacifists, 329
Chun Ah Ngon, 362n29
Chung, Margaret Jessie, 351
churches, 69, 190–91, 342. See also clergy; religion; religious organizations; specific churches
Churchill, Mrs. S. J., 62, 69
Citizen Bird (Wright), 127
citizenship: of African Americans, 345; of birds, 127–28; and class and race divisions, xvii; and suffrage, xiv–xv, 195, 203, 237; of Twentieth Century Club members, 181, 186, 194–98, 200–203. See also civitas
Citizens' League for Justice (CLJ), 213, 222–24
City Federation of Women's Clubs, 297
"The City Profitable, the City Livable" (Flanagan), 354
Civic League of Improvement Clubs, 294, 296, 298
civic work. See civitas
Civilian Advisory Commission, 315–16
civil rights, 309, 310, 331, 340, 344–45, 354

INDEX

Civil Rights Act, 361n24
civil service reform, 238, 240, 332n3
Civil War, 312
civitas, 176, 177, 183, 187, 189, 191–92, 194, 199–203. *See also* citizenship; community services; municipal activism
Claremont Hotel, 191
Clark, Mrs. O. P., 240
class: and charity work, 31, 53n26, 341, 344; differences among clubwomen, 353; divisions in California, xii, xvi, xvii; and minimum-wage law, xiv, 113, 114, 268–70, 279, 280, 353; and red-light abatement bill, 256; reduction of conflicts through conservation, 154–55; role in dance hall regulation, 303; and San Francisco graft prosecutions, 220–24; and streetcar strike, 219–20; and suffrage, xiii–xiv, 113, 211–12, 216, 226–29, 353–54; and temperance movement, 60–61; and Twentieth Century Club membership, 178–79, 181; unification in San Francisco settlement, 101–4, 113. *See also* elite women; middle-class women; unionists; working class; working-class women
Clear Lake, 5
clergy, 31, 53n25, 248, 249, 290, 291. *See also* churches; religion; religious organizations
Cleveland, Frances, 82, 85
Cleveland OH, 59
"closed" dance halls, 290, 294–97, 303. *See also* dance halls
club movement, xiii, 78, 151–52. *See also* charitable organizations; clubwomen
The Clubwoman as Feminist (Blair), 211, 347
Club Woman's Franchise League, 224
clubwomen: on alcohol sales restrictions, 191; A. L. Saylor's praise of, 198–99; A. L. Saylor's work with after legislative term, 200; on Berkeley City Charter, 186–87; in bird-protection movement, 123–24, 128–30, 135, 136, 138, 142–43; in Chicago, 202; and child labor legislation campaign, 112–13; in Citizens League for Justice, 222; and cleanup of San Francisco vice districts, 293, 298, 299; comparison to abolitionist women, 182; comparison to South Park Settlement women, 103; comparison to women philanthropists, 82; culture of, 179, 192; as dance hall supervisors, 296, 300, 302, 303; disinterest in politics, 153; Dorothea Moore's involvement with, 104–5, 110; gender ideology of, 152–54; in Humboldt County, 161–65; interest in nature, 153, 154; interests of minority, 342–45, 347–55; *Labor Clarion* on, 97–98; leadership of campaign against dance halls, 290–91; legislative agenda of, 237–40; and minimum wage, 114, 277–78, 281; P. A. Hearst's association with, 90–91; political views of, 154–55, 199, 202–3; public procedures of, 185; in redwoods campaign, 159, 160, 166–69; reform efforts of, 345–47; resistance to partisanship, 176; role in red-light abatement act, 190, 238, 241–57, 289; segregation in Berkeley, 178–79; on suffrage, xiv, 153, 170n8, 187–89, 210–13, 224, 231n13; types of, 180–81; and unemployed dance hall workers, 294; unity of California, 151–52, 183; wartime work of, 192–94. *See also* club movement; elite women; lady managers; middle-class women; *specific clubs*
Coast Miwok, 8
Coast Seamen's Journal, 110, 225
Coffin, Lillian Harris, 211, 212, 213, 222, 224
Colby, Mrs. William, 190
Coleman, Willi, 344, 345, 347
College Settlement Association, 100
Collier's magazine, 331
colonization, 3, 6, 7, 13, 16
Colored Women's Federation, 299, 348
Columbia Kindergarten Association, 83
Columbia University, 99, 114
Coman, Katherine, 100, 110
Committee of Vigilance, 217
Committee on Far Eastern Questions and Pacific Questions, 320
Committee on Women in Industry for California, 316
Commonwealth Club, 294
Community Property measure, 181–82
community services, 50, 153–56, 177, 182–84, 191–92, 344–45, 352. *See also*

379

community services (cont.)
  civitas; municipal activism; social welfare services
Condor magazine, 129, 130
Conference on the Limitation of Armament, 309–10, 318–21
Congdon, Mrs. M. E., 70
Congress of Reform in Berkeley, 213
conscientious objectors, 328–30, 336n83. *See also* military
conservation: allying of groups in California, 133; definition of, 153; discussion at GFWC convention, 154; division of movement after damming in Yosemite, 163; as feature of progressivism, 168–69; ideology in bird-protection movement, 138, 142; legislation on, 332n3; political power of, 166–69; reclamation as component of, 155, 170n13; surge of activism, 126; of Twentieth Century Club, 194, 200, 202; women's involvement in California, 142–44, 155–69, 238. *See also* bird-protection movement; environmental movement; food-conservation program; nature preservation; redwoods; water conservation
Conservation Day, 141. *See also* Arbor Day; Bird Day
consumer activism, 98, 211, 313
Consumers' League, 110, 139
Coolidge, Mary Roberts Smith, 106, 114, 241, 247, 251
Cooper Ornithological Club, 128, 129, 130
Cooper, Sarah B., 81
Cornelius, Richard, 235n67
Corona CA, 134
corporate welfare strategy, 271
cost of living, 270, 271, 273, 276, 277
Cott, Nancy, 91–92, 189, 192, 239
Council of Jewish Women, 299
Council of National Defense, 315–16
Council of the Save the Redwoods League, 167
Council on International Relations, 351
counternarratives. *See* testimonios
Craft, Mabel, 178
crime. *See* vice and crime
Crocker, Charles, 81
Crocker, Mary, 81

Crocker, Ruth Hutchinson, 353
Crowley, Tim J., 242
Cuban revolution, 2
Culver, Mrs. L. M., 300
Cumberland Presbyterian Church, 78, 79
Cumberson, Frances (Mrs. C. E.), 325

dairies. *See* pure milk campaign
Dakin, Susanna Bryant, 340
dance halls: after Howard Street incident, 297–98; Anti-Saloon League's investigation of, 253; clubwomen's campaign against, xiii, xvii, 289–91; demand for closure of, 299–300; distinction between commercial and noncommercial, 290; regulation of, 302, 346; restrictions on alcohol sales in, 292–94; sense of community in, 290; supervision of, 291, 294–97, 299, 300. *See also* Barbary Coast (San Francisco); business interests; dancing; moral reform
dancing, 289, 290, 292, 294, 304n16. *See also* dance halls
Dashaway Association, 61
Daughters of California Pioneers Society, 222
Davis, Katherine Bement, 105
Day, Clive, 103
Deane, C. T., 34, 54n43
death penalty, 179–80, 199, 321, 347
Decker, Sarah Platt, 151
decolonial imaginary, 3, 7. *See also* colonization
Democratic Party, 49, 80, 226, 229, 246–47, 314
department stores, 271
de Vries, Marion, 156
Dewey, John, 105
Dickstein Nationality Bill, 350
Dinnan, Jeremiah, 217
direct primary law, 332n3
discrimination, 343, 345, 348, 354, 361n28
Disloyal Mothers and Scurrilous Citizens (Kennedy), 328
district attorneys, 246, 249
District of Columbia, 280
Division of Industrial Welfare. *See* California Division of Industrial Welfare

divorce laws, 238, 240. *See also* marriage
Dohrman, Frederick W., 103
Dohrmann, A. B. C., 271, 276
domesticity: and bird-protection movement, 124, 127, 139; class differences over, 263; of clubwomen, 153; in conservation movement, 138, 155, 168; education in, 117n14; K. P. Edson's concerns about, 310; of middle-class women's reform efforts, 346; program at University of California, 87; Twentieth Century Club on, 193–94, 200; of WCTU, 60, 62–63, 70, 71. *See also* home; maternalism; motherhood
domestic workers, 32, 301
Donahue, James, 31
dope selling, 295, 296
Dorr, Sara J., 247–49, 255
Dorsey, Kurk, 136, 140
Doughty, Robin W., 126
draft law, 328, 329. *See also* military
Drury, Newton B., 163–64, 167
Dry State campaign, 251
Dublin, 336n89
Duisburg, Germany, 336n89
"Dungeons in America" (Park), 330
Dunlap, Thomas, 126
Durand, E. Dana, 106
Dutcher, William, 141
Dyerville Flat, 165, 167

earthquake (1868), 39, 41
earthquake (1906), 49, 114, 115, 182–83, 216, 289, 322
Eaton, A. B., 30
Eaves, Anna Ruth, 105
Eaves, Lucile, 108; background and career of, 98–99, 105–6, 115; on child labor, 110–12; collaboration with labor organizations, 107–10, 113–14; departure from South Park Settlement, 114; dissertation of, 99; in political sphere, 105–7, 110, 111, 115; praise of, 97–98; reports on working women and children, 121n81; scholarship on, 353. *See also* South Park Settlement
Ebell Club, 151, 167
Economic Consequences of the Peace (Keynes), 318
economy: addressed at South Park Settlement, 103, 107; and cleanup of San Francisco vice districts, 293; effect of Sailors' Home on San Francisco, 37–40; effect on charitable organizations, 33; and minimum-wage law, 273, 276; reform through conservation, 168; of San Francisco social welfare services, 43–50; and wine industry in California, 69. *See also* business interests; poverty
Edson, Charles, 312, 331
Edson, Katherine Philips, 311; on arms limitation, 318–21; attempt to balance interests, 271–73; background of, 310–21; comparison to Alice Park, 330; concern about women, 310, 313, 319, 331; decline of authority of, 281–82; as food commissioner, 317; on government repression, 318, 331; investigation of women's wages, 268–69; leadership of Industrial Welfare Commission, 263–64; masculine qualities of, 312, 314–15, 330–31; on milk regulation, 240; patriotism of, 309; political activism of, xiii; progressivism of, 310–12, 314–15; and red-light abatement bill, 244, 247, 248; on reduction of minimum wage, 276–80; relationship with A. B. C. Dohrmann, 271; wartime commission work of, 315–21; on West's interest in European matters, 314; on working women's well-being, 310, 313, 317–18, 320–21
education: about prostitution, 251; at African American women's clubs, 347; Alice Park on, 321–22, 325; and bird-protection movement, 123, 124, 126–27, 134–35, 137, 139–40, 143, 347; of Bole Maru children, 340; California board of, 190; at Chinese women's clubs, 349; compulsory law for, 110–11, 113; on conservation, 154; in labor movement, 107, 109; in middle-class white women's political activism, 354; P. A. Hearst's devotion to, 77–79, 81, 83–88, 90; on political issues, 239; San Francisco Center on, 290; and South Park Settlement, 101, 106; Twentieth Century Club's interest in, 193; WCTU's involvement in, 59, 68, 69, 72; of

381

education (cont.)
  women in Alta California, 16; women philanthropists' interest in, 344; on women's legislative agenda, 238, 240; women's political, 239. See also kindergartens; public schools; scholarships; specific colleges and universities; teachers
Egan, Eleanor Franklin, 319–20
egrets, 125, 137
Eichelberger, Eunice, 350
Eighteenth Amendment. See Prohibition
eight-hour work day: in canning industry, 272; employers' attitudes toward, 271; K. P. Edson on, 315; legislation under Hiram Johnson, 332n3; WCTU's promotion of, 59; Western women on, 195; for women's protection, 263, 265, 267, 274, 275, 282
elderly, 180, 199, 272, 332n3, 347
electoral politics, xiii–xiv, 340. See also ballots
Electrical Linemen's Union, 233n41
elite women: charitable activities in San Francisco, 100; in club movement, 153, 181; concerns of, 345–56; European travel of, 80; philanthropy of, 77–78, 81, 344; protection of children and redwoods, 152; in settlement movement, 109; in Town and Gown, 177. See also class; clubwomen
Elliot, Ellen Coit, 325
Elwood (Indiana) Public Library, 198
Emanu-El Sisterhood Polyclinic, 84
Emergency Peace Federation, 324
Emerson, Ralph Waldo, 154
employers' liability, 238, 332n3
Employers' Liability Act, 332n3
employment, 32, 37, 39, 275. See also minimum wage; unemployment; working class; working-class women
Emporium department store, 271
Enewah lodge, 87
England. See Great Britain
Englander, Susan, 113, 353
English language, 1–2, 5, 18, 344, 350. See also language
environmental activism. See bird-protection movement
environmental movement, xiii, 143–44, 237. See also bird-protection movement; conservation; redwoods

Episcopal Mission of the Good Samaritan, 102
equal guardianship. See joint guardianship
Espionage Act, 328
Ethington, Philip J., 103
ethnicity, xii, 29, 62, 220–24, 341, 352. See also immigrant communities; immigration
Eureka CA, 161
Eureka Chamber of Commerce, 161–62
European Americans: to California during Gold Rush, 341; Californianas' resistance to, 4–5; exploitation of indigenous peoples, 11–12; immigration of, xvi; testimonios on arrival of, 13–15; treatment of Californianas and Native Americans, 1, 9–10, 18; on woman's experiences, 339. See also mestizos; Osos; whites

Fanny Jackson Coppin Club, 347
Fargo ND, 329
farmers, 134, 136, 137, 139–40, 317–18
feather trade. See millinery trade
Federated Courier, 135
Federation of Women's Clubs, 249, 300
Fellowship of Reconciliation, 329
feminism, 18, 59–60, 192, 239, 264, 283, 331, 347. See also womanhood
Ferguson bill, 190–91
"Festival of Nations," 351
Fetter, Frank, 104, 106
Fickert, Charles, 224
Field, Sara Bard, 188–89
Filipinas/os, 351–52
Finn, Thomas, 244, 246
fire (1906), 49, 114, 182–83, 216, 289, 323
Fisher, Eleanor, 301
Flamming, Douglas, 348
Flanagan, Maureen, 201–2, 354
Flynn, Elizabeth Gurley, 229
Folsom prison, 186, 193
Foner, Eric, 181
food-conservation program, 152, 193, 194. See also conservation
Ford, Henry, 325–26
Ford Neutral Conference, 326
Ford Peace Ship Expedition, 309, 324–26, 328, 329

382

Ford, Tirey, 221
forestry, 154, 155, 162. *See also* nature preservation; redwoods
Forty-First District Suffrage Club, 210
Foster, Margaret, 222
Frances Willard Junior High School, 206n66
"Frank Chapman and His Legion of Women" (cartoon), 129, 130
Frankfurter, Felix, 317
Franklin County MO, 78
fraternal organizations, 29. *See also* men's civic organizations
Freedman, Estelle, 353
Frémont, John C., 1, 12, 14, 15, 17–18
French, 192, 193
French, Rose Morgan, 324
French, Mrs. Will, 227
Fresno CA, 134
Fresno Republican, 249
Friday Morning Club, xiii, 240, 312–13, 333n11; and Committee on Public Health, 240, 313. *See also* Los Angeles CA
Frobel, Friedrich, 81
fujinkai, 350
fund-raising, 38–40, 344, 349, 351, 352
Furuseth, Andrew, 235n67

Gabrieleños, 340, 356n6
Gage, Henry T., 154–55
Gamage, Mary H., 211, 222, 224
Gamber, Wendy, 125
gambling, 211, 340
game laws, 134–37. *See also* hunting
Gandier, D. M., 248
garbage collection, 193, 195
Gardner, Gilson, 314
garment industry. *See* United Garment Workers' Union (UGW)
Garrett, Mary, 77
Garrison, C. K., 32
Garvanza CA, 134
gas and electric service, 221
Gates, Lee C., 244, 245
Gee See, 362n29
gender ideology: in Bear Flag Revolt accounts, 6; in bird-protection movement, 124–25, 127, 129–30, 134–35, 138, 143; in California civil rights, 345; in California politics, xii, 340–41; and charitable organizations, 29, 34, 44–46, 48, 341, 344; and conservation, 152–55, 168, 169; of K. P. Edson's and A. Park's activism, 330–32; in labor movement, 264–65; in San Francisco's political structure, 28; and temperance movement, 59–61, 63; in testimonios, 14–17; in Twentieth Century Club, 181, 184, 200; of Wappo-speaking peoples, 8–9; and wartime activism, 310; and woman suffrage, 71–72; in women's political activism, 353–54. *See also* men; womanhood
"Gender, Race, and Culture" (Castañeda), 340
General Federation of Women's Clubs (GFWC): in bird-protection movement, 130; California Club's affiliation with, 231n11; C. B. Burdette with, 151–52; convention in Los Angeles, 97, 154–55; meeting in New York, 90; racial segregation in, 178; and redwood protection, 157, 165, 167–68; representation on arms limitation committee, 319; structure of, 237; suffrage debate at convention of, 187–88; Twentieth Century Club's joining of, 181
George, Henry, xvi
Gerberding, Elizabeth, 213, 222–25, 269
Germans, xvi, 62, 102, 109, 214, 310
Germany, 81, 196, 336n89
GFWC. *See* General Federation of Women's Clubs (GFWC)
Gibson, Mary, 112–13, 185, 187–88
Giddings, Franklin, 114
Gilded Age, 59, 71, 80
Gilman, Charlotte Perkins, 182
Ginzberg, Lori, 31, 53n26, 341
Girls' Advisory Council, 295
Girls' Union, 84
Glendora CA, 134
glove industry, 315
Godkin, E. L., 324
Golden Gate Kindergarten Association, 81
Goldman, Anne E., 340–41
Gold Rush, 28–30, 52n15, 60, 289–90, 339–42
Gompers, Samuel, 264, 316, 320

González, Deena, 3
Gospel Society Fukuin Kai, 349–50
Grace Cathedral (San Francisco), 92
graft, 49, 220–26, 228, 235n67, 291
Grant-Bohnett bill, 242–45, 247–48. See also Bohnett, Lewis D.; Grant, Edwin E.
Grant, Edwin E., 242–47, 249–51, 255. See also Grant-Bohnett bill
Grant, Madison, 163, 164
grassroots political work, 123, 124, 138, 142–44, 160, 165–67, 237
Graupner, Mrs. A. E., 293
Graves, Henry, 164
Great Britain, xvi, 125, 196, 320, 323
Great Depression, 50
"Greater Mexico," 19n6
grebes, 125
Greene, Mrs. M. V., 271
Greenfield, Rev. George, 329, 330
Grinnell, George Bird, 128
Grosser, Philip, 330
The Grounding of Modern Feminism (Cott), 91–92
Growing Up Nisei (Yoo), 350
Guatemalan civil war, 2
Guidotti-Hernandez, Nicole M., 341
Gullett, Gayle, xiii–xiv, 178, 187
Gutiérrez, David, 19n6

Hadden, Mrs. E. J., 202
Hagan, Sarah, 264–66, 268–70, 272, 277, 278, 280, 282
Hague, 323–25
Hague Congress of Women (1915), 324, 335n70
Haight, Anna, 32
Haight, Henry, 31, 32
Hale, Sarah, 216
Hamilton, Mildred Nichols, 344
Handbook of Settlements (Russell Sage Foundation), 117n6, 366n65
Hankuk Puin-boe (Korean Women's Association), 349
Hans, George, 244
Hardin, Reverend Floyd, 329, 330
Harding, Warren, 318–19
Harper, Ida Husted, 106
Harris, Mary "Mother Jones," 215
Harrison, Jarrod, 346
Harrison Street Boys' Club, 100

Hastings College of Law, 221
Hawaiian Islands, 110, 325
Hawes, Horace, 31
Hawkes, C. E., 103
Haynes, Fred E., 99–100
Hays, Samuel P., 126, 355, 367n70
Head, Anna, 123, 127, 132, 141
health certificates for marriage, 238, 240
Hearst Domestic Industries (HDI), 87
Hearst Free Kindergarten Building, 81
Hearst, George, 77, 79–80, 82–84
Hearst Hall, 87
Hearst Memorial Mining Building, 88
Hearst, Phoebe Apperson: background of, 77–79; in California Club, 130; in Century Club, 230n11; contributions to University of California, 86–90; contribution to San Francisco Settlement Association, 101; courtship and marriage, 79–80; death, 92; European travel of, 80–82, 86; financing of women's education in Europe, 84; influence on public policy, 77, 78; interest in arts and literature, 78–80, 82, 84, 90; interest in kindergartens, 81–83; legacy of, 92–93; on parenting, 85; philanthropic interests of, 78, 344; political activism of, xiii; promotion of women's interests, 77–78, 86–92; on protection of redwoods in Big Basin, 160, 166; on suffrage, 90–92; in Town and Gown, 177; as University of California regent, 77, 78, 88–90, 89; on women's independence, 83–84. See also philanthropy
Hearst press, 293
Hearst, William Randolph, 79, 80, 83, 103–4
Heidenreich, Linda, 339
Henderson, Sandra L., xiii, 347, 350
Heney, Francis J., 223–24, 226, 249
herons, 125
Hetch-Hetchy Valley, 163, 170n13
Hichborn, Franklin, 106, 241–42, 244, 246, 248–53, 255, 257n9
Higuera Juárez, María, 3, 4, 6–7, 12, 15–19
Hill, Andrew P., 158, 166
Hindus, 352
The Hippodrome (Barbary Coast), 254
history, 3, 4, 6, 7, 10, 15, 17–19, 339. See also testimonios

384

History of California (Bancroft), 4
Hittell, Catherine, 123, 130–32, 136, 222
Hittell, Theodore Henry, 132
Holland, 326, 329
Holloway Jail, 323
home, 85, 183–84, 238. See also domesticity
Home for Aged and Infirm Colored People (Oakland), 347
Home of Friendless Children, 42
Homestake Mine, 83
Home Telephone, 221
Hoover, Herbert, 106, 152, 194, 199, 320
Hoover Institution Archives, 324
Hopkins, Mark, 346, 348
Hosford, Hester, 162
hospitals, 28–30, 41, 51n6, 341. See also specific hospitals
Hotel Sacramento, 239, 245, 257n9
Houck, Daisy, 270
housing, 32, 350. See also boardinghouses
Houston, David, 164
Howard, George, 106, 115
Howard Street incident, 297–98
"How to Dress on $12.50" (cartoon), 278
Hudson, Lyn, 343, 344
Hughes, Charles Evans, 279, 314
Hughes, Bishop Edwin Holt, 249
Hull House, 77, 101, 102, 104. See also Addams, Jane
Hull House Maps and Papers (Addams), 99
Humane Society, 131, 134
Humboldt Chamber of Commerce, 162, 164, 165
Humboldt County, 161–67
Humboldt County Board of Supervisors, 167
Humboldt County Federation of Women's Clubs (HCFWC), 162
Humboldt Redwoods State Park, 161–65
Humboldt Standard, 162
Humboldt Times, 161
Hume, Mrs. James B., 178, 188
hummingbirds, 125
Hungarian immigrants, 64
hunting, 123, 125, 126, 134–37, 143
Huntington Library, 335n56
Hurley, Teresa, 346
Hurtado, Albert, 340
Hyatt, Edward, 141–42

Idaho, 105
Illinois, 120n68, 329
immigrant communities, xvi, 102, 214, 220–24. See also ethnicity
immigration, 63–65, 72, 109, 317–18, 343, 350, 361n29. See also ethnicity; specific countries
Immigration and Housing Commission. See California Immigration and Housing Commission
Imperial Valley, 318
India, 66, 352
Indiana, 198
Indiana State Federation of Women's Clubs, 198
Indiana Union of Literary Clubs, 198
indoor relief, 45–46. See also relief work
Industrial Accident Commission, 315
Industrial Association of San Francisco, 258n23
Industrial Mediator for California, 317
Industrial Welfare Commission (IWC): attempt to balance interests, 271–73; creation of, 266; government preemption during World War I, 273–74; investigations conducted by, 270; K. P. Edson with, 268, 309, 313–15, 319; progressivism of, 263–64; on reduction of minimum wage, 276–80; sympathy for employers, 276, 277; weakening of, 280–82; working women's attitudes toward, 267, 275
Industrial Workers of the World, 140
infant-feeding practices, 104
inflation, 273. See also economy
influenza epidemic, 92, 195
"Intelligence Office," 32
Inter-Allied Conference, 329
International Conference of Women Workers to Promote Permanent Peace, 325
International Congress of Women, 324
internationalism: Alice Park on, 329, 330, 332; of K. P. Edson, 318, 330, 332; of Twentieth Century Club, 176, 177, 179, 180, 190, 192–96, 201, 347; of wildlife protection, 136; of women during World War I, 310, 314
International Typographical Union Local 21, 104, 109; Woman's Auxiliary #18, 226

INDEX

International Women's Suffrage Alliance Congress, 323, 325
International Workers of the World, 229
Iowa, 323
Iowa injunction, 241, 242. See also red-light injunction and abatement act
Ireland, 336n89
Irish, xvi, 102, 109, 214, 298
Irwin, Mary Ann, 341
Italians, xvi, 64, 102, 214, 291, 292, 298, 342
IWC. See Industrial Welfare Commission (IWC)

Jackson, Helen Hunt, 340–41
Jaffa, Meyer, 104
jail (San Francisco), 28, 45. See also prisons and prisoners
Japan, 310, 327, 349
Japanese, xv, 64, 110, 178, 348–51. See also Asians
Japan Society of Northern California, 351
Jarvis, Annie, 340
Jeffrey, Julie Roy, 182
Jensen, Joan, 324
Jews, 64, 292, 293, 296
Jim Crow restrictions, 343, 348. See also discrimination
Johns Hopkins University, 77
Johnson, Bascom, 253
Johnson, Grove L., 213, 228
Johnson, Hiram: appointment of Alice Park to suffrage congress, 323; on bird protection, 137; on League of Nations membership, 318; on logging, 161; on minimum-wage bill, 244, 266, 268–70; progressivism of, 310, 332n3; and red-light abatement bill, 247, 249; relationship with K. P. Edson, 312, 313, 315, 320; support of labor, 263
Johnson, Leigh Dana, 342
Johnson, Mrs. R. R., 64
joint guardianship, 190, 238–40, 321, 330. See also children; men; motherhood
Joint Guardianship Bill, 190, 238–40
Jones, Louise C., 159, 159, 160
Jones, William Carey, 186
Jordan, David Starr, 133, 158, 242, 325
Jordan, Jesse Knight, 325
Josefa (Latina), 341

Jow Ah Yeong, 362n29
Juárez, Cayetano, 16, 17
Juárez Rose, Vivien, 15, 17, 24nn80–81
Juilliard, Louis, 244
Junior Audubon Society, 134, 135, 141, 143. See also Audubon societies
Juvenile Protective Association, 292, 293, 299
juveniles: alcohol sales to, 304n16; A. L. Saylor on crime prevention among, 199, 347; court system for, 105, 113, 176, 186; at Magdalene Asylum, 43, 56n76; social welfare services for, 28, 46; Twentieth Century Club's campaigns on behalf of, 179–80. See also children

Kashaya Pomo Indians, 340
Kazin, Michael, 109, 225–26
Keating, M. J., 49
Kehoe, William, 245
Keith, Mary McHenry, 123, 130–31, 210, 211, 213, 223, 323, 327
Keith, William, 131
Kelley, Florence, 120n68, 269
Kellogg, Martin, 88, 90
Kellogg-Briand Pact (1928), 180, 198
Kellor, Frances, 105
Kelsey, Benjamin, 14
Kennedy, Kathleen, 328
Kent, William, 162–63, 164
Kerber, Linda, 353
Keynes, John Maynard, 318
Kieffer, Mrs. Stephen E., 184
kindergartens, 50, 59, 68, 78, 80–81, 83. See also children; education; public schools
King, James, of William, 217
Kinney, 185
Kleehammer, Michelle, 347
Koreans, 348–49. See also Asians
Korrol, Virginia Sánchez, 357n9
Kraft, Barbara, 326
Kreider, Marie L., 62

Labor Clarion: on clubwomen, 97–98; on confrontation of K. P. Edson, 279; on graft prosecutions, 225; on labor-settlement partnership, 112; Lucile Eaves's contributions to, 107–9, 113; Lucile

Eaves's photo in, 108; on saloon license fees, 214; on Waitresses Local 48, 226; "Women's Department" column in, 227; on women's wages, 273

labor organizations: on alcohol, 214–15; betterment of society through, 97; and Chinese immigration, 106, 353; concerns about graft trials, 225, 235n67; decline of influence in 1920s, 282; deterrents to, 266, 268, 271, 275, 276, 281, 282; in Europe, 214; K. P. Edson's representation of during war, 316–18; for laundry and restaurant workers, 280; Lucile Eaves's history of legislation regarding, 99, 115; postwar surge in women's, 273–74; press attacks on K. P. Edson, 276; press on character of working women, 268; press on female reformers, 269; press on minimum wage, 271, 280; relationship with middle-class reformers, 97–98, 107–10, 112, 226–29; relationship with social scientists and settlement movement, xiii; scholarship on Latina activity in, 340; self-sufficiency through, 216, 263, 264, 269–70, 275, 279–83; sophistication of, 264, 265; South Park Settlement's cooperation with, 101, 104, 107–10, 113–14; as special interest groups, 355. *See also* San Francisco Labor Council (SFLC); unionists; Union Labor Party (ULP); working class; working-class women

Ladies' Benevolent Society, 345

Ladies Pacific Accumulating and Benevolent Society, 345

Ladies Protection and Relief Society, 84

Ladies' Seamen's Friend Society of the Port of San Francisco, 36–40

lady managers, 27–28, 48, 50. *See also* clubwomen

Lake County region, 4

Lambin, Maria, 289, 295, 296

language, 5, 7, 8, 18. *See also* English language; sitio y lengua; Spanish language

LaRue, Louise, xiii, 212–13, 215, 219–20, 225–28, 265–66

Lasch-Quinn, Elizabeth, 353

Lathrop, Reverend C. N., 222

Latinas/os, xiv, xv–xvi, 102, 340–43, 357n9, 357n11, 358n13. *See also* Californianas/os; Chicanas

Laughlin, Gail, 210, 230n6

Laughlin, J. Laurence, 105

laundry workers, 32, 216, 219, 267, 274, 280

Law Enforcement League, 253

Law, Mrs. F. G., 167

Lead SD, 83

League of Nations, 180–82, 196, 318, 329

League to Enforce Peace, 182

Leavenworth KS, 105

Lebsock, Suzanne, 353

Lee, Erika, 343

Leese, Jacob, 12, 13

legislation: agenda of 1913, 179–80, 189–92, 237–40, 290, 346, 347; on agricultural labor, 110; on alcohol sales, 215; Chinese women on immigration, 350; effect of woman suffrage on lobbying for, 237–40; for organized labor, 98–99, 107, 109, 110; progressive under Hiram Johnson, 310, 332n3; to protect birds, 123–24, 131–40, 143, 347; protective during World War I, 273, 315; for redwood protection, 156, 157, 160–62, 166; research on minimum wage, 267–69, 313–14; Twentieth Century Club's agenda, 176, 179–80, 187–92, 201, 347; and WCTU, 69, 71; for women's benefit, 237–40, 267–68, 270; for working class, 216, 227, 228, 263, 264, 267–68, 282–83. *See also* California legislature; U.S. Congress; U.S. government; U.S. Supreme Court; Women's Legislative Council (WLC)

Leland Stanford, Jr., University. *See* Stanford University

Leonard, Karen Isaksen, 351–52

letter-writing campaigns: for arms limitation, 320; of Chinese women, 350; on minimum wage for women, 277; for Panama-Pacific International Exposition, 191; on red-light abatement bill, 242–43, 247–50, 255; for redwoods, 156, 160, 167; of Twentieth Century Club, 177; of WCTU, 69

Libby, Gretchen, 141

The Liberator, 224, 226

libraries, free, 50, 83, 102, 195
Lick, James, 31
Lick School of Mechanical and Industrial Arts, 322
"life boat benevolence," 30
Lincoln-Roosevelt League, 312, 313
Lissner, Meyer, 312, 314, 315, 320, 330–31
literature: about birds, 123, 126–28, 135–37, 139–43; by Alice Park, 321, 323, 324, 327, 328, 330; clubwomen's interest in, 153, 154; Lucile Eaves's review of labor, 107; in middle-class white women's political activism, 354; on red-light abatement bill, 241, 248, 250–52; in revitalized suffrage campaign, 224; and WCTU, 59, 66, 68–70. See also newspapers
Liu Yilan, 349
Local Option Bill, 214, 230n4. See also alcohol
Lochner, Louis, 328
Locke, John G., 321
logging, 154, 156, 158–66
London, 125
London, Jack, xvi, 118n22
Long Beach CA, 187–88
Los Angeles Audubon Society, 130, 140, 141
Los Angeles CA: Asian women's clubs in, 348–49; foundation of Friday Morning Club in, 333n11; GFWC meetings in, 97, 154, 178; Japanese women's clubs in, 351; Junior Audubon Society in, 134; K. P. Edson in, 312; National Federation of Women's Clubs in, 348; pure milk campaign in, 240; sedition trials in, 330; Victoria Reid in, 356n6; women's civic associations meeting in, 151; women's legislative agenda conferences in, 238; working women in, 216, 274. See also Friday Morning Club
Los Angeles Chamber of Commerce, 112
Los Angeles Citizen, 279
Los Angeles City Charter Revision Committee, 240, 313
Los Angeles County, 134
Los Angeles County Board of Health, 240
Los Angeles Museum of Ornithology, 137
Lovell SD, 314
Loyal Temperance Unions, 68

Lubin, Simon, 315
Lucy (free black female), 342
Lummis, Charles Fletcher, 104
Lusitania, 310
Lux, Charles, 81
Lux, Miranda, 81

Mabalon, Dawn Bohulano, 352
Macarthur, Walter, 110
MacLean, Annie M., 105
Magdalene Asylum, 43, 56n76
Mahan, Laura, 162, 164, 165, 167, 168
Mahan Trail at Dyerville Flat, 165
Mammoth Grove Hotel, 155–56
Marin County, 162–63
marriage, 238, 240, 340, 352
Martin, Ann, 106
Martin, Irving, 249
Mason, Bridget "Biddy," 342–43
Massachusetts, 133, 275, 313, 319, 321
Massachusetts State Republican Club, 319
maternalism, 200, 263, 266–67, 341, 344. See also domesticity; motherhood
maternity homes, 238
Mather, Stephen, 164
Mathewson, Walter, 271, 272
Matsumoto, Valerie, 348, 351
Matthews, Lillian, 215–16, 233n41
Maybeck, Bernard, 87
McBroome, Delores Nason, 344
McCarthy, Kathleen D., 80, 344
McCarthy, P. H., 225–26, 291, 300
McCracken, Josephine, 124, 131, 133, 134, 158
McGerr, Michael, 354
McKinley, William, 156
McLaughlin, Donald H., 89
McLaughlin, Emma Moffat, 296, 297, 299–300
McLean, Fannie W., 100
McLeran, Ralph, 297
meadowlark, 132, 136–37
Meadowlark Preservation Act (1901), 136–37
Mead, Rebecca, 113, 353
men: in Audubon Society, 129–30, 135; and bird-protection movement, 139, 143; charities and services for, 36–40, 46; clubs for Asian, 349–52; fraternal organizations of, 29; health

certificates for, 240; K. P. Edson on women's political and legal equality with, 248; and National Congress of Mothers, 85; number of voters in San Francisco, 256, 261n54; objection to minimum wage, 266; parental responsibilities of, 238; in redwoods campaign, 160, 347; in saloons, 214; in San Francisco unions, 265; and suffrage, 210, 345; support for women's political endeavors, xvii; in temperance movement, 60–61; wages in cannery industry, 273; WCTU on double standard for, 63; on women workers, 263, 269, 279–80. *See also* gender ideology; joint guardianship; men's civic organizations

Menchú, Rigoberta, 2

Mendocino County, xvi

Men in War (Latzko), 330

men's civic organizations, 290, 293–94, 298. *See also* fraternal organizations; men

mental health system, 176, 180, 199, 238, 240, 347

Mercantile Library, 84

Merchant, Carolyn, 138, 143

Mercy Hospital, 41

Merriam, John C., 163, 164

mestizos, 340, 341. *See also* European Americans; Native Americans

Mexican-American War, 310

Mexicans, xvi, 8, 317–18, 340, 352, 357n9. *See also* Californianas/os

Mexico, 1, 13, 19n6, 310, 322, 342, 357n6

middle-class women: bird-protection movement of, 123, 124; on child labor, 113, 114; in club movement, 153; comparison to minority groups, 344–45; disapproval of waitresses union, 215–16; education and professions of, 82; life in South Park Settlement, 102; and opposition to minimum-wage law, 270, 281; political focus of, 354–55; protection of children and redwoods, 152; relationship with labor, 97–98, 107–10, 112, 113, 209–10, 215–16, 219–20, 222–24, 226–29, 233n45, 263, 265–69, 283, 353; response to minimum wage reduction, 277–78;

scholarship on in California politics, 341; on streetcar strike, 218; in Twentieth Century Club, 177, 181; in WCTU, 60, 62; women as concern of, 346. *See also* class; clubwomen

Migratory Bird Treaty (1916), 136

military, 294–96, 298, 299, 324, 325, 328, 329. *See also* conscientious objectors; sailors; U.S. Army

Millar, John, 275

Miller, John, 82

Miller, Oliver Thorne, 134

"Milliner's White List," 139

millinery trade, 125–26, 128, 131, 137, 139. *See also* business interests

Mills, Darius Ogden, 31

Mills College, 92, 187, 196

minimum wage: Alice Park on, 323; California industries improved by, 274–75; class divide over, xiv, 113, 114, 268–70, 279, 280, 353; comparison to dance hall regulation, 303; employers' attitudes toward, 271–72; gender divide over, 264–65; labor objection to, 266–67; legislation under Hiram Johnson, 332n3; passage and enforcement of, 270; public interest in, 277–78; and red-light abatement bill, 243–45, 263, 267, 269–70; reduction of, 276–80; research on legislation, 267–69, 313–14; Supreme Court on, 280–82; Western women on, 195; on women's legislative agenda, 238; Women's Legislative Council on, 190. *See also* employment; working-class women

Minneapolis MN, 329

Mission District, 114, 220

Mission Dolores. *See* Mission San Francisco de Asís

Mission San Antonio, 13

Mission San Francisco de Asís, 8, 9, 16

Mission San Gabriel, 356n6

Missouri, 77, 78

Mitchell, John, 108

Miwok territory, 340

Montecito CA, 134

Monterey CA, 1, 12

Monterey County, xvi

Moore, Dorothea, 104, 110, 112, 130

Moore, Ernest Carroll, 104

moral reform: and alcohol sales restriction, 215; and bird-protection movement, 123, 127; in California women's politics, xiii, 255–57; clubwomen's commitment to, 291; directed at working women, 267–68, 303; and graft prosecutions, 223, 224; influence of European travel on, 80; of military stationed in San Francisco, 294–96; at Sailors' Home, 36; of temperance, 59, 66, 69; through elite women's philanthropy, 81; through protective legislation, 263; through South Park Settlement boys' and girls' clubs, 103; whites' focus on, 345–46. See also dance halls; red-light injunction and abatement act; temperance; vice and crime
Morgan, Julia, 200
Moses, Bernard, 99, 104
Mosgrove, Alicia, 299–301
motherhood, 63, 64, 68–69, 251, 267–68, 331. See also domesticity; joint guardianship; maternalism
mothers' associations, 78, 85
Mother's Congress, 238
mothers' pensions, 190, 238, 240, 290
Mount Vernon Ladies' Association, 82–83
mourning dove, 133, 137
Mowry, George, 314
Mt. St. Joseph's Infant Asylum, 42, 56n69
Muir, John, 132, 142, 154, 157, 163
Muir Woods National Monument, 163
Mujeres Activas en Letras y Cambio Social, 18
municipal activism, 181, 186, 191–92, 198, 200, 290, 350. See also civitas; community services
Munson, Lida. See Hume, Mrs. James B.
Murphy, Timothy, 13
Murray, Annie, 162
Musante, Attilio, 292
Musician's Union, 106, 221
Myers, Harriet Williams, 123, 124, 127–28, 134, 135, 137

Napa Recorder, 6
Napa region, 1, 4–6, 8, 15–18
Nash, Roderick, 126
National American Women's Suffrage Association (NAWSA), 131, 209, 210, 327, 331
National Association of Audubon Societies (NAAS), 128, 138–42
National Association of Colored Women's Clubs, 348
National Association of Settlements, 115
National Cathedral Foundation, 84
National Congress of Mothers, 85
National Conservation Congress, 130
National Consumers League (NCL), 244, 269
National Federal Suffrage Association, 324
National Federation of Women's Clubs, 348
nationalism, 193–94, 340, 349. See also nativism; patriotism
National League for Woman's Service, 316–17
National League of Women Voters, 318–19
National Playground Congress, 187
National Woman's Suffrage League (San Francisco), 213
National Woman Suffrage Association, 91
National Women's Party, 230n6
National Women's Trade Union League (NWTUL), 227, 228, 279, 281
Native Americans: in Berkeley, 178; in California politics, xiv; California work department for, 65; European American violence toward, 1, 15; histories of, 3, 10–12, 18; interaction with Italian immigrants, 342; Mexican land grants to, 357n6; population in California, xv–xvi; resistance strategies of, 7, 18–19; scholarship on politics of, 339–42; servitude of, 13, 18. See also mestizos; Nez Percé Indians; Patwin-speaking peoples; Pomo Indians; Wappo-speaking peoples
Native Daughters of the Golden West, 159
Native Sons of the Golden West, 159, 161–62
nativism, 60, 63–64, 72. See also nationalism; patriotism
nature preservation, 152, 154, 155, 158. See also conservation; forestry
nature study, 124–28, 133, 137, 141–42
NAWSA. See National American Women's Suffrage Association (NAWSA)
needlework, 87, 193

neighborhood improvement associations, 290, 292, 293, 298
Nelson, Charles, 296–97
Nelson, H. C., 243, 247
Nevada, 79, 135
New Deal, 264
New England Kitchen, 39
Newkirk, Garrett, 133
newspapers: Alice Park's speeches on, 329; Alice Park's war protest in, 327, 328; on Bear Flag Revolt, 5–6; on child labor legislation, 112, 113; on Ford Peace Expedition, 326; on graft prosecutions, 221; on Hearsts' lifestyle, 82; on minimum wage for women, 277, 278; on protection of redwoods in Big Basin, 158–60; on red-light abatement bill, 245–46, 251; on San Francisco Settlement's activities, 115; on streetcar strike, 217–20; WCTU's promotion of "pure," 59, 63; on women's charities, 32; women's testimonios compared to, 18. See also literature; *specific titles*
New York: antiwar parade in, 324; Audubon societies in, 133; and Audubon society in New York City, 128; conscientious objectors in, 336n83; Ford Peace Ship Expedition from, 325; garment workers' strike in, 233n45; General Federation of Women's Clubs meeting in, 90; labor law-compliant factories list in New York City, 139; Lucile Eaves in New York City, 114; People's Council meeting in, 329; settlement movement in, 99, 100, 104, 353; suffragists in, 228; use of bird plumage in, 125; women's hours and wages in, 275
New York Times, 83, 92
New York Tribune, 85, 90
Nez Percé Indians, 105
Ngai, Mae M., 343
Nickliss, Alexandra, 82, 87
Nienburg, Bertha von der, 317
Noel, Frances, 278, 280–81
Nolan, John I., 228
North Beach Promotion Association (NBPA), 292–93
North Beach (San Francisco), 81, 104, 249. See also San Francisco CA
Northern California Campaign Committee for the Red-Light Abatement Bill, 248–49, 251–53
Nunis, Doyce B., Jr., 340
nurses, 238, 240, 350. See also professions, women's

Oakland CA: African American women in, 178, 345, 347; alcohol sales restrictions in, 191; cannery workers' strike in, 273; clubwomen's response to earthquake and fire, 183; laundry workers' wages in, 274; opposition to woman suffrage in, 71, 188; P. A. Hearst's support of college in, 92; Republican Party convention in, 226; survey of women and child wage-earners in, 110–11
Oakland Enquirer, 92
Oakland Tribune, 191, 198–99; *Oakland Tribune Magazine* of, 194–95
Oakland Tribune Magazine, 194–95
O'Brien, Daniel, 298
O'Connell, Daniel, 328
O'Connell, John A., 300
Odd Fellows, 29
O'Donnell, Minna (Mrs. E. H.), 226–28
Older, Fremont, 253
Old Peoples' Home, 84
Olin, Spencer, 314
Olmstead, Margaret T., 143
oölogy, 125, 137
The Order of the Sons of Temperance, 60
ornithology, 124, 125, 128–31, 139, 142
orphans and orphanages, 30–32, 42, 240, 341. See also children; San Francisco Protestant Orphan Asylum (SFPOA)
Orr, Mrs. J. W., 222, 249
Osborne, Henry Fairfield, 163
Oscar II, 325. See also Ford Peace Ship Expedition
Osio, Antonio María, 14–15
Osos, 1, 5, 6, 17–18. See also European Americans
ospreys, 137
ostriches, 125
Otis, James, 31
Our Lady's Home for Old and Infirm Women, 102
Outdoor Art League, 211
outdoor relief, 30, 33, 45–46, 49–50, 52n17, 54n39. See also relief work

Overland Monthly, 100
overtime pay, 274, 275

the Pacific (dance hall), 300
Pacific Ensign, 59, 64
Pacific Gas and Electric, 221
Pacific Lumber Company, 164, 165, 167
Pacific States Telephone and Telegraph Company (later PT&T), 219, 221, 233n41
Paddison, Joshua, 346
Padilla, Genaro, 2, 14, 17
Page Act (1875), 361n29
Page, Horace F., 361n29
Palo Alto CA, 99, 323, 324–25, 327–30
Palo Alto Community House, 330
Palo Alto Women's Club, 222
pamphlets. See literature
Panama-Pacific International Exposition (PPIE) (1915), 92, 179, 188–89, 191, 206n68, 253, 291, 293, 325, 347. See also tourism
Pankhurst, Emmeline, 192, 323
Pardee, George, 112, 114
Paredes, Américo, 19n6
parent-teacher associations, 85, 298
Paris, 125
Park, Alice L.: background of, 321; and bird-protection movement, 123, 132; in California Club, 130–31; in California Equal Suffrage Association, 211; and graft prosecutions, 222; lectures of, 323, 326, 328; memorabilia of, 335n56; patriotism of, 309–10; peace activism of, 321, 323–32; personal advertising of, 322, 323; political interests of, xiii, 321–32; protection of meadowlarks, 136; and revitalization of suffrage movement, 224; suffrage campaign of, 323–24; threats to in California, 329; on United States in war, 314; on women's rights, 310, 331–32
Park, Dean W., 322, 323
parks, 156, 158–65, 195, 226, 350. See also recreation; tourism
parliamentary procedure, 179, 184–85, 201
Parmer, Carrie, 264
parole houses, 240. See also psychopathic parole
partisanship: and election of judges,

332n3; James Rolph on, 291; and red-light abatement bill, 247; and special interests, 355, 367n70; women's resistance to, 176, 188–89, 199, 202, 239
Pasadena CA, 133–34, 177
The Past Is Father of the Present (Juárez Rose), 17, 24n81
patriotism, 193–94, 309, 330. See also nationalism; nativism
Patwin-speaking peoples, 5, 6, 8–9, 11, 16
peace: Alice Park for, 321, 323–32; Chinese women's clubs for, 350; K. P. Edson for, 310, 316, 318–21, 330; Twentieth Century Club's campaign for, 179–81, 192–93, 196–98, 347; on women's legislative agenda, 190, 238. See also arms limitation
Peace Society, 350
Peace Treaty of Versailles, 181, 196
peacocks, 125
Peffer, George Anthony, 343
Peixotto, Jessica, 100
pensions, 50, 190, 238, 240, 290
People's Council, 324, 328–29
Peréz, Dona Eulalia, 356n6
Pérez, Emma, 3, 7
Perkins, George C., 156, 157
Perry, Elisabeth, 304n16
Pershing, John J., 320
Peru, 322
Petaluma CA, 61
petition campaigns, 69, 71, 157, 162, 167, 177, 242, 248–50, 354
Philadelphia PA, 329
philanthropy, xiii, xiv, 77–84, 92, 312, 344. See also charitable organizations; Hearst, Phoebe Apperson
Philippine Commission, 99
Philippines, 352
Philips, William, 312
"Phoebes," 86
Pie del Monte lodge, 87
Pierce, Franchesca, 224
Pinchot, Gifford, 142, 153
Pinkham, Harriet Brown, 321
Pinther, Mrs. Theodore, Jr., 212
Pinther, Mrs. Theodore, Sr., 212
Pioneers of California, 5–7
Pioneers' Society, 159
Pita, Beatrice, 2

392

Pitelka, Linda, 342
playgrounds, 50, 104, 113, 187, 195, 211, 226, 350
Pleasant, Mary Ellen, 343, 355, 361n28
Pleasanton CA, 92
Plehn, Carl, 103
Ploeger, Louise, 216
police matrons, 69
Polish immigrants, 64
political activism: of California labor movement, 263; by California WCTU, 60; effect of suffrage on, 189, 237; gender ideology in, 353–54; history of, xiv; justifications for WCTU's, 71–72; of K. P. Edson, 312–13, 319; of middle- and upper-middle-class white women, 123, 124; of P. A. Hearst, 90–91; racial differences in, 345–46; structures of California women's, xii; of Twentieth Century Club, 175, 180, 182, 185–86, 192, 195; of women during World War I, 309, 310; women's charities as, 34, 39–41, 45, 48, 49
political culture: of saloons, 214; strength of Progressive Era women's, 131, 138, 143; of Twentieth Century Club, 175–77, 179, 181, 185–86, 200–203
Political Economy Club, 103
Political Equality League, 187
political patronage, 30, 49, 52n17, 291
political prisoners, 330. *See also* prisons and prisoners
politics: definition of, xi, 175, 339; scholarship on women in, xi, xviin2, 339–42
Pomo Indians, 5, 8, 340
poolrooms, 299
Porter, Stephen G., 320
Portland or, 105, 323, 330
postcards, 191
poverty: beliefs about in San Francisco, 100–101; in California population, xvi; and conservation, 154, 155; education as way out of, 82; relief in San Francisco, 28, 29; San Francisco Settlement Association on, 98; WCTU's response to, 63–64; women's charities for, 27, 32–33, 45–46, 344–45. *See also* economy
PPIE. *See* Panama-Pacific International Exposition (PPIE) (1915)
Presbyterian (Chinese) Mission Home, 42

The Presidential Election of 1916 (Lovell), 314
Price, Jennifer, 125
Pringle, Ella S., 64–65
prisons and prisoners, 59, 68, 180, 186, 193, 199, 238, 240, 321, 347. *See also* jail (San Francisco); political prisoners
private sphere, 41–50, 59, 71, 166, 184, 200, 344. *See also* public sphere
prizefighting, 297, 298
professions, women's, 77, 78, 80, 82–84, 344. *See also* nurses; teachers
Progress and Poverty (George), xvi
progressive era reform, 77, 131, 138, 342–55
Progressive Party, 247, 312. *See also* Republican-Progressives
progressivism: of Alice Park, 321; of California labor movement, 263–64; of California legislation, 310, 332n3; of clubwomen, 211–12, 347; conservation as feature of, 168–69; definition of, xviin3; history of, xiv; of K. P. Edson, 310–12, 314–15, 318, 330–31; and labor conflict, 219, 233n45; of labor legislation, 267; of middle- and upper-middle-class white women, 123, 124; of minimum wage campaign, 281; P. A. Hearst's interest in, 78, 82; in red-light abatement bill campaigns, 255–56; relationship to suffrage, xii, 227, 237; and San Francisco graft prosecutions, 220, 225–26; and success of Audubon Society, 128–30; of Twentieth Century Club, 175, 176, 181, 186, 188, 199–203; of Western women, 195
prohibition, 60, 71, 76n79, 190–91, 251–53, 255. *See also* alcohol; temperance; Woman's Christian Temperance Union (WCTU)
Property Owners' Protective Association, 248, 249, 250
property rights, 190, 238, 242, 245–51, 253, 342
prostitution: association with alcohol, 216; Chinese women accused of, 343, 361n29; class views on, 256; containment through segregation, 241, 246, 252, 253, 256–57, 291; and corruption in San Francisco's social welfare services, 49; and dance hall problem,

393

prostitution (cont.) 289, 295, 296, 303; education about, 251; effect of red-light abatement bill enforcement on, 253–57; legislation on, 237, 238, 241–57; link to low wages, 244–45; sailors' Society on, 37; WCTU on, 69, 346. See also brothels; business interests; red-light injunction and abatement act; white slavery
Protestant culture, 18, 59, 60, 66–69. See also religion
Protestants, 31, 32, 44, 62, 293, 296. See also religion
Prudón, Colonel, 14
psychopathic parole, 238, 240, 347
Psychopathic Parole Society of Los Angeles, 240
Public Dance Hall Committee of the San Francisco Center, 289, 295–96
publicity campaigns, 247–49, 251, 255. See also letter-writing campaigns; literature; petition campaigns
public schools: alcohol sales restrictions near, 190–91; battle for integration of, 345; bird-protection movement in, 130, 133, 134, 137, 140–43; K. P. Edson on, 318; military training in, 325; segregation of San Francisco, 343; in Washington DC, 83; WCTU's involvement in, 68; on women's legislative agenda, 238; Women's Municipal League on, 226. See also children; education; kindergartens
public speaking, 65–66, 184
public sphere: clubwomen's advances in, 152–53; Lucile Eaves in, 107; P. A. Hearst on women in, 90–92; success of elite white women in, 344; Twentieth Century Club in, 184, 200; WCTU in, 59, 62–63, 65–66, 71; women's entry through suffrage, 237; women's involvement in through conservation, 168. See also private sphere
Punjab province, 352
pure-foods reforms, 190, 195, 332n3
pure milk campaign, 194, 238, 240, 290, 313, 346
purity, 59, 60, 62–64, 71
Purity Sunday, 248, 249

Quijas, Father, 10

race: in California politics, xii, xiv, xvii, 339–45, 354–55; in California population, xv–xvi; of clubwomen, 344–55; and labor problems, 109; and Twentieth Century Club, 176, 178–79, 181; violence based on, 341
racism: of Berkeley clubwomen, 178–79; in California, 348; of immigration legislation, 350; of WCTU, 60, 63, 64, 70, 72, 346
railroads, 65, 161, 221, 332n3
Raker, John, 162
Ramabai, Pundita, 66
Ramírez, Gonzálo, 10
Ramona (Jackson), 340–41
Ranchito CA, 134
rape, 14–15, 43, 323. See also violence
Reagan, William, 41
reclamation, 154, 155, 158, 170n13
Record of Twenty-Five Years of the California Federation of Women's Clubs (Gibson), 112–13
recreation, 290, 293–96, 300. See also parks; tourism
Recreation League, Dance Hall Section, 293–94
recuerdos, 10. See also history; testimonios
Red Cross, 193
Redlands CA, 133
red-light injunction and abatement act: Alice Park on, 323; debate of, 244–46; enforcement of, 253–57; link to minimum wage, 243–45, 263, 267, 269–70; referendum, 248–53, 256, 261n49; San Francisco Center on, 290; Senate resolutions on, 243–44; as women's political issue, 190, 238, 241–57, 289, 346; women's role in passage of, 247–48, 251, 255–56. See also brothels; moral reform; prostitution
Red Scare, 298
"Redwood Park Committee," 162
redwoods: California Club's protection of, 152, 211; campaign to save, 155–69; clubwomen's attitudes toward saving, 151, 161–65; collaboration on campaign to save, 346–47; comparison to bird-protection movement, 132; public interest in protection of, 164; state funding of conservation, 160, 165;

women's influence on public policy for, 166, 238. *See also* conservation; environmental movement; forestry
Regan, Daniel, 244
Reid, Hugo, 356n6
Reid, Victoria, 340, 356n6
Reinhardt, Aurelia, 196
relief work, 192–93. *See also* indoor relief; outdoor relief
religion: Alice Park on, 321; and charitable donations, 31; in Gold Rush California, 341; of P. A. Hearst, 78; and support of charitable organizations, 34, 40, 44, 49; WCTU on purity of, 60, 63–65. *See also* Catholics; churches; clergy; Protestant culture; Protestants; religious organizations
religious organizations, 101, 290–93. *See also* churches; clergy; religion
Rennecourt Relief, 193
Republican National Committee, 312, 318–19
Republican National Convention, 312, 318
Republican Party: A. L. Saylor's affiliation with, 198; conservation interests of, 158; Gail Laughlin in, 230n6; and graft prosecutions, 221; K. P. Edson's association with, 312, 314, 318–19; on red-light abatement bill, 241–42, 246–47; Twentieth Century Club's support of, 176, 188, 199; union women's lobby of, 226, 229
Republican-Progressives, 247. *See also* Progressive Party
resistance, 2, 5, 6, 7, 14–15, 17–19, 34, 339–40, 343
restaurant industry, 280. *See also* Waitresses Local 48 (San Francisco)
Resthaven, 240
"Reviews of Labor Literature" (Eaves), 107
Reyes, Bárbara O., 2, 3
Rhode Island, 321
Rhode Island State Normal School, 321
Richards, John E., 158
Richardson, Friend W., 275, 281–82
Richmond Camp, 219
Richmond district, 218, 220
Rincon Hill, 79
Riverside CA, 62
Robert's Rules of Order, 185

Robins, Margaret (Mrs. Raymond), 279, 281
Robinson Bequest, 45
Roche, Theodore, 292, 294, 301
Rodes, Daniel W., 210
Roland, Carol, 81, 100
Rolph, James "Sunny Jim," Jr., 199, 253, 282, 291–92
Roman Catholic Orphan Asylum, 31, 42, 56n69
Roman Catholic Sisters of Mercy, 41, 43, 44, 46, 56n69. *See also* Catholics
Roman Catholic St. Joseph's Youth Directory, 42
Roosevelt, Theodore, 85, 142, 157, 163, 312
Ross, Edward A., 98, 103, 106, 109, 114
Rowell, Chester H., 249, 312, 315, 316
Ruef, Abraham, 221, 223, 225
Ruiz de Burton, Maria Ampara, 340–43
Ruiz, Vicki L., 3, 357n9
Russell Sage Foundation, 117n6, 366n65
Russia, 196
Russians, 62, 64
Ryan, James, 246

Sacramento CA, 14, 136, 238, 239, 245, 255, 257n9, 350. *See also* California legislature
Sacramento St. (San Francisco), 66
Sacramento Valley, 11
sailors, 68–69, 294–95. *See also* military
Sailors' Home, 36–40
Sailors' Union of the Pacific (SUP), 69, 110, 235n67
Salem District Public School, 79
saloons, xvii, 69, 213–15, 253, 292, 294. *See also* alcohol
Salvation Army, 299
Salz, Mrs. Ansley K., 297
San Bernardino Woman's Club, 135
Sánchez, Rosaura, 2–3, 6
San Diego CA, 134, 278
San Diego High School, 105
San Francisco Benevolent Society (SFBS), 45
San Francisco Board of Supervisors, 221, 225
San Francisco Boys' and Girls' Aid Society, 84

San Francisco Boys' Club Association, 103
San Francisco Bulletin, 217, 244, 277
San Francisco CA: African American charities in, 344–45; Alice Park in, 322–23; attempt to restrict child labor in, 98; Audubon Society in, 134; bar association in, 299; barrooms in, 59; beliefs about in poverty in, 100–101; bird-conservation activism in, 132; California Civic League in, 239; California Club's activities in, 152; CFWC conference in, 189; Chinese merchant immigrants to, 362n29; Chinese population of, 342; Chinese resistance to segregation in, 343; Chinese women's clubs in, 349, 350; conditions on waterfront in, 37–38, 101, 102; corruption in social welfare system of, 48–49; cross-class alliances in, 353; and damming in Yosemite, 163; demography of, xvi, 28, 30; detrimental effects of vice in, 293; effect of Sailors' Home on economy of, 37; enforcement of red-light abatement bill in, 253–57; George Hearst's funeral in, 83; graft prosecutions in, 220–26; Hearsts' move to, 79; Japanese women's clubs in, 349–51; kindergartens in, 81; Korean clubs in, 349; K. P. Edson's commute to and from, 313–14; K. P. Edson's speech on peace and labor issues in, 320–21; legislators on red-light abatement, 244–47; Lucile Eaves in politics of, 106–7; medical facilities in, 28, 51n6; military bases in, 294–96; Northern California Campaign Committee for the Red-Light Abatement Bill headquarters in, 248, 249; occupations survey in, 272; opposition to woman suffrage in, 188; origins of temperance movement in, 59–61; P. A. Hearst's influence in, 77, 80–82; People's Council meeting in, 328; private-welfare model in, 28–30, 41–50, 344; promotion of PPIE in, 179, 188–89, 191; racial segregation of public transportation in, 343; railroad from Eureka to, 161; real estate interests in, 247, 248; redwood conservation in, 164, 167; report of K. P. Edson confrontation in, 279;

role of women's charities in, 27–32, 41; saloon license fees in, 213, 214; scholarship on influence of women's charities in, 341; social welfare expenditures, 43–50; strength of labor establishment in, 263, 265; strikes in, 216–21, 225, 228, 229, 273; suffrage organizations in, 209–14; suffrage vote in, 71, 209; temperance in, 213–15; Twentieth Century Club members from, 177; Twentieth Century Club's response to earthquake and fire in, 182–83; unfavorable reputation of, 38; vice and crime in, 289–300; voters on red-light abatement bill, 250–52, 256; wages in, 110–11, 272, 274, 282; WCTU in, 62, 66; Woman's Peace Party in, 324, 325; women's club movement in, xiii, 90; women's legislative agenda conferences in, 238; women voters in, 256, 261n54. *See also* Barbary Coast (San Francisco); California Club; North Beach (San Francisco); South-of-Market district (San Francisco)
San Francisco Call, 227
San Francisco Center, 290, 293–97, 299–302. *See also* California Club
San Francisco Chamber of Commerce, 39
San Francisco Chronicle, 217, 218, 220, 297, 298
San Francisco City Hospital, 28, 42–44, 44, 46, 48, 49. *See also* hospitals
San Francisco Daily News, 267, 270
San Francisco Equal Suffrage League, 210–13, 219, 224, 227–29, 353
San Francisco Examiner: on bird conservation, 132, 139; campaign to abolish vice districts, 293, 294, 302, 303; on P. A. Hearst, 92; on red-light abatement bill, 243; on streetcar strike, 217–19; on supervision of dance halls, 297; support of George Stoneman, 82; on temperance and suffrage, 213
San Francisco Female Hospital (SFFH), 34–35, 54n43. *See also* hospitals
San Francisco Free Public Library, 102
San Francisco Home for the Care of the Inebriate, 61
San Francisco Industrial School, 28, 42–43, 45–47, 47, 57n91
San Francisco Labor Council (SFLC):

INDEX

accusations of A. B. C. Dohrmann, 271; brand of unionism, 107, 119n49; cooperation with settlement association, 107, 110–14; and dance hall closures, 300; and graft prosecutions, 225; house organ of, 97; legislative standards for men and women, 264; meeting place of, 215; on minimum wage, 269, 277; on saloon license fees, 214; sponsorship of Louise LaRue, 226–27; on streetcar strike, 217, 218, 233n43; on telephone operators' strike, 233n41. *See also* labor organizations

San Francisco Ladies' Protection and Relief Society (SFLP&RS): donations to, 31, 32; expenses for Home, 46–47, 47, 56n90; formation of, 30; Home of, 35; indoor and outdoor relief provided by, 33, 45–46, 54n39; number of occupants in Home, 33; opening of Home, 32; public opposition to, 35–36; transfers from public institutions to Home of, 41–42; winning of support for, 34

San Francisco League of Women Voters, 199

San Francisco Merchants' Association, 104, 112

San Francisco Methodist Episcopal Church, 249

San Francisco Post, 43

San Francisco Presidio, 4, 16

San Francisco Protestant Orphan Asylum (SFPOA), 27, 30–34, 33, 41–42. *See also* orphans and orphanages

San Francisco Recreation League, 290

San Francisco School Board, 90, 223

San Francisco Settlement, 114–15. *See also* South Park Settlement

San Francisco Settlement Association, 97–100, 106, 107, 110–14, 353. *See also* social welfare services

San Francisco's Twenty-First School District, 111

San Francisco Superior Court, 280

San Francisco Women's Vigilant Committee, 348

San Joaquin Delta region, 352

San Joaquin Valley Commercial Association, 156

San Jose Board of Trade, 158, 166

San Jose CA, 242, 272–73

San Jose Woman's Club (SJWC), 158–61, 159, 166, 168

San Pedro CA, 134

San Quentin prison, 186

Sansome Hook and Ladder Company, 31

Santa Barbara CA, 329

Santa Barbara Chamber of Commerce, 112

Santa Clara County, 133

Santa Cruz Audubon Society, 131

Santa Cruz CA, 314

Santa Cruz (CA) trade board, 158, 166

Santa Cruz Ladies' Forest and Songbird Protective Association, 133, 134, 138

Santa Cruz Mountains, 158

Santa Cruz Surf, 158

Santa Rosa CA, 298

Sargent, Aaron A., 211, 231n12

Sargent, Ellen Clark, 211, 213, 222

Sarris, Greg, 340

Satiyomi, 8, 10

"Save the Redwoods Day," 164

Save-the-Redwoods film, 164

Save the Redwoods League, 163–65, 167–68, 347

Saxton, Alexander, 109

Saylor, Anna Louise McBride, 179–80, 195–200, 197, 202, 347

Scandinavian immigrants, xvi

Schlesinger, B. F., 271, 276

Schloss, Mrs. Aaron, 167, 195–96, 207n94

Schmitt, Milton, 245

Schmitz, Eugene E., 106, 221, 223

scholarships, 77, 78, 86, 104, 192. *See also* education

schools. *See* kindergartens; public schools; *specific colleges and universities*

Schwimmer, Rosika, 325, 326, 335n70

Science magazine, 126

"scientific" labor movement, 107. *See also* unionists

Scientific Temperance Instruction Law, 68, 69, 72

Scott, Anne Firor, 80, 341

Seattle WA, 323, 329

Secor, Lisa, 326

Sempervirens Club, 159, 159–61, 166

Sem Yeto, 8–11

Senkewicz, Robert M., 2

397

sequoias. *See* Calaveras "Big Trees"; redwoods
Serbian refugees, 192
settlement movement, xiii, 97, 99, 108–9, 117n6, 353, 366n65
Severance, Caroline, 333n11
Severance, Sarah M., 70, 71
sex education, 321
sexual purity, 63, 346
Shattuck, David, 31
Shaw, Anna Howard, 209
Sherman, Mary, 167–68
Shinn, Millicent, 100
"shop girls," 211
shore birds, 137
Silver Street Kindergarten, 102
Simmons College, 115
Simons, May Wood, 229
Sinao (Suisun), 5
sisterhood of women, 229
Sisters of Charity, 56n69
Sisters of Mercy. *See* Roman Catholic Sisters of Mercy
sitio y lengua, 7, 15, 18. *See also* language
Skinner, Mrs. M. E., 246
Sklar, Kathryn Kish, 353
Skocpol, Theda, 341, 344
slavery, 342–43. *See also* white slavery
Slavics, 298
Small, Albion, 105
smallpox outbreak, 44
Smith College, 321
Smith, Mrs. E. O., 160, 161
Smith, Mary Roberts. *See* Coolidge, Mary Roberts Smith
Smith, Mary Rozet, 77, 344
Smith, Reverend Paul, 253, 255
Smith, Peter, 43–44
Smith, Robert, 342
sociability, 115, 180, 182–83, 185, 186, 201, 347, 349, 350
"social boxes," 352
social conditions, study of, 104
socialism, 267, 278
social purity, 63–64, 346
social reform: agenda of California WCTU, 60, 66–69; lack of San Francisco settlements' after 1906, 114–15; by Lucile Eaves, 98; P. A. Hearst's interest in, 78, 82, 88; San Francisco Center on, 290; through conservation, 168–69

social scientists, xiii, 108–9
social welfare services: corruption in San Francisco's, 48–49; of dance hall supervisors, 297; funding of San Francisco public, 28–29; private in San Francisco, 28–30, 41–50, 344; San Francisco Center on, 290; scholarship on California, 341; through Buddhist women's association, 350; through Korean clubs, 349; through women's charities, 27–30, 40–50; Twentieth Century Club's campaign for reform of, 179, 186, 189; for women, 27, 29–30, 32–33, 35–36, 41, 45–46, 50. *See also* charitable organizations; community services; San Francisco Settlement Association; South Park Settlement
social workers, women, 78
Solano, Isidora Filomena, 3, 4, 6–12, 15
Solidarity, 229
Sonoma County, 83, 298
Sonoma region, 1, 4, 6, 9, 13, 14, 16
South Asians, 351–52. *See also* Asians
Southern California League, 239
Southern California Political Equality League, 313
Southern Pacific Railroad, 69, 81
South-of-Market district (San Francisco): demography of, 102, 220; description of, 118n22; and graft prosecutions, 221; Sailors' Home in, 37; schools in, 81; South Park Settlement residence in, 101–2; study of children in, 111; women's influence in, 352–53. *See also* San Francisco CA
"South of the Slot" (London), 118n22
South Park Settlement: academic studies of, 104–5; changes after earthquake and fire, 114–15; friendship offered by, 102–3; goals of, 101, 113; history of, 97–99; lectures at, 103, 109–10; location of residence, 101–2; Lucile Eaves's departure from, 114; as "neutral territory," 109, 114; participation in local politics, 104–5, 113; relationship with labor organizations, 101, 104, 107–10, 113–14. *See also* Eaves, Lucile; San Francisco Settlement; social welfare services
Spain, 324

Spaniards, 8, 13, 339, 356n6. *See also* Californianas/os
Spanish language, 1–2, 18. *See also* language
spears, 15–18
special interest groups, 168, 355, 367n70
Spencer, Anna Garland, 327
Spencer, Dorcas J., 60, 65, 66, 69, 70
Spencer, Maude, 253
Sperry, Mary S., 211, 213, 222, 224
Square and Circle Club, 349, 350, 355
The Squatter and the Don (Ruiz de Burton), 340–41
Stanford, Jane Lathrop, 81, 91, 106
Stanford, Leland, 81
Stanford University: Alice Park's children at, 322, 323; Alice Park's commencement speech at, 331; Big Basin redwoods meeting at, 159; D. S. Jordan at, 133, 242; founder of, 81; Frank Angell at, 100; Jane Addams's visit to, 99; Lucile Eaves at, 98, 105–6; M. R. Coolidge at, 114, 241; and study of San Francisco Settlement district, 104; and Twentieth Century Club international relations conference, 196; Woman's Peace Party connections at, 325
State Board of Health, 301
State Bureau of Labor, 247
State Civil Service Commission, 240
State Council of Defense, 316, 317
State Federation of Women's Clubs, 178, 242–43
State Fish and Game Commission, 137
Steam Laundry Workers Union, 219
Stebbins, Lucy Ward, 196
Steelville Academy, 79
Steinson, Barbara, 309, 331
Stephens, William D., 165, 315, 316
Stevenson House, 79
St. Francis of Assisi Catholic church, 249, 291
St. Louis MO, 324
St. Mary's Hospital, 102
Stockholm, 326
Stockton CA, 226, 317, 352
Stockton Record, 249
Stoneman, George, 82
Story of the Session of the California Legislature of 1911 (Hichborn), 241

Stow, Joseph W., 39
Stow, Marietta, 54n42
Street Carmen's Union. *See* Carmen's Union
streetcars, 216–20, 225, 228, 229, 343, 361n26, 361n28
strikes: by cannery workers, 272–73; coal (1902), 108; effects of violent in San Francisco, 106; at Emporium department store, 271; and minimum-wage law, 270; police protection during waterfront (1901), 221; in postwar San Francisco, 298; of San Francisco streetcars, 216–20, 225, 228, 229
Sturtevant-Peet, Beaumelle, 71
St. Vincent's Orphan Asylum, 41, 42
"The Subjective Necessity of Social Settlements" (Addams), 99
suffrage: Alice Park on, 321, 323–24, 327, 330, 331; association with temperance, 210, 213–16, 227, 228; and citizenship, xiv–xv, 195, 203, 237; as class issue, xiii–xiv, 113, 211–12, 216, 226–29, 353–54; clubwomen's attitudes toward, xiv, 153, 170n8, 187–89, 210–13, 224, 231n13; comparison to bird-protection movement, 124, 131, 132, 143; comparison to dance hall regulation, 303; and conservation efforts, 168–69; of Humboldt County women, 167; K. P. Edson on, 313, 330, 331; labor support for, 265; leadership of California movement, 209–10; legislation under Hiram Johnson, 332n3; of male immigrants, 64; P. A. Hearst on, 90–92; and parliamentary procedure, 185; and protective legislation, 263; and red-light abatement bill campaigns, 243, 255–56; relationship to progressivism, xii; San Francisco Center on, 290; in state of California, xii, 71, 76n79, 135, 187–89, 195, 209, 237, 291; statistics on men's and women's in San Francisco, 256, 261n54; and Twentieth Century Club, 175–77, 187–89, 201; union women's efforts toward, 226–29; WCTU's promotion of, 59–60, 63, 70–72; William Philips's involvement in movement, 312; and women's activism during World War I, 309; as women's political issue, xi, 346

399

suffrage organizations, 34, 54n42, 187, 209–14, 224, 355. See also specific organizations
Sun Yat-sen, 349
Sutherland, William, 247
Sutter County, 69
Sutter, John A., 11, 14
Swain Bakeries, 31–32
Swan, Marion, 237–39, 257n9
Sweden, 326
Swedish chapter of WCTU, 62
Switzerland, 336n89
Syrians, 192

Taeban Puin Kuje-boe (Korean Women's Relief Society), 349
Taeban Yoja Aikuk-dan (Korean Women's Patriotic Society), 349
Taft, William Howard, 99
Tait, John, 296
Talbot, Marion, 105
Tape, Mary and Joseph, 343
taxes, 27–29, 42, 88, 193, 332n3
"taxi-dance" halls, 290. See also dance halls
Taylor, E. R., 221
teachers, 78, 81, 83, 134, 159, 318. See also education; professions, women's
Tea Committee, 182
Teamsters Union, 235n67
Tehachapi Mountains, xv
Telegraph Hill, 81
Telegraph Hill Neighborhood Center, 115
telephone operators, 219, 233n41, 297–98
Telephone Operators Union, 233n41
telephone service, 221, 225
Telling Identities (Sánchez), 3
temperance, 60–62, 210, 213–16, 227, 228, 345–46. See also alcohol; moral reform; prohibition; Woman's Christian Temperance Union (WCTU)
Temperance Arithmetic (WCTU), 68
Temple Emanu-El, 292
terns, 125
testimonios, 2–4, 6–7, 13–14, 16–18. See also history; recuerdos
testimony ban, 342, 360n22, 361n24
Texas, 342, 350
Texas Alien Land Bill, 350
Thalia, 254

Thanksgiving baskets, 348
Thoreau, Henry David, 154
Todd, Helen, 269
Toll, Mrs. Charles H., 167
Torres, Lourdes, 4
tourism, 154–58, 164–66, 289, 293. See also Panama-Pacific International Exposition (PPIE) (1915); parks; recreation
Town and Gown, 177
tuberculosis, 194, 238, 240, 313. See also pure milk campaign
Tulocay Rancho, 24n80
Tuttle, Adella. See Schloss, Mrs. Aaron
Twentieth Century Club Bulletin, 181, 186, 196
Twentieth Century Club of Berkeley (TCC): A. L. Saylor in, 198–200; association with other women's clubs, 181–83, 200–201; civic work of, 176, 177, 186, 189–92, 201; conference on international relations at clubhouse of, 196; connection to WCTU, 191, 206n66; Current Events section of, 186–88, 198, 201; efforts to reshape public policy, 179, 194; "Federation Days" lectures of, 182; first Year Book, 183; legacy of, 201–2; legislative agenda of, 176, 179–80, 187–92, 201, 347; link to CFWC, 200–201; In local politics, 176; membership of, 177–81; mobilization for war effort, 192–95; organization and goals of, 177, 191–92, 200, 201; parliamentary procedure in, 179, 184–86, 201; Peace Committee of, 192, 193; political culture of, 175–79, 193, 346; in postwar period, 194–98; sections of, 186; sewing by, 193; significance of clubhouse of, 179, 182–85, 183, 201; in state-level politics, 176, 177, 179, 181, 182, 191–92, 200–203. See also Berkeley CA
"Twin Evils, Intemperance and Tobacco" essay contest, 68
Tygiel, Jules, 234n49
Tzu-Chun Wu, Judy, 350, 351

Underwood, June, 195
unemployment, 277, 292–93, 294, 298, 300–301. See also employment
unionists: on alcohol, 215–16; male support of women, 263; meetings at

400

INDEX

South Park Settlement, 110, 114; on minimum-wage legislation, 263; on protective legislation, 264; and San Francisco Labor Council, 107; as special interest groups, 355; strength in California, xvi, 265, 267; and suffrage, xiv, 212–13, 216, 225–29. *See also* class; labor organizations; *specific unions*; working class; working-class women
union label, 98, 265
Union Labor Party (ULP), 106–10, 213, 221, 222, 224–26, 228, 234n49. *See also* labor organizations
United Garment Workers' Union (UGW), 216, 264–65, 269, 272, 279, 280
United Mine Workers, 108, 215
United Railroads, 216–21, 235n67
United States: anti-vice legislation in, 293; Audubon societies' spread in, 133; bird-protection movement in, 123, 125, 135–36, 138, 142–44; border with Mexico, 19n6; Chinese population in, 350–51; declaration of war on Spain, 324; effect of women's activism in, 143–44; entry into war, 309, 310, 327–28; eradication of prostitution in, 241; Filipina/o population in, 352; interest in redwood preservation in, 163, 167; Japanese clubs in, 351; Korean organizations in, 349; K. P. Edson on labor legislation in, 315; linking of women's clubs in, 181; organization of WCTU in, 59; ornithological clubs in, 128; political forms in Chinese clubs, 349; redwoods as asset to, 157; San Francisco women's influence on political culture in, 28; scholarship on benevolence work in, 341; settlements in, 99, 117n6, 366n65; suffrage campaign in, 209, 309; union meetings in, 215; women on involvement in war, 314; women on League of Nations membership, 180–82, 196, 318, 329. *See also* U.S. government; West
United States Commission on War Training Camp Activities (CWTCA), 294–96
United States Interdepartmental Social Hygiene Board, 299
Universal Peace Congress, 323–25
University of California: alcohol sales near, 69, 190–91; Bernard Moses at, 99; Catherine Hittell at, 132; Ernest Carroll Moore at, 104; food-conservation efforts, 194; Jane Addams's visit to, 99; Jessica Peixotto at, 100; John Merriam at, 163; Lucile Eaves's fellowship from, 115; P. A. Hearst as regent of, 77–78, 88–90, 89; P. A. Hearst's contributions to, 86–88; recognition of P. A. Hearst's death, 92; scholarship at, 77; and Twentieth Century Club international relations conference, 196; and Twentieth Century Club membership, 177; Twentieth Century Club's interest in girls at, 192
University of California Agricultural Experiment Station, 104
University of California Press, 99
University of Chicago, 105
University of Nebraska, 115
University of Pennsylvania Department of Archaeology and Paleontology, 86
University of Southern California College of Physicians and Surgeons, 351
University Settlement (New York), 104
"University Settlements and Trade Unions" (Eaves), 109
urbanization and industrialization, 125, 126, 142, 154
U.S. Army, 1, 5, 295, 320. *See also* military
U.S. Congress: aid to Sailors' Home, 39; and California's demand for fortifications, 327; House of Representatives Committee on Foreign Affairs, 320; legislation on kindergartens, 83; on minimum wage, 281; passage of "Anthony Amendment," 231n12; passage of Nineteenth Amendment, 231n12; and redwood protection, 156, 158, 160, 162–63, 166; representation on arms limitation committee, 320; on social hygiene of military, 299; Twentieth Century Club's lobby for peace, 196; war resolution of, 315. *See also* legislation; U.S. government; U.S. Senate
U.S. Congress House of Representatives Committee on Foreign Affairs, 320
U.S. Constitution, 211, 231n12, 281, 361n24
U.S. Department of Agriculture, 125, 157

401

U.S. Department of Justice, 329
U.S. Department of Labor, 317–18
U.S. Employment Service, 273
U.S. Food Administration, 194
U.S. government: aid to Sailors' Home, 39; on cleanup of San Francisco dance halls, 299–300; contracts during World War I, 315–17; K. P. Edson's work with agencies of, 315–21; preemption of IWC during war, 273–74; role in wage regulation, 266, 269, 271, 274–75, 280–83; Twentieth Century Club in politics of, 176, 177, 201; and women's legislative agenda, 238. *See also* United States; U.S. Congress
U.S. Labor Commission, 107
U.S. Marine Hospital, 36, 39, 41, 51n6
U.S. Navy Department, 316
U.S. Senate, 82, 332n3. *See also* U.S. Congress
U.S. Supreme Court, 273, 280–82. *See also* legislation
U.S. War Department, 316
Utah, 135, 342

Vallejo de Leese, Rosalía, 1–4, 6–7, 12, 12–17, 23n61
Vallejo, Mariano Guadalupe, 3–4, 9–10, 13, 14, 16
Vallejo, Salvador, 10, 14, 15
Veblen, Thorstein, 105
venereal disease, 240, 246, 291, 294, 299
Vera, Arleen de, 351
Vera, Manuel, 5
vice and crime, 252, 289–93, 295, 297–300, 302, 303. *See also* moral reform
violence, 1, 5, 12, 14–16, 18, 341. *See also* rape
Vittoria Colonna Club, 292, 293, 299
Voigt, Bessie, 300
voluntarism, 28, 29, 31, 47, 53n26, 316, 347, 349–50. *See also* charitable organizations
Von der Nienburg, Bertha. *See* Nienburg, Bertha von der
Vrooman, Rachel. *See* Colby, Mrs. William

Wage Earners Suffrage League (WESL), 226–29, 230n6
Waitresses Local 48 (San Francisco), 213, 215–16, 219, 225, 226, 265. *See also* restaurant industry
Walden, Adelaide, 266–67, 275
Walker, Lizzie, 41
Walker, Mary, 41
Wallace, Albert, 245
Waller, Elizabeth, 30, 32
Waller, Roy, 30, 31
Walter, Carrie Stephens, 158–60, 159
Wappo-speaking peoples, 5, 6, 8–9, 11, 16
War Labor Policies Board, 317
Warner, Amos G., 106
Washington, George, 82–83
Washington DC, 82–85, 156, 309–10, 318–21, 325, 327
Washington State, 224
water conservation, 153, 155, 157, 160, 170n13, 332n3. *See also* conservation
Watson, Elizabeth Lowe, 211
Way, W. Scott, 133, 134
Webb, Ulysses S., 249
Weeks-McLean Act (1913), 136
Weights and Measures Law, 332n3
Welke, Barbara Y., 343, 344, 345
Wells, Michael R., 62
West: conservation concerns in, 153, 155, 168–69, 170n13; K. P. Edson on peace issue in, 314; multiracial environment of, 341–42; views of war in, 327, 332; war contracts in, 316; woman's suffrage in, 195. *See also* United States
Western Addition district (San Francisco), 218, 220
Western Journal of Education, 111
Wheeler, Benjamin Ide, 89, 89–90
Wheeler, Mrs. Benjamin Ide, 177, 230n11
Wheeler, O. C., 31, 53n25
White House, 82, 85
White House Conference on Child Health and Protection, 199
White, J. E., 248, 249, 255
White, Laura, 152, 154, 156, 157, 160, 166, 168
Whitemire, Drucilla. *See* Apperson, Drucilla Whitemire
White, P. J., 43
whites: advantages in politics, xvii, 344; in California population, xiv, xv, 341; comparison to African Americans, 344–45; kindergartens for, 83; political

focus of, 345–46; subjugation of indigenous peoples through alcohol, 11; and WCTU, 60, 62, 70. *See also* European Americans
Whiteside, Robert P., 155–56, 157
white slavery, 246, 268. *See also* prostitution; slavery
Whitney, Charlotte Anita, 249, 260n37
Whitney v. California, 249, 260n37
Whittier CA, 56n76
Willard, Frances, 59, 60, 66, 70, 186
Willey, Samuel H., 31, 53n25
Williams, Albert, 31, 53n25
Wilson, Ann Marie, 353
Wilson, J. Stitt, 188
Wilson Ornithological Club, 128
Wilson, Woodrow, 162, 196, 314, 327
wine industry, 65, 68, 69, 136, 251. *See also* business interests
Winter Garden Dance Hall, 297
Winter, Mrs. Thomas G., 319
Winthrop, John, 64
Wolfe, Edward, 250
Wollenberg, Lucile, 295
womanhood: in California politics, xii; conservation of, 138–39, 238; "organized" in movement to protect birds, 124, 143; P. A. Hearst's conception of, 90–92; WCTU's organized, 71, 72. *See also* feminism; gender ideology
The Woman's Bulletin, 239, 242, 251
Woman's Christian Temperance Union: Alice Park in, 323–24, 330; on California exceptionalism, 62, 64–65, 71; coffee houses and reading rooms of, 62, 66, 68; Congress of Reform, 213, 223; connection to Twentieth Century Club, 191, 206n66; Department of Viticulture, 65; members of California, 61–62; motto of, 186; newspaper of, 59; political focus and power of, xiii, 59–64, 66–72, 346; on purity, 64, 346; on red-light abatement bill, 241, 242, 247–48, 251, 253, 255; responsibilities of, 64–65; strength in Berkeley, 191; on suffrage, 70–72, 210; support of Francis Heney, 224; Twentieth Century Club members from, 177; and women's legislative agenda, 238, 239. *See also* alcohol; prohibition; temperance

"Woman's Exchange," 178
Woman's Journal, 324
Woman's Peace Party (WPP), 309, 324–29, 335n70, 336n89
Woman's Political League, 294
Woman's State Suffrage Association, 34
Woman Suffrage Party, 213, 224–25
Woman's Vigilant Committee, 299–302
women. *See* clubwomen; elite women; feminism; middle-class women; womanhood; working-class women
Women's Bureau, 274, 275
women's clubs. *See* clubwomen; *specific clubs*
Women's College Alumnae, 238
Women's College Suffrage Club, 249
Women's Committee for World Disarmament, 319–21
Women's Educational and Industrial Union (WEIU), 115, 121n81
Women's Federation in Stockton, 317
Women's International League for Peace and Freedom (WILPF), 336n89. *See also* Woman's Peace Party (WPP)
Women's Land Army of California, 317–18
"Women's Legislative Agenda" (1913). *See* legislation
Women's Legislative Council (WLC), 181, 189–90, 238, 239, 245, 346. *See also* legislation
Women's Muncipal League (WML), 226
Women's Save the Redwoods League, 164–65, 167, 347. *See also* Save the Redwoods League
Women's Union Label League (WULL), 265
Women Voters of California, 324
Wood, Mrs. J. H., 206n68
Woodruff, C. A., 193
working class: attitudes toward alcohol, 214–16; effect of streetcar strike on, 220; and graft prosecutions, 221; on red-light abatement bill, 256; South Park Settlement situated among, 101–4; suffragists on legislation for, 227, 228; support of Union Labor Party, 221, 234n49; unification of men and women in, 264–65. *See also* class; employment; labor organizations; unionists

403

working-class women: care during war, 316; characterizations of, 263; in dance halls, 290, 292–94, 296, 297, 300–301, 301, 303; education and professions of, 82; effect of World War I on wages of, 273–74; effects of protective legislation on, 282–83; implications about morality of, 267–68; increasing organization of, 265; K. P. Edson's concern for, 310, 313, 317–18, 320–21; Lucile Eaves's study of, 110–11, 121n81; men's criticism of, 279–80; and minimum wage, 266–69, 271, 275, 276; relationship with middle-class women reformers, 97–98, 107–10, 112, 113, 209–10, 215–16, 219–20, 222–24, 226–29, 233n45, 263, 265–69, 283, 353; and suffrage, 209–10, 216; wages and hours of, 244, 268–69; WCTU's boardinghouses for, 59, 62, 68. *See also* class; employment; labor organizations; minimum wage; unionists

working conditions, 265–66, 272, 275, 313

workmen's compensation, 238, 269

Works, John D., 328

Works Progress Administration (WPA) Writer's Project, 202

World Court, 196

World War I: Alice Park during, 323–32; A. L. Saylor during, 198; bird-protection movement during, 140; California women on United States in, 314; cannery workers' strike during, 273; C. B. Burdette during, 152; Chinese women's activities during, 350; and dance hall problem, 294–96, 302; K. P. Edson's attitude toward, 314–18, 330–32; profiteering during, 271, 318; prohibition of prostitution during, 255; reaction to in California, 310, 314; Twentieth Century Club's mobilization for, 180, 192–95, 198–99

World War II, 352

World Woman's Christian Temperance Union (WCTU), 66

Wright, Carroll D., 107

Wright, Leroy, 244

Wright, Mabel Osgood, 127

Wyllie, George W., 241, 245

Yerba Buena CA, 13

Yoo, David, 350

Yorke, Father Peter, 218

Yosemite National Park, 163, 170n13

Young, C. C., 199, 249, 282

Younger, Maud, 228, 230n6

Young Men's Christian Association (YMCA), 84

Young Women's Christian Association (YWCA), 92, 238, 271, 350, 351

Yung, Judy, 343, 349, 350

Zimmermann, Arthur, 310

www.ingramcontent.com/pod-product-compliance
Lightning Source LLC
Chambersburg PA
CBHW021814300426
44114CB00009BA/170